TWENTY STUDIES THAT REVOLUTIONIZED CHILD PSYCHOLOGY

Wallace E. Dixon, Jr.

East Tennessee State University

Prentice
Hall

Prentice Hall, Upper Saddle River, NJ 07458

Library of Congress Cataloging-in-Publication Data

Dixon, Wallace E.
    Twenty studies that revolutionized child psychology / Wallace E. Dixon, Jr.—1st ed.
      p. cm.
    Includes bibliographical references.
    ISBN 0-13-041572-3
    1. Child psychology.   2. Infant psychology.   3. Child development.   4. Child rearing. I.
Title.

BF721 .D59 2002
155.4—dc21

2002074982

VP/EIC, English/Psychology: *Leah Jewell*
Senior Acquisitions Editor: *Jennifer Gilliland*
Editorial Assistant: *Blythe Ferguson*
AVP/Director of Production and Manufacturing:
  Barbara Kittle
Production Editor: *Nicole Girrbach*
Managing Editor: *Joanne Riker*
Manufacturing Manager: *Nick Sklitsis*
Prepress and Manufacturing Buyer: *Tricia Kenny*
Art Director: *Jayne Conte*
Cover Designer: *Bruce Kenselaar*
Cover Image: *Ken Davies/Masterfile*

Director, Image Resource Center: *Melinda Reo*
Manager, Rights & Permissions: *Zina Arabia*
Interior Image Specialist: *Beth Boyd-Brenzel*
Cover Image Specialist: *Karen Sanatar*
Image Permission Coordinator: *Debbie Latronica*
Photo Researcher: *Jerry Marshall*
Production/Formatting/Art Manager:
  Guy Ruggiero
Electronic Art Creation: *Mirella Signoretto*
Director of Marketing: *Beth Mejia*
Senior Marketing Manager: *Sheryl Adams*
Marketing Assistant: *Ron Fox*

Credits appear on pp. 290–291, which constitute a continuation of the copyright page.

This book was set in 10/12 point New Baskerville by TSI Graphics and was printed and bound by RR Donnelley & Sons Company. The cover was printed by Phoenix Color Corporation.

© 2003 by Wallace E. Dixon, Jr.
Pearson Education, Inc.
Upper Saddle River, New Jersey 07458

Printed in the United States of America

10 9 8 7 6 5 4 3 2

ISBN 0-13-041572-3

Pearson Education LTD., London
Pearson Education Australia PTY, Limited, Sydney
Pearson Education Singapore, Pte. Ltd
Pearson Education North Asia Ltd, Hong Kong
Pearson Education Canada, Ltd., Toronto
Pearson Educaión de Mexico, S. A. de C. V.
Pearson Education–Japan, Tokyo
Pearson Education Malaysia, Pte. Ltd

> **Dedicated to Michele, Rachel, and Sarah, who inspire me every day.**

CONTENTS

PART III: THREE STUDIES THAT REVOLUTIONIZED CLINICAL CHILD PSYCHOLOGY

PART IV: FOUR STUDIES THAT REVOLUTIONIZED HOW WE DO AND THINK ABOUT CHILD PSYCHOLOGY

RANK 7

PREFACE

I don't claim to have any special knowledge of how the field of child psychology operates. I'm just an average Joe trying to make a living doing what child psychologists do. One of the most important things they do is read the work of other child psychologists. Over the two decades or so that I've been reading these works, I've developed a fairly comprehensive classification scheme for what I think are the most important research topics, who are the most influential child psychologists, and which are the most revolutionary scientific publications. In fact, I've gotten to the point that whenever I read the work of another child psychologist, the second thing I do is look over the References section (the first thing I do is read the title and abstract). The reason I turn to the references first is that I believe I can get a good sense of the tone, the purpose, and the outcome of the article, just by seeing who gets cited in it. My predictions are usually right on target.

But about 5 years ago, I began to wonder whether other child psychologists had developed their own mental classification schemes, and whether their schemes were similar to mine. For example, I wondered whether other researchers considered the works of Robert Fantz and Renée Baillargeon as revolutionary as I believed they were. So in the summer of 2000, I launched a major research project of my own in an attempt to uncover the major child psychology research projects published in the second half of the 20th century. I asked child psychologists from all walks of life to nominate and vote on the studies they believed were the Most Important, Most Revolutionary, Most Controversial, and Most Fascinating. This book describes the 20 Most Revolutionary Studies.

The project was a major undertaking, and I would be remiss if I didn't acknowledge the contributions of a number of generous individuals. I must first acknowledge the overwhelming effort put forth by Debbie Hoffman. Deb was involved in this project every step of the way; she pulled names from the Membership Registry of the Society for Research in Child Development, typed up mailing labels, taped gold coins to individual recruitment letters, helped tally the results, and reviewed my entire book for typos and grammatical errors. I am extremely grateful to her. Thanks also go to Chuck Moon, who helped me come up with the research design for the data collection portion of the project. Thanks are due to a number of individuals who read, commented on, or otherwise provided guidance for how I might approach individual chapters, including Timothy Anderson, Daniel Cruikshanks, Margaret Evans, Brian Haley, Michele Moser, and Ken Porada. Relatedly I thank a number of people who provided useful information: Steve Velazquez, Bob Berg, Ayako Tabusa, Xiaoming Huang, and Muthoni Kimemia. Thanks also to the following reviewers:

Tara Kuther, Western Connecticut State University; Judy Payne, Murray State University; Joseph D. Sclafani, The University of Tampa; and Roger Van Horn, Central Michigan University. Finally, I wish to acknowledge a number of the Top 20 authors and their close acquaintances for giving me direction and suggestions for ways to approach the book; among these are Joe Fagan, Emmy Werner, Renée Baillargeon, Arnie Sameroff, and Ursula Bellugi.

A number of people deserve special mention for providing me with the mental fortitude to pursue the project: Esther Strahan for telling me my book-writing future was inevitable, Peg Smith for telling me it was about time I wrote a book, Wallace Dixon, Sr., for telling me book writing is where the real money is, Tim Lawson for outdoing me and writing his own book first, and Jennifer Gilliland for her continued support and encouragement and for telling me I was a "great writer." Finally, special thanks with sugar on top go to my wife, Michele Moser, and my daughters, Rachel and Sarah, for giving me up on all those late, late nights when I went into the office and word-processed till the wee hours of the morning.

WALLACE E. DIXON, JR.

1

Introduction

Congratulations! You've taken your first step into the exhilarating world of child psychology. Of course, I may be a little biased. After all, I've been doing child psychology for nearly 20 years, and my livelihood depends on getting others to believe what I do is important. (If my employers didn't think so, I'd be out of a job!) Still, the reason I got involved in this field in the first place was partly because it was so exciting and partly because new scientific findings in child psychology seemed to occur more rapidly than a firing neuron. In fact, I remember in my college days being puzzled that everyone else wasn't majoring in child psychology. After all, in what other profession can you get paid to play with toys and cute little babies (and no stinky diapers)? Who could want to do anything else?

But as I took upper-level child psychology courses, the drawbacks of the field became more apparent. I found that not all of child psychology is balloons and rainbows. Clinical and applied child psychologists have to deal with supremely frustrating elements of children's development. They work on problems such as repairing children who've been damaged by physical abuse and neglect, and improving the quality of life of children born with Down's syndrome or autism. These developmental disabilities can be devastating, and to work with them every day must require an emotional constitution of steel. Still, the work needs to be done, and the fact that I'm part of a field that addresses these overwhelming challenges makes me proud.

Despite my own excitement about child psychology, I'm willing to concede that other folks may not see things the same way I do. Over the years I've also found that a lot of people don't like to play golf, most people don't like to play chess, and very few people besides marine biologists and saltwater aquarists care about the difference between a soft and a stony coral. So it's not surprising that from time to time I've come across a few individuals who find the topic of child psychology an invitation to snooze, although it's still completely beyond me.

After giving the matter some thought, I think part of the reason that some people aren't exhilarated by the field can be traced to how most child psychology textbooks are written. Let's face it, child psychology texts don't exactly read like Harry Potter. If the truth be told, I've yet to find a child psychology textbook as absorbing as the field it describes. This is not to blame the textbook authors—quite the contrary. Child psychology textbook authors are extraordinarily competent professionals who've taken upon themselves the colossal task of summarizing an entire field in less than 700 pages. Now you might think 700 pages are a lot. But Piaget wrote over 700 pages in just 2 of his 100+ manuscripts, and Piaget is just one of several thousand child psychology researchers who've actively published in the field in the last 50 years. To me, at least, it's easy to understand the impossibility of the task confronted by the child psychology textbook author. Just for a moment, imagine yourself in his or her position. On the one hand, you'd want to be as complete in your coverage as possible; but on the other hand, you'd have some serious space limitations. Would any nondelusional person expect to sell a 520,000-page textbook? So, through some sort of a textbook version of Darwinian natural selection, textbooks have evolved into a dense collection of research findings held together by the organizational glue provided by the creative talents of the authors.

The problem can also be traced to the plight of the child psychology instructor. Now, trust me when I say, without any bias whatsoever, that you can't find better people on a college campus anywhere. Child psychology professors are wonderfully talented individuals. They work hard. They study hard. But they also get caught up in a couple of inescapable binds. First, as with textbook authors, instructors have the daunting task of covering a virtually infinite range of information in a conspicuously finite amount of time. At the completion of every semester, I'm amazed at how little I actually accomplished in my 40 hours of class time. Instructors are further obligated to meet the needs of a wide variety of students. If an instructor deviates too much from the textbook material, she risks dissatisfaction from students who fume over spending $115 on a textbook the professor didn't use. Yet if she deviates too little from the textbook, she offends a different group of students who are fuming over having spent $1,000 on a course when all they needed to do was read the textbook. It's a no-win situation.

Even if students actually read the textbooks, and even if they actually pay attention during class, it's no trivial matter that many theories and findings in child psychology are simply beyond a normal student's grasp. For one thing, students have to overcome the "common sense" hurdle. Many people come to a child psychology course confident in their expectation that the course will confirm what they already know. After all, they were kids themselves once. Some students even have their own children. Obviously, parents must know a lot about child psychology, right? The obstacle presents itself when many findings in child psychology contradict commonsense beliefs and child-rearing folklore. I'll never forget the middle-aged woman who came up to me after class one day (back in my youthful days when I still got carded when buying beer) just to tell me that I didn't need to feel intimidated by her extensive personal child-rearing experience.

On top of all this, child psychology theories undergo considerable refinement and revision from year to year. Understanding contemporary child psychology theory is like hitting a clay pigeon with a blunt arrow at a hundred paces. Some theories have gotten so complicated and so far removed from the children they describe that they're not even recognizable as child psychology theories anymore! I remember covering one such theory in class about 7 years ago. This theory, which child psychologists call "information processing theory," is a modern approach that uses the computer as a metaphor for thinking about children's thinking. One day, to get my students to grapple with how this theory might be relevant to children's thinking, I gave them a schematic of the general parts of a computer, including a keyboard, a printer, the RAM, and a hard drive. I broke the class into groups and had each group trace the path on the diagram, from input to output, that they thought best described how information moves through a computer. Most of the duty-bound students engaged the task eagerly. However, after about 10 minutes, in front of the whole class, an exasperated student burst out, "What does this crap have to do with kids?" I was stunned by the question, not because of its boldness, but because the connection was completely obvious to me. *I* thought students would surely see that computers process information in ways that parallel children's thinking. But this connection was completely lost on my students. The connection between information processing theory and real live children was so remote, so disconnected from how the students thought children thought, that they missed the point entirely. These days I realize that child psychology instructors must take a few steps backward from their intensely passionate immersion in child psychology if they're going to have any hope of being effective instructors. Followers of Piaget would describe this as becoming less egocentric.

In order to be effective, child psychology instructors really have to work hard at making connections between the unfamiliar, sometimes even bizarre theories and facts in the discipline and the children who are the objects of study. I think instructors would spend their time much more wisely if they tried to construct bridges to reach the minds of students rather than expecting students to build bridges to reach the minds of instructors. Unfortunately, as we've just seen, such a task is exceedingly challenging. There's just too much information in child psychology to share it effectively.

Now, left in the wake of the frontline child psychology instructors, the hardworking textbook authors, and the confused students, are the unsung heroes of child psychology, the sources of all those tidbits and factoids that fill the pages of child psychology textbooks: the research studies themselves. Here are some of the most ingenious innovations ever constructed in all of psychology, if not all of science. With them, the revolutionary advancements in our understanding of child development that have taken place in the last 50 years are unparalleled in all of human history. Yet, for whatever reason, the beauty of the studies, coupled with the ingenuity and driving motivations of the researchers who created them, are often left behind like clippings on the editing room floor. Instead, instructors sometimes get caught in a rut of asking students to memorize the facts and findings, the stages, ages, and phases (SAPs) of research investigations. I admit to doing so myself on many occasions. But this focus places disproportionate value on the outcomes of child psychology research, at the cost of ignoring everything that went into producing it. I think we could excite students of child psychology about the field a lot more if instead of pelting them with trivia, we bathed them in the ingenuity of a few of the most powerful studies. It seems to me that students whose interest is piqued through this method will pick up the trivia on their own.

Oh sure, sometimes individual studies are covered in great detail. For example, many child psychology students remember that Piaget's research on cognitive development was prompted by detailed observations of his own three children.

And no doubt, somewhere on the planet, students' eyes are glazing over as they recite Piaget's four main stages of cognitive development. But I wonder if students would find Piaget a more interesting figure if they knew he initially had no interest in studying children. He was actually more interested in mollusks. And although he eventually tripped over a career opportunity involving the observation of children, even then he really didn't find his job all that interesting, at least not at first. I also wonder if students would be fascinated to find out that Piaget coauthored his first professional article, not as a psychologist, but as a biologist, before he entered puberty. And in fact, as a result of the popularity he obtained from that article, he was put in the unfortunate position of having to turn down a job as a curator of the mollusk collection at the Museum of Natural History in Geneva, Switzerland, at age 15 (because he had to finish high school). My notion is that this kind of background information places Piaget's accomplishments in a much more interesting light, and that by providing child psychology students with this kind of "gossipy" background information, we might just find that they view the rest of what Piaget had to say much more interesting. And, if all goes well, they might remember it better to boot.

I'm willing to bet that once students have a fuller understanding of the person or studies behind the theory, they'll feel more immersed and more involved. They'll begin taking the issues more seriously because they're connecting with them. You can tell when students are connecting when they say things like, "How can a theory of all children be based on observations of only three children?" Or, with regard to Sigmund Freud, "How can we trust the theory of a coke-head?" (referring to Freud's cocaine habit). And of course this is my point. By inviting students backstage, child psychology instructors can hope to show students the motivating forces behind child psychology research. When students understand these motivations, they can better place the field in a broader context against which they can evaluate, embrace, and experience its parts.

In writing this book, I hope to spread my enthusiasm for child psychology by laying out the field in the context of 20 studies that have revolutionized our way of thinking about children. My objective is to give you something of the child psychologist's perspective on doing child psychology, after which I think it'll be hard for you *not* to share my enthusiasm. In the process of gaining this perspective, you'll have to learn something about the various histories of the field. You'll have to know what things were like in the old days before we knew about babies' newfound superpowers, before we knew that even newborns could understand, organize, and think about things. If I can get you to appreciate the methodologies of these research studies as well as their historical contexts, I think it will be impossible for you not to apply the term *exhilarating* to the field of child psychology yourself. All I ask is that you read this book, think about what I say, and raise questions about this stuff in the classroom. If you do all this, I won't guarantee it, but I think you'll have a pretty good chance of getting an A in the course.

Before we begin, there are a few things we should discuss and a few assumptions we should reveal about the field of child psychology. First, I feel I have to point out that child psychology, like psychology more generally, and like biology, chemistry, astronomy, and physics, is above all else a science. It is a *true* science in every possible sense of the word. Saying this is in some ways saying very little and in some ways saying a great deal. It says very little because it only points out that child psychology follows the scientific method. That is, child psychology obeys the rules of scientific questioning, reasoning, procedures for data collection, data analysis, and theory revision. Child psychology does all the things you've heard science does ever since your eighth-grade science class. However, saying child psychology is a science is in many ways heretical! Many people in our society question the wisdom of analyzing children, as if doing so will reveal some secret, mysterious plan. Others argue that child psychology isn't a science at all because human beings aren't subject to the same kind of scientific laws and scientific scrutiny that nematodes, chemical reactions, and meteor showers are. To this attitude I respond, "Hogwash!" The scientific method is a procedure, a way of inquiring about the world, and knows nothing of the content of its application. So you can apply the scientific method to just about any topic of study. Predicting the direction and velocity of a 10-kilogram child toddling down a garden path may not be as precise as predicting the direction and velocity of a 50-gram sphere on a 20° plane, but child psychology is just as much a science as any other method of inquiry that obeys the scientific method. The important thing is that, because child psychology is a science, we can't make our beliefs about children true just by thinking them. Facts about child psychology have to be well supported by sound reasoning and strong evidence. Students in my classes know very well, after hearing me recite it countless times, that opinions about children in the absence of systematically obtained data are scientifically worthless. Claims about what children do, think, know, and feel have to be backed up by scientific data.

Another erroneous belief is that findings in child psychology can't be valid unless they apply to every child. But this belief also reveals ignorance about the way science works. It would probably be most accurate to say that child psychology applies to all of the children some of the time, some of the children all of the time, but never to all of the children all of the time. Because children are so different from one another, and because their life circumstances are so varied, child psychologists don't realistically believe that their scientific findings will always apply to all kids. They merely do their best to explain as much about children as they can for as many children as they can under as many circumstances as they can. So when child psychologists conduct scientific investigations with children, they strive to include as many children as possible. However, many laypeople don't seem to appreciate the need for a large sample size. In fact, some laypeople seem to believe that one encounter is sufficient for a comprehensive understanding of some aspect of psychology. Their argument goes something like this: "Psychology is about people. I've been around people; therefore, I know about psychology." Now sometimes this approach is okay, but sometimes it can get you into trouble. For example, if you knew someone who snorted cocaine and then became a successful business executive, would you conclude that all people who snort cocaine will become successful business executives? I doubt it. Just because you might be aware of someone or some case that violates some child psychology finding somewhere, it doesn't mean that you can dismiss the scientific finding as untrue. There are going to be exceptions.

THE WAY IT WORKS

It wasn't until I was a sophomore in college that it finally occurred to me that the studies being referred to by news anchors when they said, "Recent studies have shown . . ." were often studies conducted by psychologists. This discovery was very exciting to me. As a psychology major, it meant that I might one day conduct a study that could make the evening news! Of course, not every study rates a mention on the evening news. The study has to be a good one, and it has to be exciting to people outside the field. But most importantly, when a study finally makes the news, it has usually undergone a very long and excruciating period of development and evaluation beforehand.

Conducting a scientific study involves a lot more than meets the eye. First, a scientist has an idea about how something works. At this point it's just an idea, and the scientist's idea is no better or more valid than anybody else's. However, unlike nonscientists, the scientist goes on to test the accuracy of her idea by collecting information from the world that has some bearing on it. This is called data collection. The scientist's original idea is usually framed in such a way as to ask a specific question. And data are collected so as to answer the question. Once the question is answered, the idea that generated the question is either proven wrong or not. The researcher might then go on to test additional questions generated by the idea. As this idea→question→data collection process cycles through a few times, a more fully elaborated idea develops. At this more sophisticated level, the idea can be called a theory. Most textbook authors define a theory as a set of statements that accounts well for an existing set of data. A good theory should also make accurate and specific predictions about the future.

But finding a desirable answer to the initial question isn't the last step. The last step is called "dissemination." Dissemination is the way scientists get their work known by their peers and colleagues in the scientific community. The dissemination step itself has several procedures that have to be followed. First, the study and its results have to be "written up." The document that gets written is called a manuscript. The scientist then submits her manuscript to the editor of a professional scientific journal for publication. However, before publishing the manuscript, the journal editor sends the article out to be reviewed by other people who know a lot about the scientist's field. These people are called reviewers. The reviewers read the manuscript, find everything wrong with it that they possibly can, then summarize the manuscript's faults in a letter back to the journal editor. If there aren't too many problems with either the study or the manuscript describing it, the journal editor may decide to publish the manuscript in the journal (after the scientist revises it once or twice). Once the manuscript gets published in the journal, all the scientists in the world can read about the study and its findings. Some textbook authors may even wish to include the results of the study in the latest editions of their textbooks.

ARTICLE STRUCTURE

Articles that get published in scientific journals have a fairly well standardized look. Psychology articles might have a slightly different appearance than articles published in other disciplines, but the general structure is the same. First, there is an introduction section, followed by a method section, followed by a results section, and ending in a discussion or conclusion section. Each of these four sections has a specific purpose in the article. Because journal articles are so standardized, readers know just where to look if they have a specific question about the article.

Introduction Section

The introduction section of an article is the place where the scientist, now the author, describes the reason for doing her scientific study in the first place. This section is where the author tells her readers why they should be interested in the study she's describing. The scientist also tells the readership what work has already been done on that topic, what the limitations are of that previous work, what work has yet to be done, and how her own study will make a contribution to the existing body of child psychology knowledge.

Method Section

To use a dessert metaphor, the method section can be likened to the recipe used for baking a cake. Here the author gets down to the nitty-gritty of specifying how the actual study was conducted. For one thing, here is where the author can describe the organisms she studied: how many there were, what age they were, their gender distribution, their ethnicity (if they're human organisms), their species, and how they were recruited to participate. (Human animals are usually recruited. Other animals are usually, shall we say, strongly encouraged.) In the old days we used to call the subjects of psychological research simply "subjects," but these days we call them "participants," especially if they're human. This change in phraseology reflects psychology's discipline-wide efforts toward treating people as people, rather than only as objects of study. But no matter what you call human participants in a psychological investigation, they're still the objects of study in the investigation.

The method section is also the place for the author to explain how she "operationally defined" all the abstract psychological concepts that she studied. The idea of an **operational definition** is essential for scientists because it allows them to state in clear, unambiguous terms how they measured an otherwise abstract concept. If you wanted to study the intellectual development of first-graders, for example, you couldn't just look at a group of first-graders and know how intelligent they were. You would have to *measure* their intelligence in some way. Typically, you might use an IQ test of some sort. An IQ test score in this example would be the operational definition of intelligence. When a scientist operationally defines an abstract concept, she isn't implying that her way is the best way to measure the concept; she's only declaring that it's her way. Other scientists can use other ways to measure the same abstract concepts if they want. The point of the method section is to let the reader know how *this* scientist measured *this* abstract concept on *this* occasion.

The method section describes not only the ingredients the scientist used (the participants and the operational definitions) but also how she mixed them together (the methodological procedure). Here the author specifies things like how the measurements were taken, when they were taken, the various conditions under which they were taken, how many times they were taken, and the order in which they were taken. If you've ever baked a cake, you know that the order of procedures makes all the difference. You wouldn't put the cake pan in the oven before mixing the ingredients, for example. Well, in specifying her experimental procedure, the researcher is telling the reader how and in what order she mixed together her ingredients. Because the author divulges this information, any reader who doesn't like the taste of the cake (the outcome of the study) can at least attempt to bake his own, making modifications to the ingredients or the mixing procedures wherever he wishes. The fact that such recipes are so public and so open to scrutiny is one of the best features of science. Scientists don't walk around in secret societies conspiring to overthrow all that is good and sincere. Science is exquisitely public, which makes it open to public scrutiny, to public criticism, and to people who think they can do it better. The result of such openness is continued scientific progress.

Results Section

If the participants, operational definitions, and procedures of a study can be likened to the ingredients for baking a cake, then the results can be likened to its taste. In the results section of a journal article, the scientist presents a detailed account of the data she collected from the participants using the operational definitions and the procedures that she described in the method section. Usually, you'll see a lot of statistics here! Even advanced psychology majors are overwhelmed at the mathematicalness of journal articles; and there are all those weird F, t, and p thingies throughout results sections too. Well, it's no coincidence that psychology majors usually have to take at least one statistics course as part of their major. The results sections of psychology journal articles are loaded with descriptive statistics, inferential statistics, p-values, F-ratios, degrees of freedom, and betas, etas, lambdas, and deltas. It takes at least one, but usually many more, courses in statistics to begin to understand the statistics presented in results sections of journal articles.

Of course, I can't go into much detail here in explaining what all the various kinds of statistics mean; but I can say that most researchers don't include statistics in their journal articles just for the heck of it. There is in fact a very important goal in presenting all those statistics: They are meant to demonstrate to the reader that the findings obtained were unlikely to have happened by accident. Consequently, the job of the scientist in writing up the results section is to review each of the initial research questions, to present statistics that guide her in answering each of her questions, and to determine whether any of the correlations or differences that she found for each of the questions was accidental. The scientist then describes to the reader her interpretations of the statistics in light of the initial research questions.

Discussion

Continuing along with our cake-baking metaphor, the discussion section provides a venue for the scientist to reflect on how good the cake tasted and how good a job she did in baking it. Here she can describe what ingredients she wished she'd used instead, how she might like to focus next on baking a chocolate cake rather than another yellow one, whether she would like to bake the thing at a different temperature, or even whether she would prefer to use a completely different oven. The scientist also uses this section to describe to the reader how her findings can be integrated into the field as a whole, and to make suggestions for future studies that might help fill in the gaps in understanding left empty or even created by her study. My graduate adviser told me to think of the discussion section as a place to "ride off into the sunset." I think what she meant is that every study has a silver lining, and the discussion section should act like a happy ending for the story of the research study. I know, it may sound corny, but the author who publishes a scientific study really is telling a story. It's a story with a beginning, a middle, and an end. There are characters and props. There is a narrative leading up to some goal (the introduction), a means set up to achieve the goal (the method section), a climax (the results section), and a denouement (the discussion section). Viewed in this way, the discussion section really should leave the reader with a sense of accomplishment and a sense of success. The reader should walk away feeling happy.

MY TACK

The purpose of my book is to share the field of child psychology with you by presenting 20 of the most revolutionary studies ever published in the field. In reviewing each of these 20 studies, where possible, I will take some time to familiarize you with each study by reviewing the four major areas with you. That is, I will review why the author wanted to do the study, what the author hoped to accomplish, how the study was conducted, what was found, and how the findings revolutionized the field. Where possible, I'll indicate how the findings from the original study are still relevant to the field of child psychology today or to modern society more generally.

Not all the studies that made the Top 20 list are traditional scientific studies of this sort, however. In four cases, the revolutionary contribution was made in the absence of a scientific study. In three of these articles, the "study" was more of an essay in which the author reflected on the state of child psychology and made a number of suggestions for ways to improve it. In these cases, I tried to capture the major focal points of the author, and when possible made mention of how the essay had a practical impact on how future studies should be conducted.

Now, because I believe so strongly in the role of science in producing new knowledge, I didn't want to be a hypocrite by relying on my own intuition in deciding which studies to include in this book. I think I have a pretty good sense of the field of child psychology, and I think I could do a pretty good job of selecting most of the revolutionary studies on my own. But I thought a far more accurate list of the revolutionary studies could be determined by taking a scientific poll of professional scholars in the field. So I undertook a scientific investigation of my own. I began by surveying over 1,000 randomly selected members of the leading organization of child psychologists, the Society for Research in Child Development (SRCD). I simply asked people to nominate up to three studies they thought had revolutionized the field of child psychology. This was the "open-ended" portion of my survey. Over 75 different studies were nominated in this portion of the survey. Because such a variety of studies had been nominated, I decided to do a follow-up survey to narrow down the list. This time, I sent a list of the 30 most frequently nominated studies to a second random sample of 500 SRCD members. In this "closed-ended" version of the survey, I asked respondents to rank order what they believed were the top 5 most revolutionary studies. These results allowed me to narrow the list down to the 20 you'll read about in this book. It is these studies you'll find described in the pages to follow.

THEMES

Many traditional child psychology textbook authors make a point of highlighting common themes that operate throughout the whole of child psychology. You'll note a number of common themes that run through the revolutionary studies described in this book as well. Some of these themes are no doubt the same as described in other child psychology textbooks, but there are also a few that are probably unique to our revolutionary studies. The prominent themes running through these 20 studies include:

The Theme of Nature Versus Nurture.   Perhaps the most popular theme running throughout these 20 revolutionary studies is that of "nature versus nurture." As you're probably aware, the nature/nurture issue has to do with the extent that children are the product of their own genes versus being a product of their unique environments. As described in Chapter 19, where Anne Anastasi attacks the nature/nurture question head-on, the issue is much less of a debate these days than a compromise. Researchers no longer ask whether genes or environment is exclusively responsible. Instead, they ask how much of each is responsible. The authors differ quite a bit in how much time they spend dealing with the nature/nurture issue, at least in terms of the works presented in this book, but most address the theme to some degree. Researchers who tend to fall on the nature side of things include Fantz (Chapter 5), Baillargeon (Chapter 6), Chomsky (Chapter 8), Harlow and Harlow (Chapter 10), Bowlby (Chapter 11), and Ainsworth (Chapter 12). Researchers who tend to fall on the nurture side of things include Vygotsky (Chapter 4), Baumrind (Chapter 13), and Bandura, Ross, and Ross (Chapter 14). Researchers who place greatest focus on the interaction between nature and nurture include Piaget (Chapters 2 and 3); Thomas, Chess, and Birch (Chapter 16); Werner and Smith (Chapter 17); Sameroff and Chandler (Chapter 18); Anastasi (Chapter 19); Bell (Chapter 20); and Hubel and Wiesel (Chapter 21).

The Theme of the Active Child.   It's also a common theme in child psychology textbooks to point out that children play an active role in their own development. Piaget (Chapters 2 and 3), for example, talks about how children are endowed by biology with certain starting points for knowledge and how they build on this knowledge by virtue of their own sensorimotor activity. And Sameroff and Chandler (Chapter 18) address the issue of how the unique behavioral profiles of some children may actually contribute to their own likelihood for being abused. Other studies that address how children play an active role in their own development include Bowlby (Chapter 11); Thomas, Chess, and Birch (Chapter 16); Werner and Smith (Chapter 17); Anastasi (Chapter 19); Bell (Chapter 20); Hubel and Wiesel (Chapter 21); and Bronfenbrenner (Chapter 22).

The Theme of Evolutionary Theory.   One theme that may be less emphasized in standard child psychology textbooks is the extent that theories and research are based on Darwin's theory of evolution. In a number of studies reported here, however, Darwin's theory of evolution played a central role. It becomes very clear in Chapter 1, for example, that Piaget's entire theory of cognitive development was based on his application of evolutionary theory to children's intellectual development. Bowlby's entire attachment theory (Chapter 11), as well as Ainsworth's adaptation of it (Chapter 12), is similarly deeply rooted in evolutionary theory. Fantz (Chapter 5) suggested that babies might be "built" by evolution to prefer to look at human faces. And Premack and Woodruff (Chapter 7) give us reason to believe that part of human success is due to the human ability to realize that other people have thoughts and beliefs.

The Theme of Perspective.   It appears that a number of studies were revolutionary because they brought a new or different perspective to the field of child psychology. For example, Piaget (Chapters 2 and 3) made great progress in child psychology largely because he approached the field from the perspective of a biologist. Vygotsky's (Chapter 4) claim to fame had a great deal to do with the fact that he applied Marxist ideologies to the cognitive and language development of children. Chomsky (Chapter 8) made his mark on child language development because of his training in linguistics, whereas Roger Brown's (Chapter 9) work on child language was informed by his training as a social psychologist. Like Brown, Bandura (Chapter 14) was a social psychologist, and so he explored children's aggression as a socially learned phenomenon. And finally, Gilligan revolutionized child psychology, and perhaps all of social science as well, by virtue of her feminist perspective (Chapter 15).

The Theme of Rebellion.   If there's a theme that's particularly conspicuous among studies that revolutionized a field, it's the theme of rebellion. Many of the studies described in this book had a revolutionary impact on child psychology precisely because they were rebelling against the status quo. Behavioral psychology was a common target of many of these revolutionary researchers. For example, the works of Fantz (Chapter 5); Chomsky (Chapter 8); Harlow and Harlow (Chapter 10); Bandura, Ross, and Ross (Chapter 14); and Thomas, Chess, and Birch (Chapter 16) were all inspired by a common rejection of mainstream behavioral psychology.

Other revolutionary researchers were more idiosyncratic in whom they rebelled against. For example, Baillargeon (Chapter 6) set out to disprove Piaget. Chomsky (Chapter 8), in addition to rejecting the behaviorists, also sought to disprove Piaget. But Brown (Chapter 9), in turn, was motivated by his dissatisfaction with Chomsky's theory. In contrast, the Harlows (Chapter 10); Bowlby (Chapter 11); and Thomas, Chess, and Birch (Chapter 16) all had Freudian theory in their crosshairs, whereas Gilligan's feminist theory of moral development (Chapter 15) was motivated a great deal by Kohlberg's "masculine" theory of moral development.

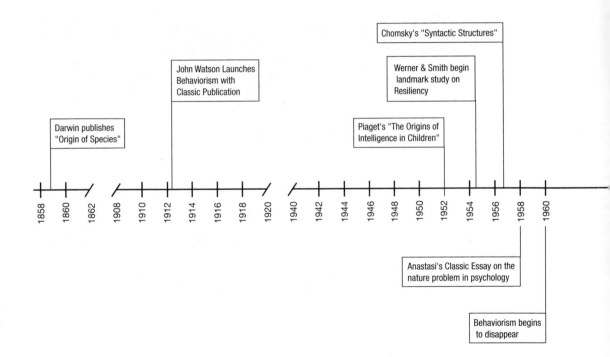

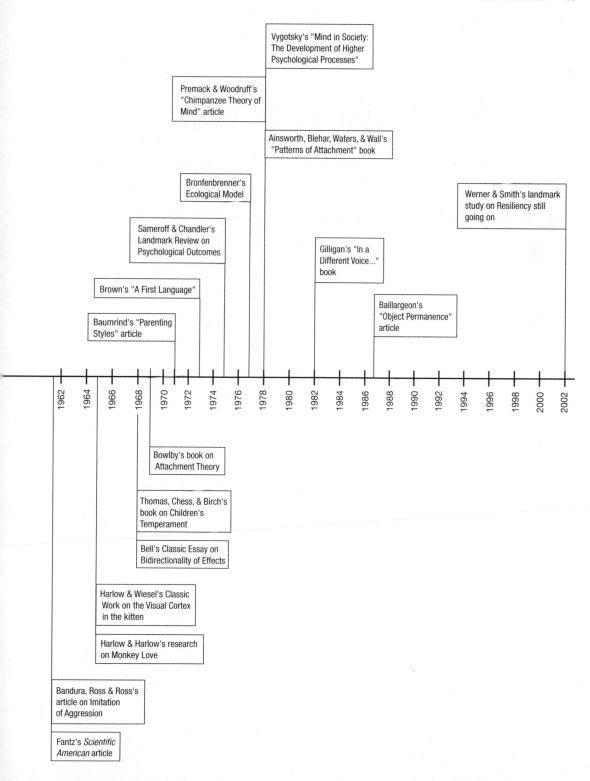

Vygotsky's "Mind in Society: The Development of Higher Psychological Processes"

Premack & Woodruff's "Chimpanzee Theory of Mind" article

Ainsworth, Blehar, Waters, & Wall's "Patterns of Attachment" book

Bronfenbrenner's Ecological Model

Werner & Smith's landmark study on Resiliency still going on

Sameroff & Chandler's Landmark Review on Psychological Outcomes

Gilligan's "In a Different Voice..." book

Brown's "A First Language"

Baillargeon's "Object Permanence" article

Baumrind's "Parenting Styles" article

1962 1964 1966 1968 1970 1972 1974 1976 1978 1980 1982 1984 1986 1988 1990 1992 1994 1996 1998 2000 2002

Bowlby's book on Attachment Theory

Thomas, Chess, & Birch's book on Children's Temperament

Bell's Classic Essay on Bidirectionality of Effects

Harlow & Wiesel's Classic Work on the Visual Cortex in the kitten

Harlow & Harlow's research on Monkey Love

Bandura, Ross & Ross's article on Imitation of Aggression

Fantz's *Scientific American* article

2

From Mollusks to Rugrats:

Biological Principles and Psychological Ideas

Anyone who knows anything about child psychology has heard the name Piaget (pronounced "pee-ah-JAY," with a very soft *j* sound). In fact, the first question I ask my students (besides "Is there anyone here who's not scheduled to take Child Psychology 206?") is "How many of you have heard the name Piaget?" Almost all the hands go up! This in itself is interesting because the students have obviously not completed a child psychology course yet, but they still recall his name. Then I ask, "How many of you with your hands up remember what Piaget did?" Just as quickly, all the hands go down! After about 10 seconds or so of silence, someone raises her hand feebly and says, "Didn't he do something with stages?"

Stages. Ugh. Of the hundreds of books and articles written by Piaget and his colleagues, the one item that students are likely to recollect is that the old codger did "something" with stages. Now this is ironic because if you ask me, his contributions to the idea of developmental stages are among the least interesting things he did. Yet high school and college students nationwide learn in the child psychology section of their courses that according to Piaget, children develop through four qualitatively different stages, in order, until adolescence, at which time they apparently stop. If you're going to say that Piaget's main thing was "stages," you might as well call Michelangelo's Sistine Chapel "a painting." You see, Piaget's contributions to science are much, much further reaching. I would even argue that the total of Piaget's work amounts to perhaps the single most intensive, coherent, sweeping theoretical integration of all the life sciences that the world has yet seen!

Having said that, I can still understand why students only remember Piaget's stages. For one thing, the concept of stages is easy to remember; and Piaget offered only four of them. It's a lot easier for child psychology teachers to teach four stages than it is for them to lecture about a comprehensive integration of all the life sciences. Second, Piaget's writings are so dense and so complex that they bring even the most able-minded doctorate-level child psychology scholar to her knees. In graduate school I used to think that Piaget's books were so difficult because they were translated from their French originals, until I learned that people who read the French originals found them just as difficult! A comprehensive effort at relating Piaget's ideas to child psychology classes would probably take months. Since the typical child psychology text usually allots just a single chapter to Piaget, which translates into about three 50-minute class periods, full coverage of the man's ideas is obviously impractical. Given the space limitations, reviewing Piaget's four stages seems a more attainable goal. But then the essence of Piaget's genius is missed; and students' understanding of Piaget as a brilliant integrator is replaced with an understanding of Piaget as "that stage guy."

What I propose to do in the next few pages is to provide a middle ground. I'd like to review two courses of the full Piagetian feast. The first review outlines Piaget's purposes and goals in doing research on the psychological development of children. The second deals more directly with the research methodology and findings excerpted from his 1952 book *The Origins of Intelligence in Children*. It was this book that was voted #1 in my list of the top 20 studies that revolutionized child psychology. To review these two topics, I'm afraid I must deviate somewhat from my goal of dedicating a single chapter to a single study. I'll be presenting the Piaget material in two chapters. The first chapter will focus on the theoretical Piaget; you know, the kind of stuff that describes what Piaget was all about. Here you'll get a sense of what made Piaget tick, where he was coming from, and why his ideas were so comprehensively integrating. The second chapter will be more typical of the sort of pattern I'll be following throughout the remainder of the book—that of presenting a single study and describing its revolutionary impact on the field of child psychology. Given the depth and breadth of Piaget's impact on the field as a whole, I think it's only proper that Piaget get two whole chapters to himself.

PIAGET: THE CHILD BIOLOGIST

Let me go back to my claim that Piaget's efforts were really aimed at integrating the whole of the life sciences. To understand such a claim, you really need to understand that Piaget was first and foremost a biologist. His initial interests were in biology, his professional training was in biology, and most of his early scientific publications dealt with biological organisms of the nonhuman sort. When I say "early" work, I mean *really, really* early. As a young child in turn-of-the-century Neuchâtel, Switzerland, Piaget published his first professional paper—on the topic of a partially albino sparrow he once saw while playing in a local park—when he was only 10! At 12 years of age he developed an intense interest in collecting mollusks, and by the ripe old age of 13 Piaget was working as an assistant to Paul Godet, the director of a nearby natural history museum. In exchange for being his assistant, Godet gave Piaget various mollusk specimens to add to his own collection. Godet befriended Piaget, and shared with him the excitement of science and of cataloging the huge varieties of mollusks and shells the museum had amassed. So Piaget spent many of his childhood days measuring, recording, and categorizing mollusk shells. Now you might think it incredibly nerdy that any young child would spend his spare time staring at and categorizing mollusk shells. But there were at least two driving forces behind Piaget's motivations.

First, as Piaget himself described it, he had a troubling childhood, primarily as a result of having to deal with a profoundly religious, and mentally ill, mother. Given Piaget's prodigious experiences in doing science, coupled with his admiration for his historian father who was devoutly nonreligious, it was probably not a bad idea for family harmony for him to steer clear of intellectual battles with his mother. For Piaget, collecting mollusks and working at the museum was an escape from this otherwise difficult life. And I suspect that, all things considered, Piaget's form of escape was probably a lot less dysfunctional than other forms of escapism he could have chosen.

Even so, it's probably not fair to call Piaget a nerd. His interests in categorizing mollusks really reflect nothing more than a natural tendency of all living organisms to categorize their surroundings. You yourself have been categorizing things since you were a baby. Babies put things in their mouths all the time. When babies put things in their mouths, it's as if they have a primitive little category of "things you suck on." Ask your parents how many different things you put in your mouth when you were little. Would you classify yourself as an infant nerd because you spent your time categorizing the world into suckable things? Older children also like to categorize stuff. When my oldest daughter, Rachel, was 3, she got the odd idea that she should gather up all her yellow toys and put them together in one tidy little pile. Red and blue toys weren't permitted to join the party. She ran up and down the stairs with glee, gathering everything she could find that was yellow. When she was done, she sat back and admired her golden conglomeration. The point is that categorizing things is natural, it's fundamental, and we do it throughout our lifetime. And if we do it objectively and systematically, we call it science. Why shouldn't a young boy like Piaget be allowed to do his own science if he found it so enjoyable?

Very soon afterward, in his early adolescence, and after looking over a lot of mollusk shells, Piaget began making his own scientific discoveries. Now here I'm not really sure that Piaget showed any particularly unique genius. I imagine that anyone who looked over enough shells for a long enough time would start to notice patterns of similarity and difference. But, with the encouragement of Godet, Piaget ran with his observations. He presented his work at various learned societies of the times (ones Godet took him to), and before long, Piaget's reputation was so well known around the world that he received an offer to be the curator of the mollusk collection at the Natural History Museum of Geneva! The people who offered Piaget the job didn't even know he was just a 15-year-old kid! Piaget probably figured he'd better finish puberty, so he turned down the position. Anyway, as you can see, Piaget was well entrenched in the biological sciences long before he attended college, and not surprisingly, the major tenets of the field of biology became infused into Piaget's personal outlook on the meaning of life.

PIAGET CARRIES THE TORCH FOR EVOLUTIONARY THEORY

Now, if you recall from your eighth-grade science class, a central guiding focus of the biological sciences is the theory of evolution through natural selection. And so it was that Piaget brought this notion full force into his conceptions of the psychological development of children. He held these beliefs very strongly. To Piaget, it made no sense to think that some parts of the natural world would develop according to one set of laws, while other parts would develop according to different laws.

To him, all life must follow the same developmental laws, whether it be the lowly mollusk or the intelligent human. It also made no sense for him to think that intellectual development would take place any differently from physical development. Again, he believed that all biological development must proceed according to the same set of rules, period.

For Piaget, then, the distinction between biology and psychology was in some ways arbitrary and trivial. To him, the theory of evolution through natural selection was an equal opportunity employer; and studying the psychological development of children reflected nothing more than his continuing interest in the biological sciences. But this still doesn't explain why Piaget gave up on his study of mollusks. Personally, it wouldn't surprise me if he just got bored with the whole mollusk thing. But why was he so interested in studying the psychological development of children? Of all the things that he could've chosen as his next topic of study, why children? It wasn't because he marveled at his own children, because when he first entered the field of psychology he was childless. The trigger for Piaget's shift of interest seems to have come from his godfather, who thought Piaget was just too narrowly focused. After all, is it normal for a child to obsess over mollusk shells exclusively? So to broaden Piaget's horizons, his godfather, Samuel Cornut, gave him a philosophy book by a guy named Bergson. The rippling effect of this relatively innocent act was to change the science of children's psychological development forever.

The book that got Piaget so fired up dealt with the topic of **epistemology**. Okay. Whoa. Back the train up. What is epistemology? Well, epistemology is a branch of philosophy that deals with the meaning and origins of knowledge. Epistemologists deal with deep questions like "What is knowledge? Where does it come from? What can be known, and can known things be known for sure? Is knowledge constant or changing?" Apparently, Bergson got Piaget to begin thinking about whether human knowledge development conformed to the principles of evolution through natural selection. Piaget's logic might've gone something like this: If evolution through natural selection is fundamental to biology, and if humans are biological organisms, and if the development of knowledge is a product of those biological organisms, then knowledge development itself should be subject to the principle of evolution through natural selection. There's no reason to believe that the mental would be any different from the biological.

Now, the reason organisms evolve at all is that it helps them fit into their surrounding environments better than their ancestors did. If you pull a fish out of water and drop it into your boat, it'll flop around for a while and eventually suffocate. Of course, the reason for the fish's death is simply that fish have evolved to extract oxygen from water, and they don't fare so well when asked to extract it from air. Fish have adapted to survive in watery environments. Presumably, human intelligence evolved for much the same reason: to allow humans to better fit into their environments.

The problem confronting Piaget in studying the evolution of human intelligence was rather large. Evolution takes place over hundreds of thousands of generations, and more complex species such as *Homo sapiens sapiens* take especially large numbers of generations to evolve. Although Piaget was a great scientist, he wasn't immortal. So he had only one lifetime to address the matter of the evolution of intelligence. He couldn't very well follow human evolution for a few million years. To remedy this problem, he began by adopting the old adage "Ontogeny recapitulates phylogeny." Although it sounds fancy, all this phrase really means is that the development of the individual (**ontogeny**) mirrors the development of the species (**phylogeny**). So Piaget believed that all he had to do to study the development of intelligence in the human species was to study the development of intelligence in the human individual. Moreover, because intelligence begins in infancy, or maybe even before birth, it made sense to study psychological development in children. In other words, children represented the ideal starting point to understand the evolution of intelligence. The primitive intellectual functioning of modern human children probably reflected the primitive thinking of archaic human adults. Anyway, I hope you can get a sense of why Piaget's interests shifted from mollusks to children. To him, both types of organisms, mollusks and children, served as vehicles for studying the same general principles of evolution that were so central to his view of the world.

EVOLUTION IN CHILDREN'S INTELLECTUAL DEVELOPMENT

Now we can focus on Piaget's interests in intellectual development more specifically. Recall that a key outcome of evolution is adaptation. If a species or an individual organism is to survive in any given environment, it must be able to adapt to changes in the environment. A species that can't adapt will become an extinct one. If environments change slowly, say over thousands or millions of years, then evolution through natural selection has a chance to work. But if environments change very rapidly or very drastically, then there is a good chance that whole groups of species could be wiped out. One popular theory for the extinction of the dinosaurs is that a huge meteor smashed into the Earth and kicked up the biggest dust storm the Earth had ever seen. Because dinosaurs weren't prepared to extract oxygen from dust particles, they died out; and apparently they did so rather suddenly. However, sometimes environments can change rapidly but not drastically. When this happens, some members of a species might die, and others might survive. The members of the species that survive live to see another day and, importantly, reproduce. If the offspring of these individuals possess the same characteristics as their parents, they too may be capable of surviving in the changed environment. This is why they call it natural selection: Some natural catastrophe happens, and the surviving organisms are more or less "selected" to survive.

Humans are pretty successful at being able to survive fairly radical shifts in surrounding environments. How many other species of plants or animals can live and reproduce in the +120 °F heat of Kenya, the –90 °F cold of Antarctica, the atmosphereless outer space, and the airless underseas? Of course, the reason humans are so successful at surviving such huge environmental changes is their intelligence. The intelligence of humans permits them to create tools. They can use tools and some more intelligence to build technologically advanced buildings and other structures. And they can use these buildings and other structures, along with still more intelligence, to create whatever climate-controlled environments they need. Of course, infant humans aren't capable of creating climate-controlled environments, and neither were prehistoric adult humans. So how is it that modern infant humans, whose greatest intellectual talent amounts to being able to produce spit bubbles, are capable of developing into intellectually sophisticated adults? For Piaget the answer was simple: **intellectual adaptation**.

Piaget's idea of intellectual adaptation can be thought of as a sort of sped-up version of evolution through natural selection. However, instead of the species as a whole evolving, it is the intelligence of the individual that evolves. The parallels between intellectual evolution and species evolution are enormous. Just as poorly adapted members of a species might die off when confronted with environmental adversity, so might poorly adapted ideas in one's intellect die off when confronted with logical inconsistency. So for Piaget, the task of explaining children's intellectual development really amounted to observing the conditions under which ideas die off, as well as the conditions under which they survive.

Piaget believed that almost all of a person's intelligence resulted from that person's unique history of interacting with a wide variety of environments. He thought that over the course of an individual's lifetime, particularly during early childhood, ideas that were goofy or unadaptive would become "extinct," whereas ideas that proved useful and helped the individual negotiate through a variety of environments would remain "alive." In infancy, the idea that the mother's breast should be sucked is a good one because it results in the baby's getting fed when she's hungry. So the baby would no doubt find breast sucking adaptive, and would likely maintain the breast-sucking idea among her collection of viable ideas—at least for a while. But if the baby kept this idea too long, say into late childhood, she would probably get teased by her friends and would eventually abandon this idea.

The result of keeping the good ideas and getting rid of the bad ideas is the essence of what Piaget meant by the adaptation of intelligence. Piaget thought of intellectual adaptation as an *equilibrium* between the action of the organism on the environment and the effects of the environment on the organism. (*Equilibrium* just means that a system is in balance.) For human intelligence, intellectual equilibrium means that humans strive to make sure their intelligence is in balance with their surrounding environment. Breast sucking in infancy provides a good source of nutrition, and so with this idea the child is in balance with the environment. Breast sucking in late childhood is very odd and results in a certain amount of antagonism coming from the environment, perhaps in the form of teasing, and so reflects an imbalance between the child and the environment.

Still, not all intelligence can be acquired through experience. Piaget believed there must be some important inborn characteristics as well, some kind of starting point. After all, other biological systems are in place and working at birth, or before birth, so why should intelligence be any different? For Piaget, the starting point for intellectual development was assumed to be similar to the starting points for other biological things that develop. In biological development, for example, we know there are preexisting *structures* and inborn *processes*. If you're talking about the biological *process* of digestion, for example, there are many *structures* in place at birth to aid a baby in extracting and using nutrients from the environment. Let's see, we have a mouth, a stomach, a large and small intestine, and a whole series of fluid-secreting glands. There are also a whole bunch of *processes* in place that encourage the extraction of nutrition from the environment. Just a few of the processes that come to mind include swallowing, peristalsis (moving food along the digestive tract), and enzyme secretion. These digestive *processes* use the preexisting digestive *structures* (like the stomach and the glands) for the adaptive purpose of taking nutritional elements from the surrounding environment and putting them into the biological functioning of the individual organism. Of course, digestion isn't the only biological thing happening. As another example, the biological act of breathing involves preexisting *structures* (lungs, diaphragm) and preexisting *processes* (muscular contractions of the diaphragm, extraction of oxygen from the pulmonary capillaries). Did you notice the words *structure* and *process* in the last few sentences? I've used them frequently and even italicized them because understanding both structure and process, as well as knowing the difference between them, is crucial for getting a grip on Piaget's theory.

To get back to the main point, Piaget believed that this basic pattern of preexisting processes acting on preexisting structures in biological adaptation to the environment must also underlie intellectual development to the environment. Remember, Piaget's goal was to show that intellectual development is just another manifestation of the basic principles underlying all of biology. However, there was one major difference between biological and intellectual adaptation that Piaget had to deal with. It goes something like this: Although you can easily see the basic structures and processes for the biological activities of digestion and breathing, you can't very easily see the basic structures and processes for the biological activity of intelligence. So Piaget had to more or less "invent" them. (Well, he didn't actually invent them, he sort of borrowed them from an American psychologist, James Mark Baldwin, but this fact tends to get lost in popular accounts of Piaget's theory.) The concept that Piaget ended up adopting as the most fundamental *structure* for intellectual development was the **schema**, and the fundamental *processes* for intellectual development were **assimilation** and **accommodation**. Piaget's notion of a schema is rather abstract and kind of difficult to follow; but that's primarily because you don't yet have a schema for the concept of the schema! So let's develop one, shall we?

SCHEMAS, ASSIMILATION, AND ACCOMMODATION

In some ways, the schema is to intelligence as the stomach is to digestion. Just as the goal of eating is to put food into your stomach so that digestion can take place, the goal of learning is to put information into your schema so that intelligence can take place. And in both digestion and intelligence, the stomach and schema are present even before birth. But here the similarities end. For example, in digestion you have only one stomach, but in intellectual development you have hundreds and thousands of schemas. And while your basic digestive structures pretty much stay the same over your entire lifetime (except that they may get bigger), your basic intellectual structures are changing continually. Schemas do get bigger, but they may also get smaller. They may subdivide like body cells, they may aggregate like Cheerios dancing on the surface of the milk in your morning bowl of cereal, or they may subsume each other like so many Pac-Men chomping down power pills through a videonic maze. A schema may be a reflex, such as sneezing or blinking; or it may be a highly complex understanding of subatomic particles of quarks and neutrinos. But no matter how you look at it, intellectual development happens when the basic, primitive schemas, which are present even before birth, evolve toward the very complex and highly interrelated schemas that exist in our adult-level thought processes. The question Piaget addressed, and it took pretty much the rest of his lifetime, was how this evolution took place.

THE DEVELOPMENT OF BABY INTELLIGENCE

Piaget began by assuming that there had to be some basic knowledge schemas in place before any new learning could happen. Without these basic schemas, there would be no "place" for an organism to put the very first information it encountered. It would be like a baby eating, but not having a stomach for the food to go into. So Piaget had to come up with some idea of what the first schemas probably looked like. Piaget found the answer to his dilemma in basic **reflexes**. I'm quite sure you know what reflexes are, especially if you've ever coughed, sneezed, or startled in your lifetime. But to be a bit more technical, we can define reflexes as more or less genetically determined, hardwired, organized patterns of behavior that usually occur in response to some environmental event. The sucking reflex, the grasping reflex, and the orienting reflex are just a few of the dozens of reflexes that human babies bring to the world with them. And it is through these basic reflexes that babies first understand the world.

So babies' first understanding of the world isn't a "blooming, buzzing confusion" as psychologist William James once suggested. Rather, babies are prepared by nature to understand the world in terms of how their reflexes can act on it. Remember earlier when I talked about how babies seem naturally predisposed to categorize the world into things that are suckable and unsuckable? This is the essence of the idea that Piaget was going for! Reflexes are babies' first schemas. Although they don't do it intentionally, babies spend much of their time reflexively responding to events taking place around them. Of course, it doesn't take long for babies to start modifying their reflexes. Once a baby figures out that a reflexive schema doesn't fit particularly well here or there, she begins to modify the schema slightly. Sucking car keys takes slightly different lip formations than sucking nipples, and both of these acts require different tongue action and lip formation than sucking a finger. Even though these differences are very slight, the process of adjusting existing schemas to be more consistent with the demands of the surrounding environment is the very essence of intellectual development, according to Piaget. Adjusting one's schemas to fit the environment is also a reflection of the very kind of evolutionary adaptation that Piaget thought made intellectual development completely consistent with the general principles of biology.

The next step, then, is to explain how schemas get adjusted. The key to understanding this kind of intellectual adaptation is in understanding the complementary processes of assimilation and accommodation. These processes work as a team, and their common goal is to ensure that an individual's internal schemas about the external world are *in balance* with the actual external world. Unfortunately, the terms *assimilation* and *accommodation* are very easily confused. They are closely related to each other in meaning, and they describe highly abstract concepts that you can rarely see in real life and that you really can't even imagine all that well. In a feeble attempt at illustrating the difference between assimilation and accommodation, let me go back to my favorite type of analogy: food.

Imagine that you want to make a peanut butter sandwich (my youngest daughter's favorite!). The first step is to spread peanut butter on a slice of bread. Now notice three things about this very mundane activity. First, you are spreading the peanut butter on the bread—not on your nose, not on a banana, not on your television screen.

The very concept of making a peanut butter sandwich requires that the peanut butter be put on the bread. If it were put on something else, you would no longer have a peanut butter sandwich. Instead you'd have something like "peanut butter nose" or "peanut butter TV." Second, after you spread the peanut butter on a slice of bread, the bread really isn't just bread anymore—it's bread with peanut butter on it. The very essence of that piece of bread has changed forever. Sure, the bread is still there, but it's not the same bread that was there without the peanut butter. The peanut butter has permanently changed the essence of that piece of bread. The bread is no longer just bread; it has become part of a peanut butter sandwich. Third, notice that you can't put the peanut butter on the bread without the bread also having some peanut butter put on it.

If you're following my wacky train of thought here, then you understand the basic concepts of assimilation and accommodation. But let me try to explain them in the sense of how they can be applied to intellectual development. Assimilation and accommodation are the processes responsible for making sure that a baby's understanding of the world is consistent with what he experiences in the world. And remember that a baby's first understanding of the world is through the basic schemas he possesses. Well, every time that a baby attempts to understand new parts of the world, he first tries to apply schemas that he already has in place. For very young babies, this might mean trying to suck the new stuff. If a baby tries to suck something he has never sucked before, say a dog biscuit, then we would say he is assimilating the dog biscuit into his sucking schema. By the act of sucking the dog biscuit, he is in a very real sense learning about the dog biscuit, and he is learning about it in this case by assimilating it into his sucking schema (and not to any other existing schema). Had he attempted to assimilate the dog biscuit into any other schema, then he wouldn't have been sucking on it. Notice that this is similar to the requirement that to make a peanut butter sandwich, you have to put peanut butter on bread. If you put peanut butter on something else, you wouldn't be making a peanut butter sandwich. To make a peanut butter sandwich, the peanut butter has to be more or less assimilated to the bread.

But when the baby starts sucking the dog biscuit, the sucking schema itself gets permanently changed. It is no longer a sucking schema that has never sucked a dog biscuit before; it is a sucking schema that has had experience with sucking dog biscuits. This experience converts the sucking schema into somewhat of a dog-biscuit-sucking veteran. A baby who has experienced dog biscuit sucking has a sucking schema that is more sophisticated than the sucking schema of a baby who is a dog-biscuit-sucking virgin. The fact that the schema changes in some way every time it encounters some new experience demonstrates the idea of accommodation. When a baby sucks a dog biscuit, he is assimilating the biscuit to his sucking schema (and not his grasping schema); but at the same time, the sucking schema accommodates the new information about the world that the dog biscuit provides. The fact that an existing schema gets permanently changed by every piece of new information that is assimilated into it is in some ways similar to how the bread in a peanut butter sandwich gets permanently changed by the peanut butter that is spread on it. To restate these ideas more succinctly, assimilation happens when new information is forced into existing schemas, and accommodation happens when existing schemas are adjusted to allow for the new information. To make a peanut butter sandwich, you have to put peanut butter on bread, but the very act of putting peanut butter on the bread changes the bread from being just bread to being part of something larger than itself—being part of a peanut butter sandwich.

DEVELOPMENT FROM HERE ONWARD

Now all this talk about primitive reflex schemas, assimilation, and accommodation is just the starting point. To say that babies have intellectual structures like schemas and have intellectual adaptive processes like assimilation and accommodation is only to say that babies have some basic tools that they can use to learn about the world from the very beginning. And even then, saying that babies have these things doesn't really say much about what babies do with them. Here is where the idea of stages often is introduced. Stages are a way of describing how far along babies are in the development of their schemas.

Now, before going any further, let me ask those of you who remembered that Piaget had "something to do with stages," don't you find it interesting that you've spent a whole chapter reading about Piaget and it's only now that I'm saying anything about stages? I think the reason for this, as I mentioned before, is that stages aren't really the most interesting part of his theory. To me the most interesting parts of his theory are the ones that tie intellectual development to basic biological functioning and evolutionary theory.

Still, I suppose I should say a few words about stages since most college textbooks spend so much time describing them. Let me start by saying that stages are really overrated. A stage is really just a shorthand way of describing a single point in time, but as you might imagine, it's not particularly useful to talk about a single point in time unless you know what happened before and what's going to happen afterward.

Let me give you an example by having you recite the alphabet to yourself. Now when you get to K, let me know. Are you there yet? Okay, now stop reciting. I hereby declare that you are in the "K-stage" of reciting the alphabet. Aren't you excited? I hope not, because being in the K-stage doesn't really do much for you, does it? What's useful about the alphabet is not that there is a K somewhere along the line, but that the alphabet can be used in highly productive ways for communicating with others through writing. Similarly, what's useful about children's intellectual development is not that there are points along the line where you can stop counting and say that a child is in a particular stage. Rather, what's useful is that intellectual development as a whole can be used in an attempt to explain how a child is able to learn about and survive in the world.

Still, as child development scientists we have a tendency to try to pigeonhole children into one of Piaget's main stages—the Sensorimotor, the Preoperational, the Concrete Operational, or the Formal Operational—or even more finely into one of his substages. (Remember my point earlier about our natural tendency to categorize?) But whether we need to talk about stages in order for the science of child psychology to make progress is questionable. Yes, Piaget talked about stages and substages. But how much importance he placed on them is highly debated. It seems that we Americans are the ones hung up on stages. In fact, I've even heard the debate about the importance of stages called "the American problem." Piaget's followers who studied under him in the Genevan tradition (i.e., people who worked with him in his own lab in Geneva, Switzerland) seem to think that the stages themselves are far less important than the structures and processes that contribute to intellectual development. Nevertheless, it is entirely true that if you take a snapshot of intellectual development at any particular point of time, it will appear that a child is at a specific stage of development. I guess that places you at the "end of Chapter 2" stage of this book!

Bibliography

Beilin, H. (1992). Piaget's enduring contribution to developmental psychology. *Developmental Psychology, 28*, 191–204.

Cairns, R. B. (1992). The making of a developmental science: The contributions and intellectual heritage of James Mark Baldwin. *Developmental Psychology, 28*, 17–24.

Ginsburg, H. P., & Opper, S. (1988). *Piaget's theory of intellectual development.* Englewood Cliffs, NJ: Prentice Hall.

Messerly, J. G. (1996). *Piaget's conception of evolution.* Lanham, MD: Rowman & Littlefield.

Piaget, J. (1950). *The psychology of intelligence.* London: Routledge & Kegan Paul.

Piaget, J. (1952). Piaget. In E. G. Boring, H. S. Langfeld, H. Werner, & R. M. Yerkes (Eds.), *A history of psychology in autobiography.* Worcester, MA: Clark University Press.

Vidal, F. (1994). *Piaget before Piaget.* Cambridge, MA: Harvard University Press.

Questions for Discussion

1. Would Piaget's impact on the field of child psychology have differed had he not been trained as a biologist?

2. Would child psychology look different today if Piaget had gotten along better with his mother? Why or why not?

3. Why is it important for the laws of psychology to correspond to the laws of biology? In general, how important is it for laws to correspond across any group of scientific fields?

4. No one has ever seen a mental schema, and it's unlikely that anyone ever will. Given this fact, can the notion of a schema have any scientific usefulness?

3

When Thinking Begins

THE ORIGINS OF INTELLIGENCE IN CHILDREN.
Piaget, J. (1952). *New York: International University Press.*   (RANK 1)

I must admit at the outset that by including this 1952 book in my list of the 20 studies that revolutionized child psychology, I embrace a certain amount of chronological dishonesty. Now it's not like I robbed the campus bookstore or anything. But keep in mind that the whole premise of my book is to showcase revolutionary child psychology research that has taken place since 1950. Although *The Origins of Intelligence in Children* (hereafter called simply *Origins*) really was published in its English version in 1952, the book was originally published in its French version in 1936. In fact, the data presented in *Origins* were originally collected in the 1920s! So why include it among my post-1950 list? Well, there are at least three reasons; feel free to choose whichever one you like best. First, this is my book, and I can handle it any way I want to, so there. Second, I'm an American elitist and as far as I'm concerned, science really isn't science until it's translated into English (just kidding). Or third, *Origins* was quite simply the most frequently nominated study in my empirical survey. In fact, it was nominated by almost all of the scholars who nominated Piaget at all, so obviously members of the child psychology research community view the book as really important.

Okay, so why do they view this book as so important? I think that much of the popularity of *Origins* was because it was here that Piaget summarized his most significant theoretical points about early intellectual development. And he coupled

25

his theoretical claims with real-life observations that helped create and support them. Unlike other epistemologists of the time, many of whom were armchair philosophers, Piaget, eminent scientist that he was, was very aware of the need to present scientific data in support of his beliefs. I think the book's popularity also came from the fact that it was the first of a trilogy of Piaget's books that exploded on the American scene right at a time when American developmental psychologists were trying to escape from the twin asphyxiating grasps of Freudian psychosexual theory and Watson's/Skinner's behaviorism. For many scholars Piaget's general biological approach, which was largely captured in this initial work, was truly a breath of fresh air!

INTRODUCTION

Because I was able to use much of the preceding chapter to describe the forces driving Piaget's theory, along with many of the central principles of the theory, I have, in essence, already given you the introduction to this study. And so I have much greater latitude in dealing with Piaget's findings. But let's review very briefly the main points of the previous chapter in a rough logical order. (1) Piaget was an evolutionary biologist. (2) Therefore, he believed that all organisms must adapt to survive. (3) Adaptation takes place at the species level *phylogenetically*. (4) Adaptation also takes place at the individual level *ontogenetically*. (5) Intelligence happens in biological organisms. (6) Therefore, intelligence is a biological process. (7) Therefore, intelligence adapts. (8) Because intelligence adapts ontogenetically, we should be able to observe it in the development of children. (9) The ontogenetic adaptation of intelligence in children might give a good approximation of the phylogenetic adaptation of intelligence that took place in the species since at least 300,000 years ago.

So Piaget's grand theoretical framework was pretty much laid out. But the busy work of finding evidence to support his notions had only just begun. All he had to do was collect the data. In *Origins*, Piaget set out on the task of determining the starting point of it all. And one of the very first questions Piaget had to contend with was "When does intelligence begin?" Or, to say it in a more biologically oriented way, "When do intelligent adaptations begin?"

METHOD

Participants

The participants that Piaget observed for this book were two girls and one boy, all siblings. For *Origins* they were essentially observed several times a day, almost every day, from birth to about 2 years of age. Jacqueline was born in 1925, Lucienne was born in 1927, and Laurent was born in 1931. So from Jacqueline's birth through the time Laurent reached 2, Piaget made detailed recordings of at least one kid pretty much constantly for 3,000 days! Although this would be a Herculean effort for anybody, Piaget's efforts were reduced somewhat because the three siblings were his own children. At least the participants in his study lived in the same house! And even Mrs. Piaget helped out on occasion. It's been said that she used to carry a small notebook attached to her necklace so that she could record observations of her children as needed.

Procedure

Because Piaget was a pioneer in the scientific investigation of children's development, and because he was dealing with very, very young babies, there really weren't many existing methodologies at his disposal that he could use to measure babies' thinking abilities. Compounded with this problem was the fact that 1-week-old babies are notoriously difficult to carry on a conversation with. This means that almost every method Piaget used to measure the thinking abilities of babies was his own creation. Have you ever heard the saying "Necessity is the mother of invention"? Well, Piaget invented dozens of methods to test out his various hypotheses, many of which are still used to this day. Unfortunately, I don't have the space to describe every type of observational technique Piaget developed, but I can at least share with you a couple of examples. Neither task was particularly sophisticated—no computers were involved, no high technology was employed. But nobody ever said doing experiments with babies had to be fancy. As the great philosopher and baseball coach Yogi Berra once said, "You can observe a lot just by watchin'."

Means-Ends Task.   In the typical means-ends task, babies are observed to see whether they can perform one action in order to do a second action. The second action is usually the more desirable action. When one act is necessary to do a second act, we call it **means-ends sequencing**. Means-ends sequencing is essential for our existence, and we do it all the time. For example, you engage in means-ends sequencing every time you remove the cap in order to take a swig of Pepsi-Cola. And about 30 minutes after drinking the Pepsi, you engage in means-ends sequencing when you push open the door to enter the restroom. Means-ends sequencing is essential to adult intellectual functioning because it's what allows us to make plans about the future. But from a developmental point of view, one might wonder when means-ends sequencing first happens. Hence, on several different occasions at several different ages, Piaget employed various forms of means-ends tasks with his kids.

For example, when Jacqueline was just over 12 months of age, Piaget placed a series of objects on a shawl, just outside of her reach. Although she couldn't reach the objects, the shawl was close enough to grab. Each time an object was placed before her, Jacqueline first tried to reach the object directly. But she quickly realized that a better way to get the objects was simply to pull on the shawl. In this way, bringing the shawl near was the *means* toward obtaining the *end* of getting the objects. The means-ends task is not overwhelmingly popular these days as a measure of intellectual competence, but for many years it was used as *the* standard measure of intellectual performance. In fact, many researchers believed performance on the means-ends task was a good indicator of infant IQ, although it should be said that performance on the task was never strongly correlated with "real" assessments of IQ in later childhood.

Object Permanence Task.   The **object permanence** task is actually just an extension of the means-ends task, but it's used more specifically to discover how well children understand that an object continues to exist even when they can't see it. You may have heard of object permanence in your high school or introductory psychology class. The basic idea comes from the notion that as adults, we function under the assumption that things continue to exist even when we no longer sense their presence. We assume that our bed will still be there when we get back home after a 12-hour shift of hard labor. We assume that the turkey we put into the oven at 6:00 a.m. on Thanksgiving Day will still be there when we go to take it out at 1:00 p.m. In fact, it's hard to imagine what the world would be like if we didn't know that objects continue to exist when we don't see them. Just as with our ability to use certain means to reach certain ends, our adult understanding of the permanence of objects is extremely adaptive. But again, we are left wondering when babies first show that they understand the permanence of objects.

In another display of ingenuity, Piaget again demonstrated that you don't need a high-tech procedure to measure object permanence. Basically, what he did was cover up an interesting toy with a cloth until it was no longer available to the baby's senses. The key question was whether the baby would remove the cloth in order to retrieve the toy. If so, the baby was assumed to have some form of understanding of the permanence of the object. If not, it was more likely a case of "out of sight, out of mind."

RESULTS

Piaget's results in *Origins* were not neatly summarized into a single, concise "Results" section, as would typically be found in professional journal articles. Instead, they were pretty much scattered throughout the book in various sections and subsections, brought into play as Piaget needed them to make some theoretical point about intelligent adaptation. It took him some 419 pages to tell the story of all his data. What I will attempt to do in my much shorter redescription of his results is to profile his major findings in the same order he presented them.

Remember that in *Origins*, Piaget was investigating intellectual development in babies from birth to about 2 years of age. So his results are pretty much presented in chronological order, starting with the intellectual adaptations of newborns and ending with the intellectual adaptations of 2-year-olds. He breaks this 2-year time frame into six different substages. (Remember that he calls the first major stage of development the sensorimotor period. But in this book, he breaks down this bigger period into even smaller chunks of developmental time, which we can call substages.) In describing each of these substages, Piaget focused on one or more of the major developmental breakthroughs demonstrated by his children during this time frame. Let me say one more time that in my opinion the interesting feature of this developmental story is not that children achieve and eventually graduate from these stages, but that their intellectual functioning represents adaptation through natural selection just as in all other aspects of biology.

In the pages that follow, I will run through the six substages that Piaget delineated. In doing so, I would like to give you a flavor of Piaget's writing style, so I will reproduce excerpts from the observations he made of his own children. This is something you don't get in a typical introductory child psychology text. But I think it will give you a better sense of the way that Piaget thought about things. Throughout these excerpts, you will see references to the children's ages during certain observations that look something like this: 1;4 (14). This is Piaget's shorthand for noting that the child was 1 year, 4 months, and 14 days old. Obviously, Piaget was quite a stickler for detail. And many times he would make observations of exactly the same behaviors on several days in a row.

The First Substage: The Use of Reflexes.   In some ways, the believability of Piaget's entire theory came down to how well he could account for children's thinking in the very first days of life. You see, it's one thing to say that adult thinking can be traced to its roots in childhood thinking; but this just takes a difficult problem at one level (adulthood) and moves it to another level (childhood). And as much as one might wish to keep moving the problem to earlier and earlier periods in human development, for example from late childhood to early childhood, then from early childhood to toddlerhood and so on, eventually one has to pay the piper. At some point, we have to account for the very first thinking. But this is like a chicken-and-egg problem. As the old conundrum goes, you can't have a chicken without an egg, but it takes a chicken to lay the first egg. Similarly, you can't have thinking without the first thought, but you can't have the first thought without also thinking. So Piaget carried quite an intellectual burden in trying to explain the very first thinking. Let's see how he dealt with it.

If you remember from the previous chapter, Piaget's problem really amounted to explaining where children get their first schemas. Schemas are the knowledge structures that underlie all thinking, and so what he had to do was account for the very first ones. Undoubtedly, one important breakthrough took place when Piaget realized that early schemas didn't need to look much like adult ones at all. In fact, the earliest schemas could look quite different from later ones. The key similarities between the first schemas and later schemas were to be found not in their structures, but in their function, in what they allowed the baby to do. Remember, thinking is a biological process that helps the organism adapt to the world. All Piaget had to do was figure out what babies brought with them into the world that would allow them to adapt to it. Piaget's solution to the problem was simple: *REFLEXES!*

Although all reflexes are essentially "hardwired" in the brain, they aren't impervious to environmental experience. In fact, many reflexes require the environment for their very existence. One of Piaget's favorite reflexes to talk about was the sucking reflex. In one of his earliest diary entries, he wrote: "Observation 1.— From birth sucking-like movements may be observed: impulsive movement and protrusion of the lips accompanied by displacements of the tongue, while the arms engage in unruly and more or less rhythmical gestures and the head moves laterally, etc. Observation 3.—The third day Laurent makes new progress in his adjustment to the breast. All he needs in order to grope with open mouth toward final success is to have touched the breast or the surrounding teguments with his lips. But he hunts on the wrong side as well as on the right side, that is to say, the side where contact has been made."

Already you can see that Piaget emphasizes "progress" in the adaptations of reflexes to the environment; in this case, of sucking. The sucking schema doesn't stay the same for long; it adapts to the environment right from the start. Within a few weeks, children begin coordinating the sucking schema with environmental input from other senses. For example, in later substages vision takes on a key role in babies' abilities to fire up the sucking reflex. Consider the following observation: "Observation 27.—Jacqueline, at 0;4 (27) and the days following, opens her mouth as soon as she is shown the bottle. She only began mixed feeding at 0;4 (12). At 0;7 (13) I note that she opens her mouth differently according to whether she is offered a bottle or a spoon. Lucienne at 0;3 (12) stops crying when she sees her mother unfastening her dress for the meal. Laurent too, between 0;3 (15) and 0;4 reacts to visual signals. When, after being dressed as usual just before the meal, he is put in my arms in position for nursing, he looks at me and then searches all around, looks at me again, etc.—but he does not attempt to nurse. When I place him in his mother's arms without his touching the breast, he looks at her and immediately opens his mouth wide, cries, moves about, in short reacts in a completely different way. It is therefore sight and no longer only the position which henceforth is the signal." So the point is that over time, and with experience, the sucking reflex ceases to be a slave to tactile stimulation, and becomes much more responsive to visual stimulation. This clearly illustrates developmental maturity of the sucking schema.

As an aside, I'd like to bring to your attention the incredible detail in Piaget's diary records. Could you imagine sitting around staring at the mouth movements of your children just to see if the mouth takes on a slightly different shape before sucking a bottle versus a spoon? I wonder if Piaget's respect for this level of detail can be traced back to his childhood when he sat around all day staring at mollusk shells!

The Second Substage: The First Acquired Adaptations and the Primary Circular Reactions.
The first substage was very short-lived in Piaget's mind—about a month—because babies' reflexes so quickly start adapting to the surrounding environment. Once a reflex changes as a result of coming into contact with the environment, in even the tiniest way, then the reflex is no longer exactly the same as it was. In other words, we can say the reflex has accommodated. In watching his kids, Piaget noticed that sometimes, beginning in about the second month, they would exercise their schemas apparently just for the enjoyment of the exercise. These kinds of behaviors indicated that the actions were no longer purely reflexive, because there was nothing around that stimulated them. Instead, it was as if the activity was self-generated. Sucking, for example, could often be seen even in the absence of any reflex-causing trigger—that is, without anything actually touching the lips. In Observation 14, Piaget wrote: "During the second half of the second month, that is to say, after having learned to suck his thumb, Laurent continues to play with his tongue and to suck, but intermittently. On the other hand, his skill increases. Thus, at 0;1 (20) I notice he grimaces while placing his tongue between gums and lips and in bulging his lips, as well as making a clapping sound when quickly closing his mouth after these exercises." Here you can see how Laurent seems to be content simply to play with his mouth and tongue muscles. Nothing in the environment caused the muscles to go into action, Laurent just seemed interested in activating them himself.

At about this time, Piaget also noticed that his children would often try to activate their own reflex schemas by stimulating them with other parts of their own body. At first, they usually did so accidentally. For example, as their arms flailed about randomly, their hands would sometimes smack into their face and accidentally make contact with the lips. Their fingers would then slip into their mouths and they would suck them. Of course, in this case, sucking was initially being activated reflexively as the fingers rushed in uninvited. But if the fingers fell back out, the babies would seem to try to "coordinate" the sucking reflex with the movements of the arm as if trying to repeat the chance occurrence. "Observation 20.—At 0;1 (5) and 0;1 (6) Laurent tries to catch his thumb as soon as he awakes but is unsuccessful while lying on his back. His hand taps his face without finding his mouth. When he is vertical, however . . . he quickly finds his lips." Clearly, you can see that the sucking schema is no longer a reflexive island, passively responding to environmental stimulation, but is being coordinated with other activities of the child's own body. And the fact that the children frequently reinstated the initial chance encounter showed that there was a certain amount of circularity involved. That is to say, an action happened by accident, the baby seemed to find it interesting, so he tried to make it happen again. For this reason, Piaget called this kind of coordination between existing schemas and body activity a "circular reaction." But because the next substage also involved these kinds of circular activities, Piaget wanted to make a distinction between the kinds of circular reactions that involved only the child's own body and those that involved other objects. Therefore, the kinds of circular reactions that take place on the child's own body, Piaget called "primary"; and so putting all these terms together, we get Piaget's term **primary circular reaction**. The primary circular reactions are most common from about the 1st month to the 4th month. But afterward, their frequency dies down and kids start showing **secondary circular reactions**.

The Third Substage: The Secondary Circular Reactions and the Procedures Destined to Make Interesting Sights Last.   As his children moved past about the 4th month, Piaget observed that they not only tried to reenact interesting experiences that took place on their own body, but they often tried to incorporate outside things into their schemas as well. If you think about it, there's little difference in *how* you can apply your basic schemas either to your own body or to other things. Does your sucking reflex really care whether it's activated by your own fingers or a set of car keys? So we would say that the sucking schema is **functionally invariant**; that is, it works the same no matter whether the baby is sucking on his fingers or a Barbie Doll. But by and large, as Piaget found, babies' efforts to incorporate external objects into existing schemas tended to occur later in time. This is why Piaget created the third substage, which is pretty much the same as the second except that external objects are now the focus of the schemas.

Although I've been focusing on the sucking schema as a primary means that babies learn about the world around them, this schema was only one among many that Piaget talked about. Another major player among infants' first knowledge schemas involved vision, or as we called it in the previous chapter, the orienting reflex. As an example of how babies coordinated their orienting reflex with outside objects, Piaget noted that his children would often perform some action, again usually accidentally at first, and the action would have some effect on the surrounding environment that the kids observed. They would then try to re-create the interesting event. Take, for example, Observation 94: "At 0;3 (5) Lucienne shakes her bassinet by moving her legs violently (bending and unbending them, etc.), which makes the cloth dolls swing from the hood. Lucienne looks at them, smiling, and recommences at once. These movements are simply the concomitants of joy. When she experiences great pleasure Lucienne externalizes it in a total reaction of leg movements." So here you see that a random body movement causes some external object to move about, which Lucienne sees (meaning that she incorporates it into her visual orienting schema), and she tries to make it happen again. This is a circular reaction of a secondary sort, but involving vision. A similar kind of reaction can be seen with Lucienne's hearing schema: "Observation 102.—. . . At 0;4 (15) Lucienne grasps the handle of a rattle in the shape of a celluloid ball. The movements of the hand in grasping the rattle result in shaking it and producing a sudden and violent noise. Lucienne at once moves her whole body, and especially her feet, to make the noise last. She has a demented expression of mingled fear and pleasure, but she continues."

In all of these examples, Piaget's goal is to provide evidence that schemas are present at birth in the form of reflexes, and that they slowly but surely get incorporated into grander and grander patterns of behavior that will give babies a fuller and better understanding of the world. Development isn't all-or-none. It takes place gradually—as later schemas build on earlier ones—with each passing experience the child has. But incorporating body actions and environmental experience into preexisting schemas is only the beginning. The really serious sensorimotor intelligent adaptations start emerging in the fourth substage. Up through substage 3, babies do something accidentally, and they try to make it happen again. Remember, these are the circular reactions we've been talking about. But in substage 4, babies start showing that they can do things on purpose. Here, they start demonstrating *intention*! And it is here that we start seeing the integration of some schemas into the service of other schemas. For the first time, babies show a capability for means-ends action.

The Fourth Substage: The Coordination of the Secondary Schemas and Their Application to New Situations.

In substage 4, which Piaget thought began at about 8 or 9 months of age, babies take a major intellectual leap forward. All along they've been developing individual, isolated schemas that have been informed by environmental feedback. They have schemas for seeing things, hearing things, sucking things, grabbing things, shaking things, pulling things, and hitting things. But before now, babies haven't coordinated two or more schemas in order to carry out some planned action. Before now, babies pretty much just reacted to things. But in substage 4, instead of only being mostly reactive, babies start being proactive. They start acting on the world, intentionally, in order to accomplish something.

Consider the following: "Observation 124.—At 0;8 (8) Jacqueline tries to grasp her celluloid duck but I also grasp it at the same time she does. Then she firmly holds the toy in her right hand and pushes my hand away with her left. I repeat the experiment by grasping only the end of the duck's tail: she again pushes my hand away. At 0;8 (17) after taking a first spoonful of medicine, she pushes away her mother's hand which extends to her a second one. At 0;9 (20) she tries to place her duck against the wicker of the bassinet but she is bothered by the string in her right hand and moves it to the far side of the left arm (the arm holding the duck), and consequently where the string no longer is an obstacle." What Piaget is describing here is that Jacqueline can use one schema, something like a pushing-away schema, in order to help her enact another schema, something like a pulling-toward schema. This is intellectual adaptation of the best kind—getting what you want! It also demonstrates a serious intellectual advantage over earlier behaviors. Previously, babies only attempted to reproduce actions that had happened by accident—the so-called primary and secondary circular reactions. Now, however, babies manage to use old schemas in new ways. Old schemas aren't activated for their own sake, they are activated for the sake of making other schemas possible. When babies move an obstacle out of the way to get an interesting thing, such as a celluloid duck, they aren't merely trying to reproduce an interesting effect they've already observed. Rather, they're dealing innovatively with a problem they're just now encountering for the first time!

We also see in this substage evidence of the emergence of object exploration for the sake of "understanding" the object. When confronted with some new object, babies in this stage will attempt to incorporate the object as much as possible into as many of the existing schemas as possible. It's as if they're saying to themselves, "Hmm. Can I suck it? Can I grab it? Can I shake it? Can I hit it?" "Observation 138.—Lucienne, at 0;8 (10) . . . examines a new doll which I hang from the hood of her bassinet. She looks at it for a long time, touches it, then feels it by touching its feet, clothes, head, etc. She then ventures to grasp it, which makes the hood sway. She then pulls the doll while watching the effects of this movement. Then she returns to the doll, holds it in one hand while striking it with the other, sucks it and shakes it while holding it above her and finally shakes it by moving its legs." So it appears that babies not only can sequence one schema in the service of another, as we saw in the means-ends behaviors above, but babies can also chain together a whole series of schemas, maybe five or six in a row, to better understand a new thing.

The Fifth Substage: The Tertiary Circular Reaction and the Discovery of New Means Through Active Experiments. The progress of intelligence through the first four substages has more or less involved the application of familiar schemas to new situations. In substage 2, reflexive schemas are applied to accidental encounters with one's own body and are reproduced to make them last. In substage 3, the same schemas are applied to accidental encounters with outside objects, but they are still reproduced to make them last. In substage 4, familiar schemas are intercoordinated to achieve some new ends. But in substage 5, there is a new push to use old knowledge to achieve novel results, at an even higher level. This time, existing schemas are used in the pursuit of novelty itself. This **tertiary circular reaction** is a pattern of behavior that Piaget observed frequently in his own kids when they were between 12 and 18 months of age.

The circular reactions of substage 5 have much the same flavor of the circular reactions of substages 2 and 3 in that they're repeated over and over. But in those more primitive substages, the circular reactions pretty much just reproduced the *same* interesting effect each time. Substage 5 circular reactions, on the other hand, are aimed at producing a different interesting effect each time. Here an old schema is applied—dropping, for instance—but the schema is not reproduced just to get the same effect that has just occurred. Rather the goal is to produce a series of novel effects. True, the same *general* schema is enacted over and over, but the specific details vary. Consider Laurent's behavior: "Observation 141.—At 0;10 (11) Laurent is lying on his back but nevertheless resumes his experiments of the day before. He grasps in succession a celluloid swan, a box, etc., stretches out his arm and lets them fall. He distinctly varies the position of the fall. Sometimes he stretches out his arm vertically, sometimes he holds it obliquely, in front of or behind his eyes, etc. When the object falls in a new position (for example on his pillow), he lets it fall two or three times more on the same place, as though to study the spatial relation; then he modifies the situation."

It seems as if the goal is not just to learn about the object, as it was in substage 4, but to learn about how the object interacts with the world, to learn about *relationships* between objects. And a good way to find out how the object interacts with a variety of aspects of the world is to vary the ways in which the object is given the *opportunity* to interact with various aspects of the world. In this substage, the baby is a little scientist! He drops an object from a variety of locales, noting the different behaviors of the object each time it is dropped. Not only is he learning about the behavior of the object with respect to the world, he is learning about the world with respect to the object. In so doing, the baby is learning about gravity (when an object falls), friction (when an object slides down another object), solidity (when one object collides into another object), bounciness (when one object bounces off another), mass (when a big object comes into contact with a smaller object), and so on.

In substage 5, the baby's little mind makes a huge leap. If you think about it, she's learning about many of the same topics that are covered in a high school physics class. However, there is at least one major difference between the intellectual abilities of 15-month-olds and those of 15-year-olds. The babies' understanding of objects in the world is limited to what they can do with them in the immediate present. They can't, for example, think about what might happen in advance of it happening. They also can't imagine it happening in the absence of any real objects. It's not until substage 6 that these kinds of abilities start to emerge.

The Sixth Substage: The Invention of New Means Through Mental Combinations.
The biggest innovation that takes place in this substage, which Piaget located sometime around the 18th month, is the *internalization* of schemas that previously had to be enacted physically. In other words, schemas go mental. This achievement provides some serious adaptive advantages over previous behaviors. For one thing, babies don't have to actually perform an action in order to know something about the world. Instead, they can more or less anticipate what will happen by imagining it. Piaget called this "pre-vision." Through pre-vision, babies can figure out how to solve some kinds of problems without the consequences of trial and error. One of my favorite examples of this kind of thinking comes from Lucienne Piaget in Observation 180. Piaget writes, "Here begins the experiment which we want to emphasize. I put the chain back into the box and reduce the opening to 3 mm. It is understood that Lucienne is not aware of the functioning of the opening and closing of the matchbox and has not seen me prepare the experiment. She only possesses the two preceding schemata: turning the box over in order to empty it of its contents, and sliding her finger into the slit to make the chain come out. It is of course this last procedure that she tries first: she puts her finger inside and gropes to reach the chain, but fails completely. A pause follows during which Lucienne manifests a very curious reaction bearing witness not only to the fact that she tries to think out the situation and to represent to herself through mental combination the operations to be performed, but also to the role played by imitation in the genesis of the representation. Lucienne mimics the widening of the slit. She looks at the slit with great attention: then, several times in succession, she opens and shuts her mouth, at first slightly, then wider and wider! Apparently Lucienne understands the existence of a cavity subjacent to the slit and wishes to enlarge the cavity."

This observation so clearly illustrates the transition from thinking on the outside to thinking on the inside that I don't think Piaget could've captured the moment better with a Polaroid snapshot. Let's recap. First, Lucienne had a problem that she needed to adapt to. She needed to get a small chain out of a partially opened match-box. To solve this problem, she first tried out a couple of good ol' schemas that worked for her in the past: her "turning-over" and "finger-poking" schemas. But this time, the schemas failed her. The chain was still stuck inside the matchbox. So Luci-enne bumped up her intellectual efforts a couple of notches and represented the problem in a different way—using her imagination. Once she removed the problem from its physical form and represented it mentally, she was able to invent a solution that wasn't previously possible. She pretended her mouth was the slit of the match-box. By bringing this mental image into play, Lucienne was able to manipulate the image in a new way. Specifically, she was able to pretend she was opening and clos-ing the matchbox by opening and closing her mouth. And once she was able to do this, she made the connection that to get the chain out of the matchbox all she had to do was open the matchbox wider than it already was. Voilà, success!

To summarize: By the end of the sensorimotor period, intelligence is no longer bound to actions on the world in conjunction with the sensory feedback they produce. The most adaptive schemas at this point are those that are capable of being repre-sented mentally—freed from the here and now. Because schemas can be invoked mentally without needing real-world objects to act upon, children in the sixth sub-stage have some serious intellectual advantages over children in the more primitive substages. For one thing, they don't have to actually do things in order to gain knowl-edge; instead, they can gain knowledge just by imagining things. Does it make for an adaptive advantage to be able to use your imagination? Heavens yes! Consider, for example, how long it would take you to learn about weight differences if you still had to physically lift a watermelon and an orange in order to know which was heav-ier. A second advantage of having your schemas go mental is that they allow you to invent solutions to problems that wouldn't have occurred otherwise. This is where Piaget's phrase "invention of new means through mental combinations" comes into play. Mentally, schemas can be combined with each other in ways that could never happen in reality. For example, imagine flying a Volvo 740 to Lake Erie to go fishing for whales and sharks. Of course, none of this could happen in reality, but they can happen very easily in mentality! Obviously, once schemas go mental there's a whole new range of possibilities for intellectual adaptation to the world. Piaget believed that once schemas became mentally represented, they were able to assimilate one another not only rapidly, but spontaneously—almost automatically.

SUMMARY

Piaget's single goal in *Origins* was to present data that showed that intelligent adapta-tion as a result of experience takes place, and that it takes place in a manner consis-tent with the basic tenets of evolutionary theory. In achieving this goal, Piaget developed a framework for describing how babies' intelligences adapted, and the framework applied equally well throughout infancy; from the earliest, most primitive reflexive "thoughts" of newborns to the most advanced mental combinations of 2-year-olds. The keys to his theory were the "functionally invariant" roles played by the adaptive processes of assimilation and accommodation. By "functionally invariant" adaptive processes, I mean that although the specific items that were assimilated and accommodated to might change over time, the processes themselves worked the same way no matter what the items were or how old the child was. It doesn't matter if you're assimilating a car key to your sucking schema or a matchbox opening to your mouth-opening schema, assimilation is assimilation is assimilation.

CONCLUSIONS

As I mentioned previously, Piaget gets so much space in this book because he was so important to the field of psychology. Piaget laid his cards down for everyone to see, and by doing so, he set the standard that everyone else would have to live up to. And, as a matter of fact, the 1960s and 1970s represented a Piagetian golden age. Everybody was testing this or that hypothesis generated by Piagetian theory. And the old master himself was still alive and kicking and doing as much as he could to further our understanding of children's cognitive development.

But as you might imagine, when you're the leader of a major revolution of any sort, it doesn't take long before other people start having second thoughts about the leadership you're providing. And so it was that a number of anti-Piagetian movements started to rise and gain momentum. The behaviorists, who, throughout the 1950s and 1960s, remained strong vocal opponents of the notion of internal mental development Piaget so clearly articulated, took potshots whenever possible. And Chomsky (see Chapter 8), who was as anti-behaviorist as Piaget, was also as anti-Piaget as were the behaviorists. Chomsky believed Piaget gave too much weight to children's own efforts at *constructing* their own mental world. As we will see in Chapter 8, Chomsky was a firm believer in the innateness of grammar; so from his point of view, there was simply no room for the Piagetian idea that children were the authors of their own mental development.

In the two decades since Piaget's death in 1980, his theory remains the target of attack of many psychologists. For example, as we see in Chapter 6, Renee Baillargeon took a huge bite out of Piaget's suggestion that object permanence doesn't fully develop until 18–24 months of age. But the result of these attacks has often been only to show that Piaget might have been wrong about *when* a particular cognitive ability emerged, not about *whether* it existed. In the end, it's a tribute to Piaget's vision, ingenuity, and comprehensiveness that his theory remains on center stage in contemporary child psychology theory. While it may be true that his theory no longer commands the attention of the entire field as it once did, his ideas remain so central to modern child psychology as to be almost invisible.

Questions for Discussion

1. What might be some limitations of basing an entire theory of cognitive development on observations of only 3 children?
2. What might be some strengths of basing an entire theory of cognitive development on observations of only 3 children?
3. Compare and contrast the concept of development with the concept of differentiation, as they apply to basic reflexive schemas.
4. Why is the concept of functional invariance important for a developmental theory?

4
A Marxist Revolution in Psychology

MIND IN SOCIETY: THE DEVELOPMENT OF HIGHER PSYCHOLOGICAL PROCESSES.
Vygotsky, L. S. (1978). *Cambridge, MA: Harvard University Press.*   (RANK 2)

And now, finishing in second place among the most revolutionary studies in child psychology published since 1950, the famous work of the Russian psychologist we all know and love, Lev Semenovich Vygotsky! What? You've never heard of Vygotsky? Well, you're not alone. Vygotsky (pronounced "vih-GOT-skee") gets so little coverage in most textbooks, if he gets mentioned at all, that you'd be in the minority if you actually had heard of him. In fact, I'd bet that some psychologists wouldn't even recognize the name. So it's somewhat surprising that Vygotsky's work was regarded as so revolutionary by so many child psychologists, with only Piaget's work rated more highly. For one thing, Vygotsky's book *Mind in Society* has been accessible to English readers for only about the last two decades—which means that Vygotsky's book gave up a 26-year head start to Piaget's. Moreover, Vygotsky has been dead for almost 70 years! It's not like he's been able to hobnob with the intellectual elite or anything. Piaget lived to the ripe old age of 84 and got the chance to revise and refine his theories until 1980. No, whatever revolutionary fires Vygotsky ignited, he did so with about half as many matches as Piaget. Nevertheless, in recent years Vygotsky has exploded onto the scene.

Like Piaget's, Vygotsky's interests actually extended far beyond the world of child psychology. In his doctoral work, he was especially interested in law and literature. In fact, before he even began his studies of children, he earned a law degree and went on to write a doctoral dissertation on William Shakespeare's famous work *Hamlet*. Vygotsky was well read indeed! But even when he began his investigations of children's mental development, he was always working from within the philosophical-political perspective of Karl Marx's theories on government and labor. Marx's writings consistently emphasized the importance of people within a community working together toward the greater, common good. Marx believed that the common good could be obtained through cooperative labor, including the use of tools. The idea was that if everyone worked together toward achieving the values of a society, society as a whole would be far better off than if individual members of the society competed with one another in promoting their own individual self-interests. Vygotsky believed that Marx's ideas should be applied to the science of psychology as well. Unfortunately, the psychology of Vygotsky's time tended to focus on the individual. So he set out to revolutionize psychology by creating a science in which the development of the individual was always considered in the context of the individual's surrounding physical and social environments.

COMPARISONS BETWEEN VYGOTSKY AND PIAGET

Before diving into Vygotsky's work more deeply, I'd like to point out a number of similarities between him and Piaget. Perhaps by understanding their commonalities, we can begin to appreciate what it takes to achieve greatness in the field of child psychology. First off, both Vygotsky and Piaget were juvenile geniuses. Vygotsky scholar James Wertsch writes that when Vygotsky was an adolescent, he and his teenage buddies used to act out fictional debates between historical figures of great intellectual prominence, such as Aristotle and Napoleon. Given these kinds of antics, it seems to me that if Vygotsky and Piaget had met each other on the playground, which was physically possible since both were born in 1896, they might have developed a great friendship! Both of them seemed to enjoy doing odd, nerdy things. It is also noteworthy that Vygotsky, like Piaget, worked tirelessly and published massively at a very young age. By the time of his premature death of tuberculosis at the age of 37, Vygotsky had already published or written over 180 scientific works. Unfortunately for the rest of the world, many of his writings remained hidden from the English-speaking public for many decades by the long arms of Stalin's communist regime. Only in the last 20 years or so has the collection of Vygotsky's writings become generally accessible, including the release of a multivolume series published in the mid-1980s.

A second and perhaps more important similarity was that both Vygotsky and Piaget were struggling with issues much larger than child psychology itself. Whereas Piaget was coming from the point of view of Darwin's theory of evolution, Vygotsky was coming from the point of view of Karl Marx's theory of government and labor. Still I find it ironic that although Vygotsky and Piaget were rated as the two most revolutionary scientists in child psychology, neither one of them had child psychology as their primary interest! Both scientists viewed child psychology as only a small, if essential, piece of the much larger puzzles they were working on.

Another interesting similarity is that Vygotsky's *Mind in Society*, like Piaget's *Origins*, was first written in various forms many years before 1950. It wasn't until Vygotsky's writings were translated into English, making them available to the vast

American psychological community, that his ideas began taking the field of child psychology by storm. And since then, Vygotsky's works have attracted as much attention as an ice cream vendor on a hot summer day. A simple check with the PsycINFO database shows that the number of articles written about Vygotsky and his theories in the last 5 years outnumbers all other articles written about him combined.

It's important to point out that *Mind in Society* wasn't a direct translation of a Russian version of the same book. Rather, as noted by its editors, the book was more of a compendium of a number of different chunks of Vygotsky's writings. They were masterfully interwoven by the editors to tell the story of Vygotsky's psychology to the rest of the world. And like Piaget, Vygotsky apparently had a very difficult style, so the editors admitted to taking liberties with pieces of his work so as to best represent his intention without misrepresenting his meaning. So what's all the excitement about? Let's take a look.

INTRODUCTION

In the beginning of the book, Vygotsky indicates that the purpose of any psychology should be to explain the relationship between humans and their surrounding environments. Here you can see Marx's influence. There are two types of environments that humans (and the psychologists who study them) have to deal with. First, there is the physical environment. The physical environment consists of all the stuff humans come into contact with: trees, rocks, ponds, chairs, screwdrivers, and so on. Second, and perhaps far more importantly, there is the social environment. By their very nature, humans are social creatures. Vygotsky believed that this fact had to be acknowledged as a basic tenet of psychology. Any psychology that failed to recognize the social nature of humans was doomed. Understanding the nature of humans without taking into account their socialness is like playing baseball without the bases. And language was one aspect of the social environment that played an especially important role for Vygotsky, particularly in terms of the development of what he called the *higher psychological processes.*

Now, keep in mind that when Vygotsky was doing his psychology thing in the early 1900s, the science of psychology was still pretty young. Psychologists around the globe were still trying to figure out what psychology should do and how it should do it. So there were lots of different opinions about the best way to do psychology. According to Vygotsky, there was at least one way *not* to do psychology. The way not to do psychology was to start by isolating a research subject from his or her natural surroundings. In other words, you should never bring anyone into the laboratory.

Unfortunately, this was exactly how much of the rest of the field of child psychology chose to proceed. These psychologists wanted to study kids in the laboratory because they thought human environments were too rich, too complex, and too varied to be able to make much sense about how kids behaved in them. They believed that doing psychology was like looking for a needle in a haystack, where the human behavior was the needle and the environment was the haystack.

Vygotsky would've called these psychologists "artificialist psychologists," because they seemed to be focusing on constructing artificial environments in the laboratory, and pulling children out of their natural surroundings. Still, the goals of the artificialist psychologists made some sense. For example, have you ever tried to listen to a weak

AM radio station? Sometimes it's hard to even hear what song is playing unless the radio station's signal is relatively strong compared to the amount of noisy static in the background. Well, the goal of the artificialist psychologists was to reduce the "noisy static" of children's surrounding environments by bringing the children into laboratories. These psychologists reasoned that by using a laboratory, they would be able to reduce the "noisy static" of the environment, and increase the signal of human behavior. As a result, artificialist psychologists believed, true human nature would be much easier to detect. And in fact, this logic was typical of scientists in all other scientific disciplines. Consider the biologist who cultures bacteria in a petri dish. Although bacteria can grow in lots of other places, it's easy to culture specific bacteria under the artificial, highly controlled conditions that are found in a petri dish. Doesn't it make sense that psychology should adopt such tried-and-true methods too?

Well, Vygotsky completely rejected this approach. He believed that any psychology that artificially removed its subject of study from its natural surroundings was bound to be wrong. For psychology to be right, he argued, it would have to take into account not only the people themselves, but where they lived, what they ate, whom they dated, and how they talked to one another. People simply must be studied within their natural surroundings before a valid psychology could even become possible.

Tool and Symbol in Child Development

Vygotsky began his Marxist-based psychology by trying to identify the kinds of things that were uniquely and truly human, and that were responsible for promoting the welfare of human society. One of these things was the relationship between tool use and speech. By "tool use," Vygotsky meant the ability to use some part of the environment to solve a problem. By "speech," Vygotsky meant the symbols and signs humans use to communicate with each other about ideas as well as about objects and events in the world. Vygotsky believed that tool use and speech were essential to the development of human societies as a whole, and so he sought to investigate their influence on the development of the individual.

Vygotsky was fascinated by the work of some of his contemporaries with chimpanzees. He believed that chimps provided psychology with a very interesting, and essential, comparison group. On the one hand, chimps, like humans, were capable of using tools to do certain kinds of things. For example, chimps have long been known to poke skinny tree limbs into termite mounds in order to pull out gobs of deliciously tasty termites. On the other hand, chimps lacked speech. So as similar as chimps and humans were to one another in tool use, humans were still the champs as a result of their speech-using capability. So an analysis of the similarities and differences between chimpanzees and human children (before and after the onset of speech) could shed some powerful light on truly and uniquely human forms of intelligence.

Of course, human babies don't pop out of the womb using tools or speaking. Rather, these capacities develop only after several months of postnatal experience—after the child matures a bit physically, and after he accumulates a good deal of learning about his physical and social worlds. Babies use tools? Sure! We've already considered one example of the tool use of human babies. Remember Piaget's means-ends task? In the means-ends task, infants are able to pull one object (like a pillow) to get at another object sitting on top of it (like a bell). In this case, the pillow is being used as a tool.

Vygotsky believed that although the capacities for tool use and speech followed relatively separate developmental paths in human babies, when a child became capable of doing both, something very magical happened. When the tool-using infant develops into the speech-using preschooler, she becomes catapulted into a whole new level of intellectual functioning. Vygotsky called this whole new level of intellectual functioning a **higher psychological process**. A higher psychological process is simply something that can be accomplished only by humans. He noted: "[T]he most significant moment in the course of intellectual development, which gives birth to the purely human forms of practical and abstract intelligence, occurs when speech and [tool use], two previously completely independent lines of development, converge."

Vygotsky spent a lot of time studying children's problem-solving abilities as they gained proficiency at speech. He believed that the problem-solving abilities of pre-speech children were more or less like those of chimpanzees. But when children become good at speech, they leave the world of the lowly chimp and enter the world of higher psychological functioning. Why was speech so important? For one thing, it gives rise to a whole new level of intellectual freedom. With speech, whether they speak aloud or not, children can talk about things that don't exist, they can make plans about the future, and they can recall mistakes they made in the past. Because words are internal devices used to signify external things in the world, children can use words to think about the things they signify in the absence of the actual things themselves. Prespeech children, like chimps, can think about things only by acting on them directly. There is a striking similarity here with Piaget's idea of sensorimotor intelligence. Speech also gives children the means to "talk through" a problem before implementing the specific strategies necessary to solve it. Creatures without speech are more or less stuck in the here and now. They are imprisoned by the limited information provided to them by their senses in the immediate situation, and so they can pretty much solve problems only through trial and error.

Vygotsky found that one of the first ways that speech helps children use tools is when, after failing to solve a problem on their own, they seek outside assistance. To get help from somebody else, children often have to describe the problem verbally. This is what Vygotsky called the **interpersonal function of speech**, which means that speech between two people is needed to solve a problem. But as children gain lots of experience speaking with others, they eventually become capable of speaking to themselves. Then they can use their own speech to help themselves through the problem. Vygotsky called this the **intrapersonal function** of speech; and at this point, speech is said to be internalized. With this so-called **inner voice**, children have a whole new level of psychological awareness available to them; and they become capable of the higher psychological functions available only to humans. To recap using Vygotsky's own words: "Signs and words serve children first and foremost as a means of social contact with other people. The cognitive and communicative functions of language then become the basis of a new and superior form of activity in children, distinguishing them from animals."

Speech and Signs

The intrapersonal function of speech has extremely powerful effects on a number of psychological abilities. Vygotsky gives examples of how the inner voice improves children's perception of the surrounding environment, their memory for past experiences, and their ability to pay attention. But when you get down to the nitty-gritty, the reason internalized speech transforms children's intellectual functioning isn't so much because of the specific speech that is used, it's because of the signifying function that individual words and sentences serve. In Vygotsky's terms, words are a type of sign. And the importance of signs is that they signify something. Notice that the word *sign* makes up the first part of the word *signify*? Which signs we use to communicate an idea isn't as important as the idea itself. It's the capacity for using signs to signify ideas that makes all the difference in the world.

Just the other day I was driving down the road in our minivan, with my youngest daughter, Sarah, buckled snugly in the back seat. We caught a red light at the intersection next to the local police station, and after several seconds Sarah said, "Look, Daddy, she has a fuzzy driving center." Of course, I didn't know what Sarah meant, nor who "she" was, but I began scanning all four corners of the intersection to see if I could catch a glimpse of exactly how fuzzy the driving center was. Obviously, Sarah was trying to share an idea with me, although I had no clue as to what it was. Eventually I caught Sarah's line of visual regard, and noticed that she was looking at the driver in the car next to us. After briefly scanning the interior of the car, I realized that Sarah was using the signs "fuzzy driving center" to signifying the fuzzy steering wheel cover being used by the female driver of that car. Of course, it helps when one person uses a sign that's understandable by the other person, but it's the fact that children can use signs in the first place that matters.

Vygotsky believed that when children become capable of using words to signify, the important thing is not that they are using words, but that they are using arbitrary symbols to stand for other things. If you think about it, when we say a word, we are really just producing a certain pattern of sounds. This pattern of sounds signifies the underlying idea. The specific pattern of sound really doesn't matter. Take the word *car*, for example. The sounds we make when we say "car" have no necessary connection with the meaning of the word *car*. Different languages use different patterns of sounds to signify the meaning of "car." In Spanish we would say "auto" (pronounced something like "OW-toe"), in German we'd say "Wagen" (pronounced "VAHG-n"), in Japanese we'd say "kuruma" (pronounced "kuh-roo-MA"), and in Swahili we'd say "gari" (pronounced "GA-ree"). The fact that speaking children are speaking is important because it means that they have reached the point where they can use an arbitrary pattern of sounds to stand for something else. If something as simple as a pattern of sounds can stand for an idea, then other things can stand for an idea too. Right now while you are reading these words, you are seeing patterns of black ink on a white background. Clearly, these patterns of black ink, like the sound patterns we just talked about, signify things. There is no special meaning in the black lines, curves, and dots, it's all in the fact that they can be used to signify. In sum, when children start using signs to stand for things, they are entering the world of higher psychological processes.

In the experiment I'm about to describe, Vygotsky set out to explore just how well arbitrary signs can help children function in the world, particularly as they can be used to enhance basic memory. Now here Vygotsky talks about two different types of memory: natural (or immediate) memory and sign-assisted (or mediated) memory. The distinction is a difficult one to grasp, but I'll do my best to explain it.

Natural memory is a very basic type of memory, and it is pretty much driven by our senses. Vygotsky described it as "very close to perception, because it arises out of the direct influence of external stimuli upon human beings." I think the kinds of memories Vygotsky is talking about here are the kinds I get when on certain occasions I get a whiff of a particular type of perfume. Whenever I smell one certain perfume, I get an immediate flashback, sort of a mental photograph, of my old girlfriend from high school. Come to think of it, there's another type of perfume, but one I rarely encounter anymore, that brings up an image of a girl I used to have a crush on in junior high! These kinds of memories pop up automatically, they are immediate, and they appear to me as visual images of the kind I might have if I were looking right at these people.

The other kind of memory Vygotsky talks about is the kind that is mediated by signs. What this means is that sometimes our memories can be aided by something external to the memory itself. He uses the example of how even primitive peoples put notches in sticks to help them remember quantities of things. Another example, commonly seen in movies, is when a prisoner makes marks on the prison or dungeon walls to remind him of how many days he has been incarcerated. Vygotsky points out that no other animal, not even the higher primates, have ever given any evidence of using this kind of sign-enhanced memory. Therefore, it must be a uniquely human process. And as a uniquely human process, it results from humans' essentially social nature. The following experiment, conducted under the leadership of A. N. Leontiev in Vygotsky's lab, sought to investigate children's use of signs to enhance memory. In the experiment, the investigators played a version of the popular parlor game "Taboo." If you've never played the game before, the goal is to get partners on your team to say a particular word. The catch is that there are certain words that you are not allowed to say when prompting your partner. If you were supposed to get your partner to say "key," for example, you might not be permitted to say "lock" or "ignition switch." The version of this game used in Vygotsky's lab was only slightly different. The experimenters asked children a series of questions, some of which would have color words as their answer. A sample question was "What color is the floor?" The children were expected to provide an answer even though sometimes they were told that certain color words could not be used. Of course, if the floor was green, and the child used the taboo word "green" to answer the experimenter's question, an error would be recorded for this child's response. Vygotsky and Leontiev wondered whether giving children cards with colors on them would help reduce the number of oral errors they ended up making. In essence their question was, Would children use the color cards as external signs to help them answer the question correctly?

METHOD

Participants

Vygotsky doesn't give us much detail about the participants who were involved in this study. But we know that at least four age groups participated. There were 7 participants in the 5–6-year-old age range, 7 in the 8–9-year-old age range, 8 in the 10–13-year-old age range, and 8 in the adult category (ranging in age from 22 to 27 years of age).

Materials

The only materials needed for this experiment were a series of 9 color cards. The colors on the color cards were black, white, red, blue, yellow, green, lilac, brown, and gray.

Procedure

Vygotsky's description of the procedure was pretty straightforward, so I'll let him describe it to you: "Children were asked to play a game in which they were to answer a set of questions without using certain words in their answers. As a rule each child was presented three or four tasks differing in the constraints placed upon the answers and the kinds of potential stimulus aids the child could use. In each task the child was asked 18 questions, seven of which had to do with color (for example, 'What color is . . . ?'). The child was asked to answer each question promptly using a single word. The *initial task* was conducted in exactly this fashion. [Dixon's note: Notice that in this initial task the experimenters were testing how well children could answer the questions without any taboo words. This could be called a baseline condition.] With the *second task*, we began to introduce the additional rules that the child had to follow in order to succeed. For example, there were two color names the child was forbidden to use, and no color name could be used twice. [Dixon's note: Notice here that even though there are some taboo color words, children weren't yet given the color cards to help them answer the questions.] The *third task* had the same rules as the second, but the child was given nine colored cards as aids to playing the game ('these cards can help you to win'). The *fourth task* was like the third and was used in cases in which the child either failed to use the color cards or began to do so only late in the third task. Before and after each task we asked the child questions to determine if she remembered and understood the instructions.

"A set of questions for a typical task is the following (in this case green and yellow are the forbidden colors): (1) Have you a playmate? (2) What color is your shirt? (3) Did you ever go in a train? (4) What color are the railway-carriages? (5) Do you want to be big? (6) Were you ever at the theater? (7) Do you like to play in the room? (8) What color is the floor? (9) And the walls? (10) Can you write? (11) Have you seen lilac? (12) What color is lilac? (13) Do you like sweet things? (14) Were you ever in the country? (15) What colors can leaves be? (16) Can you swim? (17) What is your favorite color? (18) What does one do with a pencil?."

RESULTS

The actual results from the study can be found in Table 4.1. In that table, you will notice that the individual age groups are listed on the left side of the table. Then, to the right of the age groupings, you can see the average number of errors for the second and third tasks. Comparing the errors on only these two tasks is important because they stand for the participants' scores on the trial when the color cards weren't used and the scores on the trial when the color cards were used. Remember, the research question was whether the availability of signs (the color cards) would improve children's ability to answer the questions. On the far right side of the table

TABLE 4.1   AVERAGE NUMBER OF ERRORS IN ANSWERING THE QUESTIONS WITH AND WITHOUT THE AVAILABILITY OF COLOR CARDS

Age	Number of Participants	Task 2 Errors	Task 3 Errors	Difference
5–6	7	3.9	3.6	0.3
8–9	7	3.3	1.5	1.8
10–13	8	3.1	0.3	2.8
22–27	8	1.4	0.6	0.8

you can see the difference between the scores when the color cards were or weren't used. Notice that for all age groups, having the color cards handy helped the participants make fewer errors than not having the color cards.

Because Vygotsky summarized the results very clearly, I'll again let him use his own words: "Looking first at the data from task 2, we see a slight decrease in errors from ages five to thirteen and a sharp drop in adulthood. For task 3 the sharpest drop occurs between the five-to-six and eight-to-nine-year-old groups. The difference between tasks 2 and 3 is small for both the preschool children and the adults [Dixon's note: Vygotsky's "preschool" children are what today we would call kindergartners and first-graders]. The difference is largest for school-age children."

DISCUSSION

According to Vygotsky, the results of this study indicate that there are three basic stages in the development of mediated memory. Among the youngest children, having the color cards simply did not improve memory. (I should point out here that although there is a 0.3-point improvement in the scores when these youngest children used the cards, the difference was apparently not important to Vygotsky.) At this stage, external signs aren't used profitably to aid memory. In the second stage of development, when children are between 8 and 13 years old, having the cards improved memory tremendously. That is, children became capable of using the color cards as external signs. The number of errors for children at this stage dropped quite a bit. Notice in Table 4.1 that the number of errors dropped by 2.8 points for these children (the 10–13-year-olds) when they were allowed to use the color cards as external signs, compared to when they weren't allowed to use the color cards. Finally, in the third stage, being allowed to use the color cards once again failed to improve performance. Look at the scores of the adults. Having the cards really didn't help them perform any better than not having the cards. Why would this be? Apparently, it was because the adults' performance was so high to begin with. The adults didn't seem to need the cards. It's as if they were using their own internal "mental" signs from the outset. Because they already had their own internalized mental signs, having the color cards didn't give the adults any special advantage. Vygotsky wrote, "The external sign that school children require has been transformed into an internal sign produced by the adult as a means of remembering."

The evidence produced by this experiment helped support Vygotsky's notion that the development of the higher psychological processes resulted from the progressive internalization of signs that are originally available only externally, through social communication. Of course, one limitation of this study is that we can't be sure the adults were actually using internal signs. Still, the outcome of the experiment was consistent with what we would predict if adults were capable of using internal signs to assist, or mediate, memory.

Something Else that Vygotsky Was Famous for (or Practical Everyday Applications of Vygotsky's Theory)

The experiment I just described was focused on only a very small part of Vygotsky's grander theory of the development of the individual within the larger societal context. Something else which Vygotsky talks about in the book, and which also earned him quite a bit of fame, was his notion of the **zone of proximal development**. The zone of proximal development directly reflects Vygotsky's driving interests in applying his theoretical ideas to real-life situations. Modern educators still spend considerable effort incorporating the zone of proximal development idea into their educational systems.

So what is this zone thing? To define it, it is basically the gap between what you can do on your own and what you can do with the help of somebody else. We already mentioned this idea briefly when we talked about how young children may seek out adults to help them solve problems they can't solve on their own. In this way, the zone of proximal development is an interpsychological process. But let's explore some of the ramifications of the zone of proximal development.

Suppose we have two 8-year-old children who are just learning how to skateboard. Zachary and Joshua have never really skateboarded before, but they have played lots of skateboarding video games on their Sony Playstations, and they're ready to give it a try in real life. Suppose you catch a glimpse of them trying out some skateboard moves in the parking lot at the local library after you've just returned your latest edition of the Harry Potter series. You notice that neither one seems to be having much success in completing whatever tricks he's attempting. Although they seem to be getting the hang of standing and balancing on their boards, and they do fairly well at pushing off the ground to get the boards moving, neither one seems to come close to doing a 360 or an Ollie, and neither can "grind" the fence-rail along the wheelchair ramp (all typical skateboard moves). As far as you can tell, both children seem to be performing age-appropriately, and about equally well, but neither is particularly impressive at doing any tricks.

Now imagine another boy comes along who looks to be about twice the age of Zachary and Joshua. This boy is also carrying a skateboard, but you get the impression that he has a little more experience than the other two boys. Sure enough, the older boy thrills and amazes the two younger ones with all sorts of tricks, jumps, and spins. He seems to be interested in helping the younger boys learn one simple trick, and so starts to teach them some basic strategies for learning how to grind the edge of one of the library's landscaping walls. In very short order, Joshua seems to get the hang of grinding, and he starts grinding practically everything that has an edge.

Zachary, on the other hand, has much less success. He gains slightly better balance, and so stays on his board longer. But whenever he tries to grind something, he falls down. Zachary never quite demonstrates the same skill at grinding that Joshua does. Very soon, Zachary skins his knee and decides to go home.

This example demonstrates one of the fundamental features of the zone. First, at the beginning both boys were pretty much at the same level of functioning. They both could get on their boards and ride, but neither could do much else. Vygotsky would call these initial abilities their "actual developmental level." The actual developmental level is the level of performance a child is capable of on his own, without the help of adults or more capable peers. Second, notice that Zachary and Joshua performed better under the guidance of the 16-year-old. Vygotsky would call this their "potential levels," which is the level of performance a child can achieve under the guidance of another person. Vygotsky calls this boost in ability an interpsychic process (because it involves the interactions between two people). The gap between what children do on their own and what they do with somebody else's help, or the distance between their actual level and their potential level, is what Vygotsky called the zone of proximal development. The larger the child's zone, the more prepared he is to move on to higher levels of performance. "What is in the zone of proximal development today will be the actual developmental level tomorrow." In our example, Joshua's zone was much larger than Zachary's, and so he is poised to move at a faster pace than Zachary, at least in the area of skateboarding. So even though you'd probably guess that Joshua and Zachary were at the same actual developmental level, based on observing them without the help of the older peer, there is something appreciably different about them in terms of their developmental potential. Wouldn't you say?

Now the zone of proximal development sounds like a pretty basic, intuitive idea. But it raised some important issues in its time, and it still raises some important concerns for educators today. Consider standardized testing. In American political circles there seems to be an obsession with inflicting standardized testing on American schoolchildren. Politicians seem to believe that if children are given standardized tests on a regular basis, then American taxpayers can be sure that children are being given the education they deserve. President George W. Bush has made clear his intention to impose standardized testing on American schoolchildren regularly. And even as I write these words, the legislature of the state of Ohio is planning on doubling the number of annual standardized testing sessions to be imposed on all Ohio public school children. What's ironic is that educators and psychologists oppose standardized testing.

What's wrong with standardized testing? Well, even 70 years ago, Vygotsky had a number of reasons to oppose it. For one thing, standardized testing places far too much emphasis on the achievements already made by children. When we use standardized testing we are really only measuring children's *actual developmental levels.* We're measuring what they've already achieved. And when schools are preparing their students to take the standardized tests, their focus is on getting the kids to memorize content that is likely to be on the test. Wouldn't it be much more meaningful, as we saw in the case of Zachary and Joshua, to measure children's developmental potential? Wouldn't it be much more meaningful to measure what children are capable of accomplishing in their social contexts? Vygotsky would think so. The question we should be asking is not, "What are American children's actual developmental levels?" Rather, we should be asking, "What are American children's potentials for success?" The zone of proximal development, which is ignored by standardized testing, represents an intellectual preparedness that is real, that is important, and that probably has greater implications for the successful adaptation of children to their environments than the actual developmental levels measured by standardized tests.

The idea of the zone also has important implications for how educational instruction should take place. When a schoolteacher instructs a child, she is working within the child's zone. She is making it bigger, mostly by increasing the child's level of potential development. Have you ever had the experience of taking an exam in one of your classes, only to find out that you didn't understand something as well as you thought you did? This frustrating encounter demonstrates your own personal experience with the zone of proximal development. What you understood perfectly well in class with your teacher by your side, you understood rather poorly when she wasn't there to guide you. As another example, I frequently give homework assignments to my students when I teach statistics. On the day the homework is due, it seems that without fail a student will come up to me with an incomplete homework assignment, saying that she understood what I was talking about in class, but got completely lost when she tried to do it on her own.

Clearly, people can perform better when working with other people, which was Marx's, and hence Vygotsky's, central point. And the American educational system can benefit by revising its educational practices accordingly. Rather than focusing on competitive, individualized academic achievement, perhaps we should focus on cooperative group-based learning. Fortunately, there have been fairly significant changes in the way education is delivered in both primary and secondary educational settings these days. Education is moving more and more away from a teacher-centered approach, where the teacher knows and tells all and the student copies down everything the teacher says; to a student-centered approach, where students discover knowledge on their own while working with their teachers or with groups of their peers. Grade schools, junior highs, and high schools have been doing a much better job at this kind of discovery-based learning than colleges. But even many colleges are jumping onto the discovery-based learning bandwagon these days. Have you noticed an increase in group-based learning exercises lately? In the old days, you might have been given an assignment to complete on your own. It may have been a difficult one, and you might have had to meet with the professor a number of times to get additional suggestions for how to proceed. Then in the end, you could feel good or bad about yourself based on how well you did compared with everyone else in the class. With group-based discovery learning, a group of students gets the assignment, and the group is responsible for completing it. The basic idea behind group-based discovery learning is that each member of the group has something important to contribute to the functioning of the group. So, when an individual group member isn't able to complete all parts of the assignment on his own, others in the group can compensate for these shortcomings, and the group as a whole performs at a higher level than any individual group member could. By working in a group, individual members of the group can benefit from the strengths of other members of the group. The point is that group-based, discovery-based learning is Vygotsky's zone of proximal development in action.

CONCLUSION

Vygotsky made a significant impact on the field of child psychology, to be sure. He was at least as important for giving the field a new way to think about doing psychology as he was for producing the specific scientific findings themselves. He introduced the world to a Marxist-flavored alternative to standard European and American ways of doing psychology. And importantly, his emphasis on considering human behavior in its natural context foreshadowed the theoretical viewpoints put forth by a number of other authors described in this book.

For example, Vygotsky would probably have been very happy with the work of John Bowlby (Chapter 11). Bowlby was a child psychology researcher who studied mother-infant relationships. He was well known for his belief that mother-infant relationships were best understood in terms of the environments in which they were embedded. Bowlby argued that even though mothers and their babies were designed by thousands of years of evolution to be attracted to one another, the strength of their mutual attraction depended on their environments. Bowlby pointed out that attachment disorders are more likely now than ever before because the prehistoric environments in which attachment relationships originally evolved didn't have much in common with the kinds of environments in which today's mothers and children find themselves. Consequently, when mothers and infants find themselves in unusual or strange environments, such as the hospital or the prison, and when mothers are prevented from responding to their babies' signals in some way, attachment disorders become very real possibilities.

I think Vygotsky would also have been tickled by Urie Bronfenbrenner's theory (Chapter 22). Like Vygotsky, Bronfenbrenner believed it was silly to do research on children without simultaneously taking into account the environmental influences on those children. However, he went one step further than Vygotsky. He suggested that there were several different levels of environment, and that there were therefore several different levels of influence of the environment on children. For example, children's behavior is influenced not only by whether or not they have a lot of toys to play with, but also by whether or not they live in a free, democratic society. So Bronfenbrenner suggested that environmental influences ranged from direct, immediate impacts to indirect, long-term impacts.

It is unfortunate that Vygotsky didn't live long enough to see the explosion in child psychology that took place in the latter half of the century. So many provocative and fascinating findings about the capabilities of infants and children have come out since Vygotsky's death, one can only wonder about what Vygotsky could have done had he known about them.

Bibliography

Miller, P. H. (1993). *Theories of developmental psychology.* New York: W. H. Freeman and Company.

Newman, F., & Holzman, L. (1993). *Lev Vygotsky: Revolutionary scientist.* London: Routledge.

Wertsch, J. V. (1985). *Vygotsky and the social formation of mind.* Cambridge, MA: Harvard University Press.

Questions for Discussion

1. What role does government play in the kinds of scientific research that get done? What role does science play in the kinds of government work that get done?

2. In what fundamental way does Vygotsky's approach to child psychology differ from Piaget's? How are the two approaches similar?

3. If we are going to insist on using standardized tests as a way to assess our children, how might we modify the procedure to make it more compatible with Vgotsky's approach (particularly his notion of the zone of proximal development)?

4. Do you think it's possible for chimpanzees to enter the domain of higher psychological processes? Why or why not? What would be the limiting factor, according to Vygotsky?

5

The Eyes Have It

THE ORIGIN OF FORM PERCEPTION.
Fantz, R. L. (1961). *Scientific American, 204, 66–72.*   (RANK 19)

Stunningly beautiful! Absolute genius! And that's no hyperbole (look up *hyperbole* in your dictionary). If there's a single study that serves as a cornerstone for the development of the modern study of infant cognition, it's this one. And it was a cornerstone in more than one way. First of all, Robert Fantz was somewhat of a rebel in the kind of research he was doing; his research received a rather hostile reception from his fellow psychologists at the time. Do you remember back in introductory psychology when you studied about a group of psychologists called **behaviorists** who controlled the field of psychology from the early 1910s till the early 1960s? Well, if you were doing things the behaviorist way back then, it usually meant that you couldn't talk about inborn capacities for thinking. In fact, you couldn't talk about thinking at all! The hardcore behaviorists were only interested in studying behavior. Unfortunately for Fantz, the behaviorist way of doing things was firmly entrenched in American psychology in the late 1950s and early 1960s, when he came onto the scene. And unfortunately for Fantz, the behaviorist way didn't make an exception for his own research specialty area: perception. I imagine Fantz felt a bit like an unstarred Sneetch in a community of star-bellied Sneetches (ironically, this Dr. Seuss classic was published at about the same time as Fantz's work). In the end, however, the behaviorist way died out. And because he was still around, Fantz was granted the opportunity to "take over the wheel" and conduct research on the development of babies' internal psychological functioning.

Of course, the real importance of Fantz's work wasn't that he survived his battle with the behaviorists, it was that his work gave scientists a way to communicate with babies. And although Fantz's contributions as an innovator clearly extend far beyond his own work, Fantz the scientist was really only interested in one question: Do we have to learn to perceive? A corollary of this question, which also piqued Fantz's curiosity, was: Can babies perceive at birth?

To answer these questions, Fantz put forth an exceedingly ordinary proposition: Maybe babies can tell us something about their thinking if we simply take a look at their looking. Now, you might think that since babies were probably looking at stuff for thousands of years, and that since adults were probably watching babies look at things for just as long, we would have found out a long time ago whether infants' looking behaviors could tell us something about their thinking. We all know that by following the gaze of an adult, we can tell something about what the adult is looking at, and possibly even a little bit about what the adult is thinking. So why have we been so hesitant to pay attention to the gaze of babies? I suppose there are a number of legitimate reasons for such neglect. For one thing, I imagine it didn't occur to some of our ancestors that babies' looking behaviors were meaningful. Many historical cultures thought babies were unthinking, soul-less reflex machines. Moreover, psychology itself is a very young discipline (less than 125 years old), so prior to the arrival of psychology, scientists weren't accustomed to applying the scientific method in order to ask psychological questions. And even when psychology did hit the scene, behaviorists quickly gained control of mainstream American psychology (particularly its journals and academic departments) and dominated the field for 60 years. For whatever reason, it wasn't until Fantz's works were published in the late 1950s and early 1960s that his revolutionary idea took hold among the community of child psychology researchers. So what exactly did Fantz do that was so cool? Let's take a look.

The studies I will be describing were originally described by Fantz in 1961, in an article titled "The Origin of Form Perception" published in *Scientific American*. Fantz actually published many related articles in other venues like *The Psychological Record* and *Perceptual and Motor Skills*, but the article I'll be describing was the one that received the most popularity (or notoriety if you were a behaviorist at the time). As I already mentioned, the overarching goal of his research was to determine whether humans come with an inborn ability to perceive "form" or whether such perceptual abilities have to be learned. Fantz knew that older children and adults could tell the difference between things that were round and square, between things that were light and dark, and between things that were large and small. But what he didn't know was when the ability to make those perceptual distinctions came to be.

One possibility, of course, was that babies learned to distinguish between shapes, colors, and sizes over time, as they became experts at seeing the world. This was sort of the default view. The bias of the behaviorists at the time led them to attribute every human ability to learning through environmental experience. However, if Fantz could demonstrate that babies could tell the difference between various forms from birth, then he would've made a revolutionary discovery. He would've shown that there's more to psychological development than behavioral development, and he would've shown that babies come biologically prepared, or "hardwired" to use a popular catchphrase, to respond to the world.

There was just one small problem that Fantz had to contend with before he could get around to answering his questions about perception: No one in the history of humankind had ever successfully carried on a two-way conversation with a newborn! And of course it's rather difficult to determine what newborns perceive if you can't ask them about it. Well, Fantz did get his questions answered. But to do so, he had to invent a method for communicating with babies that was in my opinion far more important for the field of child psychology than the answers he obtained! What follows is a description of Fantz's work, wherein he describes his approach through his recounting of a series of studies.

INTRODUCTION

In the introduction of his article, Fantz reviews previous research he and others conducted using nonhuman animals. The findings from these animals were themselves rather fascinating. For example, he talks of one study where he tested the pecking behavior of 1,000 baby chickens that were raised in complete darkness from the time of hatching. Fantz wondered what would happen if these chicks were exposed to something they could see, what psychologists would call a visual stimulus. (A **stimulus**, the plural form of which is *stimuli*, is something psychologists present to research participants or subjects in order to see how they respond.) So Fantz and his colleagues presented some 100 objects "of graded angularity, from a sphere to a pyramid" to the chicks under lighted conditions. Intriguingly, Fantz found that the chicks "pecked 10 times oftener at the sphere than they did at the pyramid," and they pecked more frequently at the sphere than at a two-dimensional flat disk. Because the chicks showed this pecking behavior the very first time they experienced lighted conditions, Fantz figured that the chicks could not have *learned* to prefer spheres from previous visual experiences with food, so he concluded that chicks are born with an inborn preference for pecking at things that are likely to be edible! Of course, baby chickens are not very much like baby humans, but Fantz's findings with chicks do raise the possibility that maybe human babies have some inborn perceptual preferences as well. However, the problem of how to ask *human* babies about their perceptual preferences still remained. Human babies don't engage in much pecking behavior.

A clue to a possible solution of how to converse with human babies came from some research Fantz had done with baby chimpanzees at the Yerkes Laboratories of Primate Biology in Florida. Chimpanzees don't engage in pecking behavior either, but they are like human babies in that they do look at stuff. So Fantz and his colleagues invented a "looking chamber," into which they placed baby chimps. The chamber was like a baby crib except that it had a ceiling and solid walls. Fantz attached two objects to the ceiling of the chamber, one to the chimps' right and one to the left. Fantz writes, "Through a peephole in the ceiling we could see tiny images of the objects mirrored in the subjects' eyes. When the image of one of the objects was at the center of the eye, over the pupil, we knew the chimpanzee was looking directly at it." (Today this procedure is commonly known as the "corneal reflection technique.")

All that was left to determine was whether the chimpanzees looked longer at one of the objects than at the other. If they did, two conclusions could be drawn: (1) that the chimps could tell the difference between the two objects, and (2) that, for whatever reason, the chimps preferred to look at one of the objects more than the other. Fantz and his colleagues found that chimps did prefer to look at some objects more than others. Moreover, Fantz found similar preferences in another chimpanzee who, like the chicks described above, had been raised in complete darkness. So Fantz had evidence that chimps and chicks could distinguish between different visual forms, even without any prior visual experience. Fantz attributed these results to an inborn ability to perceive form.

I want to highlight here that in his invention of the simple looking chamber procedure, Fantz discovered what a thousand generations before him did not. He discovered how to ask babies questions in a way they could understand, and at the same time he gave babies a way to talk to researchers in a way they could understand. All that was left was to determine whether human babies would respond to the looking chamber as the chimps did. In the *Scientific American* article, Fantz describes a number of studies where he tested human babies in his looking chamber. Below are the details of the studies as summarized in the article.

Experiment 1

METHOD

Participants

Thirty infants were tested at weekly intervals from ages 1 to 15 weeks.

Materials

Four pairs of test patterns, differing in complexity, were shown to babies. From most to least complex, the pairs of test patterns were as follows. Pair 1 consisted of a set of horizontal stripes and a bull's-eye design. Pair 2 consisted of a checkerboard pattern versus either of two plain squares of different sizes. Pair 3 contrasted a cross with a circle. Finally, Pair 4 juxtaposed two identical triangles.

Procedure

Babies were placed one at a time in the looking chamber and were presented with the test pattern pairs in a randomly determined order. The total amount of time babies spent looking at each member of the stimulus pair was recorded. This measure allowed Fantz both to determine the total amount of looking time to an individual pattern or to a pair of patterns as well as to determine the proportion of looking time to one or another pattern within a specific pair.

RESULTS

Fantz found that, overall, babies looked far longer at the more complex patterns than at the simpler patterns. That is, babies looked way longer at the patterns in Pair 1 and Pair 2 than at the less complex patterns. However, a second major finding was that babies showed preferences for certain types of patterns. In Pair 2, for example, babies showed a strong preference for the checkerboard pattern over either of the plain squares. Babies also showed a strong preference for looking at one of the items in

Pair 1, but interestingly, there was an age-related shift in which item was the preferred one. Early on, the striped pattern was strongly preferred, but by 2 months of age, most kids liked to look at the bull's-eye pattern.

CONCLUSIONS

The mere detection of differences in looking time to different patterns led Fantz to a singly important conclusion. He wrote, "By demonstrating the existence of form perception in very young infants we had already disproved the widely held notion that they are anatomically incapable of seeing anything but blobs of light and dark." However, Fantz went one step further and showed that babies also tended to prefer some patterns over others! Some of these preferences, he felt, were tied to inborn perceptual processes. Still, these discoveries didn't mean that form perception couldn't continue to develop with experience or with the maturation of visual nervous pathways. It only meant that babies seemed to be able to make some sense of the visual world right after popping out. Fantz next described how he set out to measure developmental differences in babies' **visual acuity**—how well they could see.

Experiment 2

METHOD

Participants

The number and ages of infant participants are not clearly specified. However, the performances of 6-month-olds as well as babies less than a month old are described, so babies of at least these ages must have been included.

Materials

Babies saw a series of black-and-white striped patterns, each time paired with a gray square of equal brightness.

Procedure

As before, babies were placed one at a time in the looking chamber, and were presented the pairs of stimulus patterns. On each succeeding trial, the stripes became thinner and thinner. Fantz's logic was brilliant: "Since we already knew that infants tend to look longer and more frequently at a patterned object than at a plain one, the width of the stripes of the finest pattern that was preferred to gray would provide an index to visual acuity." As before, Fantz recorded the amount of time babies looked at each stimulus item in each pair.

RESULTS

Fantz found that "by six months babies could see stripes $\frac{1}{64}$ inch wide at a distance of 10 inches—a visual angle of five minutes of arc, or $\frac{1}{12}$ degree. (The adult standard is one minute of arc [or $\frac{1}{60}$ degree].) Even when less than a month old, infants were able to perceive $\frac{1}{8}$ inch stripes at 10 inches, corresponding to a visual angle of a little less than one degree." Fantz wrote, "This is poor performance compared to that of an adult, but it is a far cry from a complete lack of ability to perceive pattern."

CONCLUSION

With this study, Fantz was able to show that babies have some visual acuity as young as 1 month of age, and his results suggested that visual acuity continues to improve over time. (Experiment 1 also suggested this.) The fact that visual acuity continues to develop also supports the notion that maturation and/or experience plays a role in infants' developing visual perceptual abilities. Behaviorists would've been happy about this point. However, neither one of these preliminary studies addresses what for Fantz was the crux of the issue: Do infants come into the world with some inborn, possibly hardwired mechanisms for making "order out of chaos"? In other words, do babies come into the world seeing a "blooming, buzzing confusion," to borrow William James's oft-quoted phrase, or do they see shapes and wholes? Fantz's work with chicks suggests that at least baby chickens come into the world ready to distinguish edible things from other things. Do human infants also have some preformed categories that they can use to organize the world from chaos?

Experiment 3

In addressing this question, Fantz started out by considering what might be of utmost adaptive significance for the survival of human babies. For chicks, finding things to eat seemed to play this role. But for human babies, Fantz reasoned that social stimuli would probably be most important. Fantz gave special attention to the potential role of the human face: "Facial pattern is the most distinctive aspect of a person, the most reliable for distinguishing a human being from other objects and for identifying him. So a facelike pattern might be expected to bring out selective perception in an infant if anything could." Again, Fantz was able to use his newfangled methodology to translate his adult question into a language babies could understand. The question he put forth to babies was simply, "Do you like to look at faces more than other kinds of things?"

METHOD

Participants

The participants were 49 infants ranging in age from 4 days to 6 months.

Materials

The stimuli were "three flat objects the size and shape of a head." On one object were painted black facial features arranged against a pink background in a facelike pattern. On a second object were painted the same facial features, but this time arranged in a scrambled fashion so as to be in a nonfacelike pattern. The third object retained the same amount of blackness as used on each of the first two objects (in terms of total area), but on this stimulus the black was arranged in a dark patch toward the top of the object. Across all three objects, the features were made large enough so as to be detected by even the youngest babies with the poorest visual acuity.

Procedure

While in the looking chamber, babies were presented with all possible pairings of the three stimuli. As before, looking time to each pattern on each presentation trial was recorded.

RESULTS

Fantz found that babies preferred to look at the facial pattern slightly longer than at the nonfacial pattern, and they preferred the nonfacial arrangement over the pattern with a single black patch. Babies at all ages demonstrated these preferences.

CONCLUSIONS

Although the strength of the babies' preferences for the facial pattern over the non-facial pattern wasn't altogether impressive, the slight preference that was observed was sufficient for Fantz to conclude that "there is an unlearned, primitive meaning in the form perception of infants as well as chicks." Fantz's wording here is crucial. Nowhere in this sentence does he claim that babies are born to look specifically at human faces, at least not in the same way that chicks are born to peck at foodlike items. However, as I'll discuss shortly, he is often remembered as having made just such a claim.

Experiment 4

I'll bypass my usual outline approach in describing this last study because it was one Fantz himself described only briefly. In this study, Fantz deviated somewhat from his previous procedure and presented stimulus objects only one at a time instead of in pairs. He expected that the length of time babies spent initially looking at each item would provide meaningful information about how important that item was. Fantz showed babies a series of 6-inch-wide flat disks that differed from one another in terms of what they had on their surfaces. Three of the disks had patterns on them; three were plain. The patterned disks consisted of a face, a bull's-eye pattern, and a patch of printed media that looked something like a piece of cut-out newspaper. The plain disk stimuli were red, fluorescent yellow, and white. Fantz recorded the length of babies' initial looks to each of the objects. As in Experiment 1, Fantz found that babies looked longer at the patterned stimuli than at the plain stimuli, even though the stimuli weren't paired with one another. And as in Experiment 3, the facial pattern was the most strongly preferred among the patterned stimuli, based on the length of the initial look. Fantz used these results as evidence that social stimuli may be extremely important to babies, perhaps to the point that babies might be biologically predisposed to begin looking for faces at birth.

CONCLUSION

Fantz's genius is striking in many regards and his trailblazing efforts are recognized at many levels. Not only did he devise a technique that allowed researchers to "talk" to newborns and to "listen" to what newborns had to say, but he single-handedly challenged behaviorist assumptions that studying children's development was limited to studying the development of their behaviors. Oh sure, Fantz was also studying behaviors—he was studying looking behaviors. But rather than trying to explain the development of the behaviors themselves, he explained differences in behaviors as reflecting differences in babies' underlying perceptual abilities. He boldly suggested that babies are more than simply the sum of their experiences. He concluded, "The results to date do require the rejection of the view that the newborn infant or animal must start from scratch to learn to see and to organize patterned stimulation."

Another of Fantz's contributions is that his findings set the research agenda for a large chunk of child psychology research for the next four decades! For example, his focus on the human face as a social stimulus with special powers in attracting and maintaining babies' attention was an issue that struck a chord with child psychology researchers throughout the 1960s and 1970s. At the core of the issue was whether babies' brains were wired, before birth, to seek out human faces, or whether babies just preferred to look at faces because they happened to have the kinds of features babies liked to look at. This issue had important ramifications for John Bowlby's theory of attachment (Chapter 11). In particular, Bowlby argued that babies and mothers were biologically prepared, through evolution, to respond to one another. Mothers responded to the signals given off by their babies; and for their part, babies responded to stimuli given off by their mothers. If Fantz was right, one stimulus that could be really important for maintaining the attention of babies could be the mother's face!

Fantz's methodology also served as a foundation for researchers studying infant intelligence. Fantz's longtime colleague Joseph Fagan even developed an infant intelligence test based on the approach (appropriately called the Fagan Test of Infant Intelligence, or FTII for short). The FTII is based on the premise that babies are capable of visually discriminating between two perceptual forms. The way the test works is that babies are familiarized with one picture for a certain amount of time (depending on the baby's age), and then they are shown a pair of pictures. One picture is the old one they were just familiarized with, while the other is a completely new picture. Babies who look longer at the new picture (we call this a "novelty preference") tend to have higher IQ scores in later childhood. Babies who don't show a novelty preference are at increased risk for being diagnosed with developmental delay later in childhood.

SUMMARY

Fantz's efforts really did open the door for hundreds of child psychology researchers who were standing in line with hundreds of questions they just couldn't wait to ask babies, but who weren't sure how to phrase them. Recent developments in the field now allow us to ask babies if and when they can tell the difference between categories of things such as boys and girls, emotions such as happy or sad, or even velocities such as fast and slow. We can ask whether differences in babies' abilities to make these kinds of distinctions might be linked to their understanding of more abstract social concepts such as gender or race, to physical concepts such as time and space, or to their ability to produce and understand language. We've moved beyond showing babies pairs of individual, static objects to showing them complex, real-time visual events that are both real and fictional. Since the time of Fantz, hundreds of studies have produced thousands of pages documenting an enormous profile of infants' mind-blowing intellectual capabilities. And all this came about because Fantz didn't trivialize something as simplistic as what babies like to look at. Interesting, isn't it?

Bibliography

Fagan, J. F., III. (2000, June). *Visual perception and experience in early infancy: A look at the hidden side of behavioral development.* Paper presented at the biennial meetings of the International Conference on Infant Studies, Brighton, England, UK.

Fagan, J. F., III, & Detterman, D. K. (1992). The Fagan Test of Infant Intelligence: A technical summary. *Journal of Applied Developmental Psychology, 13,* 173–193.

Questions for Discussion

1. Fantz suggested that babies might be biologically predisposed to prefer human faces. But is it possible that babies just like to look at certain things that faces happen to have? If so, does this reduce the significance of Fantz's findings?

2. Would Fantz have made as big a splash in child psychology had he tried to publish his findings 10 years earlier? Why or why not?

3. Many people would argue that Fantz's discovery of babies' looking behavior was the result of doing little more than paying attention to the obvious. Is it fair to label Fantz a genius if he only paid attention to the obvious? Explain.

4. Why does it matter if form perception is learned or innate?

6

The Drawbridge Studies

OBJECT PERMANENCE IN 3½- AND 4½-MONTH-OLD INFANTS.

Baillargeon, R. (1987). *Developmental Psychology, 23, 655–664.*   (RANK 15)

Every now and then a scientific study comes along that defies description in ordinary scientific terms. Such a study goes beyond the mere production and reporting of empirical data and actually penetrates the social and political milieu of the scientific community itself. To capture the spirit of such a study, we sometimes have to turn to other academic fields such as the humanities and fine arts to find the right labels. Renée Baillargeon's (pronounced "by-er-JOHN," with a soft *j* sound) 1987 study is one such work. This now famous study is at once an allegory of the classic biblical tale of David and Goliath (but without the bloodshed) and an embodiment of a French Impressionist painting.

It's an allegory of the David and Goliath story because in her labors Baillargeon was like the young, wet-behind-the-ears shepherd boy whose strong convictions were sufficient to bring down the stout, dominant, and overbearing force of the Philistine giant Goliath. Baillargeon's Goliath was Piaget. The work was like a French Impressionist painting because to fully appreciate it you have to take a few steps backward and embrace the piece as a whole. If you look too closely at the detail, the essence of the piece loses coherence. But also, being of French Canadian descent, Dr. Baillargeon has a marvelous French accent that makes a wonderful impression on those who hear her speak English. (Get it? She makes a French impression.)

Piagetian Object Permanence.   To understand where Baillargeon is coming from in this study, you first have to understand a bit about Piaget's concept of object permanence.

It was Piaget's concept of object permanence that was the target of her attack. Although we spent considerable time reviewing Piaget's work in Chapters 2 and 3, we didn't spend much time on object permanence. So I'll review it briefly here.

Object permanence is a basic understanding that objects continue to exist even when they're no longer available to the senses. As adults, we have no problem with this concept. When I put a Butterfinger candy bar in my desk drawer, I know it'll be there the next time I have an urge for a sugar rush. And if it's not there when I go for it, I'll know it's because my daughter snuck it out when I wasn't looking. According to Piaget, we're not born with object permanence. An understanding of object permanence develops over time, and usually isn't fully available until about 18 months, although the beginnings of object permanence can be seen at about 9 months. Object permanence is essential for survival in the world, for without it we wouldn't be able to make plans about the future and remember the past. We wouldn't even remember what food we have in our refrigerator.

Piaget based his reasoning about object permanence on some innovative experiments he employed with his own children. He invented various techniques where he would hide one object behind another and look to see what his children would do, at different ages. As an example, he might take a rubber ducky and cover it up with his monogrammed handkerchief. If his kid failed to search for the ducky, he might pull the hanky just enough to reveal the ducky's tiny little tail feathers, and so on. When his kids failed to search for the hidden objects, he saw it as an indication that they lacked object permanence. According to Piaget, babies younger than about 9 months don't search for hidden objects because they don't yet realize (1) that objects have separate identities, and (2) that objects continue to exist even when they're outside of sensory awareness. Nine months was documented as the key age because it was at about that time that babies first began searching for objects that were hidden from view. This was pretty much the point of departure for Baillargeon's revolutionary study.

INTRODUCTION

Baillargeon begins her article by telling the reader the same thing I just told you—that Piaget thought object permanence didn't begin until about 9 months of age. But Baillargeon goes on to point out that other researchers have also questioned Piaget's interpretation of his children's performance on the object permanence tasks. The central criticism is usually that Piaget's task actually requires two separate abilities. Imagine you are a subject in one of Piaget's object permanence experiments. You are given an attractive toy to play with, say a Fisher-Price Little People figure. You look at it, you bang it on the table, and then you put it in your mouth (remember, you're only 6 months old). Now imagine Piaget takes it from you and hides it under a cloth handkerchief in the middle of the table in front of you. In order to get the object back, what do you have to do? Of course, you must first realize that the object continues to exist. If you do, you have object permanence. But if all you do is remain sitting there quietly in your high chair, no one actually knows that you have object permanence, do they? You have to do something else to *demonstrate* that you have object permanence. You have to reach out and lift the cloth hanky off the Fisher-Price Little People figure. Now, whether or not you really have object permanence, Piaget can't know that you have it until you reach out and grab the cloth. So, to the outside world, your ability to demonstrate object permanence depends on your ability to reach out and grab the cloth. If you don't have the capacity for removing the cloth and grabbing the toy, no one will have the slightest clue that you actually *have* object permanence.

Herein lies Baillargeon's major objection to Piaget's task. He required children to have two abilities (object permanence and the ability to reveal and grab a hidden object) before he was willing to give them credit for just one (object permanence). In Baillargeon's mind, Piaget's test of object permanence was just too hard. And because it was too hard, it was unfair. In sum, she believed it didn't permit the accurate measurement of object permanence.

According to Baillargeon, Piaget failed to detect "real" object permanence in children because his object permanence test required them to be capable of means-ends sequencing. If you recall from Chapter 3, means-ends sequencing happens when one action is used in order to allow another action to take place. You remove the cap from your Pepsi bottle *in order to* drink the Pepsi. That's means-ends sequencing. When Piaget required his children to remove the cloth in order to grab the hidden toy, he was requiring them to engage in means-ends sequencing. Baillargeon reasoned that means-ends sequencing might be a more sophisticated ability than object permanence. If so, then requiring a child to demonstrate means-ends sequencing in order to demonstrate object permanence would result in a serious underestimation of children's object permanence abilities.

Baillargeon's goal was to develop a simpler object permanence task to find out when children *really* understand object permanence. She would at least need a task that didn't require means-ends sequencing. But Baillargeon was confronted with one small problem: There was no other object permanence task available. So like all good little revolutionaries, she invented one, and it was ingenious. Taking advantage of the well-known measure of infant looking behavior (see Chapter 5 on Robert Fantz's work), she fashioned a method for measuring object permanence that would require little more than having children look at stuff. It was from children's looking behavior that Baillargeon purported to detect their emerging understanding of object permanence. She believed it was a much simpler task, and at least it didn't require children to engage in means-ends sequencing.

In her revolutionary article, Baillargeon conducted three related experiments. Experiment 1 looked at whether 4½-month-olds could show object permanence. Experiment 2 looked at whether 3¾-month-olds could show it, and Experiment 3 looked at whether 3½-month-olds could show it.

Experiment 1

METHOD

Participants

Twenty-four full-term infants ranging in age from 4 months, 2 days to 5 months, 2 days participated. Half of the infants were assigned to an experimental condition; half were assigned to a control condition. An additional 5 infants were excluded from the experiment either because they were fussy (3 babies), they were drowsy (1 baby), or the equipment failed (1 baby). Parents of babies who participated were offered reimbursement for their travel expenses.

Materials

Apparatus. Baillargeon used a specially designed experimental apparatus to conduct her experiments. Now describing the setup is a bit tricky since I can only use words. If I could just show you a videotape of the thing, the picture would be worth a thousand words. Instead, we'll have to rely on the next best thing—your imagination.

Baillargeon's apparatus looked a little bit like the stage for a puppet show. From a distance, it looked like a large wooden box roughly the size of a kitchen stove, with a hole cut out of the middle of the front wall for viewing the "show." If you have a viewing window in your oven door, you can get a good idea of what Baillargeon's device looked like, only Baillargeon's viewing window was larger.

If you were to look through the viewing window of Baillargeon's device, you would see a silver cardboard screen that was affixed to a metal axle. What was special about this screen was that it could be rotated on its axle toward you and away from you, through an arc of 180°. If you were to watch the screen go through its entire 180° range of motion, you would see it start out lying flat (let's say it was lying toward you), then begin to rise until it was eventually standing straight up and down, and then begin to fall backward, away from you, until it became completely flat again. As an example, if you laid this book flat on a hard surface and turned a page, you would be turning the page in a 180° arc. And if you kept flipping the page back and forth, you'd pretty much be mimicking the motions of the silver cardboard screen in Baillargeon's apparatus. Although I know some of you avoid numbers and symbols like the plague, I will use the term "180°" throughout the rest of the chapter to refer to the times when the screen in Baillargeon's apparatus rotated from one flat position all the way over to the other flat position.

Baillargeon also used a little wooden box in her apparatus, which was roughly the size of a Nerf football. The box was painted yellow, it had a little clown face painted on it, and it was placed behind the silver screen so that if the screen were leaning toward you, you would be able to see the box in the background, but if the screen were leaning away from you, the box would be hidden from your view. As you might imagine, if the screen tried to go through its full range of motion when the box was present, it would stop whenever it made contact with the box. At least this is what you would expect to happen. However, Baillargeon also fashioned a tricky little trap door under the box that would allow it to fall below the level of the surface whenever the screen contacted it. So rather than stopping when it contacted the box, the screen could be made to go through its full 180° range of motion. But if the screen did stop upon contact with the box, it would rotate through only part of its full range of motion. Specifically, Baillargeon calculated that the screen rotated through only a 112° arc.

Three Different Events. All together, three different "events" could be created using this apparatus. First, babies could just watch the screen rotate back and forth through its entire range of motion, with the little clown box nowhere to be seen. Baillargeon called this event the *familiarization event* because it served to familiarize babies with how the screen was capable of moving. When the box was present, one of two other types of events could happen. On the one hand, the screen could rotate back and forth, "contacting" the box each time. In this event, which Baillargeon called the *possible event,* the screen would rotate through only the 112° arc and would stop whenever it made contact with the box; then it would begin to rotate back in the other direction. On the other hand, the screen could be made to rotate through its full 180° range of motion, making it seem to rotate magically right through the box. Baillargeon called this the *impossible event* because, normally, solid objects can't pass through other solid objects. Of course, the impossible was made possible in this case because of the little trap door in the floor that allowed the box to be secretly removed whenever the screen passed by.

Procedure

Babies who participated in Baillargeon's study sat on their mothers' laps in front of the apparatus, with a perfect view of the events that were going to take place. The mothers were asked not to talk to their babies during the experiment. Before each "show" began, the babies were allowed to hold and play with the little wooden clown box. This allowed them to see for themselves what the box was like. I think the most important thing was that they learned the box was made out of a hard material rather than some spongy substance.

Two observers looked through little peepholes in the apparatus and watched where the babies looked. It's important to have two observers watch where the baby looks to improve the accuracy of their observations. If Baillargeon had used only one observer, she could never be sure that that observer was observing accurately. By having two observers, she could calculate the percentage of the time the two observers agreed. If the percentage agreement was high, then she could be assured that the observations they were making were accurate. In this study, agreement between the observers was high (about 88%).

Experimental Condition.   Each baby in the experimental condition first saw the familiarization event. Remember, this event was designed simply to familiarize babies with the 180° range of motion of the silver screen. The babies saw the familiarization event over and over until they became bored with it. How did Baillargeon know the babies were bored? That's easy. They just stopped watching the show. Once the babies were bored, Baillargeon began showing them the two other events: the possible event and the impossible event. She alternated her presentation of the two events so that babies would see first one event, then the other, then back to the first. In the possible event, the little wooden clown box was present. The screen would rotate to the point where it bumped into the box, it would stop, and then it would begin rotating back the other way (112° arc of motion). In the impossible event, the box was also present, but the screen would rotate all the way through its range of motion—right through where the box was supposed to be. When it rotated all the way down, it would stop and begin rotating back in the other direction (180° arc of motion).

Control Condition.   Babies in the control condition saw exactly the same sequence of events as the experimental babies, but with one major difference—the box was never present during any of the screen rotations. So these babies first saw the familiarization event until they were bored with it. Then Baillargeon alternately showed them two events, but because no little wooden clown box was present she couldn't call these events possible and impossible. Both of these events were possible. So instead, she just called them the *180° event* and the *112° event*. If you've been paying attention, you'll realize that the 180° event is really the same as the familiarization event.

Predictions. Before moving on to the results of Baillargeon's Experiment 1, I think it would help you to understand the spirit of Baillargeon's study if we were to entertain a couple of predictions about what might happen in the experimental and control conditions. The key dependent variable here is looking time. Baillargeon was primarily interested in what would happen to babies' looking times when they saw the impossible event. She reasoned that if babies are like most of us grown-ups, when they see an impossible event they should be surprised. And just like us grown-ups, when they show surprise at the impossible event, they should look at it for a relatively long period of time. At least they should look longer at the impossible event than at the possible one. But notice what it would take for these babies to be able to be surprised in the first place—they would have to recognize that the impossible event was, in fact, impossible. According to Baillargeon, to recognize that the impossible event was impossible babies would have to (1) realize that the little wooden clown box continued to exist even when they could no longer see it behind the silver screen, and (2) realize that two solid objects can't occupy the same physical space at the same time. In other words, to show surprise at the impossible event babies must have an understanding of object permanence.

On the other hand, if babies didn't recognize the impossible event as impossible, they would show no special inclination to look at it. If anything, babies might be inclined *not* to look at the impossible event because in that event the screen is rotating in a 180° arc. Remember, 180° is the same amount of rotation that they just got bored with during the familiarization period. After just seeing the 180° rotation event during the familiarization period, we would expect babies to show a preference for the possible event, where the screen is rotating in only a 112° arc. From the babies' point of view, this 112° rotation would be more interesting because it's new.

EXPERIMENT 1: RESULTS AND DISCUSSION

As you might have guessed, Baillargeon found that 4½-month-old babies did indeed look longer at the impossible event. After they became familiarized to the familiarization event, which was reflected by a decrease in looking time after seeing the familiarization event over and over, the babies showed a significant increase in looking time to the impossible event. But they showed no increase in looking time to the possible event.

Now the fact that babies showed an increase in looking time to the impossible event was interesting enough. It supported Baillargeon's belief that these babies expected the wooden clown box to continue to exist even though it was hidden from view by the silver screen. But the fact that they showed *no* increase in looking time to the possible event is also interesting. Consider why. We predicted that babies would prefer the 112° rotation because it was different from the 180° rotation they saw in the familiarization event. But they preferred the 180° rotation they saw in the impossible event, despite the fact that they had just been observing a 180° rotation in the familiarization event. It was as if their preference for the impossible event outweighed any preference for looking at a different rotation distance.

Based on these data, Baillargeon concluded that "contrary to Piaget's claims, infants as young as 4½ months of age understand that an object continues to exist when occluded." The word *occluded* is just another word for *hidden*.

Experiment 2

METHOD

Experiment 2 was designed to examine whether children even younger than 4½ months of age were capable of demonstrating object permanence. Experiment 2 was exactly the same as Experiment 1, except that younger babies were used. In this experiment, the babies were about 3¾ months of age.

Participants

Participants in this study ranged in age from 3 months, 15 days to 4 months, 3 days. Forty babies partook. As before, half the babies were assigned to the experimental condition, and half were assigned to the control condition. An additional 6 babies were excluded from the experiment because of fussiness (5) or drowsiness (1). Baillargeon wrote that she needed more babies in this experiment because the younger babies were a lot more variable in their looking behavior. Some babies consistently were short-lookers, whereas others consistently were long-lookers.

Materials and Procedure

As I already mentioned, the apparatus and procedure were exactly the same as in Experiment 1.

EXPERIMENT 2: RESULTS AND DISCUSSION

In contrast to the babies in Experiment 1, the Experiment 2 babies, as a group, did *not* look longer overall at the impossible than at the possible event. While it would have been easy enough for Baillargeon to give up and conclude that object permanence didn't exist this early, she looked a little deeper into the data and made an interesting discovery. She noticed that babies who got bored with the familiarization event very quickly mirrored the pattern of the older babies. That is, they looked longer at the impossible event than at the possible event. But the babies who took longer to become bored with the familiarization event didn't look longer at the impossible event compared with the possible event. She called the short-looking babies (those who got bored with the familiarization event rapidly) **short-habituators**, whereas she called the babies who didn't get bored with the familiarization event rapidly, **long-habituators**. For some reason, the rate at which babies got bored with the familiarization event had something to do with whether they showed surprise at the impossible event.

Experiment 3

METHOD

The fact that Baillargeon decided to run a third experiment was interesting. In part, she wanted to push the envelope further to see whether even younger babies could demonstrate object permanence. But in reading her explanation, one also gets the sense that maybe she was surprised at her own results and wanted to be sure she could replicate her findings. She wrote, "Given the unexpected nature and potential significance of the results obtained in the experimental condition of Experiment 2, it seemed important that they be confirmed. Experiment 3 attempted to do so with 3½-month-olds."

Participants

The participants in this experiment were 24 babies ranging in age from 3 months, 6 days to 3 months, 25 days. The average age was 3 months, 15 days.

Materials and Procedure

The apparatus and procedure were pretty much exactly the same as in the previous two experiments, with one very interesting difference. Rather than using the small, wooden, clown-faced box as the object, she used a Mr. Potato Head doll. Mr. Potato Head was smaller than the wooden box that was used in the previous two experiments, so the silver screen rotated further down than in the previous two experiments. More specifically, the screen rotated 135° before it made contact with the object, rather than the previous 112°.

EXPERIMENT 3: RESULTS AND DISCUSSION

Just as in Experiment 2 with the 3¾-month-olds, Baillargeon found that, as a group, 3½-month-olds did not show longer looking times at the impossible event than at the possible event. But also just like in Experiment 2, she found that there were differences between long-habituating and short-habituating babies. Short-habituating babies looked *longer* at the impossible event than at the possible event, again suggesting that they were surprised to see the silver screen pass right through good ol' Mr. Potato Head.

GENERAL DISCUSSION

The general finding from all three experiments is that babies as young as 4½, 3¾, and 3½ months of age looked reliably longer at the impossible event than at the possible event. This is evidence that babies show both an awareness that an object continues to exist when they can no longer see it and an awareness that two objects can't exist in the same place at the same time. Of course, there is an alternative interpretation of these findings. It could be that babies just liked to watch the silver screen move through the full 180° rotation in the impossible event rather than the 112° or a 135° rotation found in the possible event. But this interpretation isn't a very good one, according to Baillargeon, because of the fact that the babies in the control group did not look reliably longer at the 180° event compared to either the 112° or 135° rotations.

Based on these findings, Baillargeon takes on Goliath, er, Piaget, at a couple of different levels. First, she challenges Piaget's claim about the age when object permanence begins. Remember that Piaget believed that object permanence didn't begin until about 9 months at the earliest. But Baillargeon's data indicated the existence of object permanence as early as 3½ months of age, at least for some babies. In her view, the reason she observed object permanence in babies this young was that she didn't require them to do a fairly complicated behavior in order to demonstrate their object permanence abilities. Therefore, she is also challenging Piaget's object permanence task. By challenging the *task*, Baillargeon was making a very important distinction between children's *knowledge* of hidden objects and their ability to *search for* hidden objects. Why should we force children to go through all the trouble of searching for hidden objects, if all we want to know is whether they know about hidden objects?

The answer to this question is, "It depends on whom you ask." Don't forget Piaget's point of view. He didn't believe you could separate knowing something from acting on it. In fact, he had a whole theory that said children gain knowledge about the world by acting on the world. So it's not so surprising that he used a task that required babies to search for a hidden object in order to demonstrate they knew about the hidden object. His theory didn't allow for the possibility that babies could know about a hidden object without searching for it.

The Emergence of Nativism

Now because Baillargeon wasn't limited by Piaget's theory, she wasn't tied to his belief that you had to act on something to know about it. But what is the alternative? If you don't have to act on something to know about it, how else can you learn about it? Or more specifically, if babies don't learn about the permanence of objects by searching for hidden ones, how do they learn about it? Baillargeon suggests two possibilities. Both suggestions were so radical that Baillargeon might have been safer poking a stick into a hornet's nest!

Baillargeon's first suggestion was a simple one: Maybe object permanence is inborn. The belief that children's knowledge is inborn is called **nativism**, and so her suggestion would be called a nativist one. If this suggestion was right, then the reason Baillargeon was able to detect object permanence in babies as young as 3½ months old was that these babies had an understanding of the permanence of objects from birth. Notice that from this point of view, object permanence isn't something that develops from experience. It's something that's there from the outset.

Baillargeon's second suggestion was a little more complicated, but it still had a nativist flavor. If object permanence isn't present from birth, she thought, maybe babies are instead born with a special learning ability that allows them to create an understanding of object permanence very quickly, with relatively little experience. We might call this special learning ability an object permanence acquisition device. As evidence in support of this possibility, Baillargeon called attention to research done by other child psychologists, which showed that babies younger than 4 months of age will often perform arm extensions in the presence of objects. These arm extensions are thought to be precursors to more mature reaching and grasping abilities that are in the process of emerging. Baillargeon pointed out that if babies extend their arms in the presence of objects, they will no doubt gain experience seeing objects hidden by their own arms and hands and will also see their own arms and hands hidden by objects. These experiences may be all that's necessary for the object permanence acquisition device to kick in and establish an understanding of object permanence within the baby.

CONCLUSIONS: POKING A HORNET'S NEST

In the original David and Goliath story, once David took out Goliath, Goliath's army put its tail between its legs and ran away. And David, well, he eventually became king. But the story wasn't quite the same for Baillargeon in her efforts to dethrone Piaget. Challenging even this one small part of Piaget's theory agitated the child development research community into a frenzy. Attack after attack was leveled at both Baillargeon's methodology and her interpretations. Of course, the attacks weren't directed so much at Baillargeon herself as they were at the nativist claims she was making. And to be sure, Baillargeon had a number of allies on her side as well. But because Baillargeon's study was so prominent (it was voted the 15th most revolutionary study published in the last 50 years), it may have taken on a disproportionate burden of criticism.

Attacks on Baillargeon's claims have been at two levels. At the level of theory, Baillargeon was criticized for her suggestion that object permanence could be innate. At the level of methodology, Baillargeon has been criticized for overlooking some minor perceptual details when she developed her rotating-screen procedure. Let's consider each level of criticism in turn.

The Problem with Innateness

It's a good bet that anyone who criticized Baillargeon's nativist speculations would be equally critical of any other nativist explanations for how knowledge gets into children's heads. It's not that these kinds of critics believe nothing is present at birth, it's just that they think there are far too many claims for things that are. Antinativists view nativist explanations for children's thinking as at best unhelpful and at worst deceptive and misleading. "Where does Baillargeon get off claiming object permanence is inborn," they might rant, "when every kid she's looked at has been at least 3 months of age?" As critic Elizabeth Bates pointed out, 3-month-olds "have had 90 days, approximately 900 waking hours and 54,000 minutes, of visual and auditory experience." By the time these kids get into Baillargeon's experiments, they're not newborns anymore, and therefore claims of innateness aren't justified.

But what if Baillargeon is right? What if object permanence really is present from birth? Then could we say that object permanence is innate? Well, maybe. But critics of nativism would still argue that calling object permanence innate doesn't do anything to advance science. In fact, they would even argue that explaining object permanence by calling it innate isn't an explanation at all. At best, it only moves the explanation of object permanence from one level to another, from a postbirth phenomenon to a prebirth one. But nothing is explained by calling it innate. Critic Linda Smith writes, "Stopping at only one level of analysis—no matter how well motivated—just is not good enough if we want to understand how change really works, if we want to understand it well enough that we can alter the causal chain to a good end. Stopping short of real causes is not 'good enough' for developmental psychology either." So even if object permanence really does turn out to exist before birth, developmental psychologists will simply have to try harder to explain it, even if it means they have to start looking at it prenatally.

Overturning the Drawbridge Studies: Drawing on the Principle of Parsimony

Besides the criticisms Baillargeon's work provoked by her nativist claims, additional attacks have been levied at her methodology. Over the years, Baillargeon's rotating-screen experiments have received a great deal of attention. In fact, sometimes they're endearingly called the "drawbridge" studies because of the resemblance of her rotating screen to a drawbridge. But researchers are still struggling to come to grips with her findings to this day.

You see, the problem amounts to this. In science we are trained to follow a rule called the **principle of parsimony**. The principle of parsimony states that if two different theories are equally good at accounting for children's behavior, then the simpler theory is preferred. Baillargeon's theory was that *object permanence* caused her babies to look longer at the impossible event. But recently researchers have begun testing the possibility that the babies in her experiments looked longer at the impossible event for reasons having nothing to do with object permanence. "Could there be something else," they wondered, "that would make babies look longer at the 180° rotating screen than at the 112° rotating screen?" Maybe there was just something about the 180° rotating screen that attracted babies' interest, and maybe it had nothing to do with object permanence. (Isn't it interesting how 15 years after Baillargeon's study was published, researchers are still preoccupied with it? Revolutionary studies have quite an effect on people!)

In a recently published study, Thomas Schilling tested this possibility. He started out by giving Baillargeon the benefit of the doubt and assumed that her data were not flawed. He was willing to accept that her babies really did look longer at the impossible event than at the possible event. But he wasn't willing to go along for the ride and assume it was because the babies had object permanence. Rather, he thought it might have something to do with the way babies look at things, the way they *visually process information*. To fully understand what Schilling was saying, we need to back up a bit and introduce the concept of **information processing**.

Whenever you and I look at something, we need to "process it" in order to understand it. The way we use the term in psychology, processing something simply means that we take in information from the thing; maybe to recognize it, to observe its shape or colors, or even to realize that we've never seen anything like it before. Everything we pay attention to gets some level of processing. Sometimes we process things a lot; sometimes we process things very little.

Consider the following case of information processing. Suppose you go out for an evening of dining and dancing sometime around mid- to late December. At Wallenda's

Italian restaurant, the hostess seats you at a table where you get a clear view of a largish white man seated across the room from you. He has a full white beard and moustache, a velvety red coat hemmed in white fur, plump rosy cheeks, and a belly that jiggles like a bowl full of jelly when he laughs. How interested would you be in looking at this man? Especially if you were dining on Christmas Eve? You'd probably be so fascinated by this man's wardrobe that you'd have to force yourself not to stare! But truth be told, you'd probably be fascinated by the way this man was dressed any other day of the year too. Now suppose instead that the situation was exactly the same, except that the man you saw was normal in size, was wearing a sweater typical for an early winter evening, had no rosy cheeks, and had a belly that didn't jiggle. How interested would you be in looking at this man? My guess is that this man would appear so normal (at least in the United States) that you wouldn't even notice him, unless he was the only other person in the restaurant.

Now the question is, why did the St. Nick look-alike attract your interest? And why were you inclined to look at him longer than at the more typical man? Was it because you recognized the man in the velvety red coat as Santa Claus? Or was it simply because he wore clothes and facial hair that were unusual? A Baillargeon-type explanation might be that the man attracted your interest because you recognized him as looking like Santa Claus. But a more parsimonious (simpler) explanation would be that your interest in looking at the man was based on his unusual clothes and facial hair. Why is this a more parsimonious explanation? Well, people who knew nothing about Santa Claus might still find this man interesting to look at, based on his visual appearance alone. Knowing about Santa Claus requires an additional level of knowledge, and so is a more complicated explanation.

Now back to Schilling's experiment. Schilling thought that Baillargeon's 3½-month-olds preferred to look at the impossible event more than the possible event not because of the impossibility of the event, but because of the 180° rotation of the screen. If you remember from the procedure section, Baillargeon first showed all her babies a rotation event where the screen rotated 180° without the box. She familiarized them with this event *prior* to showing them the rotation events with the box. Although exposing babies to this event may very well have familiarized them with the motion of a 180° rotating screen, they may not have had enough time to *fully* process the motion of the 180° rotating screen. Schilling argued that if a baby is given too brief an exposure to something, she will prefer to look at it again the next time she gets a chance—probably so she can finish processing it. However, if a baby is given a long enough exposure to something the first time, she will no longer need to keep looking at it to finish processing it. Schilling suspected that Baillargeon's babies preferred to look at the impossible event, not because it was impossible, but because they didn't get a chance to fully process the 180° rotating event during the familiarization period. The impossible event, where the screen was again rotating 180°, gave the babies a chance to finish processing the event. And it was for *this* reason that babies looked longer at the impossible event.

To test his hypothesis, Schilling replicated Baillargeon's experiment exactly, except that he varied how many familiarization rotations the babies saw. Baillargeon had babies observe the familiarization period only until the babies began looking away, and her babies might have differed from one another in how many familiarization rotations they observed. Schilling, however, exerted much more control over the specific number of familiarization rotations babies watched. In his experiment, half the babies saw the screen rotate 180° exactly 6 times, while half the babies saw the screen rotate 180° exactly 12 times. His results were also fascinating. Babies with the short familiarization periods were the only ones who looked longer at the impossible event (where the screen also rotated 180°, but this time through a wooden box). Babies who received the longer familiarization period actually looked longer at the possible event! Schilling reasoned that babies who were familiarized with the 180° rotating event 12 times had fully processed it, and so wanted to move on to something new. Therefore, the 112° rotation event (the possible event) was more interesting to them. Babies who observed the 180° rotation 6 times didn't process the event fully, and so preferred to look at the impossible event so that they could finish processing the 180° rotation.

If Schilling is right, then Baillargeon's conclusions about the existence of object permanence by 3½ months of age become questionable, her findings appear to be artifacts of the procedure she used, and babies' interests in the impossible event are not due to object permanence but simply to how far the screen rotates. Is this yet another example of the David and Goliath story, only this time with Baillargeon starring as Goliath? Well, Baillargeon hasn't given up the ship yet.

In an article published in the same journal and issue as Schilling's, Baillargeon defends her position strongly by pointing out a number of shortcomings with Schilling's "replication." For one thing, she notes that she gave her babies a chance to touch and explore the box prior to the experiment. Schilling didn't. This finding alone could've been enough to account for their different results. As a result of this difference, maybe Schilling's babies didn't realize his box was a solid, three-dimensional box and that it was capable of stopping the screen from rotating. But there were other differences too. Baillargeon's box had a big clown face painted on it, whereas Schilling's didn't. Baillargeon's box was also bigger. These two differences could've drawn more attention to Baillargeon's box than to Schilling's, resulting in babies' being more attuned to the impossibility of the screen passing through the box in Baillargeon's version of the experiment. The bottom line is that the differences between the two studies were sufficient to call into question Schilling's questioning of Baillargeon's results.

Based in large part on the reception her study received, controversial or otherwise, Renée Baillargeon has assumed a leadership role alongside Piaget within the child development research community. She did so by taking Piaget's object permanence task to task. It was a bold move for her to take on Piaget, given that when her study was published she was only 6 years out of graduate school and hadn't even been promoted to associate professor yet. But take him on she did. And the consequence was that she revolutionized child psychology.

Bibliography

Baillargeon, R. (2000). Reply to Bogartz, Shinskey, and Schilling; Schilling; and Cashon and Cohen. *Infancy, 1*, 447–462.

Bates, E. (1999). Nativism versus development: Comments on Baillargeon and Smith. *Developmental Science, 2*, 148–149.

Schilling, T. H. (2000). Infants' looking at possible and impossible screen rotations: The role of familiarization. *Infancy, 1*, 389–402.

Smith, L. (1999). Do infants possess innate knowledge structures? The con side. *Developmental Science, 2*, 133–144.

Questions for Discussion

1. Is it more important to demonstrate that children *have* an ability or that children can *demonstrate* an ability? Why? What's the difference between the two?

2. What's an advantage of claiming that an ability or behavior is innate? Does calling something innate contribute to scientific progress?

3. Piaget claimed that object permanence emerged in full bloom at about 18–24 months of age. Baillargeon argued that it was more like 3.5 months of age, or even earlier. Why does it matter how early object permanence exists?

4. Baillargeon had a scientific "coming out party" at an extraordinarily early point in her career. However, other scientists never achieve Baillargeon's success. What kinds of factors do you think influence the notoriety and stature of individual scientists?

7

"Do You Know What I Know?"

DOES THE CHIMPANZEE HAVE A THEORY OF MIND?

Premack, D., & Woodruff, G. (1978). *The Behavioral and Brain Sciences, 1, 515–526.* (RANK 20)

Human beings have a particularly interesting knack for playing language games when it comes to talking about mental states. By "mental states," I mean things like believing, knowing, wanting, and thinking. We all have mental states. We all have beliefs, knowledge, wants, and thoughts. And, of course, to communicate our mental states we use mental state words. When I say something like, "I *believe* you," I'm using the word *believe* to describe the internal mental state I'm having in response to something you've said. In this case "I believe you" means that I accept what you said to be true. I also could've said, "I don't believe you," which means that my internal mental state is one of disbelief, where I don't take what you say to be true. My use of **mental state words** in this case is my way of letting you know what I think about what you said.

Now it's easy enough to use a single mental state word to talk about a single mental state. I have no problem constructing a sentence with one mental state word, and you have no problem understanding it. "I love you" may suffice to make the point. I could even bump up the level of complexity a bit by combining two mental state words into a single sentence, as in "I *want* to believe you." In this case, I'm not saying that I believe you and I'm not saying that I don't. I'm saying that I have a desire to accept what you say is true. Using two mental state words in one sentence is a tad harder to follow, but it's still something we do all the time. You just have to pay closer attention to keep track of what I'm saying. But what if I boosted the octane of complexity even further by adding a third mental state word to the sentence? How would you fare with something like, "I *think* I want to believe you?" In this sentence, I'm not saying I want to believe you and I'm not saying that I don't. I'm only saying that I'm *leaning toward* wanting to believe you. Although this sentence is more complicated, I'm sure you can still understand it, provided you think about it a little bit.

The rules of language provide very few limits as to how many mental state words we can string together. We're probably limited only by the number of internal mental states we're capable of having. We can combine mental state words in all kinds of ridiculously complicated ways. It's probably not till we get to something on the order of four mental states that we start stretching the limits of our understanding. What would you take me to mean, for example, if I said something like, "I'm *not sure* if I *think* I *want* to *believe* you"? Grammatically, there's nothing wrong with this sentence; it's perfectly acceptable. But the meaning of the sentence certainly requires some additional cerebration to comprehend. As I was growing up, I learned that my mother was the master of using mental state words. She's always been one to spend hours talking on the phone with her family and friends. As a child, I was never quite sure of what the person at the other end of the line was saying. But my mother, well, come to think of it, I was never quite sure what she was saying either. She would produce sentences that to this day baffle me. She would say things like, "I just don't think Marge knows Jeffrey believes Carol wants to hear an apology," or, "I really hope Ted understands that his boss believes Helen didn't know what Ted thought about Helen's last wishes." Huh? I think I need a flowchart.

As humans, we're in a unique position among the species not only to be aware of internal mental states, but in being able to communicate them to other people using language. We use mental state words to talk about our own thoughts, beliefs, and desires, but we also have the capability for talking about and understanding other people's thoughts, beliefs, and desires. Moreover, we can use language to talk about how our own mental states relate to the mental states of other people. By saying something as simple as, "I know what you are thinking," I'm communicating to you that my mental state is connected to your mental state. We may be the only species on Earth with this capability!

Modern child psychologists who study how children learn about mental states are said to be studying children's **theories of mind**. As adults, we all have a mind theory. What this means is that we have the ability to understand mental states, both our own and those of other people, and we can use our knowledge of mental states to make guesses about what people are going to do based on the mental states we *think* they have. If I know you *want* some candy, then based on my theory about what it means to *want* something, I can anticipate that you'll do something in order to get some candy. In this way, a theory of mind is a lot like a scientific theory. Scientific theories use abstract ideas to make predictions about what's going to happen, when it's going to happen, and under what conditions it will happen. And our personal mind theories use our abstract understanding of mental states to make predictions about what people are going to do, when they're going to do it, and under what conditions their behavior will happen. Of course, if adults are capable of having a theory of mind, the child psychologist wants to know whether children are capable of having a theory of mind. And if not, when does the capacity develop? Theory of mind research is extremely popular these days. It's so hot that in 1997 it was granted its own official PsycINFO database Thesaurus entry. It's just too bad that theory of mind research isn't listed on the NASDAQ stock exchange. I'd cash in my 401(k) and invest it all!

In an interesting twist of fate, the article that seems to have started all the ruckus about the development of children's theories of mind wasn't even about children. It was about a chimpanzee, and that chimp was named Sarah. In their 1978 study, voted 20th most revolutionary in child psychology since 1950, chimp researchers David Premack and Guy Woodruff launched a whole new era of research on children's understanding of mental states. They started with a simple question: Do chimps have a mental life?

INTRODUCTION

Premack and Woodruff began their article by talking about chimpanzees' well-known problem-solving abilities. For example, chimps are able to stack boxes on top of each other to reach fruit hanging from a ceiling, or they can put two short sticks together to make a stick long enough to rake in some food from outside their cages. And they can solve both these problems on first exposure, without having to be taught the solution. It's as if they have a sudden insight about how to manipulate their environments to satisfy their own desires.

Although these are nice examples of chimps' abilities to manipulate the physical world, Premack and Woodruff were more interested in what chimps knew about the psychological world. They wondered about the possibility that chimps might have a theory of mind. They wrote, "In saying that an individual has a theory of mind, we mean that the individual imputes mental states to himself and to others. A system of inferences of this kind is properly viewed as a theory, first, because such states are not directly observable, and second, because the system can be used to make predictions, specifically about the behavior of other organisms."

Premack and Woodruff cautioned their readers that it would be premature to question whether chimpanzees' theories of mind were at the same level as humans' theories of mind. In other words, it wasn't important to them "whether the chimpanzee's theory is a good or complete one, [and] whether he infers every mental state we infer and does so accurately . . . on exactly the same occasions we do." It was good enough for them just to see if chimpanzees impute mental states at all. (Just as a sidebar, the word *impute* more or less means to assign. If I say, "You are happy," then I am assigning, or imputing, the mental state of happiness to you.) As we've already seen, even humans have cognitive limits when it comes down to how many mental states they can have in mind at one time. Humans start having trouble when about four mental states are linked together, as in "Mary thinks John believes that Francine is happy about Jim's knowing the truth" (although I think my mother would have no trouble with this one). So it was good enough for Premack and Woodruff just to see if a chimp could impute a single mental state.

In what follows, I describe three related studies conducted by Premack and Woodruff to investigate the nature of chimpanzees' theories of mind. Although the authors actually describe more than three studies, the three I talk about here seem to do a pretty good job of illustrating the range of methodologies they used to try to understand the scope of chimps' theories of mind.

Experiment 1

METHOD

Participants

As I already mentioned, there was only a single participant in this study. Sarah was a 14-year-old African wild-born female chimpanzee. She had been used in a number of other experiments conducted by Premack, and she had gained international fame for being taught to "talk" using plastic symbols on a magnetic board when she was only about 5. Although Sarah had no prior experience with the tasks used in this experiment, Sarah had been tested on a variety of cognitive tasks 5 days a week for the previous 10 years. Importantly for this study, she also had lots of experience watching commercial television!

Materials

The materials used to test Sarah's theory of mind included four 30-second videos of a human actor inside a cage similar to Sarah's. In each video, the caged human actor was shown struggling to reach some bananas that were just out of his reach. Each video portrayed the bananas being out of reach in a different way:

Video 1: The bananas were attached to the ceiling and were vertically beyond the grasp of the human.

Video 2: The bananas were outside the cage wall and were horizontally beyond the grasp of the human.

Video 3: The bananas were again outside the cage wall, but this time they were within reach. The problem was that there was a box along the inside wall of the cage that acted like an obstacle to getting the bananas.

Video 4: This was the same setup as in Video 3, only the box was covered with heavy concrete blocks.

In addition to the videotapes, Premack and Woodruff took still photographs of the actor engaging in actions that would solve each of the problems. For Video 1, the photograph was of the actor stepping up onto a box. For Video 2, the photo showed the actor lying on his side and reaching outside the cage with a rod. For Video 3, the photo portrayed the actor pushing the box to the side. And for Video 4, the photo showed the actor removing the concrete blocks from the top of the box.

Procedure

Sarah's understanding of each of the problems was tested by showing her a video, and pausing it just before the last 5 seconds were played. Then she was given a pair of photographs. One of the photographs showed the actor engaging in the correct solution to the problem, the other showed the actor pursuing one of the other solutions. Each video was shown a total of six times, each time paired with the correct photo and an incorrect photo. The way Premack and Woodruff gave the pairs of photographs to Sarah was interesting. Rather than just handing them to her, they placed them in a box. By putting the pictures in a box, they could avoid giving Sarah any unintentional social cues about which picture was the right choice.

Sarah's job was to take out the two photos, choose between them, and place the one she believed contained the right answer next to the TV. After she made her choice, she rang a bell, indicating that she had decided. This was Sarah's way of saying, "Final answer." The trainer then entered the room and said, "Good, Sarah, that's right," or, "No, Sarah, that's wrong," using a tone of voice "like the one we would use with a young child." At the end of each session, the trainer gave Sarah some yogurt, fruit, or other favorite food.

RESULTS

Sarah identified the correct solution on 21 of 24 trials. When Sarah made a mistake, it was always on the video involving the concrete blocks. Premack and Woodruff made the humorous observation that for an adult chimpanzee such as Sarah, moving the blocks was probably an unnecessary step before pushing the box to the side. Only puny humans would be so weak as to be unable to push the box aside with the concrete blocks on top. So for this video, from Sarah's point of view, she was presented with two still photos that both depicted incorrect solutions!

DISCUSSION

The question, of course, is, Why was Sarah correct so often? Was it because she had a theory of mind? Was she smart enough to know what the actor wanted? This was a distinct possibility. If Sarah did have a theory of mind, it would mean that she was capable of imputing (there's that word again) two mental states to the actor. She would know (1) that the actor had a *purpose* in mind, and (2) that the actor *knew* how to solve the problem. This would've been a very cool finding, indeed. If nothing else, it would mean that humans aren't alone in the world when it comes to knowing something about mental life. Unfortunately, there was also a second, much less interesting explanation for Sarah's behavior. Premack and Woodruff called this second explanation "classical associationism."

The logic behind the classical associationism explanation goes something like this. When a human or smart animal watches a familiar action of some kind, and they see the action interrupted, their natural tendency is to complete the action. If an animal has previous experience with a problem, she not only knows what happens in the beginning part of the action, but she also knows how the action should conclude. In other words, the animal has learned to associate the first part of the action with the last part. Premack and Woodruff admit that Sarah had lots of experience with these kinds of problem-solving activities, although she had never seen a human do them before. So when Sarah saw the human actor faced with the problem of trying to reach the bananas, she knew what the solution was. Consequently, when she selected the photograph that depicted the correct solution, she may have based her decision entirely on her *own* experience of "what comes next" in the sequence.

If this is what Sarah was doing, then realistically Sarah didn't need to know anything about the mental states of the human actor.

To help them decide between the theory of mind explanation and the classical associationism explanation, Premack and Woodruff conducted a second study. The purpose of the second study was to expand on the first one by increasing the range of problems. All of the problems presented to Sarah in the first study revolved around the actor trying to get some food (the bananas). In the second study, a number of less familiar kinds of problems were represented, where the solution to the problem didn't revolve around getting food.

Experiment 2

METHOD

Participants

Sarah.

Materials

Videotapes of a human actor were again used. The actor was confronted with four different problems.

Video 1: The human actor is shown trying to escape from a locked cage.

Video 2: The human actor is shown kicking a malfunctioning heater, looking at the heater wryly, and clasping his arms around his chest while shivering.

Video 3: The human actor is trying to play a record on an unplugged turntable (Premack and Woodruff called it a "phonograph," but I wasn't sure if you knew what that was).

Video 4: The human actor is trying to wash a dirty floor, but the hose he is using isn't connected to the faucet.

Still photographs were again taken of the "proper solutions," but this time they didn't include the actor engaging in any activity. Instead, they were just pictures of objects that could be used to solve the problems. For Video 1, a photograph of a key was the correct answer. For Video 2, a lit cone of paper was correct (the kind we would use to ignite the pilot flame of a furnace). For Video 3, the correct photograph was one that showed an electrical cord plugged into a wall outlet. And for Video 4, the correct answer was a photo that showed a hose properly attached to a water faucet.

After testing Sarah's skill at solving problems using these photos, Premack and Woodruff conducted the study a second time using a second set of photographs. The second set of photos were meant to increase the difficulty of the task. Instead of simply requiring Sarah to choose from among pictures of a key, a burning cone of paper, a plugged-in AC cord, or an attached hose, Premack and Woodruff gave Sarah several versions of each correct solution. For Video 1, there were three "key" photos: one of an intact key, one of a twisted key, and one of a broken key. For Video 2, there were three photos of the wadded cone of paper: one of the paper burning, one of the paper not yet lit, and one of the paper already burnt out. For Videos 3 and 4, the pictures were of the electrical cord (or the hose), either plugged in (or attached to the faucet), not plugged in (or not attached to the faucet), or plugged in but cut (or attached to the faucet but cut).

Procedure

The procedure was the same as in the first experiment. Sarah watched all but the last 5 seconds of each videotape. She was then given a choice of two pictures. One picture was counted as the correct solution to the problem; the other was counted as an incorrect solution to the problem. For the first set of photos, the incorrect photograph was simply one of the other three photos (photos that would've been correct for the other three problems). But for the second set of photos, the incorrect photo was of the correct object, but in an incorrect state. For example, the photo of the intact key was paired with the photo of the broken key.

RESULTS

For the first set of pictures, "Sarah made no errors whatsoever." Apparently, this set of pictures was way too easy for Sarah. That's why Premack and Woodruff went ahead and used the second set of pictures.

The second set of pictures presented Sarah with many more difficult choices. She couldn't simply choose the picture of the key in response to Video 1, for example, because there were always two different pictures of the key. To solve this problem, Sarah would not only have to know that a picture of a key was the right answer, she would also have to know which picture of a key was the right answer. Amazingly, despite the greater difficulty of the choices, Sarah made only one error. And when she made that error, it was probably because the quality of the photograph was poor. To make the photos, Premack and Woodruff shrank 8″ × 10″ photos to a 3″ × 4″ size. Apparently, the quality of the reduced picture of the twisted key wasn't very good, which made it look a lot like the intact key, and so Sarah chose the twisted key as the correct answer.

DISCUSSION

Premack and Woodruff took the results of the second study as evidence against the classical associationism explanation because the pictures Sarah had to choose from didn't depict the human actor completing any actions. They were simply pictures of solid objects. This gives greater weight to the possibility that Sarah really did have a theory of mind and *knew* what the actor *wanted* to do. Still, when Sarah chose the correct pictures, it was possible that she was choosing on the basis of her own personal preferences. In other words, it's conceivable that she didn't realize that the correct pictures stood for the solutions to the problems. Instead, it's possible that she just liked the correct pictures better. But Premack and Woodruff dismissed this possibility because why would Sarah just happen to like only and all of the correct photos? This doesn't seem very probable. Thus, Premack and Woodruff were left with the very real possibility that Sarah was making her choices on the basis of her knowledge of the desires of the actor. Maybe Sarah had a primitive theory of mind after all.

Premack and Woodruff next wondered whether Sarah had made her choices on the basis of her wishes to see the actor succeed. As it turns out, the actor in all the videotapes was a guy named Keith, who was one of Sarah's favorite trainers. Once Sarah realized what Keith's desires were in each of the videos, maybe she selected the proper photos because she wanted to see Keith succeed in his task. This raised the question of what Sarah would do if she were given problem solutions for someone she didn't like so much. Premack and Woodruff tested this possibility in a third experiment.

Experiment 3

METHOD

Experiment 3 was set up just like Experiment 1, except that a new set of videos and photos was made using a new actor, whom Premack and Woodruff named "Bill" (the names have been changed to protect the innocent), to accompany the original set of videos and photos. Bill was a real trainer in Sarah's everyday life, but Sarah didn't seem to be especially fond of him. To test whether Sarah would choose different problem solutions for good Keith and bad Bill, given the chance, Premack and Woodruff used two types of still photographs. There was one set of photos that showed the actors engaging in the successful solution, which Premack and Woodruff labeled the "good" outcomes. And there was a second set of photos that showed the actors failing to achieve the desired solution, and in some cases even experiencing some mishap. The good photographs consisted of the same photos used in Experiment 1, except that now some of the photos included Bill as the actor. The bad photos are described below.

Participants

Sarah.

Materials

The original set of videos depicting Keith in the four problem situations were used in this experiment, but a new set of four videos were made portraying Bill in the same four problem situations. Just as a reminder, the videos showed either Keith or Bill (1) trying to reach the bananas overhead, (2) trying to reach the bananas outside the cage with a rod, (3) trying to reach the bananas outside the cage with a box in the way, and (4) trying to reach the bananas outside the cage with a box in the way, with concrete blocks on top of the box.

The four "good-outcome" photos were the same type as used in Experiment 1: (1) either Keith or Bill was shown stepping up on a box to reach the bananas, (2) either Keith or Bill was shown lying on his side using a long rod to reach the bananas outside the cage, (3) either Keith or Bill was shown pushing the box to the side, and (4) either Keith or Bill was shown removing the concrete blocks on top of the box.

The four "bad-outcome" photos were new to Experiment 3, and showed either Keith or Bill in a situation involving some form of failure. For Video 1, the bad outcome showed the actor's foot stepping right through the box. For Video 2, the bad outcome showed the actor lying on his side and reaching for the bananas with a rod that was too short. For Video 3, the bad outcome showed the actor falling over the box. And for Video 4, the bad outcome showed the actor lying on the floor with the concrete blocks lying on top of him.

Procedure

The procedure was the same as in Experiment 1. Each videotape of each actor was shown to Sarah, with the videotape paused during the last 5 seconds. When the videotape was paused, Sarah was asked to choose between the good and bad outcome photos for each actor. After each session, the experimenter came back into the room and praised Sarah for either choice. In other words, neither choice was treated as wrong.

RESULTS AND DISCUSSION

Amazingly, Sarah chose the good outcome eight out of eight times when Keith, her preferred trainer, was the actor. But when Bill was the actor, she chose the bad outcome six out of eight times. It was almost as if she was asking herself, "Hmm, what would I like to see happen to people I like and to people I don't like?" In sum, it seems that Sarah is able to understand what an actor wants to do, that is, she knows something about the actor's mental state, but also that Sarah has some ideas as to what *she* would like to see happen to people based on how much she likes them.

GENERAL DISCUSSION

The results of these experiments led Premack and Woodruff to the very tentative conclusion that chimps may have the capability for forming at least a very simple theory of mind. Although this isn't exactly a ringing endorsement for the mental strength of chimps, scientists are notoriously cautious when it comes to making bold revolutionary claims. Before a stronger conclusion could be drawn, Premack and Woodruff recommended a number of additional studies that would need to be undertaken. Unfortunately, I don't have space here to review them all. But most of the studies impressively anticipated a great deal of the research that child psychologists are conducting on children's theories of mind today.

For example, Premack and Woodruff noted how their procedure could be easily adapted to find out if chimpanzees *know* something about the mental state of *knowing*. As we've already seen, their research with Sarah suggested that chimps are capable of imputing the mental state of *desire* to human actors. That is, Sarah knew what Keith and Bill *wanted* to do. But that study said nothing about Sarah's *knowledge* of what Keith and Bill *knew*. Consequently, Premack and Woodruff suggested that future research could test whether chimpanzees can tell the difference between an adult's and a child's *knowledge* about a problem-solving situation. If a chimp saw a very young child engaging in some of the banana-seeking problems, for example, would the chimp be more inclined to anticipate failure than if the chimp saw an adult engaging in the same banana-seeking problem? If so, then we would have evidence that chimps *know* that human children don't *know* as much as adults. Such a finding also might mean that chimps *know* something about how knowledge *develops*!

Relatedly, Premack and Woodruff showed how chimps could be tested about their knowledge of whether a human is a liar or is just a fool (their terms). At the time their 1978 article was published, they were actually in the process of testing chimps' knowledge of lying. Their procedure involved a chimp trying to find a container that held a reward from among 100 opaque containers. The trick was that before the chimp made a selection, she was advised by either a "liar" or a "fool" about which container to choose. The "correct" container was the one that contained the reward (although it's not exactly clear what was used as the reward). The difference between the liar and the fool in this study was that the chimp knew that the liar knew which container had the reward because the chimp observed the liar to be present when the reward was hidden. The chimp also knew that the fool didn't know which container held the reward because she observed that the fool wasn't present when the reward was hidden. Both the liar and the fool made wrong suggestions to the chimp about which container to choose; the liar was wrong 100% of the time and the fool was wrong 99% of the time (because the fool would occasionally get lucky). The important question was, Would the chimp develop different attitudes toward the two people? Apparently so. As Premack and Woodruff described it, "After only two or three experiences with the [liar], [Sarah's] aggressive displays toward him were such that we thought it dangerous to continue the experiment. Toys and other objects lying about the cage, many of them sharp and hard, sailed out under the mesh at dangerously high speeds, narrowly missing the [liar]." With these results, it's hard to avoid the conclusion that Sarah *knew* what the liar *knew*, and became angry when the liar acted as if he didn't *know* it.

CONCLUSIONS

Although it's difficult to pinpoint the precise beginnings of the modern theory of mind research bandwagon, there's little doubt that wherever they were, Premack and Woodruff's 1978 article is to be found nearby. I'm inclined to give it the nod as the most formative article, based on its nomination and selection frequency as one of the most revolutionary studies by so many child psychology researchers. But don't take it from me; what do I know? Noted theory of mind researcher and historian John Flavell also locates the origin of the theory of mind wave of research with the Premack and Woodruff article.

But it's also clear that other studies were a driving force in contributing to the theory of mind hoopla. Central among these was a famous study conducted by Austrian psychologists Josef Perner and Heinz Wimmer in 1983. Their classic study, probably every bit as ingenious as Premack and Woodruff's, was based on the simple question, What do children think other children think? Flavell describes research in the Perner and Wimmer tradition nicely:

> A developmental psychologist shows a 5-year-old a cookies box with a picture of cookies on it and asks her what is in it. "Cookies," is the ready answer. The child then looks inside the box and to her surprise sees that it actually contains crayons, not cookies. "What would another child who had not yet opened the box think was in it?" the experimenter now asks. "Cookies!" says the child, amused at the trick. The experimenter then tries the same procedure with a 3-year-old. The answer to the first question is the expected "cookies," but the response to the second is unexpected: "crayons." Even more surprising, the child also maintains that he himself had initially thought that the box would contain crayons.

In this typical case scenario a 5-year-old is able to understand that another child would be fooled by the picture of the cookies on the outside of the box. She also realizes that the other child would hold a different belief about the contents of the box than she herself held. In other words, this child knows what another child knows (or in this case doesn't know). In contrast, the 3-year-old seems unable to separate his own beliefs from the beliefs of another child. He doesn't seem to grasp the idea that someone else could have a different mental state than himself, or that someone else could lack the knowledge base he has. And even more interestingly, he doesn't seem to realize that the current state of his own knowledge differs from his previous state of knowledge. Even though he initially thought the box contained cookies, he seemed to forget that fact once he found the box actually contained crayons.

What Flavell is describing is commonly called a "false-belief task." Theory of mind researchers took to the false-belief task like flies to honey. A recent 1999 review article, which summarized false-belief research up to that time, found that in 77 published research articles, 177 separate studies were conducted, comprising 591 false-belief conditions! The false-belief task has occupied such a principal role in theory of mind research because it gives researchers a perfect window into children's understanding of what other people believe. With the false-belief task, you can set in motion some kind of physical transformation witnessed only by the child, and then probe that child about what she thinks other people who didn't witness the event will think. The false-belief task comes in all shapes and sizes. In one of its most famous versions (the one used by Perner and Wimmer), two children are in a room with two containers. Both children watch as the experimenter places a toy in one of the containers. One child leaves the room, and while she is gone, the experimenter removes the toy from the first container and places it in the second. Of course, the remaining child witnessed the toy transfer. The key question asked of the child who witnessed the transformation is, "Where will the other child look for the toy?" The same kind of age difference reveals itself. It's not till about 5 years of age that children *think* other children will *think* the toy is still in the first container. Younger children *think* other children will *think* the toy is in its new hiding place. These kinds of findings have led researchers to conclude that it's sometime between the ages of 3 and 5 that children begin developing their personal theories of mind, at least theories of mind that include belief as one of the mental states children are capable of imputing.

So how would a chimp fare on the false-belief task? Based on Premack and Woodruff's work, we know that chimps are capable of imputing something like *desire* or *purpose*. But would a chimp be able to understand that someone else could hold a false belief? Premack attempted to answer that question in a book chapter he published in 1988. Sarah's cage was rigged so that a cabinet was attached to one of the walls. On the left side of the cabinet were stored all kinds of goodies, particularly pastries, that Sarah's trainer Bonnie shared with her during their daily teatime. On the right side of the cabinet were stored all kinds of bad things, including rubber snakes, putrid rotting rubber, and a cup of chimp poop. The experiment was set up so that Sarah had to press a button before Bonnie could open either side of the cabinet. Every day for 18 days, Bonnie would walk up to the left side of the cabinet and wait for Sarah to press the button, after which Bonnie would get out the pastries and share them with Sarah. Sarah's average response time for pressing the button was 7 seconds. One day, a "villain," dressed in a mask and a gown, came into Sarah's room, broke into the cabinet with a crowbar, and switched the contents on the left side of the cabinet with the contents on the right. Fifteen minutes later, Bonnie walked in for her usual teatime with Sarah. What would Sarah do with the knowledge that the contents in the cabinet had been switched? Would she, like 5-year-old children, realize that Bonnie wouldn't know that the contents had been switched? Would she refuse to press the button so that Bonnie couldn't open the cabinet and be disgusted by the contents? Alas, no. Sarah showed absolutely no change in her behavior when Bonnie entered the room. Either Sarah didn't realize that Bonnie's knowledge was different from her own, or she knew but didn't care. What's clear is that Sarah's behavior provides no evidence that chimps are capable of using *belief* in whatever theory of mind they might have.

Since the publication of his 1978 article with Woodruff, Premack had a chance to reflect on the scientific revolution he helped launch 10 years earlier. In the 1988 book chapter, he revisited the issue of whether chimpanzees could be viewed as possessing a theory of mind. He concluded, in a noncommittal sort of way, that if chimps do have a theory of mind, they are bound to be weaker than mind theories found even in human 5-year-olds. Chimp theories are probably based on more elementary mental states like seeing, wanting, and expecting. Chimps may know what others see, and they may be able to make predictions about others' behaviors based on that knowledge, but they don't seem capable of understanding what others believe. *Belief* may be an altogether different mental state, one that our closest cousin in the animal kingdom isn't capable of entertaining.

Premack and Woodruff's 1978 article was revolutionary because, in part or whole, it launched a whole new movement in child psychology. At child psychology research conferences, it's very easy to get the impression that everybody's doing theory of mind research. It has the flavor of a fad that never died out. Flavell likens the way theory of mind scientists are dominating child psychology today to the domination enjoyed by Piagetian scientists a generation ago. Why all the interest in children's theories of mind? Probably because mental life is so darn important in defining what it means to be human. Imagine what it would be like if we didn't impute mental states to other people. Flavell gives the example of how another famous theory of mind theorist, Alison Gopnik, likes to put it: Imagine what it would be like for you to give a lecture to an audience if you had no conception of mental states. The audience might appear to you as bags of meat with two small holes at the top. You would see these bags and the shiny things in their holes shift around unpredictably in a way that perplexes and terrifies you, although, of course, you don't realize that you are perplexed and terrified because you have no sense of what mental states are.

Bibliography

Flavell, J. H. (2000). Development of children's knowledge about the mental world. *International Journal of Behavioral Development, 24,* 15–23.

Hughes, C. (2001). Essay Review: From infancy to inferences: Current perspectives on intentionality. *Journal of Cognition and Development, 2,* 221–240.

Premack, D. (1988). "Does the chimpanzee have a theory of mind?" revisited. In R. W. Byrne & A. Whiten (Eds.), *Machiavellian intelligence: Social expertise and the evolution of intellect in monkeys, apes, and humans.* New York: Oxford University Press.

Questions for Discussion

1. How might having a theory of mind provide humans with a selective survival advantage over other species?

2. Why would chimps have difficulty knowing about the *beliefs* of others, when they seem to do just fine knowing about the *intentions* of others? What's the difference between belief and intention?

3. Premack's chimp Sarah really had two lives as a research subject. In the first life, she was trained intensively to learn a language composed of plastic symbols. In the second life she was tested for her knowledge of the mental states of others. Might Sarah's performance on theory of mind tests during the second part of her life have been influenced by her language training during the first part of life? Why? How might other chimps have performed differently than Sarah during the theory of mind testing?

8

Language Development and the Big Bang Theory

SYNTACTIC STRUCTURES.
Chomsky, N. (1957). *The Hague: Mouton.*   (RANK 5)

It's difficult enough to be a revolutionary in any single scientific discipline. Revolutionizing a discipline requires a lot of dominoes to fall over in just the right order. You have to be the first one to come up with an inspirational and provocative new idea, and the idea has to be inspirational and provocative to other people besides yourself. If your idea represents some new theory, your theory has to make sense of all the data that already exist, and it has to do it better than all the previous theories. Your theory must generate a lot of new avenues for research and be capable of making sense of any data that might be collected in the future. But to be revolutionary, simply having a good idea is not enough. You need a matching personality. You have to be bold enough to believe other people want to hear your idea. You have to be persistent enough to get your idea past all the doors that will be slammed in your face. And you have to be callous enough to withstand all the personal attacks your idea is going to generate. Let's face it, revolutionaries aren't revolutionary because they play the fiddle and get everybody out on the dance floor. They're revolutionary because they ridicule out-of-date, old ideas and sometimes even the old people who believed those ideas. Being a revolutionary takes a strong personality indeed. But in addition to having a revolutionary idea and a strong personality, you simply have to have good timing. Your idea needs to be unveiled at a time when the field is mentally prepared. If your revolutionary idea comes out too early, no one will recognize its ingenuity. If it comes out too late, someone else has already stolen your glory. Darwin sat on his revolutionary theory of evolution for decades before he felt the time was right to cut it loose. Even then he wasn't ready to publish it; but another scientist, named Alfred Russell Wallace, was planning on publishing the same idea, so Darwin thought he'd better get on the ball.

With his publication of *Syntactic Structures*, not only did Noam Chomsky start a revolution in the field of child psychology (*Syntactic Structures* was voted the fifth most revolutionary overall), he planted the seeds of revolution in a half-dozen other fields as well! Chomsky revolutionized fields as diverse as anthropology, artificial intelligence, cognitive science, linguistics, neuroscience, and philosophy. And if that wasn't enough, he's been working on the side toward revolutionizing political theory.

In my presentation of Chomsky's work, I'm going to deviate a bit from the formula I've adopted up to this point. In this chapter, I'm actually going to focus relatively little on *Syntactic Structures*. Oh sure, the ideas ignited by *Syntactic Structures* were truly revolutionary and caused quite a stir within the child development community. But let's be real, talking about the syntax of language doesn't get the blood pumping like a good episode of "My Transsexual Lesbian Doberman Is Having an Affair with My Exhibitionist Cross-Dressing Calico" on Jerry Springer. In fact, I'd wager that you'd have more fun watching paint dry than reading *Syntactic Structures* (don't tell anyone I said that). This isn't to belittle the book's importance. The problem is that the book's subject matter is so esoteric, so remotely relevant to anything that could possibly be meaningful to your life, I don't see much advantage in spending our time trying to make syntax sizzle. I think our time would be better spent taking a look at Chomsky's radical ideas as they came out in the decades following publication of *Syntactic Structures*. Collectively, these later ideas had a profound impact on child psychology, but it all began with *Syntactic Structures*.

BACKGROUND

Chomsky's revolution focused on the nature of human language. Human language is at once childlike in its simplicity and encyclopedic in its complexity. It's childlike in its simplicity because developing a language is so easy even a child could do it. In fact, every child does it! In every corner of the world, every child with a good brain who is minimally exposed to a language will end up developing that language. In other words, the development of language is universal. The universal story of children's language development goes something like this: Children begin understanding their first words at about 8 months of age, they begin saying their first words at about 13 months of age, they start combining their first words to make simple sentences at about 20 months of age, and they begin adding the elements of grammar at about 24 months of age. So usually by the age of 2, and certainly by the age of 3, most children have at least a cursory grip on the basics of the language of their culture.

But as an object of study, language is at the same time exceedingly complex. Consider, for example, all the different rule systems you need to master in order to speak a language fluently. There are at least five of them, each one aimed at a different level of language use. First, the **phonological rule system** has to do with the sounds and sound combinations used to make up words. To master the phonological rule system, you have to be able to decipher the relevant sounds for your language, you have to be able to reproduce those sounds (or a close approximation thereof), and you have to be able to tell the difference between sound combinations that are permissible and those that are illegal in your language. Both the /s/ and the /t/ sound, for example, are relevant for English, but the phonological rules for English specify that they can be clustered together only under certain conditions. For example, /s/ and /t/ can be combined at the beginning of a word (as in *star*) or at the end of a word (as in *fast*). But the reverse order, /t/ + /s/, is permissible only at the end of a word (as in *rats*). You can't begin an English word with /t/ + /s/. Or at least when you see a word beginning with /t/ + /s/ you're not really sure how it's pronounced (as in *tsetse fly*). That's why you might not be able to say the Chinese word for car, *che* (pronounced "tsir").

Then there's the **morphological rule system**, which specifies when and how you should combine prefixes and suffixes with root words to make new words. (Prefixes, suffixes, and root words are collectively called **morphemes**, which is related to the word *morphological.*) To make plurals in English, for example, you learn there is a standard approach, for example, /car/ + /plural marker/ = cars, or /tree/ + /plural marker/ = trees. But you also learn that there are a number of irregular approaches for doing the same thing: /man/ + /plural marker/ = men, but /deer/ + /plural marker/ = deer. If you said, "I saw two mans walking across the street yesterday," you would be violating the morphological rule system. So not only do you have to learn the regular rules for combining morphemes, you also have to learn all the exceptions. On top of that, you have to be able to generalize the morphological rules that you've learned (such as how to make a plural) to words that you've never even heard before. Sometimes it's fairly easy. Consider Jean Berko-Gleason's famous example, "Yesterday I had one wug, but today I have two of them. I have two _____." In this case, most English speakers would say "wugs" because even though they've never encountered the word before, it seems to align itself closely with similar-sounding words they *have* seen before, such as *bug → bugs* or *hug → hugs*. But consider this case, "Yesterday I had one Sony Walkman, but today I have two of them. I have two _____ _____." Most English speakers would have a hard time making the plural of Sony Walkman because although the word *man* has a well-learned irregular plural form, the word *man* isn't being used in its ordinary sense. The world-famous author/lecturer Steven Pinker uses this example on his lecture circuit, and points out that Sony Corporation has a convenient way out of this conundrum. For Sony, the plural of Sony Walkman is simply "Sony Personal Stereo Systems."

The **semantic rule system** specifies how you're supposed to combine words based on word meaning. In fact, the word *semantic* means "meaning." Again, there are semantically legal sentences, such as "The man saw the robber burst from the bank carrying two bags of cash." But there are also sentences that violate the semantic rule system, such as "The blind man saw the robber burst from the bank carrying two bags of cash." You know this second sentence is semantically illegal because the meaning of *blind* excludes the possibility of being able to see. You can also take advantage of the way our semantic system works in order to create humor by creatively employing words with dual meanings. Question: What has eight wheels and flies? Answer: A garbage truck. Get it? Ha!

The **pragmatic rule system** contains the rules for how we *ought* to use language given the nature of a particular social situation. Of course, you're already familiar with most rules of the pragmatic rule system, even though you may not realize it. Consider how your speech would differ in these two social situations. In Situation 1, you're sitting around a campfire with your close friends talking about how the school year is going. In Situation 2, you're sitting around a table having dinner with your boyfriend/girlfriend's parents, and as an added bonus, they've also invited the family priest/minister/rabbi. When you're with your close friends, you use an informal and casual kind of language. You may not pronounce words perfectly, and you may use slang words known only to you and your friends. But around your boyfriend's/girlfriend's parents, presumably people you're trying to impress, you'll tend to use language more properly. Your speech will be more precise. And you probably wouldn't use slang words because you'd realize that the parents wouldn't know what they meant. If you used slang words, you'd be in violation of the pragmatic rule system. You'd also be in violation of the pragmatic rule system if you went up to the priest/minister/rabbi and said, "Bite me!" Unless, of course, it so happened that the priest/minister/rabbi was your close friend or brother, with whom you have a teasingly adversarial relationship. In any case, all these do's and don'ts of social language use represent your knowledge of pragmatics.

Finally, we have the rule system called **syntax**. As you can probably guess based on the title of his book, this is the rule system that occupied most of Chomsky's attention. Syntax specifies the rules for combining words based on the grammar of a language. English grammar, for example, specifies that the standard sentence should be of the subject-verb-object variety. The subject of the sentence comes first, the verb comes next, and the object, if there is one, comes last. If you failed to turn in an assignment to your professor, for example, you might say, "My dog ate my homework." In this case, *dog* is the subject of the sentence, *ate* is the verb, and *homework* is the object of the verb. If instead you said something like, "My dog essay ate!" English speakers would know you weren't talking right. They might think you were either not a native speaker of English, so frantic you couldn't talk straight, or under the influence of some kind of recreational substance. Although subject-verb-object is the standard syntactic order for English, other orders in English are possible when you want to produce a special effect. For example, a sentence expressing special emphasis could take an object-subject-verb form like "*Homework* my dog ate—not biscuits!" But this would be an unusual sentence, one you wouldn't ordinarily hear in English. Other languages have different standard orders altogether. In Japanese, for example, you *would* say the equivalent of "My dog essay ate," with the verb at the end of the sentence. By combining subject, verb, and object in different ways, there are six possible syntactic orders for the world's 6,000 languages: SVO, SOV, VSO, VOS, OVS, and OSV. But as it turns out, about 90% of the world's languages are made up of only three of the six orders: SVO, SOV, and VSO. Notice that in all three orders the subject precedes the object, which means that 90% of the world's languages have a common preference for a subject-before-object order. More rarely, some languages allow for the object to precede the subject in their standard sentences. As author David Crystal informs us, instances of VOS, OVS, and OSV orders have been found, but only in relatively exotic languages like Malagasy, Hixkaryana, and Jamadi. Crystal also brings up the humorous example of Yoda, the famed Jedi master, as an individual who spoke with something akin to an object-subject-verb order, with phrases such as "Sick have I become," "Strong am I with the force," and "Your father he is."

SO WHY IS LANGUAGE ACQUISITION SO HARD TO EXPLAIN?

The dilemma facing anyone dealing with children's language acquisition is precisely the fact that *all* children pick up language with ease, apparently without regard for its complexity. How can this be? At the time Chomsky arrived on the scene back in the 1950s, the story of how children acquired language was being told mainly by behavioral psychologists like B. F. Skinner. You may recall from other chapters that Skinner's theory of behaviorism assumed that all behaviors were shaped through patterns of reinforcement and punishment. Language behaviors were no exception. Phonology training, for example, was believed to begin in early infancy when parents started rewarding babies for producing sounds appropriate to their native language. And if a baby produced sounds that weren't used in her native language, she would be equivalently punished. An English baby's "oooooh" sounds might be met with smiles and applause from doting parents, but that same baby's clicking sounds might be met with frowns of disapproval. Clicks are important in some African languages, but they're not used in English. The "oooooh" sound, on the other hand, is used in English. Over an extended period of time, the pattern of reinforcements and punishments experienced by babies would ultimately shape and mold their vocalizations into a phonology that was appropriate for their language. Other rule systems such as morphology, semantics, pragmatics, and syntax would be similarly trained in the baby. Through these conditioning procedures, babies would eventually become fluent users of the language.

Chomsky's response to this behavioral story was, "Poppycock!" At 30 years of age, it was brash and bold for Chomsky to take on the whole behavioral movement, especially since behaviorism had gained a national following and was headquartered at the highly prestigious Harvard University, and especially because he was attacking psychology from within his own discipline of linguistics. The interdisciplinary nature of Noam Chomsky's attack on B. F. Skinner's theory of behaviorism would be sort of like Albert Einstein attacking Charles Darwin's theory of evolution. And by taking on Skinner, Chomsky was taking on an intellectual force as brash and bold as his own. But in a famous and somewhat vicious 1959 article titled "Review of *Verbal Behavior*," attack he did, and Chomsky's explicit and powerful rejection of behaviorism was made known to the world. (*Verbal Behavior* was Skinner's book on language learning.)

The essence of Chomsky's argument was that language development simply happens too fast to fit within the constraints of a behaviorist explanation. The long-drawn-out shaping and molding process bandied about by the behaviorists would take decades to result in language fluency in a real child. If the behaviorists were right, then every single grammatical utterance produced by a child would have to be reinforced at some point in that child's history. And every ungrammatical utterance would have to be punished. This would take way too long. Furthermore, children are always saying creative things they've never even heard before, and so how could they possibly be reinforced for these? In English morphology, for example, children often misapply the regular past-tense marker to irregular verbs. They say things like, "We goed to the zoo yesterday," or "The doggy bited me." Of course, these are sentences they've never heard spoken to them. And in the area of semantics, my daughter still says, "Turn the TV to me really." She's used this phrase for nearly 2 years to ask us to turn the TV toward her. But why she appends the word *really* to her request is mysterious. She's never heard us say it, and we've never rewarded her for saying it. The point is that mounting evidence shows children reliably produce sentences they've never heard before and continue producing them in the absence of reinforcement.

Given data like these, Chomsky reasoned that something other than reinforcement and punishment had to be responsible for language development. If language isn't learned from the environment, he thought, then it must develop *within the child* from the very beginning. But claiming that language is present within the child from the very beginning carries with it a couple of corollaries. First, language must somehow be hardwired into the circuitry of the brain (where else would it be, the elbow?). Second, language must ultimately be specified in the genes (because that's where inside things always come from). So Chomsky made the very radical claim that the source of language was not to be found in children's environments, but in their DNA!

CHOMSKY'S ACCOUNT

It was in *Syntactic Structures* that Chomsky first began publicly outlining his nativist theory of language development, and so it served as a kind of cornerstone to the theory. But the major nativist portions of his theory really weren't spelled out here. They were to evolve over the course of the next several decades in a number of other publications. (Ironically, *Syntactic Structures* was published the same year as Skinner's book *Verbal Behavior*, which, as we already pointed out, Chomsky bludgeoned with a metaphorical mallet.) Nevertheless, *Syntactic Structures* got the ball rolling, and in the book Chomsky laid out the groundwork toward explaining how a nativist theory of language could be possible in the first place.

You see, it's no explanation just to say language is inborn. Any theory worth its salt also has to say *what's* inborn. Moreover, any claim about what's inborn would have to be reasonable. It would be *un*reasonable, for example, to claim that all of the world's 6,000+ languages are individually prewired into the brains of all the world's children. For one thing, this wouldn't explain how future children could develop languages that haven't been invented yet; and linguists are well aware that new languages are emerging all the time. No, Chomsky had a relatively more sensible idea in mind. He thought that if language was going to be innately prewired in the brain, it would have to be prewired in a very, very general way. There would have to be some sort of universal language, and it would have to be in a form broad enough to support the growth of all the world's languages. In fact, it's probably not a bad metaphor to think of Chomsky's universal language as a sort of seed language. It would be this seed language that gets inherited through the genes. And out of this seed language would blossom all past, present, and future languages of the world. Which specific language grew out of the seed language would simply depend on which language the child was exposed to during her upbringing.

This was a marvelously revolutionary suggestion. First, it got rid of the need for reinforcements and punishments. But as we've seen, they didn't seem to work anyway. Second, it provided an explanation for how children were able to pick up their native languages so effortlessly. Chomsky's answer was that children didn't pick them up; the languages were, in a matter of speaking, already there. Third, it linked language directly to the mind. Language no longer had to be viewed as something *out there* in the environment. It could now be viewed as something *inside* the head, intimately connected with the rest of mental life. And finally, it explained why humans were the only creatures with a capacity for language—the seed language was part of the human genome. Although other animals develop communication systems, only humans were capable of mastering the rules of language.

Now this underlying, genetically determined seed language is a lot more palatable than having to assume that all 6,000+ languages were individually wrapped in the genes. It's also a lot easier to defend because it makes for a more parsimonious theory. (Parsimony, which means simplicity, is a delicious quality to have in a theory.) But Chomsky still had his work cut out for him. He still had to identify the gears or switches or bells or whistles or whatever that were responsible for nourishing, or coaxing out, each of the 6,000+ different native languages that people around the world were speaking. True, there's a relatively small number of subject-verb-object combinations that the seed language would have to produce. But there's a whole bunch of odd little quirks unique to individual languages. Consider, for example, the gender- and number-marking systems of Spanish and English. Even though both English and Spanish are SVO languages, Spanish marks nouns and determiners for gender and number, whereas English marks only nouns, and then only for number. In English you can use the word *the* to introduce different nouns in either singular or plural forms; you can say "the dog," "the dogs," "the window," or "the windows." But in Spanish, there are four ways to say "the" (*el, la, los,* and *las*), representing a combination of masculine and feminine forms with singular and plural forms. Which "the" you use in Spanish depends on the gender and number of the noun it goes with. So you would say "el perro" (the dog; masculine singular) or "los perros" (the dogs; masculine plural), but you would have to say "la ventana" (the window; feminine singular) or "las ventanas" (the windows; feminine plural).

No matter what system Chomsky came up with, he still had to explain how a seed language could figure out whether to grow into a gender-marking language, a number-marking language, a language that has both gender and number marking, or one that has neither. And gender and number marking are just two of a kazillion other language peculiarities that a seed language would have to contend with. Actually, a kazillion may be a bit of an overestimate; parsimony would have us look for a relatively small number of syntactic rules or principles that could be applied to *all* languages.

One tactic Chomsky employed in linking the seed language to the actual language spoken by a child was to propose that there are actually two levels of syntax. For every idea a person wants to communicate there is a beginning, underlying level, which Chomsky called the **deep structure**, and a final, expressed level, which Chomsky called the **surface structure**. The deep structure is more or less rooted at the level of the seed language, and has some unknown form. The surface structure is the form we actually produce when we put the idea into words. The problem that remains, then, is figuring out how we go about converting the deep structure into the surface structure whenever we speak, and converting the surface structure to the deep structure whenever we listen. Chomsky reasoned that there must be some set of rules that we follow, probably unconsciously, during the process of converting from deep structure to surface structure, or vice versa. Speakers of one language would all use one set of rules, whereas speakers of another language would use a different set of rules. English speakers would use the English set of rules and Spanish speakers would use the Spanish set of rules. There might even be some overlap between different sets of rules for different languages. English and Spanish, for example, might share a rule that specifies a subject-verb-object order in the surface structure.

When children develop a language, then, what they're really doing is learning the rules of their language for converting deep structures to surface structures. At least this was the idea. Chomsky argued that an acceptable set of conversion rules would have to have three essential features. First, it must be capable of generating all possible surface structures for a given language. People can produce an infinite variety of sentences, of course, so the conversion rules had to be able to generate an infinite number of surface structures. Second, the conversion rules had to generate only grammatical surface structures, which means they couldn't generate surface structures that violated the syntactic rule system for that language. And third, there had to be a relatively small, finite number of conversion rules (parsimony at work). There would be no point in trying to come up with a set of conversion rules if there were as many conversion rules as there were potential surface structure sentences. Chomsky's focus was on developing a set of rules to generate all possible surface structures, so his theory is sometimes called a theory of generative grammar.

In *Syntactic Structures*, Chomsky started out small and focused mainly on coming up with a set of conversion rules (a grammar) to describe how English syntax works. Although I say "small," English syntax is actually a huge area of study. But it's smaller than the whole of English, which includes other areas like phonology and morphology. Anyway, Chomsky intended to document a grammar of English that could generate all possible grammatical sentences and no ungrammatical ones, with as few conversion rules as possible. By the end of his book, Chomsky had a pretty good description of English grammar that met these three criteria. But remember, his motivating goal wasn't to understand English grammar, per se. Rather, he used English as more of a test case to see if a set of conversion rules could be uncovered at all. If English could pass the test, maybe all the other languages could as well.

In *Syntactic Structures*, Chomsky worked out a number of conversion rules for English. In developing these rules, which are called **phrase structure rules**, he also developed a new notational system. He used symbols like NP and V to indicate certain parts of speech (like noun phrase and verb) and an arrow ($\rightarrow$) to indicate the act of converting a sentence from one state to the next state. A typical set of phrase structure rules to move from a seed-language-based deep structure sentence to an English surface structure sentence might look like the following (accompanied by my own brief narratives in parentheses). Notice that only six phrase structure rules are needed here:

1. Deep structure sentence → NP + VP
   ("To produce an English sentence, you first have to parse the deep structure into a noun phrase and a verb phrase.")
2. NP → Det + N
   ("To produce a noun phrase, you have to first put a determiner in front of the noun.")
3. VP → V + NP
   ("To produce a verb phrase, you take a verb and put it in front of another noun phrase.")
4. Det → *a, the*
   ("A determiner in English can be either *a* or *the*.")
5. N → *man, ball, dog, house, chair,* etc.
   ("A noun in English can be any of the following list of words.")
6. V → *hit, take, eat, chase,* etc.
   ("A verb in English can be any of the following list of words.")

To produce a surface structure sentence like "The man hit the ball," then, we would follow the phrase structure rules step by step, applying them only one at a time.

0. Deep structure sentence
1. NP + VP
2. Det + N + VP
3. Det + N + V + NP
4. *the* + N + V + NP
5. *the* + *man* + V + NP
6. *the* + *man* + *hit* + NP
7. *the* + *man* + *hit* + Det + N
8. *the* + *man* + *hit* + *the* + N
9. *the* + *man* + *hit* + *the* + *ball*

Although this set of phrase structure rules was used to generate only one surface structure sentence, the same set of six rules is nevertheless capable of generating an infinite number of similar surface structure sentences. For starters, you could begin by replacing N with any number of different nouns in your vocabulary. And you could replace V with any number of different verbs in your vocabulary. But your noun and verb vocabularies are finite in size, and so this procedure would only result in your being able to produce a few billion different sentences of this form. The true power of infinite sentence generativity comes from the fact that noun phrases are embedded in verb phrases. Because noun phrases are embedded in verb phrases, you can take the whole noun phrase *the man hit the ball* and embed it in a higher-order verb phrase to get something like *I am angry at the man (who) hit the ball.* And this could in turn be embedded in a higher-order verb phrase to get something like *Sam knows that I am angry at the man (who) hit the ball.* And this could be further embedded in an even higher-order verb phrase like *You saw that Sam knows that I am angry at the man (who) hit the ball.* The rules of English place no limit on how many times we can embed noun phrases into verb phrases, although our memories may place some restrictions on how long a sentence we could actually follow and understand. So with only this small handful of six phrase structure rules, we can generate surface structure sentences to infinity and beyond.

But this is only part of the story. These are the phrase structure rules for simple sentences. There are also phrase structure rules for producing more complicated sentences, including passive sentences like "The ball was hit by the man" and questions like "Did the man hit the ball?" And so on and so forth. (Are you feeling the need to watch some paint dry yet?) Chomsky drafted phrase structure rules for these more complicated sentences too, but they get very complicated very quickly, and frankly I'd rather not wade through that pool. The point is that Chomsky succeeded in coming up with phrase structure rules for deriving surface sentence structures from underlying deep structures. And, importantly, they had the three necessary features: They were capable of producing an infinite number of surface sentences, they produced only grammatical surface sentences (sometimes with a little work), and a relatively small number of them were needed to produce an infinite range of sentences.

But some pesky problems remained. For one thing, just because phrase structure rules are possible, it doesn't mean that kids use them. And there was still the problem of explaining how children "grew" these rules in the first place. Although the universal seed language idea got Chomsky past the initial problem of explaining where language came from, it didn't explain where the phrase structure rules for individual languages came from. Never fear, Chomsky is here! Chomsky bypassed this problem the same way he bypassed the first problem: He claimed the rules themselves were contained in the genes. And he wasn't particularly concerned by the fact that the rule systems for over 6,000 languages would have to be accounted for, because he thought that all 6,000 languages probably relied on a common set of core principles. The problem, of course, was in identifying what those common principles were.

It's easy to generate what some of the principles might look like. As we've already seen, gender marking is one important feature of many world languages. Spanish, French, and Italian do it; English and Japanese don't. Another feature might be whether or not a language requires the use of determiners like *the* or *a.* English, French, Italian, and German do; Japanese, Chinese, Korean, and Vietnamese don't. If all languages could be defined by a small group of principles like these (say 500 or so), then it wouldn't be unreasonable to suppose they could all be prewired in the brain. In this case, developing a language would simply be a matter of a child's determining which of the 500 or so principles applies to her language. She could flip the gender-marking switch to the "on" position, for example, once she realized hers was a gender-marking language. And flipping the gender-marking switch to the "on" position might produce a domino effect of constraining which other switches could be flipped "on" or "off." For example, having a gender-marking language might automatically imply that you also have a language that uses determiners. You can't gender mark your language's determiners if your language doesn't use determiners. So one effect of flipping the gender-marking switch to the "on" position might be that it automatically flips the determiner-using switch to the "on" position. This procedure of flipping switches on and off for principles that are common to all languages would ultimately determine which language a child develops.

Okay, so the problem of how the main principles of languages are picked up is figured out—they're not picked up, they're there before birth. But how do children decide which of the 500 or so principles should be activated? We're talking about little bitty babies here. They can't even tie their own shoelaces. How could they have the intellectual savvy to know which switches they're supposed to turn on and which switches they're supposed to turn off? Chomsky had an answer for this question too. The children don't make any decisions, at least not consciously. Their brains do. But they don't really make a decision, they sort of respond automatically to language input received from the environment. Chomsky further proposed that built into children's brains is a device dedicated to just this task, perhaps a language acquisition device, that detects language regularities in children's environments and automatically sets the whole warehouse of switches one way or another based on what it detects in the surrounding language environment.

So yet another innovation that earned Chomsky fame and fortune was his assertion that children's brains were host to this **language acquisition device** (or LAD) thing. The LAD was claimed to be a biological organ dedicated exclusively to the task of detecting linguistic features or principles in children's surrounding environments. As it detected the relevant features of language in the child's surrounding environment, it would activate those same features in the child's head. Using this procedure, the child's native language would eventually appear. And voilà! There you have it: Chomsky's nativist theory of how language develops in a nutshell.

SUMMARY

Chomsky succeeded in revolutionizing child psychology because he developed a revolutionary way to explain the development of children's language. His explanation relied heavily on innate structures that were presumed to be genetically determined. The two most important innate structures were the seed language, which contained all the possible principles of all the world's languages, and the language acquisition device, which was responsible for selecting among all the possible principles. The environment played a relatively trivial role in Chomsky's theory, useful only for the raw language data it made available to the language acquisition device.

PSYCHOLOGY'S RESPONSE

Although Chomsky has his admirers among modern developmental psychologists, it seems many of them would rather smoke a firecracker than accept even the most rudimentary version of Chomsky's theory. Having attended child development conferences for the last 12 years or so, I don't think this is much of an exaggeration. There really is quite a bit of animosity between Chomskyan types and a number of noted developmental psycholinguists. Historically, the most vitriolic point seems to be Chomsky's overreliance on innateness. Chomsky seemed to retreat too rapidly to the safety and security of nativism at the first signs that direct reinforcements and punishments were insufficient to produce language acquisition. Developmental psychologists are quick to point out that there are a number of other ways that children can learn besides experiencing direct reinforcement and punishment. Beginning sometime around the early 1970s, psychologists all over the world began producing examples of how learning does contribute to language development. In the area of vocabulary development, for example, it's now well known that parents who talk more produce children who talk more. Parents' styles of interacting with their children also seem to influence language development; parents who are more directive tend to have children who have lower vocabulary levels.

A second sticking point has been Chomsky's claim that language is a unique property of humans. Rising to the challenge, a number of researchers have begun training chimps, gorillas, and orangutans to pick up language. If humans hold the trump card on language, then language-training studies with great apes shouldn't produce a whole lot of success. However, using the medium of sign language, a number of animals have picked up relatively large vocabularies (at least for apes)—on the order of several hundred words. There have even been some cases where apes were observed producing simple but completely novel "sentences." The most popular cases were when Washoe the chimpanzee, not knowing the word for "duck," signed "water" + "bird," and when Koko the gorilla signed "sleep" + "pictures," apparently in reference to her own dreams (she didn't have a sign for "dream"). The Chomskyan counterargument to these kinds of claims is that although apes may produce words, their words aren't used in the same way that adult humans use them. Moreover, apes give no evidence of being able to produce or understand a grammar. But even the "no-grammar" argument is currently being challenged by a chimp named Kanzi, who is reported to have a rudimentary grammatical understanding; perhaps roughly equivalent to that of a 2-year-old human.

The third point of contention has been the claim that innate language structures are specific to language—that is, that they're not used for any purposes other than those related to language. This claim has been attacked on at least two grounds. First, in a theoretical argument propounded by noted psycholinguist Elizabeth Bates, the existence of a biological organ like the language acquisition device simply doesn't make sense given what we know about evolutionary theory. A major tenet of evolutionary theory is that biological parts take on new roles as species adapt to new surroundings (over thousands of generations). Nature is stingy, and because of its stinginess, biological organs don't come out of nowhere. They evolve into new functions slowly and gradually as nature co-opts old biological structures to do new jobs. Because Chomsky's language acquisition device has no evolutionary predecessor, Bates questions how a biological organ as important for human survival as the LAD could come out of nowhere. She describes Chomsky's theory as the "Big Bang Theory of Language Acquisition."

The idea of a language-specific structure has also been attacked on empirical grounds. A number of correlational studies have shown that language development proceeds hand in hand with other cognitive abilities. For example, researchers have found that children begin to combine pretend play actions at about the same time they start combining words into sentences. Sentence formation comes about, then, not because of the functioning of some language-specific brain mechanism, but because a more general cognitive ability has made it possible for a child to begin combining symbols two at a time. These researchers argue that a more likely scenario than Chomsky's nativism would be that language development and cognitive development both depend on the functioning of a good, general-purpose brain.

CONCLUSIONS

I suppose it's safe to say that children's language acquisition remains a mystery wrapped in a puzzle rolled up in a conundrum. And while many child psychologists may not like what Chomsky had to say about language acquisition, he surely has given the field some things to think about. Ultimately, whether we collect scientific data to show Chomsky's right, or we collect scientific data to show he's wrong, our understanding of how children acquire language will improve. And the field of child psychology will be all the better for it.

Bibliography

Barsky, R. F. (1997). *Noam Chomsky: A life of dissent.* Toronto: ECW Press.

Crystal, D. (1997). *The Cambridge encyclopedia of language.* Cambridge, England: Cambridge University Press.

Harris, R. A. (1993). *The linguistic wars.* New York: Oxford University Press.

Hoff, E. (2001). *Language development.* Belmont, CA: Wadsworth.

Maher, J., & Groves, J. (1996). *Introducing Chomsky.* Cambridge, England: Icon Books.

Questions for Discussion

1. Does placing the origins of language inside the child's head rather than inside the child's environment represent progress in our understanding of how children learn language?

2. What happens to gender-marking switches and determiner-marking switches when a child is learning two languages at once?

3. Chomsky claims that syntactic rules are innately "known." Is it possible that the pragmatic rule system could also be innately known? Explain.

4. If the rules from grammar are more or less specified in the DNA, how might they have gotten there in the first place?

9

Adam and Eve and the Garden of Eden Studies

A FIRST LANGUAGE: THE EARLY STAGES.
Brown, R. (1973). *Cambridge, MA: Harvard University Press.*　　　(RANK 18)

Have you ever given any really serious thought to what it means to be human? No, I mean a really genuine, deep up to your eyebrows, mind-numbing kind of thinking? Maybe not. Many young people are still struggling to "find themselves" in their early college years. But should you ever spend some time pondering the essence of humanness, I think you'll find it's difficult to pinpoint precisely what separates us from other animals. Humans certainly aren't king of the beasts in any physical way. Relatively speaking, we're a pretty frail species. We don't have thick fur or blubber to protect us from the cold. We don't have razor-sharp claws and fangs to protect ourselves in a fight. We rank among the slowest-moving creatures in the animal kingdom. And most of us aren't even strong enough to carry our own body weight up a rope. Yet, despite all these limitations, somehow something has allowed us to survive, prosper even, in a world chock full of thick-furred, sharp-clawed, fast, physically powerful creatures.

When I pose this question to my students, they usually answer by pointing out that humans have the power of reason. But what does that mean? Doesn't your dog reason when he begs to go outside? Don't birds reason when they fly away at your approach? If these other creatures reason, then can reason be what makes humans that much different? I think that when you get down to the bottom of the matter, being human means having the capacity for language. And when humans do reason, it's language that they use in their reasoning; and it's language that allows humans to reason at a much, much higher level than other animals. Oh, I bet I know what you're thinking. You're thinking that other animals use language too. Dogs bark, birds chirp. Maybe. But they certainly don't use it to the extreme that we do. Think about what you can do with human language. You can talk about the past and make plans for the future. You can tell somebody about your new car that's out in the parking lot. You can say and understand new sentences you've never heard before. And you can lie. No other species uses its "language" to do all these things. Imagine how bizarre it would be if you were strolling through the park one day and saw a group of juvenile squirrels all sitting in a circle listening to the chatter of a larger, adult squirrel. Yet the sharing of information through language in this fashion happens in human classrooms around the world. You can get a glimpse of the power of language when you consider that all the technological developments we have at our fingertips today were the result of groups of humans communicating through language with other groups of humans across thousands of miles and hundreds of years. When you get right down to it, the essence of language is that it gives us a way to be able to create the most sophisticated and complex of ideas and to share them with other people. And it must've been these complex ideas that allowed humans to survive the dangers of the wilderness. Early technology allowed us to develop weapons like clubs, arrowheads, and spears, and through language we could easily share that knowledge with other people, especially our offspring. Despite the survival advantages language has provided for humans over the last 40,000 years (or even longer if you include Neanderthals), it's rather shocking that only in the last half-century has any serious scientific attention been paid to language, both in figuring out how it works and in understanding how it develops in children.

In his 1973 book, Roger Brown documented one of the most important and influential scientific investigations of language development in children ever conducted. It was ranked the 18th most revolutionary study in child psychology published since 1950. Being the first of its kind, and representing the *genesis* of a new era of language development research, his investigation is sometimes called the "Garden of Eden" study. In keeping with this theme, Roger Brown nicknamed the three children in his study Adam, Eve, and Sarah. One of the most striking features of this study was that it benefited from some of the greatest minds in the field of child language research. Because he was at Harvard, arguably one of the grandest institutions of higher learning in the world, Brown gained access to the best and brightest student minds in the world. Many of these students have since gone on to establish their own world-renowned careers in the field of language development. Mention the names of Dan Slobin, Melissa Bowerman, Jill de Villiers, Steven Pinker, Jean Berko-Gleason, Ursula Bellugi, or Laura Pettito at any major child development conference and eyes will pop open and ears will perk up. In a wonderful group of essays published collectively under the apt title *The Development of Language and Language Researchers*, they all reflect very fondly on their years at Harvard studying under the mentorship of Roger Brown.

Roger Brown had a very simple goal in mind when he began his study—to catalog how children make their first sentences. But what seems simple on its face can sometimes have the complexity of rocket science. In fact, I'd venture to say that understanding rocket science is probably easier than understanding language development. In any case, Brown's study was the first major attempt at documenting language development from a psychological point of view. Noam Chomsky, a popular linguist during Brown's time, also had some things to say about how children acquired language (see Chapter 8). But Chomsky's theories were concerned with the structure of a perfect language. Brown was more interested in documenting how children actually talked. And where Chomsky was interested in describing the development of syntax, or grammar, Brown was more interested in describing the development of semantics, or meaning, as expressed in children's first sentences.

INTRODUCTION

In the first part of his book, Brown begins by introducing his readers to the "five aspects of sentence construction." Any theory of language development would have to be able to explain how children eventually master all five of these aspects. In later portions of the book, he describes how his three language newbies, Adam, Eve, and Sarah, began to construct sentences using the first two of the five aspects. As I walk you through each of these five aspects, many of the ideas and concepts Brown used will sound very strange and foreign. But keep in mind that even though these ideas may have weird-sounding names, as a language-using expert you yourself have already mastered them.

Relations or Roles Within the Simple Sentence

Whenever you say something or hear someone else say something, the words of the sentences you say or hear have a **semantic relation** with one another. In sixth-grade English class, where we spent a lot of time diagramming sentences into subjects, verbs, and objects, we were focusing on identifying the *grammatical* parts of sentences. But Brown means something else altogether when he talks about the *semantic relations* among words in a sentence. He's referring to the meaning elements, or *roles*, assumed by the words in the sentence. There are about eight different types of semantic roles that words can take in a simple sentence. First there is the *relation* word, which is usually the verb, but it can be an adjective too. The sentences "Harriet sang" and "The men laughed" have *sang* and *laughed* as the relation words. All sentences have to have at least one relation word.

Then there are the nouns. The semantic roles of nouns are very tricky because they can take on several different semantic roles, depending on how they're used in the sentence. In the two sentences above, *Harriet* and *men* both play the role of the **agent**. The agent role applies to any noun that is doing some action. Agents and relation words are the most popular semantic roles that occur in sentences. But in the sentence "The men laughed at Harriet," *Harriet* is no longer taking on the role of agent as in "Harriet sang," because Harriet is no longer doing anything. Instead, Harriet is the target of the men's laughter, and so Harriet is now described as being the **beneficiary** of the action in this sentence. In all, Brown describes seven semantic roles that can be taken on by nouns:

Role	Definition	Examples
Agent	Someone or something that causes or instigates an action or process. Usually animate but not always, an agent must be perceived as having its own motivating force.	*Harriet* sang. *The men* laughed. *The wind* ripped the curtains.

Patient	Someone or something either in a physical state or suffering from a change of state.	*The wood* is dry. He cut *the wood.*
Experiencer	Someone having a mental or perceptual experience or having a mental or emotional disposition.	*Tom* saw the snake. *Tom* wanted a drink.
Beneficiary	Someone who is the recipient of a state or process, including possession.	*Mary* has a convertible. Tom bought *Mary* a car.
Instrument	Something that plays a role in bringing about a process or action but that is not the instigator; it is used by an agent.	Tom opened the door with a *key.* Tom used *his knife* to open the box.
Location	The place or location of a state, action, or process.	The spoon is in *the drawer.* Tom sat in *the chair.*
Complement	The verb names an action that brings something into existence. The complement, on a more or less specific level, completes the verb.	Mary sang *a song.* John played *checkers.*

As you can see, there are quite a few different semantic, or meaning, roles that nouns can take in our sentences. Notice also that the descriptions are very abstract—but they have to be in order to apply to the full range of possibilities. The point is that when you add meaning to the equation, it becomes far more complicated to manage than dealing with just the subject or the object of the sentence. And, of course, when you're studying this stuff with kids, you want to know (1) when do children start understanding and using the various semantic roles in their sentences, and (2) how do they do it?

Modulations of Meaning Within the Simple Sentence

Not only do children have to learn when and how to use semantic roles in their speech to describe the world around them, they have to fiddle with the words they use to change them very slightly in various ways according to the details of what they're trying to say. In Brown's terms, they have to learn to modulate words, for example, for noun plurality, verb tense, and definiteness. We know that when we hear the word *cookie*, we understand that just one cookie is being talked about. But if for some reason it's important to know whether we're talking about one cookie or two cookies, we have to know how to use the plural. Imagine how disappointed little Johnny would be if he wanted two cookies but didn't know how to form the plural for the word. And on a snowy winter day, there's a big difference between finding out that my student is going to throw a snowball at me and that she's going to throw snowballs at me.

We also have to learn how to conjugate verbs and to change them according to "tense." It's very important to know whether the snowball throwing is going to happen tomorrow, or whether it might have already happened and I didn't even notice. So there's a great deal of difference in the meaning of the sentence "I bombarded you with snowballs today" as compared with the sentence "I am going to bombard you with snowballs today." As schedule dependent as we are in our hectic daily lives, modifying verbs according to their tense is essential for us to communicate our plans to the important people around us.

Modalities of the Simple Sentence

Children learning their first language also have to learn how to take basic sentences and rephrase them in various ways, to make a question or to make a sentence negative. As on the TV game show *Jeopardy*, we can choose a number of different ways to phrase a sentence in the form of a question. One way we can do it is by adding new words at the beginning of the sentence. If we use this tactic, we produce the so-called "yes-no" questions and the *wh-* questions. But we can also change the pitch of our sentences to indicate that they are meant to be interpreted as questions, as in "The men laughed at Harriet?" Consider the following examples.

Yes-No Questions.   One way we can make a yes-no question is to start out with a sentence like "Lizzy Borden took an axe and gave her mother 40 whacks," add a helping verb like *did* to the beginning, and then change the tense of the main verbs in the original sentence to the present tense. For example: "*Did* Lizzy Borden *take* an axe and *give* her mother 40 whacks?" When we follow this rule, the time of the event, which in this case was sometime in the past, is embedded in the helping verb we place at the beginning. So even though the original sentence used the words *took* and *gave*, which are past-tense forms of *take* and *give*, we remove the past tense from these words and allow the helping verb *did* to carry the tense. (If you didn't follow this, go back and reread the words slowly, taking time to process the main points in each sentence.) This is just one of the rules we've learned automatically, without even trying, even though it might seem weird that we use it. Another way we can form a yes-no question is simply to *tag* a question to the end of the otherwise unchanged sentence: "Lizzy Borden took an axe and gave her mother 40 whacks, *didn't she?*" Notice that if we form our yes-no question this way, we leave the past-tense forms of the main verbs (*took* and *gave*) intact, even though the helping verb *do* also carries the past tense.

Wh- Questions.   *Wh-* questions are basically questions that begin with *wh-* words like *who, what, where, when, why, which,* and *how.* Of course, *how* doesn't begin with a *wh-,* but we let it hang out with the *wh-* words anyway. We use *wh-* questions whenever we aren't sure about all the information in a particular sentence and would like to find out about the missing information. Which *wh-* word we use in the sentence depends on which information in the sentence is missing. So we could ask the following types of *wh-* questions, when we're interested in finding out the following missing pieces of information:

Question Form	*To Find Out . . .*
Who took an axe and gave Lizzy Borden's mother 40 whacks? *Or . . .*	To find out the *agent* of the action.
Whom did Lizzy Borden give 40 whacks to?	To find out the *patient* of the action.
What did Lizzy Borden use to give her mother 40 whacks?	To find out the *instrument* of the action.
Which axe did Lizzy Borden use to give her mother 40 whacks?	To find out more about the *instrument.*
Where did Lizzy Borden give her mother 40 whacks?	To find out the *location* of the action.
When did Lizzy Borden give her mother 40 whacks?	To find out the *time* of the action.
Why did Lizzy Borden give her mother 40 whacks?	To find out the motivations of the *agent.*

The basic rule for making a *wh-* question is to add a helping verb like *did* to the beginning of the simple sentence, allowing it to carry the tense of the main verb, and to place one of the *wh-* words in front of it.

Negatives.   Just as children have to figure out how to make a sentence into a question, they also have to figure out how to make the negative of a sentence. As an expert language user, you may already have realized that in making the negative of a sentence, you're basically adding words like *not* or *no* to deny, reject, or undo something. In making sentences negative, either (1) you're saying that something doesn't exist (example: "There wasn't any axe"), (2) you're rejecting something (example: "I don't want to hear about Lizzy Borden anymore"), or (3) you're pointing out that something about the sentence is untrue (example: "It wasn't an axe she used, it was a knife; and it wasn't 40 whacks, it was 39 slices"). The rules for making the negatives of a sentence are pretty complicated. But since you do it all the time, I'm sure you can generate lots of your own examples. The point is that you can make the negative of a sentence, even if you yourself aren't aware of the rules for how to do it. But most importantly for Brown, children learn to do it too.

Imperatives.   Imperative forms of sentences usually have the function of demanding that somebody do something. In other words, they are commands. However, unlike "normal" sentences, imperative forms of sentences usually begin with a verb: "Stop or I'll shoot," "Go away," "Pass the salt." In civilized society, of course, we can't go around making demands all the time. So we have developed softer versions of imperatives that actually don't look like imperatives at all. For example, in the sentence "Would you mind turning down the stereo," we aren't really asking somebody if they mind turning down the stereo. We're really *telling* them to turn down the stereo, but we're doing so in a softer, gentler kind of way. So although this sentence looks like one of the *wh-* questions on the surface, in reality it has the impact of an imperative. If children are ever going to learn to get along in society, this is one of the more subtle and difficult rules they're going to have to master.

Embedding of One Sentence Within Another

Because of our highly sophisticated minds, we are capable of generating some fairly complex sentences sometimes. By "complex sentences," I'm referring to sentences that are actually the result of two sentences being combined into a single sentence in some way. In general, we know we have a complex sentence when it contains more than one main verb. The Lizzy Borden sentence I used earlier is an example of a complex sentence. It represents a combination of two simpler sentences: (1) "Lizzy Borden took an axe," and (2) "Lizzy Borden gave her mother 40 whacks." And many of the sentences you've been reading in this book are also of the complex kind. But still, my sentences are far less sophisticated than the ones you would find in the original works I've been summarizing. In fact, one of my explicit goals in writing this book was to present the basic findings of major research studies using as many simple sentences, and as few complex sentences, as possible. Complex sentences are efficient, but they can be quite difficult to understand. You may have noticed that professional scientists are usually extremely complex in writing up their research findings. Although a complex style of language may be appropriate for professional, scientific audiences, the message in complex sentences is often lost on the lay public. In fact, language probably doesn't get any more complex than what you find in scientific writing. But I digress.

Brown talks of complex sentences as being of two types: *embedded sentences* and *conjoined sentences*. In this section, we focus on the embedded kind. Conjoined sentences are discussed in the next section. Sentence embedding can happen in lots of different ways. Here are just a couple of examples. Just as a reminder, don't let the fancy terminology scare you. You use all these sentence types every single day.

Object Noun Phrase Complement.   This kind of embedded sentence begins with a simple sentence frame like *I hope X*, where *X* can be anything that is hoped. Of course, "I hope X" is by itself a simple sentence. But we can completely embed another simple sentence in that frame. Consider the simple sentence *Jane picks her nose*, for example. After we do the embedding, we get the complex sentence *I hope Jane picks her nose*. This kind of embedding, when a whole complete sentence is placed after a verb like *think, know, guess, tell, hope*, or *mean*, is what Brown calls "*object noun phrase complement.*" In ordinary English, this means that a whole sentence is used as the object of the verb. In our example, the whole sentence "Jane picks her nose" is the object of the verb *hope*. My apologies go to Jane.

Relative Clause.   Another type of embedded sentence occurs when a clause is inserted into an otherwise simple sentence. We can start with a simple sentence like *The man stayed a week*. We can then insert a clause that adds some information about the man, such as that he came to dinner. After the clause gets embedded, we say, "The man who came to dinner stayed a week." The two main verbs are *came* and *stayed*. Brown gives as another example: "The argument the dean made surprised the students." Here, it's the argument that surprised the students. But we also know, by virtue of the **relative clause**, that it was the argument that the dean made that we're talking about, and not some other argument like the one made by the teacher or the custodian. The relative clause allows us to do the work of two sentences in only a single sentence.

Coordination of Simple Sentences

Finally, children have to learn how to combine sentences using conjunctions, which of course is commonly done by adult users of the language. Coordinating simple sentences using conjunctions is probably a lot easier than embedding sentences because it only requires the insertion of conjunction words like *and, or, then, because,* and *but,* but they are complex sentences nonetheless because they have more than one main verb. Stringing together sentences using conjunctions allows for more powerful forms of expression than saying single sentences individually. You could say, "I hugged my dog" and then say, "My dog pulled the drowning kitten from the lake." But these two sentences separately don't carry the same meaning or expressive power as they would if you combined them with the word *because.* The meaning would be a lot more weighty if you instead said, "I hugged my dog because he pulled the drowning kitten from the lake." The element *because* gives some motivation for the first act (hugging the dog) because it was carried out as a result of the second act (the dog saving the kitten). The overall meaning of the coordinated sentences would be completely lost if not for the conjunction word *because.*

Although children eventually master all five of these aspects of sentence construction, Brown focused on only the first two. He had hoped to describe how children master the remaining three aspects in a second book. But he never quite achieved this objective. So in the remainder of this chapter we focus on (1) semantic relations, and (2) modulations of meaning.

METHOD

Brown begins his description of the methodology of his Garden of Eden study by giving credit to the colleagues who assisted him in the study from the very beginning. He specifically mentions Ursula Bellugi, Colin Fraser, Gloria Cooper, and Courtney Cazden, who were each responsible for recording the transcriptions of a single child. Bellugi was assigned to Adam, Fraser was assigned to Eve, and first Cooper and then Cazden were assigned to Sarah.

Participants

All 3 children were only children at the beginning of the study. Brown provides the details: "Adam is the son of a minister who lived at first in Cambridge and later in Boston. Eve is the daughter of a man who was at the time a graduate student at Harvard and who lived in Cambridge. Sarah is the daughter of a man who worked as a clerk, at the start of the study, and their home was in Cambridge. The parents of Adam both had college degrees; Eve's father had a college degree and her mother a high school degree; the parents of Sarah both had high school degrees."

Although only 3 children were used in the study, Brown and his colleagues originally started with a sample of over 30 children. They ended up choosing these 3 children because they could talk clearly and because they talked a lot. Unfortunately, after only 1 year into the study, Eve's family moved to Nova Scotia, Canada, so only 20 hours of her speech were recorded. But as it happened, "Eve's speech developed so much more rapidly than that of Adam and Sarah that 10 months of her transcriptions equaled about 20 months of transcriptions for Adam and Sarah."

Materials

The technologically innovative materials Brown used in his study are best described by Ursula Bellugi in *The Development of Language Research and Language Researchers*. She wrote, "Roger Brown became justly famous throughout the United States and far beyond for his new work on language acquisition; work that promised to lead to a deeper understanding of the development of the child's mind. One day, a delegation of dignitaries from Africa arrived to visit him in his elegant Harvard office. They had heard, they said, about his exciting new techniques and equipment for the study of child language, and they wanted to establish a similar center in Africa. The visitors talked on at some length. Roger listened silently and politely, with a smile. Finally, they turned to him to hear what the great man had to say about technological advancements and the impact they had made on his progress in charting this new field. 'I'll show you,' he said, and without another word, got up, went into his inner office and returned, bearing tools in hand—a large, yellow, lined pad of paper and a sharpened pencil. 'This,' he said with a smile, 'is the technology we use.' And indeed it was. Paper, pencil, also a tape recorder, and Roger Brown's intellect."

Procedure

The general procedure was that visits were made to the children's homes at least a couple of times a month. For Adam and Eve it was a 2-hour visit every 2nd week, but for Sarah it was a half-hour each week. Generally, two observers visited the home. One observer wrote down everything that was said; the other played with the child. All conversations were also audiotaped. The final official transcriptions were made by the primary observer assigned to each child, who worked with both the written transcripts and the audio recordings to produce the final record.

You can probably imagine the information overload you would get if you collected dozens of hours of recordings of children's speech. You would have thousands of speech samples to deal with. To help manage this massive information overload, Brown concocted a measure that boiled down the complexity of each child's speech into a single number. He called this measure the **mean length of utterance** (or MLU for short), and it's a measure that is still used by language researchers to this very day. The MLU is basically the average length of a child's spoken sentences at any particular point in time. But Brown wasn't satisfied with simply averaging the number of words kids used, because he realized that some words are more sophisticated than others. For example, when a child marks nouns for plurality, she is at a higher level of language sophistication than if she didn't mark them for plurality. So *cookies* would be a more sophisticated word than *cookie* because it has the plural attached to it. In more technical jargon, we would say that *cookies* is marked for plurality, or that it is *inflected* with the plural marker, whereas *cookie* is unmarked. So if a child said "more cookies please," the length of the utterance using Brown's MLU measure would be 4.00: *more* + *cookie* + plural + *please*. MLU turned out to be a beautiful measure, and it has proved to be far more useful than simply depending on chronological age as an index of language sophistication. Eve, for example, far outpaced Adam and Sarah in language sophistication even though they were the same age. The point is that MLU allows a way to compare children on a measure of language that ignores age.

RESULTS

As a starting point, Brown set up ranges of MLU that corresponded to the major achievements of sentence construction I outlined in the introduction. Each MLU range was more or less arbitrarily assigned to a particular stage, although Brown was clear in noting that he didn't wish his notion of stage to carry the same meaning of "stage" as used in other theories like Piaget's. Stage II language, for example, wasn't meant to represent a higher organization of language than Stage I, or didn't imply that Stage II children were better thinkers than Stage I children. It just meant that Stage II children's utterances were longer. The range of MLU for each of the stages goes like this:

Stage	MLU Range	Major Language Accomplishment (as Discussed in Introduction)
Stage I	1.00–1.99	Relationships or roles within the simple sentence
Stage II	2.00–2.49	Modulations of meaning within the simple sentence
Stage III	2.50–2.99	Modalities of the simple sentence
Stage IV	3.00–3.99	Embedding of one sentence within another
Stage V	4.00 and up	Coordination of simple sentences and propositional relations

Throughout the rest of his book, Brown describes children's achievements during the first two stages, Stages I and II. Remember, any MLU greater than 1.00 means that children's utterances are averaging more than 1 word in length, which is the point that marks when children are starting to produce sentences.

In making sense of his voluminous collection of utterances made by Adam, Eve, and Sarah, Brown made an additional methodological contribution to the literature. He made what he called a "rich" interpretation of their utterances. A **rich interpretation** amounts to taking into account the specific context in which children talk. Most language researchers at that time, Brown noted, tended toward a more cautious, "lean" interpretation of the things kids said. That is, they were hesitant to give too much credit to children for the sentences they produced. They were afraid of overinterpreting children's sentences, or of reading too much into them. In fact, it's a rule of thumb that child psychology researchers are usually very conservative when it comes to making sense of what kids do. Kids sometimes do amazing things, but it's always possible that they do them by accident. But Brown pointed out that when children do talk, they always talk in specific situations. And as long as an observer is in place to record the specific situations when kids say things, it's possible to discern a fuller, more comprehensive intent on the part of the child about what he *means* to say.

Stage I

The major achievements of children's first word combinations during Stage I are (1) combining words in an order that roughly approximates adults' utterance of the same meaning, and (2) producing a handful of semantic relations in their speech. Of course, word order is extremely important in English, more so than in many other languages, and the order of words in an English sentence carries a lot of weight when a listener is trying to figure out who is doing what to whom. Agents tend to appear at the beginning of sentences, and patients tend to occur at the ends of sentences. So learning how to manage word order takes children a long way toward achieving their goal of becoming fluent speakers of English. Brown noted that the children in his study produced many thousands of sentences that preserved the proper word order, but only a few hundred that violated proper word order. He took this as evidence that word order was one of the earliest achievements in children's first sentences. How did he know what the proper word order was? Through rich interpretation. Using the method of rich interpretation, Brown was able to figure out what kids were trying to say, and so knew whether or not they were using the proper word order to do it.

But perhaps much more important than word order, children's first word combinations carried particular patterns of meaning. And the number of different meanings children used to get their points across to listeners was relatively small. Or, said another way, Adam, Eve, and Sarah tended to talk about only a few semantic relationships, and all 3 tended to be interested in the same kinds of semantic relationships. Brown found that they mostly talked about only eight different "semantic relations" in their speech. Along with a couple of examples of each, they are:

Semantic Relation	Example
Agent + action	Mommy fix.
	Bambi go.
Action + object	Sweep broom.
	Hit ball.
Agent + object	Mommy pumpkin (as in *is cutting a*).
	Daddy truck (as in *is in his*).
Action + location	Write paper.
	Sit water.
Entity + location	Lady home.
	Baby table (as in *is eating at the*)
Possessor + possession	Mommy chair (as in *That is mommy's chair*).
	My nose.
Entity + attribute	Little dog.
	Yellow block.
Demonstrative + entity	That doggie.
	That ball.

One of the most interesting findings was that children's first word combinations almost always consisted of major **content** words like nouns, verbs, and adjectives. Adam, Eve, and Sarah pretty much ignored the little fill-in words that we adults use when we talk. Articles, prepositions, helping verbs, and pronouns were, for the most part, left out of their utterances. In fact, so much of the main message was preserved, and so many of the little **filler words** were left out, that scholars often call these kinds of utterances *telegraphic speech*. The term *telegraphic* comes from the old days when our primary means of communication over long distances was through the telegram.

Since when sending telegrams you got charged by the word, it was cost effective just to send the main elements of the message and leave out the less important parts. So college students sending telegrams home might simply write, "Need money send now," rather than the more eloquent and grammatically correct, "Dear Mom and Dad. It's unfortunate that I must request some additional funds as I ran out just yesterday." Of course, as children get more sophisticated in their command of the language, they eventually will start using the little filler words as well. But the first word combinations, the earliest forms of grammar, were based on combining content words that were very high in meaning. One interesting theoretical implication of this finding was the possibility that children's earliest grammars were based on meaning, and not on some abstract set of grammatical rules that some researchers thought children were born with.

Stage II

The period of Stage II combinations begins at MLU 2.00 and ends at MLU 2.50. This means that children are saying sentences averaging over, roughly, three words long. But remember, not only words are included in calculating MLU. Inflections like plural markers also count. The major development during Stage II of early sentence production then, as you might have guessed, is the greater and greater inclusion of inflections as well as those little filler words we've been talking about. Brown referred to the major achievement of this stage as the development of **grammatical morphemes** and the **modulation of meaning**. Although I haven't spent any time talking about grammatical morphemes, it's sufficient here just to say that they are the little parts of speech, inflections and filler words, that make telegraphic sentences more grammatical and make them look more like adult sentences. As adults, we use lots of different kinds of grammatical morphemes on a regular basis. Inflections are the little changes we make to nouns and verbs that change their meaning ever so slightly. And when we change the meaning of a word only slightly, you could say we are *modulating* it, which is why Brown calls this development the "modulation of meaning." We've already talked about the grammatical morpheme for plurality, as in what you add to *cookie* to make it into *cookies*, and grammatical morphemes can also be used to make irregular plurals such as in *woman* → *women*. But there are also a lot of inflections we use to modulate the meaning of verbs, such as when we mark a verb for the present progressive tense by adding—*ing*: *take* → *taking* or *give* → *giving*, or when we mark a verb for the past tense by adding *-ed*: *walk* → *walked* or *play* → *played*.

In addition to the inflections children start applying to major content words like nouns and verbs, they also start adding the separate little filler words like prepositions, articles, and helping verbs. Brown observed that 14 grammatical morphemes appeared to be most important to children's sentences during Stage II. What I find most surprising is that these 14 inflections and filler words emerged in the same order across all three children. Each of the 14 grammatical morphemes is listed below in order of appearance and with a couple of examples each. Some of the names of the morphemes sound weird, but I'm sure you'll recognize them as parts of speech you use on a daily basis in your own speech.

(Order)	Grammatical Morpheme	Example
1	Present progressive	adding *-ing* as in *Adam eating. Baby crying.*
2 & 3	*in, on*	adding prepositions: *Daddy in bed. Socks on.*
4	Plural	adding *-s* or *-es*: *Puppies! Two cookies.*
5	Past irregular	making past tense of irregular verbs without the typical *-ed* being attached: *Went bye-bye. Made a mess.*
6	Possessive	often adding *'s* to mark a noun for possession: *Adam's chair. My bear.*
7	Uncontractible copula	a copula is some form of the verb *to be* and can be used as part of a contraction or not; the first form used is the uncontracted kind: *Eve is girl. I am Adam.*
8	Articles	*A doggie. The moon.*
9	Past regular	*Walked home. It dropped.*
10	Third person regular	usually by adding *-s* as in *He sleeps. Timmy bites.*
11	Third person irregular	the exception to only adding *-s* as in *Adam does it. He has to.*
12	Uncontractible auxiliary	using helping verbs, as in *I am running. They have to eat.* but not as part of a contraction.
13	Contractible copula	the copula used as part of a contraction: *Eve's a girl. I'm Adam.*
14	Contractible auxiliary	helping verbs used as part of a contraction: *I'm running. Mom's got it.*

DISCUSSION

In Brown's final chapter, he clearly points out that much of what he has revealed about the origins of children's first sentences would probably be revised by future researchers in the field. One of the most mysterious questions that remained unresolved by the conclusion of Brown's book was precisely why children *improved* in their speech. In other words, although Brown's research showed that children's grammar did improve over time—and by "improve" he meant getting closer and closer to the adult version of grammar—it wasn't exactly clear what motivated them to do it. Are there social pressures that force children to use closer and closer approximations of adult grammar? Or could there be some sort of biological timetable that dictates when full-blown grammar unfolds as children's brains mature? Perhaps even more surprising is that even after some 30 years of research following Brown's original groundbreaking work and after thousands of further scientific studies on the topic of language development, the questions of how and why language develops in children remain unanswered.

CONCLUSIONS

Two developments that pursued Roger Brown's major findings strike me as particularly interesting, as they have occupied much of the research spotlight after Brown vacated it. The first has to do with Brown's very intriguing finding that children's abilities to use the regular past-tense marker, *-ed*, seem to emerge after their abilities to use the irregular past-tense marker. According to Brown's data, children start saying irregular past-tense verbs like *went, ran,* or *ate* before they start making regular past-tense verbs like *talked, wanted,* or *kissed*. Of course, these latter three past-tense verbs are examples of regular past tenses because they result from the standard rule of adding *-ed* to a verb to make it into the past tense. *Go, run,* and *eat* can't be made into the past tense using this "regular" rule. But even though the regular past-tense rule doesn't apply to *go, run,* and *eat,* children still produce the irregular past-tense versions of these verbs before they start producing regular past-tense versions of other verbs.

In all other grammatical morphemes, the irregular versions are picked up after the regular versions. Now this makes sense because using regular grammatical morphemes involves applying only a single rule such as "Apply *-ed* to make the past tense of a verb." So you might think irregular tenses should be harder to learn since there is no single rule for making the past tense of irregular verbs. The past-tense procedure changes with practically every different irregular verb you can make the past tense of. This raises the question, Why do children learn the harder thing first in the case of past-tense marking? Subsequent research has revealed a very interesting discovery. Children first learn irregular past tenses and say them correctly. But once they start learning the general, regular rule for making past tenses, that is by adding *-ed,* they start making mistakes on the very same irregulars that they used to say correctly. They start applying the regular past tense rule to the irregular verbs, in a process called *overregularization*. But after spending some time overregularizing irregular verbs, they eventually learn that the regular past-tense marker doesn't apply, and they start producing irregular past-tense markers correctly again. This is a fascinating development! It's as if children have to take one step backward in order to take two steps forward.

The second interesting outcome following Roger Brown's research has to do with the phenomenon of *individual differences* in grammatical development. Brown made some pretty strong claims when he suggested that (1) children start out with the same set of eight semantic relations in Stage I, (2) children acquire the same set of 14 grammatical morphemes in Stage II, and (3) grammatical morphemes are later developments than basic semantic relations. Since his work, a number of researchers have suggested that maybe not all children do follow the same path into language. While it may be true that most children follow a common path, starting out with major content words (nouns and verbs) and common semantic themes and only later adding the filler words (grammatical morphemes), other researchers have revealed that some children seem to focus on the filler words first and only later add in the major content words. You might say these children enter into grammar backward! Work by researchers such as Lois Bloom, Katherine Nelson, Elena Lieven, and Elizabeth Bates has presented some fairly convincing evidence in support of this multiple-pathway-into-language idea. Although no one has ever been able to figure out *why* some children choose the nonmainstream route, there have been some suggestions. Nelson, for example, has speculated that children might choose different pathways depending on what they view the function of language to be. Children who choose the standard route (focusing on content words first) may view language as a way to analyze and describe the world. She called these children "referential" because they use their words to refer to things and events going on around them. Children who instead focus more on the filler words may view language as a tool to facilitate social interaction. These children seem to have noticed that sophisticated language users use those small filler words, and it's as if they think they can join the social world faster if they use the small filler words too. Because these children seem more interested in expressing themselves than in describing the world, Nelson called them "expressive." Unfortunately, research on the different routes children may follow into grammar has died down recently, so we still don't know what prompts children into one path or another.

Final Remarks

It is with great hesitation that I release this chapter as a recapitulation of Brown's revolutionary study. Brown's thoughtfulness in considering all aspects of children's language during the first two stages of word combinations, and his overwhelmingly comprehensive review of the research on language development available at the time, cannot possibly be given judicious treatment in a single chapter of this size. Instead, the tactic I have pursued has been one of revealing the seeds of wisdom sown by his book that have borne the fruit for the 30 years of language acquisition research which followed. The revelation that children's first sentence constructions consisted of about eight common semantic relations and that their first grammatical morphemes tended to be of 14 different sorts which emerge in a determinable order seems to capture the essence of the harvest. It is for these contributions that his work is regarded as truly revolutionary.

And how does the story end? It turns out that Brown never did get around to publishing anything about the major grammatical developments in Stages III, IV, and V. As he wrote in his "Autobiography in the Third Person" in Kessel's book, "The planned second volume of *A First Language* that was to cover *The Later Stages* was never written. People used to ask about it but after several years that became embarrassing and developmental psycholinguists came to assume that it never would appear. Why has it not? Data collection had been complete in 1973 and so had data description in the form of unpublished grammars. Brown had an unhappy sabbatical year in which he worked on *The Later Stages* but finally had to admit defeat. The detailed analyses of presumptive Stages III, IV, and V did not yield up to Brown, then, any strong generalizations comparable to those of the early stages, and he could see no value in publishing the possibly quite idiosyncratic details available." Roger Brown died in 1997 at the age of 72. But his legacy lives on in the brilliant contributions of the many students fortunate enough to have been mentored by the creator of the Garden of Eden of language research.

Bibliography

Hoff, E. (2001). *Language development.* Belmont, CA: Wadsworth.

Ingram, D. (1989). *First language acquisition: Method, description and explanation.* New York: Cambridge University Press.

Kessel, F. S. (1988). *The development of language and language researchers: Essays in honor of Roger Brown.* Hillsdale, NJ: Erlbaum.

Nelson, K. (1973). Structure and strategy in learning to talk. *Monographs of the Society for Research in Child Development, 38*(Serial No. 149).

Questions for Discussion

1. Is there anything wrong, or anything right, with basing a whole study of language development on only three children?

2. Brown said that he never got around to describing children's language development during Stages III, IV, and V because no "strong generalizations" became obvious. Why might it be easier to make generalizations about children's early language development than to make generalizations about children's later language development? What factors might come into play?

3. Adam, Eve, and Sarah were English-speaking children. Is there any reason to believe that the first appearing semantic relations in English speakers would differ from the first appearing semantic relations in speakers of other languages? Why or why not?

4. If you could retain your intelligence, would you be willing to give up your capacity for language if you could replace it with the strength of a gorilla, the speed of a cheetah, and the flight of an eagle? Why or why not?

10

She Loves Me, but
She Loves Me Not

THE AFFECTIONAL SYSTEMS.

Harlow, H. F., & Harlow, M. K. (1965). *In A. Schrier, H. F. Harlow, & F. Stollnitz (Eds.),* Behavior of nonhuman primates: Modern research trends. *New York: Academic Press.*   (RANK 8)

"What's the deal with these monkeys? And what've they got to do with psychology anyway? Psychology is about people!" These questions erupted from the mouth of a fellow student whose name I can no longer recall, in an undergraduate class I took some 20 years ago. For whatever reason, the student was genuinely puzzled about how investigating monkeys could inform psychology about anything having to do with humans. I suppose I remember his astonishment so well because in my mind he seemed so clueless. I may have responded, in excited disbelief, with something like, "You're kidding! What can monkeys tell us about humans? Why, everybody knows that on the evolutionary ladder humans are only a couple of rungs higher than monkeys. How can anybody not see the similarities?" Well, maybe I wasn't quite that articulate at the time, but I really was puzzled about how someone could fail to see the obvious similarities between humans and nonhuman primates.

Back in those days I suppose I wasn't particularly tolerant of what seemed to me to be the ignorance of some of my fellow psychology majors. Now, in my more forgiving role as college teacher, I realize that it's not always obvious how the behaviors of the "lower" animals can bear any resemblance to the complexity of human beings. I realize that students' religious beliefs often come into play when talking about the evolutionary similarities between higher and lower primates. And as much as I want to get on my soapbox and shout with all my might that evolution is right, I think that when push comes to shove, what's most vital to consider is not that apes and monkeys are like humans, but that apes and monkeys might give psychologists something to look for when they study humans.

The work I'll be describing in this chapter, authored by Harry and Margaret Harlow, serves as Exhibit A in the case of the usefulness of studying monkey behavior for the purpose of illuminating the secrets of human behavior. You'll see in some of the other chapters in this book, especially the work of John Bowlby and Mary Ainsworth, that much of what the Harlows observed in the emotional behaviors of rhesus monkey babies and their mothers also seems to be true about the emotional behaviors of human babies and their mothers. The title of this piece, which ranked seventh among the 20 most revolutionary studies in child psychology, is "The Affectional Systems." But unless you've already had a course in abnormal psychology or motivation and emotion, I suspect that such a title doesn't send up firework displays of excitement. In fact, it's possible you've never even heard the word *affect* used as a noun before. So before I launch into a detailed description of the Harlows' work, let me suggest that whenever you see the word *affect*, you replace it with the word *emotion*; and if you see the word *affectional* you replace it with the word *emotional*. *Affect*, which when used as a noun begins with the same sound as the word *apple*, more or less means emotion. But when we get right down to the bottom of the thing, what we're really talking about is "love." The question really addressed by the Harlows is, How does infant-mother love develop? And now, on with the show.

INTRODUCTION

The Harlows had two purposes in writing their chapter. First, they set out to outline what they believed to be the five most important affectional systems of nonhuman primates. Although the term *nonhuman primate* refers to a whole bunch of species, including higher-level species such as the chimpanzee, the gorilla, and the orangutan, the Harlows spent most of their time with a particular lower-level monkey species known as *Macaca mulatta*, or more commonly, the rhesus monkey. Rhesus monkeys are primarily ground dwellers found in the wild in various parts of Asia. However, thousands of rhesus monkeys are also found in research labs throughout North America and Europe.

The Harlows' second major goal was to bring together in one place the results of a whole series of experiments on the emotional development of these monkeys. So, in their chapter, they present dozens of research findings from a number of different, previously published experiments. They use these findings as evidence in support of their theoretical ideas, but it's important to remember that the research findings were also largely responsible for helping them to generate their research ideas.

In their chapter, the Harlows describe what they believe to be five affectional systems: "(1) the infant-mother affectional system, which binds the infant to the mother; (2) the mother-infant or maternal affectional system [which ensures the mother develops a sense of protectiveness over the infant]; (3) the infant-infant, age-mate, or peer affectional system through which infants and children interrelate with each other and develop persisting affection for each other; (4) the sexual and heterosexual affectional system, culminating in adolescent sexuality and finally in those adult behaviors leading to procreation; and (5) the paternal affectional system, broadly defined in terms of positive responsiveness of adult males toward infants, juveniles, and other members of their particular social groups."

Do you notice a parallel between the affectional systems of monkeys and those of humans? You should. Modern psychology invests a great deal of effort in it, and government funding agencies have granted millions of dollars to developmental, clinical, and social psychologists who are studying precisely these same relationships between family members in *Homo sapiens sapiens* (human) families.

For all practical purposes, the system that's most relevant here is the first one: the infant-mother affectional system. Harry Harlow, in collaboration with a number of other colleagues who were also researching the development of infant bonding and security, achieved the greatest and most widespread attention with regard to this topic. Consequently, my focus throughout the rest of this chapter will be on describing the Harlows' take on the emotional development of infant rhesus monkeys, especially as it pertains to the development of the **infant-mother affectional system**.

The Infant-Mother Affectional System

At the very beginning of their discussion of the infant-mother affectional system, the Harlows point out that this particular system is probably the least variable and least flexible of all of the systems. They say this because this system is perhaps the most important one for the survival of baby monkeys, and it is probably the one most directly rooted in biology. This system, in which baby monkeys emotionally attach themselves to their mothers, is even more important than the complementary mother-infant affectional system (system number 2 above) where mother monkeys more or less attach to their babies. In some ways, this sounds rather backward. How can a baby's emotional attachment to its mother be more important than a mother's protectiveness and attachment to her baby? If a mother doesn't develop an emotional attachment to her baby, how can the baby possibly survive? According to the Harlows, the infant-to-mother attachment is more important because "many infants can survive relatively ineffective mothering, and the system will even continue with great strength in the face of strong and protracted punishment by unfeeling mothers." So even if some mother monkeys don't think too highly of their babies, the babies will increase their chances of survival if they develop a strong attachment to their mothers anyway.

The Harlows describe four normal stages in the development of the infant-mother affectional system: (1) a reflex stage, (2) a comfort and attachment stage, (3) a security stage, and (4) a separation stage. But although they separate the emotional system into four stages, they also point out that there is some overlap between them. The stages also don't necessarily begin and end at the same time, since a lot depends on the specific characteristics of the mother and the baby, as well as of the specific environment in which the baby is being raised. The point is that under relatively normal circumstances, babies progress through these four stages in order to survive to maturity, and to successfully separate from the mother when the time is right.

Reflex Stage.   The reflex stage of baby rhesus monkeys, which lasts for about the first 15 to 20 days, is a lot like the reflex substage of Piaget's sensorimotor period (which we talked about in Chapter 3). It's made up primarily of the basic reflexes needed to ensure the baby's survival. The reflexes are of two types: those pertaining to nursing and those pertaining to maintaining close physical contact with the mother. One of the nursing-related reflexes is the rooting reflex. The rooting reflex first gets activated when the baby monkey detects some stimulation on her face, especially near the mouth. This stimulation causes the baby to move her head up and down or side to side until her mouth makes contact with the nipple. Once contact is made with the nipple, the mouth engulfs it and the sucking reflex starts up (which is a second nursing-related reflex). A third reflex that might also be related to nursing is the climbing reflex. This reflex is apparently useful when the baby monkey is situated near the feet of the mother, and tries to climb up the mother until the rooting reflex enters the picture. This climbing-up thing seems to be a reflex rather than something a baby monkey does intentionally, because according to the Harlows, "If a neonatal monkey is placed on a wire ramp, it will climb up the ramp and even climb over the end of the ramp and fall to the floor unless it is restrained"! Clearly, this is a reflex that separates human babies from monkey babies. Human babies don't gain any climbing capabilities until well into childhood.

Another reflex that isn't seen in human babies is the clinging reflex, although remnants of this reflex may be seen in human babies' palmar "grasping" reflex. The clinging reflex occurs when baby monkeys cling with both their hands and their feet to the underside of their mothers' bodies. This reflex is also crucial for their survival, because without it, monkey mothers would have to use their hands and arms to hold onto their babies most of the time. Since monkeys need their hands and arms to walk, and since in the wild monkey groups may migrate several miles a day, mother monkeys wouldn't be able to keep up with the monkey group very well without their babies' clinging reflex.

The Stage of Comfort and Attachment.   As the reflex stage starts to go away, it is slowly replaced by a stage where the baby's primary goals are to maintain closeness to the mother and to feel belongingness. The Harlows mention that in monkeys this stage lasts until 2 to 2½ months of age, but that in humans it probably lasts until about the 8th month. The mother is highly protective at this stage. The baby achieves her sense of comfort and attachment primarily through two routes: nursing and physical contact. But based on experiments conducted by the Harlows, some of which I'll describe below, these two routes aren't equally important. Even though the baby must nurse to get the necessary nutrition in order to survive, physical contact seems far more important for the baby's "mental" health. As long as the baby is allowed to maintain close physical contact with the mother, the baby will slowly and gradually begin to explore her surrounding environments—first exploring the mother's body, and eventually exploring the nearby things that were otherwise out of reach.

The Stage of Security.   Baby monkeys who have bonded normally with their mothers, and who develop a sense of comfort and attachment, will next begin exploring the more remote outreaches of their environments. However, for monkey babies to engage in such exploratory behavior, the mother has to be at least accessible. When the mother is available, it's as if the baby has the courage to venture out into uncharted territory. But when the mother ceases to be available, bad things happen. Here's one description of what happens when the mother isn't accessible: "The behavior of infants change[s] radically in the absence of the mother. Emotional indices such as vocalization, crouching, rocking, and sucking increase sharply. Typical response patterns [are] either freezing in a crouched position or running around the room on the hind feet, clutching themselves with their arms." This presents a rather disconcerting image, doesn't it?

One interesting caveat is that how far away baby monkeys go to explore their environments depends partially on their mothers' social status in the monkey group. Monkeys whose mothers are highly dominant in the group can strut around freely with little fear of being assaulted or harassed by other monkeys. They can act like little monkey snobs. But the story is quite different for monkeys born to mothers who are low on the social totem pole. These babies have to maintain a high level of vigilance and constantly be on the lookout for bullying by both their same-age peers and other mothers.

The Separation Stage.   The very last stage of the infant-mother affectional system emerges when baby monkeys have matured to the point where they can leave the tightly knit bonds previously established with their mothers. Part of this impending separation results from the monkey youths' natural interest in venturing out on their own to explore the world. But separation also partially results from the mother's sort of "booting the kid out of the house." In fact, Stage 2 of the *mother-infant* affectional system, which we haven't been discussing here, is a stage the Harlows called the "Transitional or Ambivalence Stage." During this stage, the mother starts acting more and more indifferent to the presence of her child. She also starts using harsher and harsher punishments. In general, separation of the infant from the mother seems to correspond with a relative increase of negative responsiveness of the mother to her child. Eventually, it's simply in everyone's best interest if the child decreases the frequency of her contact with Mother. When separation happens, the household negativity goes away.

The Harlow Studies

The theory of rhesus monkey infant-mother affectional systems that we've just reviewed might seem so obvious that it comes across as little more than common sense. On the contrary, the theory was developed after a long series of experiments conducted by Harry Harlow and his colleagues. And fascinatingly, some of their initial findings happened by accident. For example, although Harry Harlow and his colleagues began by intentionally separating baby monkeys from their mothers at birth to investigate the outcomes of social isolation, they didn't plan on these baby monkeys developing strong attachments to the cheesecloth blankets that were used as flooring in their cages. In fact, in an article by Harry Harlow and his colleague Robert Zimmerman in 1959, they reported that the baby monkeys exhibited extreme emotional reactions when attempts were made to remove the cloth flooring.

It was this very serendipitous discovery that first raised the possibility that contact with something relatively soft and cuddly was an extremely important factor in the emotional development of these babies. Up until that point, it was common knowledge in psychology that babies became attached to their mothers either through some form of conditioning, wherein mothers were deemed attractive because they provided babies with the rewarding properties of eating, or through some form of oral satisfaction of the type Sigmund Freud always talked about. Harry

Harlow's exciting discovery suggested that feeding had nothing to do with infants' emotional attachments with their mothers. Rather, it might have something to do with skin-to-skin contact.

The Harlow and Harlow book chapter summarizes the major findings of Harry Harlow and a number of his colleagues. However, so many studies were conducted and published that it would be impossible to review them all. What I'll do instead is review the general procedures used by the Harlows, and review the major findings of some of their major studies. Just as they present their findings in the chapter, I'll do my best to extract the most interesting and most important results.

METHOD

As with other research reports covered throughout this book, detailed information about Harlow's subjects isn't readily available from the authors' own description. However, to give you a better sense of the scope of their study, I'm going to cheat a little bit and borrow the information from an earlier report published by Harry Harlow and his colleague Robert Zimmerman in the journal *Science* in 1959.

Participants

Sixty infant macaque (rhesus) monkeys were separated from their mothers within the first half-day after their births. Surrogate care for the monkeys proved successful as evidenced by the fact that these monkeys gained even more weight than the infants who were raised by their own mothers.

Materials

Two artificial **surrogate mothers** were constructed. The "cloth mother . . . was a cylinder of wood covered with a sheath of terry cloth, and the wire mother was a [cylinder commonly used to store hardware cloth]. . . . The two mothers were attached at a 45-degree angle to aluminum bases and were given different faces to assure uniqueness in the various test situations." In the photos below, you can get a sense of what these surrogate mothers actually looked like. Given this arrangement, both mothers were constructed so that they could provide food for the babies, but only one of the surrogates could provide contact comfort. Given this arrangement, monkeys with both types of surrogate mothers gained normal weight from the food they received. At the risk of providing too much information, for some reason, Harlow also reported that the monkeys raised by the wire mothers had softer stools.

Procedure

Although the exact procedures used by Harlow and his colleagues differed depending on the specific experiments that were conducted, there were a number of commonalities throughout all of them. A typical procedure would have 4 newborn monkeys being "raised" in one condition, and 4 others being raised in a different condition. Usually they were raised in a particular condition for a minimum of 165 days.

For example, in one arrangement, each of 4 newborns would be raised in isolation from other monkeys and would have both surrogate mothers present; the cloth mother would provide the milk. In a corresponding condition, everything would be the same except that the wire mother would provide the milk. In another setup, each of the infants might be raised in the presence of only a single surrogate mother. But again, 4 would be raised with the cloth mother and 4 with the wire one. In one particular version of this experiment, for example, 4 newborns were raised with a lactating (milk-providing) wire mother, whereas the other 4 newborns were raised with a nonlactating cloth mother (but were hand-fed through other means).

An important issue that persisted throughout all these "family arrangements" was how the infants would deal with anxiety-producing situations. The anxiety-producing situations themselves differed in terms of how the anxiety was produced. In some cases, a moving toy bear or dog was introduced to a chamber very near the infants' own living quarters. In other cases, the infants were introduced to a completely unfamiliar room containing a number of "stimuli known to elicit curiosity-manipulatory responses in baby monkeys." On some occasions a surrogate mother would be present during the time of the anxiety-provoking situations (and in this case it would sometimes be the wire mother and sometimes the cloth one), and on other occasions the surrogate mother would be absent.

I think you can see that the number of ways these experiments could be conducted is mind-boggling. And indeed, one of the reasons Harlow and his colleagues had some two dozen publications from this series of experiments was simply that it took that many to describe all the different kinds of studies they conducted. But throughout all the tests, at the end of the day, the question was always, What is the nature of the infant-mother affectional system?

RESULTS

Because there were so many findings reported by the Harlows, I've divided them into separate sections based on which conditions were manipulated.

Infants Raised by Both Surrogate Mothers

In this condition, half of the infants were raised with the wire mother providing the milk and half were raised with the cloth mother providing the milk. But for all the babies, both surrogates were always present. The most interesting finding here was that all the babies spent the vast majority of their time in contact with the cloth mother. Even when babies had to go to the wire mother to feed, they often did so by leaning over from the cloth mother. From 25 to 165 days of age, both sets of babies spent anywhere from 15 to 18 hours per day in contact with the cloth mother. In contrast, they spent only about 1 to 2 hours per day in contact with the wire mother.

Now there are at least two interpretations of these results. On the one hand, you could argue that the reason the infants spent so much more time clinging to the cloth mother was because the cloth mother was more comfortable to be around. Who wants to lie around on something made of wire? On the other hand, it could be that the cloth mothers provided a better sense of security to the babies than did the wire mother. If this is true, then we would expect to see the baby infants flee to the cloth mother under times of fear or distress. To test such a possibility, Harlow and his colleagues introduced the fear-provoking stimulus.

Infants Raised by Both Surrogate Mothers and Who Were Exposed to a Fear-Provoking Toy

In this condition, as before, the infants were raised with both surrogate mothers, but for half of the infants the wire mother provided milk, and for the other half the cloth mother provided milk. Then the fear-producing stimulus was introduced. In about 80% of the cases, the monkeys preferred to run to the cloth mother, regardless of which mother provided the milk. But shortly after seeking the security of the cloth mother, they would begin to venture back out into the open to explore the fear-producing toy. Harlow and Zimmerman described it graphically: "In spite of their abject terror, the infant monkeys, after reaching the cloth mother and rubbing their bodies about hers, rapidly came to lose their fear of the frightening stimuli. Indeed, within a minute or two most of the babies were visually exploring the very thing which so shortly before had seemed to be an object of evil. The bravest of the babies would actually leave the mother and approach the fearful monsters, under, of course, the protective gaze of their mothers."

Apparently, then, the babies were not spending all their time on the cloth mothers simply because those mothers were more comfortable. Based on the fact that the babies would also run to the cloth mother in times of extreme fear, it seems that the cloth mother provided a sense of security in addition to being comfortable to the touch.

Infants Raised by a Single Surrogate Mother and Exposed to a Strange Room

The next question Harlow and his colleagues investigated was what would happen if the monkeys never had a chance to develop a "relationship" with a cloth mother in the first place. To explore this possibility, a number of babies were raised with *either* the cloth mother or the wire mother, but not both. What's more, the cloth mother in this experiment was not a feeding mother, whereas the wire mother was a feeding mother. Then twice a week for 8 weeks, they were introduced to the strange room, which contained lots of unfamiliar objects. Each week, the appropriate surrogate mother was present for one of the visits but not for the other. In this experiment, a **control group** of infants was used where infants weren't even raised by a surrogate mother, but instead were only given a cheesecloth blanket for the first 14 days.

When placed in the strange room, infants who were raised by the cloth mother "rushed to their mother surrogate when she was present and clutched her tenaciously, a response so strong that it can only be adequately depicted by motion pictures. Then, as had been observed in the fear tests in the home cage, they rapidly relaxed, showed no sign of apprehension, and began to demonstrate unequivocal positive responses of manipulating and climbing on the mother. After several sessions, the infants began to use the mother surrogate as a base of operations, leaving her to explore and handle a stimulus object and then returning to her before going to a new plaything."

In sharp contrast, infants who were raised by the wire mother didn't seem to be affected by whether or not she was in the strange room, even though the wire mother had been the primary source of food for these babies. Sometimes the babies would go to the wire mother, but their contact with her was qualitatively different from the monkeys who had access to the cloth mother. Here is another graphic description of the infants' behaviors in the strange room in the presence of their lactating wire mothers: "they sat on her lap and clutched themselves, or held their heads and bodies in their arms and engaged in convulsive jerking and rocking movements similar to the autistic behavior of deprived and institutionalized human children."

DISCUSSION

The series of experiments described by the Harlows in this chapter lead to the unmistakable conclusion that one of the most important factors in the establishment of a healthy mother-infant bond is physical contact. Moreover, not just any physical contact will do. The contact has to provide comfort to the touch. In these studies, the feel of cold, hard metal on the skin just wasn't good enough to enable the close emotional connection needed between infant monkeys and their wire surrogates. Without this emotional connection, a secure sense of belongingness and security never quite seemed to develop in these babies.

All this is not to say that an inanimate, unresponsive conglomeration of wood and cloth is good enough for the emotional needs of the infant, at least not to the point where it replaces a real, live, biological mother. For all we know, from the point of view of wild monkeys in their natural monkeyland, the babies in Harlow's studies could have grown up to be dysfunctional, neurotic wrecks, even if they were raised by cloth surrogates! This is something we don't know, since to my knowledge the babies were never released back into the wild. The point is only that baby monkeys raised by cloth surrogates showed a number of behaviors that are typical of babies raised normally.

For one thing, the cloth surrogates served as a secure base for the baby monkeys. Whenever they were frightened, babies would run up to the cloth mother and maintain close physical contact. Babies raised by their biological mothers also behave this way. Similarly, after babies reestablished contact with their cloth surrogates, they felt comfortable enough to venture out and explore the fear-provoking toy and the strange room. Again, these are behaviors exhibited by monkeys raised by their real mothers.

In its entirety, the Harlow work made a strong stand against the prevailing views about theories of infant-mother affectional systems in vogue at that time. One of the most popular theories came from behavioral psychologists. Although behavioral psychologists came in all flavors, shapes, and sizes, they all believed that infant-mother connectedness came from some form of conditioned association. For example, they might argue that an infant develops an attraction to his mother because she provides food. As a result of repeated pairings between the food and the mother's face and shape, the infant begins to associate the mother with the food and ultimately goes to the mother simply because she's associated with food. Obviously, the Harlow work raised a significant challenge to this notion. The baby Harlow monkeys preferred the cloth mother over the wire mother even when the wire mother was the one that provided the food.

This same finding flies in the face of some of the prevailing Freudian views of the time. As you may recall from your introductory psychology course, Freud argued that a significant motivating influence on children's behavior was the drive to seek oral satisfaction. Because nursing was one way that babies could meet their oral needs, they would seek out their mothers primarily to nurse. Again, with the Harlow babies, any oral needs that might have been motivating them were apparently not sufficient to overcome their desires to maintain closeness to the cloth surrogate mother.

CONCLUSIONS

The Harlow work revolutionized child psychology because it was the first to demonstrate, under experimentally controlled conditions, the importance of physical contact in establishing the infant-mother affectional bond. And the findings of the Harlows played a central role in John Bowlby's development of attachment theory (discussed in Chapter 11). Interestingly, their work also anticipated controversies about the importance of infant-mother bonding that were waged decades after their earliest publications. For example, in the late 1970s and the early 1980s there was considerable concern in the child-rearing literature about whether human mothers needed to make skin-to-skin contact with their newborns immediately after birth. One argument these people made was that this initial skin-to-skin contact was essential for jump-starting the instinctual caregiving drives built into humans by hundreds of thousands of years of evolution. It's easy to imagine that a prevalent fear among new mothers at that time was that babies who didn't make skin-to-skin contact immediately after birth were doomed to experience abnormal emotional relationships with their mothers. John Kennell and Marshall Klaus were two key advocates of this position.

The impact of this line of thinking was that a burden of guilt was placed on lots of new mothers who, for one reason or another, couldn't make that initial skin-to-skin contact with their new babies. For example, imagine how you would feel if you just went through 40 hours of hard labor in delivering a baby (this is easier to imagine if you're female). How easy would it be for you to hold your baby for the next hour? Or might you think a short nap would be a good idea? Well, maybe you'd have enough energy to visit with your baby for a while. But many mothers are so exhausted after the birth of their child that they can't even keep their eyes open. And now imagine a well-meaning nurse shoving the baby in your face and saying, "Here, Doctor says you have to hold this kid for 47 minutes." Things get even worse when birth complications enter the picture. If a baby is born prematurely or with a medical condition needing immediate treatment, Mom might not get an opportunity to hold her baby even if she wanted to. Imagine the guilt these mothers would feel if they were then told that their babies will have emotional deficits because they didn't make that initial skin-to-skin contact!

Fortunately, more recent research, published in the early 1990s by Diane Eyer, suggests that immediate contact isn't necessary. As it happens, babies who don't make early contact turn out just fine emotionally. Apparently, the main reason that lack of early contact has a negative effect on the infant-mother emotional relationship is that some mothers *believe* that initial skin-to-skin contact is essential. When mothers think early contact is essential, and for one reason or another the early contact doesn't happen, a sort of self-fulfilling prophecy takes place. If a mother *thinks* that her emotional relationship with her child suffered as the result of the lack of that initial contact, she behaves differently toward her baby. It's this latter behavior, which is based on the mother's erroneous beliefs, that seems to contribute to a negative infant-mother affectional system. Funny how the mind works, isn't it?

Bibliography

Eyer, D. E. (1992). *Mother-infant bonding: A scientific fiction.* New Haven, CT: Yale University Press.

Harlow, H. F., & Zimmerman, R. R. (1959). Affectional responses in the infant monkey. *Science, 130,* 421–432.

Kennell, J. H., & Klaus, M. H. (1979). Early mother-infant contact: Effects on the mother and the infant. *Bulletin of the Menninger Clinic, 43,* 69–78.

Kennell, J. H., & Klaus, M. H. (1984). Mother-infant bonding: Weighing the evidence. *Developmental Review, 4,* 275–282.

Questions for Discussion

1. Is there much of a difference between infant-mother love in humans and infant-mother love in other primates? What specific behaviors do human infants and mothers engage in that indicate they're in love? How does this differ from the sorts of behaviors exhibited by nonhuman primates?

2. From an evolutionary point of view, what survival value would infant-mother love provide? Isn't it risky for a mother to expend all her energy caring for a baby?

3. Is it ethical to intentionally raise baby monkeys without their mothers? Can you think of any situations in which human babies would be raised in environments like those of Harlows' monkeys?

4. We know that the exploratory behaviors of rhesus monkeys depends in part on the social status of their parents in the group. Do human children experience the effects of the social status of their parents similarly?

11

The Invisible Bungee Cord

ATTACHMENT AND LOSS.
Bowlby, J. (1969). Vol. 1. Attachment. *New York: Basic Books.*   (RANK 3)

Have you ever had a chance to watch a spontaneous game of bungee-baby? Well, maybe you've never heard it called "bungee-baby," but I'm quite sure you've seen it played. The game of bungee-baby has many features in common with the extreme sport of bungee jumping. In bungee jumping, a crazed individual ties a long, strong bungee cord to his ankles and proceeds to jump off a tall building, a bridge, or a platform high in the sky. The hope is that moments before the individual crashes face first into the Earth, the bungee cord's elasticity will slow down the person's descent and snap him back up from gravity's grasp.

The game of bungee-baby is also a game of risk and daring, it involves a stationary platform, but in this case the bungee cord links a mother to her 2- or 3-year-old child. However, no real jumping takes place, and the bungee cord is invisible. You can see bungee-baby being played at public places everywhere, wherever mothers and young children can be found. The mother, who plays the role of "home base," starts the game by taking a relatively stationary position. She may sit in a chair in a doctor's office waiting room or on a playground park bench, for example. The child begins in a position very near the mother. The goal of the game is for the child to wander as far away from the mother as possible before the invisible bungee cord of anxiety and fear snaps the child back toward the mother. However, if the child isn't paying attention and wanders too far from home base, the bungee cord snaps the mother toward the child. Bungee-baby is played all the time in public places. Next time you go to a playground, an airport, or a restaurant, just sit back and watch. You'll see children and mothers moving to and fro, back and forth, toward and apart from one another. You never actually see the invisible bungee cord, but you can sense its presence because it always keeps the mom and the baby within a safe distance of each other.

John Bowlby was an enormous figure in the field of children's mental health, especially because he discovered and figured out the rules for bungee-baby. Well, okay, nobody actually calls it bungee-baby. I suppose that's my name for it. And it's not really a game either. It's just something that always happens between mothers and their young children under normal circumstances. Bowlby called the phenomenon "attachment." But you'll have a clearer picture of what Bowlby was talking about if you think about his attachment idea as if it were a game of bungee-baby.

Bowlby and his colleague Mary Ainsworth (see Chapter 12) were responsible for arguably the single most important theoretical achievement in the scientific investigation of mother-child love relationships ever, let alone the last 50 years. Jointly, the two of them established and developed a huge ideological umbrella known throughout psychology as attachment theory. Using the PsycINFO database, I conducted a search to see exactly how many articles were published on the topic of attachment. Over 5,000 pieces of work emerged! Fortunately for me, I at least have the luxury of two chapters I can use to scrape the surface of the contributions of these two world-famous attachment theorists. In the current chapter we'll be focusing on the efforts of Bowlby (who came in third among the 20 most revolutionary authors published since 1950). In the next chapter, we'll take a closer look at Mary Ainsworth's contributions (which ranked fourth).

Bowlby was trained as a medical doctor, with a specialization in psychiatry. As was typical for psychiatrists educated in the early part of the 20th century, Bowlby's clinical training was steeped in the philosophical and theoretical traditions of psychoanalysis, a form of psychotherapy developed by the famous Sigmund Freud. Due to space limitations, I can't go too much into Freud's extensive and complex psychosexual theory of personality development. But to understand the theoretical context of Bowlby's work, it helps to briefly review the typical psychotherapeutic approach employed by Freud and many of his psychoanalytic descendants.

Freud derived his method of psychotherapy, as well as his overarching theory, from his experiences with adult patients. These patients were usually women, and they often came to him with a number of unusual, and sometimes downright bizarre, psychological symptoms. One reason the symptoms were so odd was that they seemed to have no physical basis. They seemed to come from nowhere. A typical disorder Freud might encounter would be something like "hysterical paralysis," where a patient would report limited movement or sensation in one of her limbs. The term *hysterical* was often applied to conditions like these, when they had no underlying neurological explanation. Freud preferred the term *hysterical* because he found that women usually had the problems—*hysterical* comes from the Greek *hystéra*, which means uterus or womb.

Fascinatingly, Freud found that the severity of his patients' symptoms could sometimes be reduced or even eliminated just by talking with patients about their pasts. And this was how psychoanalysis generally proceeded. You start with a patient who has a psychological disorder, and you move backward in time to see if you can find the source of the pathology. Freud found that oftentimes the source of the psychological disorder could be traced to the patient's childhood relationship, or lack thereof, with her parents. But Freud's focus wasn't on whether the parents gave their child the usual amount of love and belongingness; rather, it was based on whether a child's fundamental pleasure needs were satisfied by the parents. Children who received too much or too little pleasure during early childhood were usually doomed to experience neuroses in adulthood.

Because Bowlby was trained as a Freudian psychoanalyst, he was already sensitive to the importance of mother-child relationships in establishing children's personalities. But Bowlby was a little bummed out by the fact that almost all of the psychoanalytic theory up to that time had focused on parent-child relationships **retrospectively**. In other words, Bowlby thought it was unfortunate that somebody had to have a psychological problem first before the dynamics of her relationship with her parents would be analyzed. Bowlby thought this was a pretty backward approach. He thought it would be much more useful to psychological science if the field first developed a basic understanding of the nature of the mother-child relationship. Once the basic nature of mother-child relationships was understood, then scientists could examine whether they contributed to normal or abnormal psychological development later in life.

Since no one had yet fully developed such a forward-looking approach, Bowlby was pretty much on his own. One goal of his book, then, was to draw up a set of blueprints for the methodology of a **prospective** (looking forward) psychoanalytic psychology. Not only would a prospective psychology be immensely useful for the field, he thought, but a prospective approach would also increase the scientific credibility of psychoanalysis. A prospective approach would allow psychoanalytic scientists to make predictions about future emotional functioning. In this case, expectations about a kid's future emotional functioning could be based on the quality of his relationship with his parents as he's currently experiencing it. Scientifically, this would be a lot better than the traditional Freudian method of explaining everything after the fact. In effect, a prospective approach would make psychoanalytic theories a lot more scientific. Testability is a fundamental necessity of science. Ideas that aren't testable aren't scientific. Unfortunately, much of psychoanalysis before Bowlby's time depended on probing patients' personal histories, including their own recollections of what happened to them when they were very young children. Personal recollections after they've happened simply aren't all that reliable. With his prospective approach, Bowlby was clearly on his way to revolutionizing psychoanalytic theory, because his version would allow scientists to make testable predictions about what would happen in the future based on parent-child relationships in the present.

Now, it's not as if Bowlby was contemplating these ideas in the abstract while sitting in a rocking chair sipping his afternoon tea. Bowlby was compelled to confront the broader theoretical issues of psychoanalysis when he was faced with a large number of very young children who, for one reason or another, were separated from their mothers and who were being raised institutionally, sometimes in rather serious social isolation. Bowlby himself had experienced several emotional separations from important caregiving figures. Minnie, his favorite nursemaid and primary caregiver, and who was in many ways like a mother to him, left when he was only 4 years old.

From a scientific point of view, no one really knew the prognosis for very young children being raised in relative states of maternal separation, because no prospective science had yet been undertaken. Bowlby set out to fill the gap.

INTRODUCTION

In his book, Bowlby's efforts to lay out his vision for a prospective psychoanalytic psychology began with his presentation of the "Observations to Be Explained," which was also the title of his second chapter. In laying out the observations to be explained, Bowlby gives us the sense that he wanted to avoid starting out with a presupposed set of theoretical beliefs. He acknowledged that his training was in psychoanalysis, but he also acknowledged the scientific shortcomings of that approach. Rather, he gives us a sense that he wanted to develop his new theory *inductively*. He wanted to start out with observations of what happened when children were separated from their mothers, and only then proceed to generate a theory to account for the observations.

METHOD

Participants

Bowlby gave credit to his colleague James Robertson for providing the brunt of the observations that he used to build his theory of attachment. Specific characteristics of the children filmed by Robertson were not provided, but they were all filmed during stays at institutions in or around London. Bowlby notes that Robertson's "basic data are observations of the behavior of children in their second and third years of life whilst staying for a limited period in residential nurseries or hospital wards and there cared for in traditional ways. This means that the child is removed from the care of his mother-figure and all subordinate figures and also from his familiar environment and is cared for instead in a strange place by a succession of unfamiliar people. Further data are derived from observations of [the child's] behavior in his home during the months after his return and from reports from his parents."

Materials

No special materials were used here since the research was pretty much based on "naturalistic observations" of the children during their periods of separation. What this means is that observations were made of the children in the naturally occurring, if not ideal, circumstances in which they found themselves. However, in order to make a permanent record of the observations, a camera was used.

Procedure

Similarly, nothing that could really be called an experimental procedure was used here. However, Robertson turned out to be such a gifted filmmaker of children during their separation from their mothers that his filming methods were subsequently adopted as standard protocol whenever the filming of separated children was necessary. In fact, Robertson's filmmaking prowess resulted in his making films that were shown widely throughout Europe and the United States, and which frequently resulted in hospitals' changing their visitation policies.

RESULTS

Based on his recordings, Robertson outlined what appeared to be a three-phase series of separation behaviors. This common pattern of separation behaviors was seen even among children who otherwise had a perfectly healthy and "secure" relationship with their mothers prior to the institutionalized separation. The three phases of separation behaviors described by Robertson were (1) protest, (2) despair, and (3) detachment. Bowlby notes that the children didn't necessarily experience these phases one right after the other. And the children could differ quite a bit from one another in terms of how long they spent in each phase. But the apparent universality of these phases made a significant impression on Bowlby. Here are some examples of what happened during each of the three phases.

Protest. When the children first separated from their mothers, they underwent an intense period of protest. Sometimes the protesting would start right away; other times it would wait awhile. Some children would protest for only a few hours; other children would protest for more than a week! A lot of the differences between children in how long and when they started protesting could be traced to the quality of their relationships with their mother. So although all children went through a period of protesting, the quality of their initial relationship with their mothers affected the length and intensity of protesting.

As Bowlby described it, while protesting "the young child appears acutely distressed at having lost his mother and seeks to recapture her by the full exercise of his limited resources. He will often cry loudly, shake his cot, throw himself about, and look eagerly towards any sight or sound which might prove to be his missing mother. All the behavior suggests strong expectation that she will return. Meantime he is apt to reject all alternative figures who offer to do things for him, though some children will cling desperately to a nurse."

Despair. After the period of protesting, which, from the child's point of view, obviously did not work, children gradually begin to accept the idea that their mother isn't going to return. During this phase, they develop an increasing sense of hopelessness. The energy and vigor they used during the protesting stage goes away, and they become withdrawn and rather nonresponsive. Bowlby describes it as a state of deep mourning.

Detachment. After despairing, and as they enter the detachment phase, children just sort of give up. From a behavioral standpoint, they actually seem to improve. It may even appear to the naïve observer during this third phase that a child's stress has gone away, and that he has finally come face to face with his fate. It's as if he's gotten over his mother's leaving. For one thing, he begins accepting the caregiving efforts of the nurses rather than continually rejecting them. And he may even show signs of happiness and sociability. However, as Bowlby notes, when the mother visits "it can be seen that all is not well, for there is a striking absence of the behavior characteristic of the strong attachment normal at this age. So far from greeting his mother he may seem hardly to know her; so far from clinging to her he may remain remote and apathetic; instead of tears there is a listless turning away. He seems to have lost all interest in her."

Although these observations were made with children who had to go to the hospital or who had to stay at a residential children's nursery, similar kinds of observations can be made in children who stay at home but whose mothers leave. I recall vividly how my nephew Matthew, who was 2 at the time, completely rejected his mother after she returned from only a week-long excursion. In his case, Matthew never showed any outward signs of protest or despair, probably because he was able to stay with his father during his mother's separation. But when his mom returned, I was amazed that he showed absolutely no interest in being hugged or even picked up by her. Here I expected to witness the joyful embrace of an overdue mother-child reunion, but instead I saw what appeared to be complete detachment.

DISCUSSION

Now there Bowlby was: a scientist in possession of all those observations but with little besides psychoanalytic theory to guide him as to what they meant. So he began inventing a whole new theory, primarily by taking advantage of the rapidly growing literature coming out of the field of animal ethology. **Ethology** is based on Charles Darwin's evolutionary notion of adaptation through natural selection. Ethologists study the behaviors of individual species of animals to see whether the behaviors help the species survive better in its environment. Behaviors that help a species adapt to its environment better bestow on the species as a whole, as well as individual members of the species, greater opportunity for survival. It stands to reason that if a behavior is good for a species, then the genes responsible for producing that behavior will be more likely to be transmitted to the next generation of the species, and that next generation will also engage in the same adaptive behaviors. Bowlby thought that the human mother-child relationship was a type of adaptive behavior. He believed it was so strong and so important to the developing child because it was built into the child by evolution in order to help the human species survive. And why not? The Harlows (Chapter 10) had just recently shown how important the infant-mother relationship was for the well-being of infant rhesus monkeys. Why couldn't the same be true for humans?

Borrowing From Ethology

As a science that deals with evolutionarily based adaptations of species, ethology had a heyday during Bowlby's time. Ethologists all over the world were publishing articles that documented all kinds of animal behaviors, many of which proved to be absolutely fascinating. The behaviors were often unusual and exotic, but they were almost always clearly adaptive for the species exhibiting them. Bowlby thought that maybe ethology could provide some insight into why mothers and their very young children always tried to remain in such close proximity, as if bound by an invisible bungee cord. Throughout much of the rest of his book, Bowlby presents ideas from animal ethology that he believed were probably responsible for contributing to the formation of the strong mother-infant bond in humans.

The Environment of Adaptedness.   One central ethological idea that Bowlby latched onto was something he called the **environment of adaptedness**. The environment of adaptedness refers to the specific environment that a particular system, through natural selection, was "built" to work best in. A "system" can be any number of things. For example, we can imagine a whole species as a system. Take, for example, the rainbow trout. As a system, the rainbow trout species functions best in colder freshwater environments where the water temperatures range somewhere between 44 and 75 °F. The trout species would function much more poorly in warmer tropical freshwater environments, or in saltwater environments of any temperature. And of course, rainbow trout function *extremely poorly* in waterless environments, especially the kind found in a greased frying pan hovering over a campfire.

As another example, consider something much smaller than a whole species. Take a biological system within a species for example: the human cardiopulmonary system. The job of the cardiopulmonary system is to extract oxygen from the environment and put it into the bloodstream. Human cardiopulmonary systems were built to work best under atmospheric conditions such as you might find at sea level. They work less well at higher elevations because at higher elevations there is less oxygen to be had. This is one reason so many teams in the National Football League have always dreaded playing the Denver Broncos at the old Mile-High Stadium. Players on those teams found themselves running up and down the field huffing and puffing, and slapping oxygen masks on their faces whenever they got a chance. These were athletes who were otherwise extremely physically fit. Yet, because there was so little oxygen available in the atmosphere 1 mile above sea level, their cardiopulmonary systems weren't able to work up to their full potential.

Although all systems function best in their environments of adaptedness, over time, the environment of adaptedness for a particular system can change. This change can challenge the successful survival of the system in question. Sometimes the environment changes only temporarily, such as when a goose's favorite lakebed dries up as a result of a long summer drought. However, sometimes the environment can change permanently, and it can do so as a result of a species' own intentional actions. Humans are probably most notorious for permanently changing their own environments. The environments that humans live in now are dramatically different from the original environments humans evolved to fit into. No human system was built to survive in a world of planes, trains, and automobiles, for example. Rather, the behavioral and biological systems we now have in place actually evolved to help our ancient ancestors survive in a world that by today's standards we would consider extremely primitive. So right off the bat you can appreciate the great mismatch between humans' current evolutionary state, which evolved to fit a primeval environment, and humans' current industrialized environment, which is anything but primeval.

From this ethological point of view, it's also clear that human babies raised today are relatively ill prepared for survival in modern society. Human babies were built to survive in a time and place where there were no planes, trains, and automobiles; where there were no institutions like hospitals and orphanages; and where they wouldn't ordinarily have cause to experience extended separations from their mothers. Bowlby was very clear that if we are to understand the mother-child relationship, we can't do so from the point of view of modern society. Rather, mother-child relationships must be understood from the point of view of their original environment of adaptedness. Bowlby notes, "the only relevant criterion by which to consider the natural adaptedness of any particular part of present-day man's behavioral equipment is the degree to which and the way in which it might contribute to population survival in man's primeval environment." Accordingly, to understand the survival value of the mother-child relationship today, we have to consider how it would have contributed to the survival of the species many thousands of years ago. In large part, then, the protest, despair, and detachment behaviors of children who are separated from their mothers result from the mismatch between the actual biological adaptedness of human babies and the reality of the modern environments in which these babies find themselves.

Bowlby was interested in this system idea to the extent that it could be applied to children's behavior. In this case, it would be a *behavioral system*. Bowlby had reason to believe that children had inside of them a system that served to keep them physically close to their mothers. At least their separation behaviors in an institutional setting seemed to suggest this possibility. In its full complexity, he called this system the **attachment system**.

With this idea in mind, Bowlby tried to accumulate additional evidence in support of his notion of a primeval attachment system. Not only would such evidence support the idea that an attachment system was "built into" prehistoric human babies, hence giving babies and the human species as a whole an evolutionary edge for survival, but it might also help explain babies' protesting, despairing, and detachment behaviors during periods of separation from their mothers. Since there are two parts to the equation of the mother-child relationship, we should ask two questions: (1) What factors, if any, contribute to a baby's inborn, overwhelming desire to be near its mother? (2) What factors, if any, contribute to a mother's natural urge to be near her baby? Bowlby saw potential answers to these questions in the ethological research being conducted with subhuman species.

Imprinting.   As to whether human babies have a special inborn attraction to their mothers, one of Bowlby's favorite ethological ideas was **imprinting**. Imprinting is probably best known from ethologist Konrad Lorenz's research with baby geese and ducks. Lorenz found that after baby geese and ducks hatch, they develop a preference for the nearest moving object they see. The babies will soon begin following the object around, and they do their best to stay as close as possible to it. If the object goes away, the babies will try to find it, or they may give off distress calls to beckon the object back. This is the process of imprinting; and we might loosely say that the object of desire has been imprinted on the "minds" or brains of the baby geese and ducks.

Now, in a natural environment, the imprinted object is almost always the goose or duck mother. And the imprinting process more or less ensures that the baby birds will remain near their mother. But the conniving hands of experimental ethologists have shown us that the mother bird is not the only object that can be imprinted. The imprinted object could also be a ball, a dog, or even a pair of orange socks being worn by the ethologist himself. Although the specific object doesn't seem to matter much, a number of naturally occurring factors can help strengthen the imprinting process. For one thing, the imprinted object needs to be of a particular size. Objects that are too big or too small don't trigger imprinting. Also, auditory calls given off by the object, like quacking, can further strengthen the degree of imprinting. But once one object is imprinted upon, it's very difficult for imprinting to happen with any other objects. And objects that aren't imprinted can sometimes even produce fear responses should they venture too close to the baby birds.

The adaptive value of imprinting is obvious. In natural environments, it virtually guarantees that babies will stay close to their mother. Near ponds or lakes you may have even seen the familiar trail of ducklings or goslings following their mother around in a sort of little waterfowl train. Remaining close to the mother is adaptive because it gives the babies all the protection from predators and intruders the mother can muster. I've experienced it firsthand! There's been many a time on the golf course when I've had to fend off the attack of a hissing mother goose when my errant golfball drifted a little too close to her brooding area.

Bowlby believed that imprinting had obvious implications for the human mother-child relationship. That is, maybe human babies imprint on their mothers too. Of course, there are obvious differences between birds and mammals, especially higher-level mammals like people. For one thing, human babies can't get up and follow their mothers around right after birth. So any application of the idea of imprinting to human babies will have to take place over a much longer period of time, say several months. But in a more generic sense, there are many parallels between imprinting in birds and similar behaviors in humans. For example, after human babies are a few months old, they begin showing a strong preference for some objects over others. Usually, the preferred object is the mother. Human babies also show fear responses in the absence of the mother, and they can appear incredibly frightened at the unwelcome advances of strangers. Human babies who are mobile also show a strong tendency to remain close to the mother when she's around, and to follow her as she moves about (bungee-baby!).

Bowlby wrote, "We may conclude, therefore, that, so far as is at present known, the way in which attachment behavior develops in the human infant and becomes focused on a discriminated figure is sufficiently like the way in which it develops in other mammals, and in birds, for it to be included, legitimately, under the heading of imprinting—so long as that term is used in its . . . generic sense. Indeed, to do otherwise would be to create a wholly unwarranted gap between the human case and that of other species." You can see that it was important for Bowlby to remain in keeping with the spirit of Darwin's theory of evolution in explaining human attachment. Bowlby's theory was based on potential ethological parallels between human behaviors and those found in subhuman species.

Instincts. Although imprinting may help explain babies' natural interests in maintaining closeness with their mothers, it doesn't account for any natural tendencies of mothers to stay near and care for their babies. So Bowlby borrowed another idea from ethology, that of the so-called maternal **instinct**. The question of whether any human behavior can be regarded as instinctual causes quite a bit of controversy these days. Many modern psychologists would probably argue that no human behaviors are truly instinctual. However, Bowlby disagreed. For him, maternal caregiving behavior met the criteria for being labeled instinctual. According to his criteria, maternal caregiving is instinctual because (1) it follows a similar and predictable pattern in most members of the species, (2) it is not a simple response to a single stimulus, but a sequence of behavior that runs a predictable course, (3) the consequences of the behavior are valuable for ensuring the survival of the individual or the species, and (4) the behavior develops even when there are no opportunities for learning it.

Now, because modern human society no longer reflects the original environment of adaptedness, we have to rely significantly on observations of other animals to best understand the maternal instinct. We can learn especially well from what other "ground-living primates" do. One remarkable characteristic of other ground-dwelling primates is that they are highly social. They have their own little primate societies with their own little primate pecking orders. Different members of the group have a status within the group, and each member dares not try to live at a more privileged level than her or his status provides, else the higher-level group members will put them back in their place. (Sounds a lot like American culture to me.) But one benefit of living in a highly role-differentiated society is that everyone knows what she or he is supposed to do. When the group is threatened by a predator of some kind, for example, the males all gather together to fend off the beast. Meanwhile, the females gather up the young ones and run off to safety. By the definition we've just outlined, these role-governed behaviors are instinctual. One reason that human mothers might be so protective over their babies, then, could be because the prehistoric baby-grabbing and baby-hiding behaviors during times of threat have helped the human species survive as a whole. In turn, the survival of the species has selected for genes that initiate maternal grabbing and hiding behaviors, making them behaviors that have survived alongside human societies to this very day.

Another ethological factor may also be partially responsible for arousing a desire in moms to hold and care for their babies. And that is that babies give off signals that mothers feel obligated to respond to. For example, babies inevitably cry when they need something. Infant crying has the effect of more or less forcing mothers to seek out and relieve the source of their babies' distress. Babies also smile! And smiling can bring about the most rewarding of emotions in the mother. Bowlby writes about the mother, "When she is tired and irritated with her infant, his smile disarms her; when she is feeding or otherwise caring for him, his smile is a reward and encouragement to her . . . her infant's smile so affects a mother that the future likelihood of her responding to his signals promptly and in a way favoring his survival is increased."

Finally, it's probably no small matter that babies are so dang cute! In fact, the natural cuteness of babies may bring out caregiving behaviors in all of us, not just mothers. Have you ever felt an overwhelming desire to go up and hug a really cute little baby? And they don't have to be human babies either. Puppies, kittens, baby monkeys, and even baby birds seem to bring out smiles of adoration and hugging impulses from adult humans around the world. Is it an accident that baby members of many species are so cute? Konrad Lorenz (the imprinting guy) noted a long time ago that baby members of many animal species have a number of anatomical characteristics that humans perceive as cute. Relative to adult members of their species, babies all tend to have an unusually large, rounded head, rounded cheeks, large eyes, and a large forehead. These characteristics of babyness may be found by adult members of the species to be powerfully appealing, and they may actually pull caregiving efforts right out of the adult providers. These caregiving efforts in response to the cuteness of the baby has even been given a name: the **cute response**. Anyway, although Bowlby didn't talk about the cute response himself, it may very well be another evolutionary item built into mothers to guarantee a willingness to care for their babies.

Mother and Baby: A Mutual Attraction

Bowlby's efforts at drawing on the ethology literature to establish an evolutionary, biological basis for the mutual attraction experienced by mothers and children really was a stroke of genius. No one before, or possibly ever since, has drawn together such vastly different disciplines to make such a clearly stated position. But Bowlby goes further to point out that the mother-child relationship is not biological destiny. It's not like moms and their babies are computerized machines running on software programs. Evolution might have given moms and their babies a gentle nudge toward a mutual attractiveness to one another, but there is still much work to be done by both partners to ensure a successful attachment relationship.

Mothers and babies have to be mutually responsive to one another, for example. Bowlby points out that the attachment relationship is an intensely emotional affair. If for some reason the mother is unavailable to the baby, emotionally or otherwise, or if the baby is unavailable to the mother, emotionally or otherwise, then psychological disorders run rampant. He writes, "for proximity and affectionate interchange are appraised and felt as pleasurable by both whereas distance and expressions of rejection are appraised and felt as disagreeable or painful by both. . . . As a result, whenever during the development of some individual these standards become markedly different from the norm, as occasionally they do, all are disposed to judge the condition as pathological." And this is where we came in. As we saw in the results section, children who were separated from their mothers due to some form of institutionalization inevitably displayed signs of intense emotional trauma, either in the form of protesting, despair, or worst of all, detachment.

Finally, although mothers may be the preferred attachment objects of choice, babies can also show attachments to other key figures in their lives. Just as baby ducks might imprint on and follow around Fido the dog, so might human babies imprint on and attach to fathers, older siblings, nurses, and even babysitters. There have even been rare cases where nonhuman animals have served the role of attachment figure and primary caregiver. For example, a young boy nicknamed Viktor was found in the woods in the late 18th century. He had apparently been raised by a pack of wild wolves!

The Attachment Revolution

I think it's quite fascinating that we could spend the last 10 pages talking about the theoretical ingenuity of a person who was trained as a Freudian psychoanalyst without making a big deal about Freudian psychoanalysis. As I mentioned before, this is mostly because Bowlby was dissatisfied with traditional Freudian theory. Although Bowlby originally wanted to strengthen Freudian theory by infusing it with the powerful and widely accepted findings coming out of ethology, he ended up producing an attachment theory that could pretty much stand on its own. It required very little if anything in the way of support from Freudian theory. In fact, some of Freud's more traditional followers have even called Bowlby a heretic!

Still, many psychoanalytic therapists draw significantly on Bowlby's attachment theory when they treat adult patients who have various psychological disorders. This post-Bowlbyan psychoanalytic approach begins the traditional psychoanalytic way—by starting with the current psychological problem and tracing it backward into the patient's childhood. But there is a distinctly Bowlbyan flavor to this new form of psychoanalysis. For one thing, therapy begins by examining a patient's current attachments with important social figures in her adult life, such as her husband, her children, or her best friend. If these relationships are generally poor, the next step is to consider whether they might be indicators of a poor attachment relationship with the mother way back in early childhood. Although this is still a retrospective approach of the sort Bowlby rejected, Bowlby's attachment notion clearly predominates. The goal of this new Bowlbyan psychoanalysis would be to help the patient work on reestablishing the attachment relationships through many years of intensive, hour-long therapeutic sessions—to help the patient gain insight into how her childhood attachment with her mother might have been obstructed or otherwise contaminated. Through insight, the Bowlbyan psychoanalyst can help guide the patient in taking corrective measures to reestablish the missing or damaged attachment relationship, even though the patient has long since left childhood.

The Devolution of Attachment Theory.   Although it might be said that imitation is the sincerest form of flattery, some recent "unauthorized" applications of attachment theory would probably have Bowlby turning over in his grave. There is a disturbing trend in the treatment of attachment disorders that goes by the name of **rebirthing therapy**. The idea behind rebirthing therapy is simple. An individual with an attachment disorder symbolically goes back in time and experiences "birth" again, in order to try to establish a healthier attachment relationship the second time around. Rebirthing centers are popping up all over the country. You can get yourself reborn for a meager $5,000–7,000. Just enter the terms *rebirthing* and *clinic* in your favorite search engine to find the center nearest you!

While I don't particularly oppose symbolic rebirthing, the problem is that children are dying from this therapy! Take the case of Candace Newmaker. She was a 10-year-old girl having problems getting emotionally close to her adoptive mother. Her mother paid $7,000 to a rebirthing clinic in Evergreen, Colorado, for a 2-week program that included an episode of symbolic rebirthing. The child was wrapped up in a blanket that was supposed to represent the womb. Four adults then began pushing pillows against the now-engulfed girl. The pushing was symbolic of labor contractions. According to a *U.S. News & World Report* article, Candace said seven times during the first 24 minutes that she couldn't breathe. She said six times during the first 16 minutes that she felt like she was going to die. Instead of ending the session, the therapist continued on by saying, "You want to die? Okay, then die. Go ahead, die right now." After 1 hour and 10 minutes into the session, and the failed rebirth of Candace, they unwound the cloth womb to reveal an unconscious, blue Candace—ironically, in the fetal position. She was pronounced dead the next day.

CONCLUSIONS

John Bowlby's work helped open the eyes of health care providers around the world. His work showed that if a child is denied contact with an attachment figure for an extended period of time, significant emotional trauma and long-term damage could result. The evolutionary status of human babies just wouldn't permit them to be separated from their mothers for extended periods. He also argued convincingly that mothers were much more than walking breasts that provided only basic nutritional needs to their children. Mothers supplied love. Bowlby showed that if institutions were truly interested in the mental health of their child patients, they would have to allow the children's mothers to be available on a full-time basis. And for orphaned children who had no one who could take the attachment role, special staff people would need to step in and take over. Moreover, mothers were essential for providing a secure base from which children could venture out and explore uncharted waters. So attachment was necessary not only for emotional security, but also for the kind of intellectual development that comes from learning about the surrounding world.

Mary Salter Ainsworth, John Bowlby's longtime acquaintance, colleague, and friend, in an obituary published in the journal *American Psychologist*, wrote, "John Bowlby the scientist cannot be separated from John Bowlby the human being. All those who knew him considered him a deeply warm and caring person. A good clinician, he viewed others with respect, understanding, and compassion. Some misconstrue his emphasis on parental behavior in influencing the course of a child's personality development as blaming the parents for anything that goes wrong. He knew that 'to understand all is to pardon all.' He was incapable of blame."

Bibliography

Ainsworth, M. D. S. (1992). John Bowlby (1907–1990): Obituary. *American Psychologist, 47,* 668.

Bretherton, I. (1992). The origins of attachment theory: John Bowlby and Mary Ainsworth. *Developmental Psychology, 28,* 759–774.

van Dijken, S. (1998). *John Bowlby: His early life: A biographical journey into the roots of attachment theory.* London: Free Association Books.

Questions for Discussion

1. Do human babies really imprint like Konrad Lorenz's birds? In general, how are the behaviors of baby humans and baby birds similar and different?

2. How can Harry Harlow's work (Chapter 10) be incorporated into Bowlby's attachment theory?

3. What would the attachment behaviors of babies born to chronically depressed mothers look like?

4. In what other ways is modern human society different from the environment of adaptedness? Can you think of any conditions that might arise in the future that could actually render attachment behaviors unadaptive?

12

What a Strange Situation

PATTERNS OF ATTACHMENT: A PSYCHOLOGICAL STUDY OF THE
STRANGE SITUATION.
Ainsworth, M. D. S., Blehar, M. C., Waters, E., & Wall, S. (1978). *Hillsdale, NJ: Erlbaum.*   (RANK 4)

"Utter fear" describes my emotional state the first time I visited downtown Chicago
as a grown-up. Now it's not that Chicago is especially frightening. I suspect it's no different than any other major city with a population of several million. And now that
I'm a seasoned visitor to Chicago, I'm thrilled with the cultural opportunities Chicago
provides. But for some reason, I was pretty freaked out by that first visit. After thinking about it, I think I know why. On the day that my fiancée and I arrived in Chicago,
our contact person was nowhere to be found. You see we had planned on visiting our
friend Sharon, who lived in downtown Chicago; we intended to surprise her because
we were "in the neighborhood" (actually, we were an hour away in northern Indiana,
but what's a few dozen miles?) and because we knew she wasn't away on one of her
frequent business trips. We thought we would just pop in and say "Hi." We assumed
that because she wasn't traveling on business, she would be holed up in her downtown
Chicago apartment. Seemed like a reasonable expectation to us. After all, what else
could anyone possibly do in Chicago on a sunny Saturday afternoon, right? (Just kidding, of course!) Well, she wasn't expecting us, and she wasn't home.

　　The moment I game to grips with the fact that we were alone in that very large,
noisy, towering city, a mild sense of panic washed over me. Even though I grew up in
a city (a much, much smaller city), my initial reaction was to high-tail it out of that

urban jungle and get back to familiar territory. Then it occurred to me. The reason I felt so intimidated, so vulnerable, was that we had no home turf, "no center of operations." I knew that if Sharon would just come home and open up the safety net of her apartment to us, all would be well. We would be free to make plans about which sights to see and which restaurants to try out. We could venture out safely to explore our strange new urban surroundings, with the comfort of knowing that at least we had a secure place that we could go back to if the need arose. As it turned out, Sharon came home shortly afterward, and the presence of that secure place really did make all the difference in the world.

According to the work of Mary Ainsworth, it turns out that my need for the assurance of a secure place isn't all that unusual. In fact, needing a **secure** place (or **"base"** in Ainsworth's words) may be a fundamental part of being human. In her book, which was voted the fourth most revolutionary work in the field of child psychology published since 1950, Ainsworth explores in great detail the developmental importance of having a secure base. In her book, she and her three coauthors, Mary Blehar, Everett Waters, and Sally Wall, began by reviewing Bowlby's concept of attachment (which we visited in the previous chapter), and launched on a voyage to explore the impact of attachment on children's emotional development. Ainsworth and her colleagues were especially interested in how a child's "attachment system" worked in a familiar versus a strange environment. To cut to the chase, Ainsworth discovered that children have very different kinds of attachment relationships with their parents. It was her discovery of these patterns of attachment that made her and her work so famous. Indeed, she titled her book *Patterns of Attachment*.

INTRODUCTION

As I just mentioned, Ainsworth and her colleagues began their book by rehashing the central features of John Bowlby's attachment theory. Of course, we just spent a chapter on the topic, so we don't need to talk about it again here. Suffice it to say that the feature of Bowlby's theory that most interested Ainsworth and her colleagues was the attachment system Bowlby believed existed inside all human babies. Ainsworth was especially interested in understanding the conditions that activated children's attachment systems, as well as the conditions that resulted in their termination. What's that? You say you've forgotten a bit about the attachment idea? Okay, here's a brief review. Bowlby suggested that the human infant had an inborn attachment system that consisted of an evolutionarily adaptive set of behaviors which helps a child remain close to his mother. Just about anything a child can do to bring his mother close to him and keep her there is an attachment behavior. One obvious thing a child could do would be to follow the mother around. But this isn't really an option for children who can't crawl or walk yet. To get their mothers' attention, premobile children are pretty much limited to crying or smiling. Although imperfect, these **signaling behaviors** are often good enough to bring the mother closer to the child; but even these behaviors don't work very well when the mother can't see or hear the child. After a child becomes mobile, his collection of attachment behaviors expands to include locomotion, which permits him to move toward his mother all by himself. As we noted in the previous chapter, the significance of all these behaviors is that they serve the survival function of keeping the child under the protective care of the mother. This would have been an important factor in prehistoric times, when a separated child could have become a scrumptious midmorning snack to a hungry lioness and her cubs.

Ainsworth and her colleagues were also interested in how the development of children's thinking could accompany and improve their attachment behaviors. Older children, in addition to having mobility, have the ability to think and make plans about how to stay close to their mothers. Although I ran out of space in the last chapter to discuss it, Bowlby spent a lot of time developing his notion of a **mental model**, or "cognitive map," and argued that it probably plays an important role in children's attachment systems. What is a mental model? You can think of a mental model as a set of expectations you develop based on experience. Let me give you an example. When I was a kid, everyone in my neighborhood was familiar with the sound of the ice cream truck. The ice cream truck was a vehicle that drove through our neighborhood at a very slow pace, played a pleasant melody very loudly through loudspeakers attached to its roof, and supplied all the neighborhood kiddies with as much ice cream as their parents could afford or tolerate. No matter what neighborhood games we were playing, the melody of the ice cream truck grabbed our attention, and we knew that the ice cream vendor would soon be driving by. In Bowlby's words, we had formed a mental model of the ice cream truck. Our mental model of the ice cream truck event included the sound of the melody, the sight of the truck, and the taste of the ice cream we bought if we were lucky enough to talk our parents into giving us some money. However, embedded in our mental models of the ice cream truck was also the time of year. We never had expectations of seeing an ice cream truck in the middle of winter, which in the Midwest is usually accompanied by several inches if not feet of snow. (Although I do remember one odd January day when an ice cream truck, amazingly, cruised through my neighborhood, the familiar tunes of the ice cream truck music being absorbed by the cascading snow mounds. I don't think many children bought ice cream that day!)

Anyway, both Bowlby and Ainsworth believed that children's mental models of their mothers played a fundamental role in determining when children would activate their attachment systems. Children who had mothers who always remained nearby would eventually develop mental models of mothers who were reliable. In contrast, children who had mothers who frequently wandered off would end up developing mental models of mothers who were unpredictable. Ainsworth and her colleagues wrote, "If in the course of his experience in interaction with his mother he has built up expectations that she is generally accessible to him and responsive to his signals and communications, this provides an important 'modifier' to his proximity . . . goal under ordinary circumstances. If his experience has led him to distrust her accessibility or responsiveness, his . . . goal for proximity may well be set more narrowly."

With these ideas in mind, Ainsworth and her colleagues set out to study children's attachment systems. They thought that if they could activate children's attachment systems under controlled conditions, they would understand the attachment systems better because they would have an opportunity to scrutinize the detailed inner workings of the systems. To activate children's attachment systems, Ainsworth implemented a now famous procedure known worldwide as the **strange situation**. The source of Ainsworth's ingenuity in creating the strange situation can be traced to Harlow's work with rhesus monkeys (Chapter 10). If you recall from that chapter, Harlow placed infant rhesus monkeys in an unfamiliar room, which he called an open-field chamber. The chamber was unfamiliar enough to cause a great deal of distress in the baby monkeys, especially when Harlow introduced a fear-provoking, drum-banging, walking toy bear. Although Ainsworth didn't want to freak human children out to the same extent that Harlow frightened his monkeys, she did want to present children with unusual and unfamiliar situations of the sort they might encounter in their day-to-day, real-life experiences.

METHOD

Participants

Quoting Ainsworth and colleagues, "The subjects come from white, middle-class, Baltimore-area families, who were originally contacted through pediatricians in private practice. They were observed in the strange situation at approximately 1 year of age. The total [sample] of 106 infants is comprised of four samples that were observed in the course of four separate projects."

Materials

The Physical Setup. All observations took place in one of two laboratory rooms that were connected by way of two-way mirrors. (A two-way mirror is made of a special kind of glass that looks like a real mirror when viewed from one side, but that works like a clear window when viewed from the other side.) The 9′ × 9′ experimental room was sparsely furnished with items such as a desk, chairs, a bookcase, and metal storage cabinets (the specific furniture used varied from project to project). For 13 of the subjects the floor was covered with a braided rug, but for the rest of the subjects the floor was bare and marked off into 16 squares so that the observers could make more accurate observations of where and how the children moved about the room. At one end of the room was a child's chair "heaped with and surrounded by toys." Near the other end of the room were two adult chairs, one for the mother and one for a "stranger." The two-way mirrors were on the wall nearest the two adult chairs. Observers watched everything that happened through the two-way mirrors, and dictated their observations into a Stenorette reel-to-reel tape recorder.

Personnel. Under ideal conditions, five different personnel were involved in carrying out the strange situation procedure: two observers, a stranger, an experimenter, and a greeter. The greeter's job was to meet the parents and show them to the experimental room. The experimenter's job was to time the episodes and to cue the mother and the stranger about when to enter and exit the experimental room. The observers' job was to observe and record a play-by-play narrative of everything that happened in the experimental room (two observers were used to increase the chances of getting an accurate portrayal of the events that took place). The stranger's job was to be a stranger, but also to enter, exit, and then reenter the room on cue. I guess you could say that a sixth person was also needed: the mother. The mother's job was to be a mother, and to exit and reenter the room on cue. At an absolute minimum the procedure could be carried out with as few as two staff people, with one person playing the role of greeter and observer and the other playing the role of experimenter and stranger.

Procedure

The strange situation procedure consists of eight separate episodes. Because this procedure is so well known, and is arguably among the most ingenious experimental methodologies invented in the last half-century, I'll present a fair amount of descriptive detail for each episode. However, it's interesting to note that Ainsworth didn't spend a lot of time thinking up the procedure. She and her colleague Barbara Wittig came up with the episodes and their order after chatting for only about a half-hour.

Episode 1: Mother, Baby, and Experimenter.   During this episode, Mom and Baby are introduced to the experimental room. Mom is asked to carry her baby into the room and is shown where to put her child. She is also shown where to sit afterward (one of the chairs near the two-way mirror). Observations of Baby are made during this episode, which also counts as a first introduction to an unfamiliar place.

Episode 2: Mother and Baby.   Mom places Baby down midway between her own and the Stranger's chairs. Baby is set down so as to face the toys on the other side of the room. It is okay, even expected, that the baby will explore the room (especially the toys). For the first 2 minutes, Mom is asked not to initiate any activity with Baby, although she is allowed to respond any way she sees fit to solicitations made by Baby. If after 2 minutes baby has not begun to explore the room and the toys, Mom is instructed to carry Baby to the toys and to try to stimulate Baby's interest in the toys. During this episode, observations are made of the amount and kind of exploration exhibited by the baby.

Episode 3: Stranger, Mother, and Baby.   The Stranger then enters the room and says, creatively, "Hello! I'm the Stranger." The Stranger immediately sits in the Stranger's chair (near Mom's chair) and remains quiet for one minute. She doesn't stare at the baby if the baby seems wary of her. After the 1-minute period, the Stranger strikes up a conversation with Mom. After 1 more minute, the Stranger is cued to begin interacting with Baby. After 3 minutes, Mom is cued to leave the room, making sure to leave her purse behind. Mom tries to leave at a time when Baby isn't paying direct attention to her. During this episode, observations are made of how much and what kind of attention Baby pays to the Stranger compared with the attention he pays to Mom or to exploring the toys. Observations are also made of how accepting Baby is of the Stranger's attempts to interact with him.

Episode 4: Stranger and Baby.   After Mom leaves the room, the Stranger reduces her interaction with Baby so that he has a chance to notice that Mom is gone. If Baby returns to exploring the toys, the Stranger returns to her chair and sits quietly. Observations are made of how much exploration Baby does compared to when Mom was still in the room. But if Baby starts crying, the Stranger tries to intervene by distracting him with a toy, and if this fails, by picking him up or talking to him. If her soothing efforts succeed, the Stranger tries to reengage Baby's interest in the toys. If Baby's distress isn't too severe, this episode lasts for 3 minutes. Observations during this episode are made of Baby's response to Mom's departure, as well as Baby's response to the Stranger when she tries to soothe him. After 3 minutes, Mom is cued to return to the room.

Episode 5: Mother and Baby. Mom returns to the outside of the closed door of the experimental room and speaks loudly enough to be heard by Baby. She pauses, then opens the door, then pauses again. The planned pausing is designed to permit the baby to mobilize toward the door if he is going to. Mom is instructed to take whatever actions are necessary to calm Baby down and to redirect his attention to the toys. Meanwhile, the Stranger leaves the room quietly. After 3 minutes, or whenever Baby has settled enough to begin the next episode, Mom is cued to leave. Mom chooses a moment when Baby seems happily engaged with the toys, walks to the door (again leaving her purse on her chair), says "bye-bye," exits, and closes the door behind her. Observations during this episode are aimed at Baby's response to Mom when she returns, as well as to her departure.

Episode 6: Baby Alone. Three minutes are allocated to this episode when Baby is allowed to explore the room alone. If he cries, he is given a chance to calm himself down. But if the intensity of his crying is too great, the episode is cut short. Observations are made both of Baby's emotional responsiveness to Mom's leaving and how quickly he returns to exploring the toys.

Episode 7: Stranger and Baby. Now the Stranger returns to the outside of the closed door and speaks loudly enough to be heard by Baby. She pauses, opens the door, then pauses again. As before, the pauses are planned to allow baby a chance to approach the Stranger if he is going to. If Baby is crying, the Stranger again tries to soothe him, picking him up if he permits. If the soothing succeeds, she places him near the toys and tries to interest him in them. If he plays, the Stranger returns to her chair. However, if Baby isn't crying when the Stranger enters the room, she tries to coax him to come to her. If Baby doesn't come, she approaches him and tries to interest him in playing. If he starts playing, as before, she retreats to her chair. Observations are made of how easily soothed Baby is by Stranger, whether he seeks or accepts her initiations, and whether he will play with her. Observations are also made of Baby's reactions to the Stranger's return as compared with Mom's return to the room as in Episode 5.

Episode 8: Mother and Baby. After Episode 7 takes place for 3 minutes, Mom returns to the room. Mom opens the door and pauses a moment before greeting Baby. She then speaks to the baby and picks him up.

How Do You Know Attachment When You See It?

The observers were trained to look for a lot of different attachment-related behaviors shown by the babies. Ainsworth and her colleagues thought six specific behaviors were probably most important. Here is what they called each behavior along with a brief description of each one: (1) proximity and contact seeking: reflected how hard a baby tried to get near another person; (2) contact maintaining: reflected how hard a baby worked at staying in contact with another person once contact was established; (3) resistance: this was sort of the opposite of proximity and contact seeking and reflected how hard a baby actively tried to stay away from another person; (4) avoidance: reflected not so much active resistance, as in trying to get away from another person, but rather how much babies ignored another person; (5) search: this was a lot like proximity and contact seeking except that it happened when the desired person wasn't in the room; a baby engaging in search behavior would tend to go to the door and try to open it or otherwise remain near it; and (6) distance interaction: reflected babies' efforts at interacting with a desired person from a distance, that is, even though they didn't seek physical contact they displayed an interest in establishing eye contact or smiling back and forth with a desired person.

RESULTS

Although Ainsworth achieved great fame for her ingenious innovation of the strange situation procedure, her star rose even higher when she noticed that babies' attachment behaviors could be rather cleanly grouped into one of three patterns. She called the three patterns, mundanely, "Group A," "Group B," and "Group C." One thing I remember thinking the first time I encountered these labels was why the heck Ainsworth used such boring names. They obviously didn't correspond to anything meaningful, like maybe the first letter of a name or something. As it turns out, Ainsworth chose these arbitrary labels precisely because they were nondescript. She feared that if she gave the groups labels that were more meaningful, such as "the Crying Group" or "the Happy Group," the group names themselves would end up biasing her and her colleagues into looking for certain types of behaviors and ignoring others. By choosing the arbitrary "A," "B," and "C" labels, Ainsworth could at least be sure that the names of the groups children belonged to wouldn't influence what the observers saw.

Still, Ainsworth had to distinguish between different patterns of attachment behavior somehow, and so the different group labels eventually corresponded to different patterns of attachment behaviors. Now in distinguishing among the different patterns of attachment behavior, it wasn't as if some children showed attachment behaviors whereas others didn't. There were no unattached children. Children in all three groups showed attachment-related behaviors of some kind or another. And for that reason, Ainsworth and her colleagues regarded all children as attached to some degree. Rather, children differed in the quality of their attachments. Here's a brief description of the kinds of attachment behaviors children exhibited in Ainsworth's strange situation, arranged in terms of Ainsworth's three categories of attachment.

Group A.   The single most obvious pattern of behavior for Group A babies was that they didn't seem bothered by being left alone with a strange person in a strange room, and they avoided their mothers during the reunion episodes! The general impression was that these babies didn't care whether the mother was around or not. In fact, some of these babies seemed more interested in being near the stranger than the mother! Ainsworth further classified these Group A babies into two subtypes. Group A_1 babies avoided or ignored their mothers altogether. Group A_2 babies, on the other hand, seemed to show a very slight interest in being near their mothers coupled with a strong opposing interest in staying away from their mothers.

Group B.   Babies in this group seemed to have the healthiest and most adaptive attachment relationships with their mothers. The most common characteristic of babies in this group was that they acknowledged the importance of their relationships with their mothers during the reunion episodes. However, they differed from one another in how they expressed their attachments. Some of these babies became highly distressed when their mothers left them alone, whereas others weren't bothered so much. But common to all the babies in this group was that they recognized the importance of the mother as a secure base, and they appreciated her presence. Based on how babies in Group B differed from one another, Ainsworth classified them into three subgroups. B_1 babies showed little distress during separation but showed definite signs of interest in the mother when she returned. However, these babies' interest in their mothers more or less took place across a distance. That is, they didn't try to get near their mothers, but they definitely greeted their mothers with smiles of approval when the mothers returned to the room. B_2 babies showed mild distress when mothers left the room, and they were more likely than B_1 babies to physically approach their mothers during the reunion episodes. B_3 babies differed from the other two B subgroups in that they were the most proximity-seeking of the three. During reunions, these babies sought out the mother most actively, and spent the most time near her. But these babies didn't necessarily show a lot of distress when their mothers left the room, and they weren't particularly clingy prior to the separation episodes.

Group C.   These babies were very interesting because their attachment behaviors seemed to contradict each other. During reunion episodes these babies showed a bizarre, zigzag pattern of actively approaching their mothers and then actively resisting them. They might run up to the mother during the reunion episode to be held, for example, only to immediately struggle to get loose from the mother's hug. Babies in this group either acted extremely distressed and downright angry during the separation episodes (C_1), or they appeared noticeably passive (C_2). By noticeably passive, I mean they didn't *do anything*. They just sat there motionless like a limp rag.

DISCUSSION

Ainsworth's main success in coming up with these different attachment styles was in giving the field of child psychology a handle on the different kinds of relationships that existed between children and their mothers. But there was another important outcome of Ainsworth's work: Her classification system could be used to predict successes and failures in other domains of children's later development. Wouldn't it be useful, Ainsworth thought, if we knew which type of attachment relationship led to the best outcomes? If so, then we would have some reason to intervene when we saw evidence of mother-child relationships gone bad. Let's begin by taking a deeper look at the hidden implications of having an A-, B-, or C-type attachment relationship.

Group B Is Best (Secure Attachments).   Although Ainsworth and her colleagues initially went to great lengths so as not to bias their own perceptions of babies belonging to the different attachment categories (e.g., by giving them nondescript labels such as A, B, and C), in the end it turned out that some attachment types were better than others. Clearly, attachments of the B kind are strongly preferred: "The typical

Group B infant is more positive in his behavior toward his mother than are the infants of the other two classificatory groups. His interaction with his mother is more harmonious, and he is more cooperative and more willing to comply with his mother's requests. [Group B babies] appear to be positive and unconflicted in their response to close bodily contact with the mother." In addition, Group B babies are likely to use their mothers as a secure base to explore, and they are likely to feel relatively comfortable when their moms aren't in the immediate vicinity. Ainsworth writes, "Even when [Mom] is out of sight, [the typical Group B baby] nevertheless usually believes she is accessible to him and would be responsive should he seek her out to signal her." The reason for their comfort level, Ainsworth believed, is that Group B babies have developed mental models of their mothers which included easy access to her and reliable responsiveness from her. Even when their mothers aren't around, Group B babies feel as if their mothers could be called upon if needed. Ainsworth believes the security seen in Group B babies came from Group B mothers being "sensitively responsive." Fortunately, about two thirds of babies are Group B babies.

There are a number of developmental benefits of having a Group B, or secure, attachment. For one thing, these babies are more cooperative and willing to comply with their mothers' requests. Consequently, securely attached babies are more easily socialized. An easily socialized child is a socially competent child, and a socially competent child is a popular child. Second, securely attached babies are less fearful of unknown people and things. If they are generally less fearful of new things, they will be more likely to perform well in unfamiliar situations such as on the first day of school or when taking a school placement exam. Not surprisingly, securely attached Group B babies tend to score better on a variety of different kinds of tests.

Group C (Anxious-Ambivalent) Attachment. There are fewer babies with a C-type attachment than babies in either Group B or A, but there are enough babies sharing a common set of anxious-ambivalent behaviors to justify giving them their own group. Remember that Group C babies generally cried when their mothers left them alone in the strange situation, and they seemed uncertain about whether they should hug their mothers or avoid them when mothers returned. In fact, these babies sometimes wanted to be held by their mothers and then immediately afterward wanted to avoid their mothers. These babies seemed to have opposing feelings about the whole thing. For this reason, these babies have sometimes been called "ambivalently attached." Of course, the word *ambivalent* means having opposing feelings.

As it turns out, one characteristic common to babies in this group was that they all tended to have mothers who weren't very responsive to their signals. Not surprisingly, these Group C babies spent a lot of time crying. This makes sense. If you were a baby who was crying, and your mother didn't readily respond to your needs, wouldn't that fact in itself give you something more to cry about? Also, because their mothers were relatively unresponsive to their communicative signals, these babies never quite developed a mental model of mothers being emotionally available. Instead, they developed mental models of mothers who were mostly emotionally unavailable. And, because these babies never developed mental models of having a dependable mom, they never quite developed a sense of how to use Mom as a secure base to explore the world. Lacking a secure base in turn had the effect of diminishing how much exploration these Group C babies did. And to the extent that exploration of the world translates into having knowledge about the world, you can easily imagine how these Group C babies were generally not as cognitively advanced as Group B babies.

Group A (Anxious-Avoidant) Attachment.　Ainsworth writes that the "key to understanding Group A behavior seem[s] obviously to lie in their avoidance of the mother in those very episodes of the strange situation in which the attachment behavior of other babies was activated at high intensity." Whereas Group B and C babies looked to their mothers for security (Group B babies had secure mental models and Group C babies cried intensely when their mothers left), Group A babies seemed to have a take-it-or-leave-it attitude toward their mothers. In fact, they seemed more in favor of the leave-it part. In the strange situation, they often actively avoided their mothers, especially during the reunion episodes. Were these babies cold and unfeeling? No. As it turns out, these babies' active efforts at avoiding their moms were probably quite adaptive.

You see, they had mothers who really didn't want to be around *them.* Their mothers were rather rejecting of them; they were the types of mothers who found close contact with their babies as something to be avoided. This rejection on the part of the mothers probably caused a great deal of grief in the babies, who may have developed considerable anger and resentment toward their mothers as a result. But, from an ethological point of view, chronically expressing anger toward your mother is probably not a good thing. You run the risk of her giving up on you and leaving, which would be bad because she is your protector and the primary source of your nutrition. So if you can't express your anger toward her and if she doesn't like being near you, avoiding her is probably the best thing you can do. When you avoid her, you're not risking expressing anger toward her and you're also not getting in her face. The bottom line is that Type A babies are pretty much in a bind, and their avoidant responses were probably the most adaptive behaviors they could muster under such short notice.

However, being an avoidantly attached baby comes at some interpersonal cost. The most obvious consequence is that later in life these babies may not be able to form secure, stable relationships with other important figures in their life. They run the risk of living their lives alienated from the social comforts that can be provided by healthy attachments with other people. Accordingly, they also run the risk of not being able to get along with people very well later in life. In fact, recent research has shown that children classified as having an avoidant attachment are more likely to get in trouble in school and are less likely to be able to get along with their friends.

NEW DIRECTIONS

Coming up with these attachment styles was a monumental achievement for Ainsworth, and her work launched a thousand more studies on attachment. Yet despite Mary Ainsworth's high profile as a revolutionary researcher, and despite her innovation of the strange situation and her discovery of the three attachment classifications, she was amazingly unsuccessful in securing grant funding for carrying out her work. You may not be aware of this, but at most academic research universities around the country, faculty are expected and sometimes even required to obtain funding for their research from external agencies. The United States government is the largest recipient of funding requests, with agencies such as the National Institutes of Health and the National Science Foundation supplying millions of dollars annually to child psychology researchers. Thus, there is a lot of pressure on researchers for getting money to support their own research efforts. But for one reason or another, Ainsworth didn't get to taste much of the sweetness of the fruits of external funding. According to Mary Main, Ainsworth's colleague and research collaborator, Ainsworth's grant-getting failures rested largely on the fact that her work was "peculiar in its virtually clinical focus upon individuals, and that the claims she had made regarding the import of differences in the organization of infant-mother attachment involved shockingly small-sized groupings, and were very unlikely to be replicated." Despite the granting agencies' shortsightedness, decades of attachment research have followed, mostly extending and building upon Ainsworth's original theorization and methodology. As any revolutionary study should, Ainsworth's work raised a lot more questions than it answered. And so researchers set out to answer as many of them as possible.

One of the first research goals was to see if the mother was the only adult figure that a child could form an attachment relationship with. The mother would appear to be an ideal candidate, but was she destined by nature to be the only figure to which children could attach? Or could other figures play that role as well? As it turns out, children can form secure attachment relationships with people besides their mothers, including their fathers, their grandparents, their siblings, or probably just about anyone else who serves as a primary caregiver. Apparently, the mother doesn't have a particularly important role just because she's the mother. Her importance as an attachment figure lies in the fact that she is typically the primary caregiver, and because she is in a position to be sensitively responsive to the child's needs. As you can imagine, this finding is a big relief for nontraditional families such as the increasingly familiar single-parent, father-headed household.

Another research goal was to see whether children who attended day care centers 8 hours a day were at any special risk for developing insecure attachment relationships. As you are probably aware, and as you yourself may have experienced, many preschool-aged children live in families in which the primary caregivers have to go to work 5 or more days per week. With no other relatives available to help care for the children, parents often have no choice but to place their children in all-day, every-day day care centers. For many years, there was a rampant fear that children raised in day care settings were going to develop insecure attachment relationships because they spent so much time away from their primary caregivers. Unfortunately, the research findings on this question are a lot less clear. While some research shows that children who go to day care are at risk for developing avoidant attachment relationships, other research fails to find such a risk. I suppose we'll have to hold our breath until the scientific jury finally returns an answer to this question.

But one recent research track that I think is especially interesting is the development of a methodology for measuring attachment in adulthood! There is a growing movement among attachment researchers to measure the attachment status of adults. Using a test called the Adult Attachment Interview, parents are probed about the kinds of attachments they had with their own parents back when they were children. Intriguingly, it was found that adults can also be classified into one of three attachment classifications, and these categories directly parallel Ainsworth's. And perhaps even more intriguingly, research has found that adults with particular attachment relationships tend to have similar attachment relationships with their own children. I guess this is called handing down attachment relationships across the generations. But it does raise the point that parents who had insecure attachments as children are at risk for promoting insecure attachments with their children. Attachment relationships are contagious.

CONCLUSIONS

I suppose the most important take-home message from Ainsworth's work is that the mother (or some other primary attachment figure) plays a very strong and central role in the child's formation of healthy attachment relationships. The key concept following out of Ainsworth's work was maternal **sensitive responsiveness**. While all babies are virtually guaranteed to form some kind of attachment with their mothers, only babies with sensitively responsive mothers will form secure attachments. However, this key concept is also the source of concern for many researchers on the outside of the attachment field looking in. For one thing, the sensitive responsiveness notion places an awful lot of responsibility on the shoulders of mothers (or other attachment figures). Like Bowlby before her, Ainsworth has been accused of "mother blaming" in instances in which infant-mother relationships go wrong.

Part of the problem seems to be that Ainsworth simply didn't give enough attention to differences in children's temperament. Temperament researchers have pointed out that some children might cry during strange-situation separation episodes, not because of an insecure attachment, but because of a biological predisposition to exhibit high anxiety under unusual circumstances. Harvard child psychologist Jerome Kagan is well known for his work documenting that some infants are just biologically predisposed to have a highly reactive sympathetic nervous system. What this means is that some babies cry at the slightest deviation from normality. When these babies cry, Kagan argues, it doesn't necessarily mean they're insecurely attached; they might simply be temperamentally inhibited. The point is that if children's own temperament can explain some of their tendencies to cry, then mothers don't need to take all the blame.

Although Ainsworth's work was focused on clinical aspects of children's normative emotional **development,** her work has had far-reaching impacts that have extended beyond the boundaries of normative development and emotional development, most notably on the field of developmental psychopathology. Here researchers are busy conducting longitudinal studies to see if early childhood attachment classifications are predictive of later childhood pathologies such as depression and behavioral conduct disorders. And researchers in the area of cognitive development are beginning to consider whether children's attachment relationships with their parents factor into their own cognitive growth. This is the kind of thing that makes common sense—if you have a troubled relationship with your parents at home, you won't be able to perform very well at school. But science doesn't work well when it depends on common sense. Science needs the actual data. And the next few years will reveal much-awaited data on the long-term importance of secure attachment relationships in infancy and early childhood.

The idea of attachment lies at the center of almost all contemporary thinking about children's emotional growth. I guess you could say that attachment theory provides the scientific community itself with a secure base from which it can venture out into exploring new, uncharted territories of children's psychological development. The one-two punch provided by the theoretical developments of Bowlby and the methodological-empirical advancements by Ainsworth have clearly revolutionized the field of child psychology. It's difficult, but exciting, to imagine what the next revolution in the area of children's attachment will be.

Bibliography

Ainsworth, M. D. S., & Marvin, R. S. (1995). On the shaping of attachment theory and research: An interview with Mary D. S. Ainsworth (Fall 1994). *Monographs of the Society for Research in Child Development, 60*(Serial No. 2-3), 3–21.

Bretherton, I. (1992). The origins of attachment theory: John Bowlby and Mary Ainsworth. *Developmental Psychology, 28*, 759–774.

Fagot, B. I., & Kavanagh, K. (1990). The prediction of antisocial behavior from avoidant attachment classification. *Child Development, 61*, 864–873.

Main, M. (1999). Mary D. Salter Ainsworth: Tribute and portrait. *Psychoanalytic Inquiry, 19*, 682–736.

Questions for Discussion

1. Ainsworth has been criticized for placing too little emphasis on children's own behaviors in contributing to the quality of the mother-child relationship. How might differences in children's temperament impact favorably or negatively on their attachment relationships?

2. Ainsworth's "strange situation" was truly an experimental innovation. A limiting factor, of course, is that it's restricted to being used in the artificial conditions of the laboratory. Can you think of any naturally occurring situations that resemble the "strange situation"? Would scientists be better off using these naturally occurring situations than Ainsworth's laboratory version? Why or why not?

3. Attachment theorists view the "secure base" notion as central to healthy emotional development in childhood. However, having a secure base throughout life may also be important for good mental health. Can you come up with two or three examples from your own personal experiences in adulthood in which you benefited or didn't benefit from having some sort of secure base?

13

"This Is Gonna Hurt You a Lot More Than It's Gonna Hurt Me"

CURRENT PATTERNS OF PARENTAL AUTHORITY.

Baumrind, D. (1971). *Developmental Psychology Monographs, 4(1, part 2).*   (RANK 16)

There once was a family, blue collar.
Dad worked so hard for a dollar.
Mom watched the kid,
Blowing her lid.
Dad came home only to holler.

This is a story about parenting. It's a story we're all familiar with, whether we were raised by biological parents, stepparents, foster parents, adoptive parents, robotic parents, or maybe even a pack of wolves. And we all have something to say about it too (unless we were raised by wolves, in which case we wouldn't have any language). We often defend our parents' disciplinary strategies, while at other times we vow never to raise our children the way our parents raised us. One of the quickest ways I can get a rise out of my students is to challenge how they were raised. In my most authoritative voice, I'll sometimes say something like, "*Studies show that frequent spanking produces long-term negative consequences.*" No sooner can I finish my sentence before a largish male athlete shouts, "Hey, my parents spanked me, and look how I turned out!" Smiling wryly, I usually follow up with, "How exactly *did* you turn out?" It's about then that his friends start giggling.

We all have opinions on the topic of parenting. But we don't always realize when our opinions run smack into fact. For this reason, the psychology instructor often takes a lot of grief from her students when she suggests their beliefs about parenting might be wrong. It's interesting that other sciences don't have to carry around this same kind of baggage. When our physics teacher tells us atoms are composed of electrons, neutrons, and protons, we say, "Yeah, okay." We don't challenge the physicist. How could we? We've had no experience with the insides of an atom, and most of us probably wouldn't know a proton from a protein. It may have something to do with not being able to get ourselves small enough.

But we've all been parented. And when the child psychology teacher tells us frequent spanking tends to produce long-term negative consequences, she's hitting very close to home on a topic we all know quite a bit about. But just as we listen to what the physicist has to say in a course on physical science, I think it's a pretty good idea in a class on human science to put our own stereotypes and biases aside and listen to what the child psychologist has to say. As budding scientists we at least owe it to ourselves to review the evidence on the matter, especially when the evidence had the effect of revolutionizing the field of child psychology.

In the 16th most revolutionary study published since 1950, Diana Baumrind focused on the outcomes of different styles of parenting. Among her most important findings was that some ways of parenting really are better than others, which depends in part on what you mean by "better." And she didn't rely on her own opinions in classifying parenting styles as good or bad. Rather, she examined how the children themselves turned out. "Good" parenting styles were defined as those which best prepared children to adapt to the adult world or were **socially adaptive**. "Bad" parenting styles, in contrast, were defined as those which produced children with poor survival skills. Her research was revolutionary because it scientifically documented a standard of good parenting that remains in place to this day, at least for mainstream, educated, middle- and upper-income families.

INTRODUCTION

In the introduction to her 1971 article, Baumrind doesn't give us much of a history of parenting research. She simply points out that she was conducting her study to answer a few questions raised by a couple of her earlier studies. In those earlier studies, she had already identified three different styles of parenting, which she called *authoritative, authoritarian,* and *permissive.* But they were based on children's behaviors, not on how the parents themselves actually parented. So one goal of her 1971 study was to explore parents' *actual* parenting behaviors, and to see if the same three parenting styles emerged.

Another limitation of the earlier work was that Baumrind didn't consider whether different parenting styles affected boys and girls differently. The question of male-female differences was quite an important social issue of the times. In the early 1970s the women's movement was just getting underway. Women were "burning their bras" under the banner of "women's lib." Ratification of the Equal Rights Amendment to the United States Constitution was making headlines in all the papers. And social scientists throughout the country were clamoring to explore the origins of gender differences and gender equality. So a key issue for the 1971 study was whether parenting styles worked differently for boys versus girls.

METHOD

Participants

The children in the study were all enrolled in one of the 13 Berkeley, California, area nursery schools (roughly similar to today's preschools). Baumrind required that the children had to be at least 3 years, 9 months of age and had to have an IQ score of at least 95 (in the normal range). In addition, the parents had to be willing to allow Baumrind into their homes for the "home visit phase" of the study. Sixteen black children and their families were excluded from the study because in other work Baumrind found that black parents parented differently from white parents. Although she indicated that a separate article on the parenting styles of black parents was in preparation, it's important to keep in mind that Baumrind's results, as described in this monograph, may apply only to white families, and then possibly only to high-IQ, upper-income, white families from the Berkeley, California, area. The final sample consisted of 60 white girls and 74 white boys, with an average IQ of 125 (placing them in the above-average range) and an average age of slightly over 4 years.

Materials and Procedure

As a revolutionary, Baumrind's interests in measuring parenting styles and child outcome quality meant that she was dabbling in a new area. And as a dabbler, she would have to figure out a way to measure both parenting style and quality of child behavior. What she ended up with was a very complicated set of information taken from a very complicated series of measurement instruments that she administered to both parents and children. On top of that, she used a very complicated series of statistical techniques to analyze her very complicated set of data. To give you an idea of how complicated the whole thing was, she spent 46 pages of her article describing her measurement instruments and procedures! I'll do my best to summarize these 46 pages in the next couple of paragraphs.

Child Measures.   Because Baumrind was interested in figuring out which parenting styles were better than others, she had to come up with some way to measure "better." She reasoned that a better parenting style would have to be one that produced socially adaptive behaviors in children. After all, what is the purpose of parenting if not to raise your kids to be successful on their own? So one of her first objectives was to measure socially adaptive behaviors in children. She started with a method known as **naturalistic observation**. In naturalistic observation, an observer simply watches a child in some sort of naturally occurring situation and records instances of behaviors believed to be important. In Baumrind's study, the children were observed in two situations: in their nursery school class and while taking a Stanford-Binet intelligence test.

Baumrind used seven different observers in her study, but each child was assigned only to one observer. She also used a lot of reliability checks to make sure the observers were in agreement as to how to record the behaviors. The observers were looking for evidence of seven different types of behavior. Each type of behavior was anchored at one end with a developmentally adaptive characteristic (in other words, a behavior that was viewed as relatively good) and at the other end with a developmentally unadaptive characteristic (a behavior that was viewed as relatively bad). Again, keep in mind that a behavior was defined as adaptive or unadaptive relative to the goals of a white, well-to-do, high-IQ culture. Carla Bradley, who studies African American parenting strategies, would be quick to remind us that what's adaptive for European American kids may not be adaptive for African American kids. In any case, here's a list of the seven behavior types Baumrind came up with, along with a couple of examples of behaviors at each end of the "good" and "bad" range.

Behavior Type	Examples of Adaptive Behavior	Examples of Unadaptive Behavior
Hostile-Friendly	Nurturant or sympathetic toward other children Helps other children carry out their plans	Insulting Bullies other children
Resistive-Cooperative	Obedient Can be trusted	Tries to evade adult authority Provocative with adults
Domineering-Tractable	Nonintrusive Concerned about adult disapproval	Manipulates other children
Dominant-Submissive	Peer leader Resists domination of other children	Suggestible
Purposive-Aimless	Confident Self-starting and self-propelled	Spectator Disoriented in environment
Achievement Oriented– Not Achievement Oriented	Likes to learn new skill Gives his best to work and play	Does not persevere when encountering obstacles Does not become pleasurably involved in tasks
Independent-Suggestible	Individualistic	Stereotyped in thinking Does not question adult authority

Although I've listed only a couple of examples of each category of behavior, each child was actually observed for many more specific behaviors. In fact, each child was rated on 72 different behaviors!

Parenting Measures.   Measures of parenting quality were also taken from naturalistic observation. But for the parents, the observations were done in the home. Baumrind describes it this way: "In order to achieve a standardized situation, the home visit was structured identically for each family and occurred for all families during a period commencing from shortly before the dinner hour and lasting until just after the child's bedtime. This period is commonly known to produce instances of parent-child divergence and was selected for observation in order to elicit a wide range of critical interactions under maximum stress." In other words, the observers camped out in these people's homes during one of the most difficult times of the day—the time when parents battle their children to get them into bed.

Baumrind's development of the parenting measure is a bit trickier to describe. It had two phases. In the first phase, she came up with 15 different practices of parenting that she thought would *likely* describe how parents parented. In the second phase, she conducted a sophisticated statistical analysis to reduce these 15 practices down to a more reasonable number (like 5 or 6). In addition, she also conducted the statistical analyses separately for mothers and fathers to see if the most important parenting practices for mothers differed from the most important parenting practices for fathers. I'll start out by first listing the 15 practices of parenting Baumrind initially looked for, and follow that up by listing the reduced set of parenting behaviors as they turned out for mothers and fathers separately. First, here are the 15 original practices of parenting. Keep in mind that for each practice of parenting, as with the child measures, Baumrind included a number of specific behaviors that observers could look for. For each practice, I'll list two examples of specific behaviors the observers were trained to detect. You might find it meaningful to rate your own parents on each of these scales as well (think back to when you were about 4):

1. Expects Versus Does Not Expect Participation in Household Chores.
   Examples: Parent demands child put toys away; Parent demands child dress self.
2. Provides Enriched Versus Impoverished Environment for Child.
   Examples: Parent provides an intellectually stimulating environment; Parent makes demands upon child that have educational value.
3. Directive Versus Nondirective.
   Examples: Parent has many rules and regulations; Parent assigns child fixed bedtime hour.
4. Discourages Versus Encourages Emotional Dependency on Parents.
   Examples: Parent encourages child to make contact with other adults; Parent isn't overprotective of child.
5. Discourages Versus Encourages Infantile Behavior.
   Examples: Parent discourages child from exhibiting babyish speech and mannerisms; Parent demands mature table behavior at mealtime.
6. Provides Flexibility and Clarity Versus Inflexibility and Lack of Clarity in Parental Role.
   Examples: Parent can specify aims and methods for how child should do stuff; Parent has stable, firm views about things.
7. Provides Firm Versus Lax Enforcement Policy.
   Examples: Parent uses negative sanctions when defied by child; Parent requires child to pay attention.

8. Treats Obedience as an Important Positive Value Versus Treats Obedience as an Unimportant or Negative Value.
   Examples: Parent forces confrontation with child when child disobeys; Parent willingly exercises power to obtain obedience from child.

9. Promotes Respect for Established Authority Versus Seeks to Develop a Cooperative Working Relationship with Child.
   Examples: Parent believes parents should take precedence; Parent does not share decision-making power with child.

10. Shows Confidence Versus Lack of Confidence in Self as a Parent.
    Examples: Parent regards self as competent person; Parent believes child must defer to parental expertise.

11. Encourages or Discourages Independence.
    Examples: Parent encourages independent actions; Parent asks for child's opinions.

12. Encourages Versus Discourages Verbal Exchange and the Use of Reason.
    Examples: Child disobedience results in parent giving additional explanation; Parent encourages verbal give and take.

13. Reluctant Versus Willing to Express Anger or Displeasure to Child.
    Examples: Parent feels shameful and embarrassed after expressing anger; Parent hides annoyance or impatience when child disobeys.

14. Promotes Individuality Versus Social Acceptability.
    Examples: Parent promotes individuality in child; Parent expresses own individuality.

15. Expresses Punitive Versus Nurturant Behavior.
    Examples: Parent becomes inaccessible when displeased; Parent disciplines harshly.

Whew! That's a bunch to handle. You better learn it too, because there's gonna be a pop quiz later on today. Anyway, from these initial 15 practices of parenting, Baumrind's statistical procedure found the following reduced sets of parenting behaviors to be most important for mothers and fathers. Baumrind used slightly different names here because some of the dimensions of parenting in the reduced sets arose out of certain combinations of items from the larger set. But the main point, as you can see, is that the reduced set of the most important parent practices that turned up for mothers was very similar to the reduced set that turned up for fathers, with only a couple of exceptions.

Important Parenting Practices for Mothers	*Important Parenting Practices for Fathers*
1. Firm Enforcement	1. Firm Enforcement
2. Encourages Independence and Individuality	2. Encourages Independence and Individuality
3. Passively Acceptant	3. Passively Acceptant
4. Rejecting	4. Rejecting
5. Self-confident, Secure, Potent Parental Behavior	5. Promotes Nonconformity
	6. Authoritarianism

Most of these aspects of parenting are self-explanatory. But I think a couple need a little further explanation. First, *passively acceptant* meant that parents were almost always outwardly accepting of the child, even when she disobeyed. They might get angry at the child, but if they did they hid their anger from her. And if they didn't hide their anger, then afterward they felt rather embarrassed about not doing so. Also, they tended to avoid using negative sanctions when the child disobeyed. Second, *promoting nonconformity*, which was important only for fathers, meant that some fathers tended to express their own individuality, and encouraged their children to do the same. Third, *authoritarianism*, which again was important only for fathers, meant that some fathers tended not to listen to their children and tended to take a very strict, inflexible stance whenever interacting with them.

Baumrind also discovered a third reduced set of parenting measures. She called this third set "Joint Parenting Behaviors" because they didn't so much reflect the behaviors of one of the parents as much as they reflected the *climate of expectation* established by both parents together in combination with how they structured the child's environment. These 5 joint parenting behaviors pretty much mirror the same aspects of parenting from the original set of 15. So they share the same names. They were:

Important Joint Parenting Aspects
1. Expects Participation in Household Chores
2. Provides Enriched Environment
3. Is Directive
4. Discourages Emotional Dependency
5. Discourages Infantile Behavior

RESULTS

Baumrind's first goal in the study was to identify valid patterns of parenting that could then be used in the next step to predict the child outcome measures. She started out with the three parenting patterns she had identified in her previous research (authoritarian, authoritative, and permissive); but remember, those patterns were identified from measures that came from the children. So an important question was whether or not the same parenting styles would come out of the parents' actual parenting behaviors. It turns out that by and large they did, but there were a couple of subtypes of parenting styles that emerged in this study that didn't come up in the earlier research. We'll take a look at these styles and substyles one at a time. But let me warn you. These styles were established through some complicated scoring procedures. I don't expect you to memorize the definitions of each style and substyle, but I present them here anyway so you can get a good sense of the level of parenting complexity Baumrind was dealing with. What most child psychologists remember from the Baumrind study is her main three parenting styles.

Parenting Styles

The Authoritarian Parent. The goal of the **authoritarian parent** is complete obedience. She favors forceful, **punitive** discipline when the child's will conflicts with her own. She doesn't believe in give and take and believes that her word should always be final. Baumrind found two subtypes of the authoritarian parenting style: *authoritarian–not rejecting* and *authoritarian–rejecting/neglecting*.

The *authoritarian–not rejecting* parenting style was said to describe the household when (1) both parents scored above the midpoint on Firm Enforcement, (2) both parents scored below the midpoint on Encourages Independence and Individuality, (3) both parents scored below the midpoint on Passive Acceptant, and (4) the father scored in the bottom third of Nonconformity or in the top third on Authoritarianism. Stated in less technical terms, these parents enforced rules very firmly, they discouraged independence and individuality, they didn't hide their anger or frustration, and the father demanded conformity. Ten families had this parenting style.

The *authoritarian–rejecting/neglecting* parenting style was defined as all of the above plus (1) both parents scored above the midpoint on Rejecting and (2) the family scored below the midpoint on Provides Enriched Environment. So in other words, not only were these parents as authoritarian as the first group, they were additionally rejecting of their children and they expended little effort in trying to stimulate their children's minds. Sixteen families had this parenting style.

The Authoritative Parent.   The primary goal of the **authoritative parent** is the personal growth of her child. She sets rules firmly but is willing to change them in cooperation with the child. She values her child's individuality and opinions. She also believes that when rules are set, they should be accompanied by an explanation the child can understand. Baumrind also found two subtypes of this style of parenting: *authoritative–not nonconforming* and *authoritative–nonconforming*.

The *authoritative–not nonconforming* parenting style, despite its awkward name, was similar to the authoritarian styles in two respects. It was defined as (1) having both parents score above the midpoint on Firm Enforcement or having one parent score in the upper third and (2) having both parents score below the midpoint on Passive Acceptant. But the authoritative–not nonconforming parenting style was additionally defined as having (3) both parents score above the midpoint on Encourages Independence and Individuality. In other words, these parents had firm rules and they tended to express their anger and frustration openly when they experienced it, but they also placed a very high value on promoting the emotional growth of their children as separate and autonomous people. Nineteen families had this style.

The *authoritative–nonconforming* parenting style was the same as authoritative–not nonconforming except that (1) one of the parents scored in the upper third on Firm Enforcement and one of the parents scored below the midpoint on Firm Enforcement, (2) the father scored below the midpoint on Rejecting and Authoritarianism, and (3) the father scored in the top third on Promotes Nonconformity. In other words, these parents were basically the same as the authoritative–not nonconforming group accept that the father was extremely responsive to his child and encouraged the child to question authority.

The Permissive Parent.   The primary goal of the **permissive parent** is to serve as a resource for her to child to use as he wishes. She is nonpunitive, completely accepting, and always positive toward the general whims of her child. She places few demands on her child for helping with the housework and behaving socially appropriately, believing that her child should regulate his own activities. In Baumrind's classification of the subtypes of permissive parenting, she points out that no parents fit the perfect stereotype of the completely permissive parent. Rather, they differed by degrees in one way or another from what we might normally think of as a parent who was really, really permissive.

For example, the *nonconforming* (*not permissive and not authoritative*) parenting style had many features of the prototypical permissive parent. This style was defined as having (1) at least one parent scoring below the midpoint on Firm Enforcement, (2) at least one parent scoring above midpoint on Encourages Independence and Individuality, (3) the father scoring below the midpoint on Rejecting, (4) both parents scoring in the top third on Encourages Independence and Individuality *or* the father scoring in the top third on Promotes Nonconformity, and (5) the father scoring below the midpoint on Authoritarianism. What this means in normal English is that although the parents didn't exactly enforce any household rules, they at least tried to encourage their children to be independent, and at least one of the parents tried not to be rejecting. And if both parents didn't encourage independence, the father at least tried to promote nonconformity and to encourage his children to question authority. This style characterized the parents of 15 children.

In the *permissive* (*not nonconforming*) style, a more truly permissive style of parenting emerged. This parenting style was diagnosed if (1) both parents were below the midpoint on Firm Enforcement, and (2) at least one parent was in the top third of Passive-Acceptant, and (3) at least one parent was in the bottom third in terms of Rejecting. In addition, households with this parenting style showed two out of the following three criteria: (a) at least one parent scored below midpoint on Expects Participation in Household Chores, (b) at least one parent scored below the midpoint on being Directive, and (c) at least one parent scored in the bottom third on Discourages Infantile Behavior. In other words, these parents didn't enforce rules firmly and tended not to expect children to participate in household duties. Moreover, they showed an across-the-board acceptance of their children, and they even tolerated it when their 4-year-olds acted like little babies. Are you getting the picture? Fourteen families had this parenting style.

Rejecting-Neglecting. Finally, there was a group of parents who had a rather disturbing style of parenting. Baumrind used the label "rejecting-neglecting" to describe the habits of parents who scored (1) below the midpoint for Encourages Independence and Individuality, and (2) above the midpoint for Rejecting. If both parents didn't score above the midpoint for Rejecting, then they were still defined as rejecting-neglecting if either (a) one parent scored in the top third on Rejecting, or (b) the household was scored in the bottom third on Enrichment of the Child's Environment and in the top third on Discourages Emotional Dependency. In other words, not only did these parents *not* provide very much structure for their children in the form of providing rules, but they were in fact quite rejecting of their children and provided little guidance for nurturing their independence. Eleven sets of parents had this parenting style.

Relationships Between Parenting Styles and Child Outcome Measures

After Baumrind established that it was possible to identify different parenting styles from the parents' own behaviors, she next examined whether these styles led to desirable or undesirable qualities in the children. Remember, a desirable quality was one that would help the child adapt to human society. Although she measured seven general child behavior characteristics, she combined these seven characteristics to form two even more general characteristics that she believed really got to the heart of the most important, most societally adaptive outcome measures. The first she called social responsibility; the second she called independence. Social responsibility is highly valued in most (if not all) cultures, and more or less reflects how much children respect and show concern for the well-being of other people. She created her measure of social responsibility by combining children's scores on three of the seven behavior types we talked about earlier. Specifically, she combined scores from the behavior types of *hostile-friendly, resistive-cooperative,* and *achievement oriented–not achievement oriented.* Children with the highest social responsibility scores were those who were rated as friendly, cooperative, and achievement oriented. And, of course, children with the lowest social responsibility scores were those who were rated as hostile, resistive, and not achievement oriented. Working independently is also highly valued in many cultures, especially mainstream Western culture. So she reasoned that children with high levels of independence would also be well prepared for entry into mainstream Western culture. Her measure of independence was created by combining children's scores on the remaining four of the original seven behavior types; specifically, *domineering-tractable, dominant-submissive, purposive-aimless,* and *independent-suggestible.* Children high in independence would score high on tractable, dominant, purposive, and independent, whereas children low in independence would score high on domineering, submissive, aimless, and suggestible. Let's take a look at how the children turned out as a result of the types of parents they had, in light of Baumrind's original hypotheses.

Hypothesis 1: Baumrind thought the children of authoritarian parents, relative to other children, would be lacking in independence, but not in social responsibility. In terms of social responsibility, Baumrind expected children of authoritarian parents to be no different from other children. Baumrind found that girls of authoritarian parents were, in fact, significantly less independent than the girls of authoritative parents. Boys of authoritarian parents were also less independent than the boys of authoritative parents, but not to the same degree as girls. Boys of authoritarian parents were also less socially responsible than boys of authoritative parents, not because the authoritarian boys were especially low in social responsibility, but because the boys from the authoritative households were exceptionally high in it. In addition, she found that girls with authoritarian parents were less achievement oriented than girls with authoritative parents.

Hypothesis 2: Baumrind expected the children of authoritative parents, relative to children of all other parents but authoritarian parents, to be socially responsible, and relative to children of all other parents but nonconforming parents, to be independent. As it turned out, boys of authoritative parents were significantly more socially responsible than boys with authoritarian or permissive parents. They were also more friendly than boys with nonconforming parents. Girls with authoritative parents were slightly more achievement oriented than girls with authoritarian parents. But not all authoritative parents produced children with desirable behaviors. Children from authoritative-nonconforming parents were actually rather hostile to their friends and disrespectful of adult authority!

Hypothesis 3: Baumrind expected the children of permissive parents, relative to the children of authoritarian and authoritative but not to the children of nonconforming parents, to be lacking in social responsibility. These children were also expected not to score high in independence. As she predicted, Baumrind found that boys of permissive parents were lower in social responsibility than boys from other parenting styles. Specifically, they were lower in social responsibility than boys with authoritative parents. But they weren't lower in social responsibility when compared to boys with authoritarian parents. Girls with permissive parents, on the other hand, were not especially lacking in social responsibility. However, girls with permissive parents were lacking in independence compared to girls with authoritative parents. Girls with permissive parents were no lower in independence than girls with authoritarian parents. Finally, boys with permissive parents were somewhat less **purposive** (that is, interested in obtaining goals) than boys with authoritative parents, and they were far less independent than boys with nonconforming parents.

Hypothesis 4: Baumrind believed the children of nonconforming parents, relative to the children of authoritarian and authoritative parents, but not to the children of permissive parents, would be lacking in social responsibility. She also expected that, relative to the children of authoritarian and permissive parents, but not to the children of authoritative parents, children of nonconforming parents would be more independent. Contrary to Baumrind's expectation, children of nonconforming parents were not lacking in social responsibility compared with children of any other parenting style. Moreover, boys with nonconforming parents were way more achievement oriented and way more independent than boys with permissive parents. Still, girls with nonconforming parents were less independent than girls with authoritative parents.

DISCUSSION

As you can see, the patterns of findings are very complicated. It's even more complicated when you consider that different parenting styles sometimes influence boys and girls differently. But here are some general conclusions that Baumrind made about the different socialization practices for boys and girls, and their impacts on two global types of socially desirable behaviors that children might express.

Social Responsibility

If you want your kids to be socially responsible, then your best bet is to adopt an authoritative approach to parenting. Prior to Baumrind's research, authorities on parenting believed that having a strict style of parenting would almost automatically result in aggressive and delinquent behavior. But this is obviously not the case. The parents who, in Baumrind's study, were strict produced socially responsible children so long as they accompanied their strictness with positive acceptance of their children and provided their children with explanations for their rules. But it's important that the authoritative parenting style you adopt not be of the nonconforming type. Authoritative-nonconforming parents produced children who were lacking in social responsibility.

Independence

If you want your kids to be independent as they grow up, then your best bet is also to choose an authoritative parenting style. Prior to Baumrind's research, authorities on parenting also believed that having a strict parenting style would lead to passivity and dependence. But Baumrind found quite the opposite. She wrote, "It appears that children are not that easily cowed by parental pressure." Authoritative parents tended to have a lot of characteristics that were likely to promote independence in their children. For one thing, they provided environments that were stimulating to their children. Stimulating environments are likely to promote interest and exploration on the part of the children, which, of course, is part of the definition of being independent. Authoritative parents also rewarded individuality and self-expression in their children, even when the children displayed what we might call "willfulness," so long as the willfulness didn't cause harm of some kind. Authoritarian parents, on the other hand, were more likely to punish willful children whether or not their willfulness would cause any harm. From the perspective of the authoritarian parent, disobedience of any kind was not tolerated. In contrast to authoritative and authoritarian parents, permissive parents really didn't reward children differently for displaying either a tolerable or an intolerable kind of willfulness. As Baumrind put it, "Permissive parents instead would accede to the child's demands until their patience was exhausted and then punish the child, sometimes very harshly."

The point is that strictness by itself isn't so bad, it's *how* the parent is strict that makes all the difference. If strictness is accompanied by good reasons, reasons that children can understand, then the outcome is good. Children will understand why the rules are in place, and they'll further understand when it's permissible to break a rule. Consequently, authoritative parents will understand why children are breaking the rule, and they'll tolerate a violation of it. And then when children see their parents accepting violations of the rule when there is good reason, the parents are serving as a nice model for the children themselves to emulate when they make their own transition to parenthood.

CONCLUSIONS

Baumrind revolutionized child psychology because she showed that different styles of parenting can be identified, and that different parenting styles can lead to better or worse outcomes in children. She also showed that socialization practices could affect boys and girls differently. Perhaps the single most important finding her work produced was that an authoritative style of parenting produced the best outcomes. And it should come as no surprise that once her work started getting published and circulating throughout the child development community, many parents around the country began employing parenting techniques associated with an authoritative parenting style. And why shouldn't they? Doesn't everyone want to have competent, well-adapted, successful children?

However, at the risk of sounding like a scratched CD, remember that Baumrind's parenting scheme came from a sample of white, high-IQ, highly educated, middle- and upper-class American families from the Berkeley, California, community. Although her findings have pretty much held up over the decades for white, educated, middle- and upper-class families in other parts of the United States, a number of researchers have questioned the value of an authoritative parenting style for other cultural groups. As noted before, the problem is that what counts as a "good" and adaptive outcome behavior can vary considerably from culture to culture. In the United States, for example, we value independence very highly. We all strive to "be the best we can be." We're encouraged to question authority, and to think for ourselves. In elementary school classrooms, children who know the right answers and say them aloud (provided they raise their hands first) are praised and encouraged. But this kind of independence-fostering isn't seen as a valuable socialization goal in other cultures. In many Asian classrooms, for example, children might get into trouble if they do something to distinguish themselves from their peers. In these Asian cultures, collaboration and cooperation are seen as "better" outcome measures than independence. Consequently, the same authoritative parenting style that serves many European American children well for fostering independence may serve many Asian and Asian American children poorly for the same reason. Parents from different cultures have different goals in their parenting. An Asian parenting goal includes producing children who will contribute to the cooperative efforts of the society, rather than finding ways to personally benefit from it.

Even in the United States there are some environments where children would gain little from authoritative parenting. Consider households located in high-crime neighborhoods or neighborhoods high in gang activity. Kids raised in these kinds of conditions aren't likely to benefit much from being warm and fuzzy. Rather, a parenting style that nurtures toughness and aggressiveness may be far more adaptive. And so a style of parenting that shares many characteristics of an authoritarian style of parenting may be called for.

Since Baumrind's original work, there has been a great deal of additional refinement of the basic parenting-style concepts, much of it done by Baumrind herself. These days, researchers point to two dimensions of parenting that are especially crucial in identifying four basic parenting styles. One dimension is *responsiveness*. A responsive parent is one who acknowledges, accepts, and tries to satisfy his children's needs. The other dimension is *demandingness*. A demanding parent has high expectations about the level of maturity his children display, as well as how much responsibility they take for caring for themselves and for following household rules. By crossing these two dimensions, you get four parenting styles that have much in common with Baumrind's original parenting types. In tabular form, they look like this:

	High in Demandingness	Low in Demandingness
High in Responsiveness	Authoritative	Permissive-Indulgent
Low in Responsiveness	Authoritarian	Permissive-Indifferent

The recent work also continues to show that parenting styles influence children's outcome behaviors into adolescence and beyond. Now that Baumrind's original sample of children has had a chance to grow older, it's possible to look at longer-term influences on parenting style. In a 1991 study, for example, Baumrind reported that "authoritative parents who were highly demanding and highly responsive were remarkably successful in protecting their adolescents from problem drug use and in generating competence."

　　We haven't spent much time talking about how authoritarian parents discipline their children, but given their high demandingness and low responsiveness, it's not surprising that their disciplinary tactics rely heavily on power-assertive techniques like spanking. Authoritarian parents, by definition, *make* their children obey, through sheer power if necessary. But based on Baumrind's research, we know that you may not have to cause pain in your children in order to socialize them! Except for the adaptive advantages that authoritarian parenting provides for some children in some cultures, in mainstream American culture, authoritarian parenting generally works against children's successful transition to adulthood. Authoritative parents rarely resort to spanking as a means of discipline, and their children turn out to be the happiest, most outgoing, most successful, most independent, and most socially responsible children. And authoritative parents are just as high in demandingness as authoritarian parents. If there is a moral to this story, it might be something like, "You don't have to spank your kids to get them to turn out okay." To my largish, male athlete student who says he turned out okay despite being spanked, I can't help wondering how he might have turned out otherwise.

Bibliography

Baumrind, D. (1991). The influence of parenting style on adolescent competence and substance use. *Journal of Early Adolescence, 11,* 56–95.

Bradley, C. R. (1998). Child rearing practices in African American families: A study of the disciplinary practices of African American parents. *Journal of Multicultural Counseling and Development, 26,* 273–281.

Questions for Discussion

1. There's a lot of concern among parenting researchers not to make assumptions that parenting styles for one group, culture, or ethnicity are equally appropriate for other groups, cultures, or ethnicities. Is it possible that there is any single parenting practice or behavior that would be good for all people?

2. Do you think Baumrind's findings from 30 years ago would still be applicable today? If not, why not?

3. Choose three of your favorite TV families and see if you can classify the parents in those families according to Baumrind's classifications. Do the children in the TV family resemble the children in Baumrind's study, in terms of the parents' styles of parenting?

4. Would the effectiveness of a parenting style differ in a single-parent versus a two-parent household?

14

Monkey See, Monkey Do

TRANSMISSION OF AGGRESSION THROUGH IMITATION OF AGGRESSIVE MODELS.

Bandura, A., Ross, D., & Ross, S. (1961). *Journal of Abnormal and Social Psychology, 63,* 575–582. (RANK 9)

It was the middle of the evening on a blustery November day. The warmth of summer was long gone, and the dinner bell signaled the onset of darkness as reliably as it signaled the day's final meal. My wife was working her normal lunchtime-to-bedtime schedule as one of the few clinical psychologists in town, and she wasn't due home for another 3 hours. My 2-year-old daughter Rachel was running around the house as part of her normal after-dinner routine, stopping just long enough to announce her presence at each of the various play stations we set up for her. And me, I was adjusting to my new role as evening homemaker and full-time father.

There aren't a whole lot of mid-evening recreational opportunities available to you in a small, rural, Midwestern town, especially when the cold and darkness of winter set in. And when you have a 2-year-old with more go-power than the Energizer Bunny, there's little chance she'll slip into an accidental slumber. You might as well forget about catching up on your office work. So that night, I decided to do what any rational parent would do under the same circumstances. I pulled out my Sega Genesis gaming system and resumed my career as a contender in the World Heavyweight Boxing circuit.

I was making good progress in the game, working my way up the ranks—10th, 9th, 8th. The "fights" were getting harder, but I was developing quite a reputation in the virtual world as a KO king. Then it happened. Right in the middle of a 10-round event, catching me completely off guard, my daughter caught me in the left ear with a strong right hook! Despite my pain, I began rolling with laughter. It was too funny! But where on Earth did she get this inspiration? I had never taught her to box. We had never attended a boxing match (virtual boxing is the only kind I condone). And it wasn't something she could've picked up off the street because we never let her go out onto the street. The only possible explanation was that she was motivated by the two cartoon boxers going at it on the TV screen. The power of video!

The question of where human **aggression** comes from has occupied the world's greatest thinkers for thousands of years. The popular opinion is that it's either in our genes or learned from our culture. But, hello, what other possibility is there? These were the same answers offered two thousand years ago. Fortunately, within the last half-century, scholars have made some real progress in understanding the origins of human aggression by bringing the full arsenal of science to bear on the question.

Albert Bandura has been at the forefront of these scientific efforts to explain the origins of aggression. In fact, his 1961 article, with coauthors Dorothea Ross and Sheila Ross, was largely responsible for starting the whole thing off. To appreciate the revolutionary character of this study, ranked ninth overall, you really need to have a sense of the social-scientific odds Bandura was working against when he launched his search for the origins of aggression.

At the time of the study's publication, American psychology was pretty much dominated by behavioral psychologists who firmly disavowed the importance, and sometimes even the existence, of internal cognitive processes. Basically, these behaviorists *thought* thinking was irrelevant for psychology. Ironic, huh? Although many American psychologists had heard of Piaget, the wholesale acceptance of Piaget's theory of cognitive development in the United States was at least a decade off. The prevailing view was that learning took place not as a result of the mental construction of conceptual networks, as Piaget proposed, but as a result of behaviors that were rewarded or punished. The idea was that if you did a behavior that was rewarded by someone or something, you would be more likely to do that behavior in the future. If you did a behavior that was punished by someone or something, you would be less likely to do that behavior in the future. What you thought or felt about your behaviors didn't matter. The behaviorist climate didn't have room for thoughts or feelings. In short, human activity, and the psychology that addressed it, amounted to little more than an amalgam of behaviors and the rewards and punishments that molded them. For our purposes, the behaviorist view of aggression was that aggressive people became aggressive because they were rewarded for aggressive behaviors. End of story.

Now along comes Bandura. Bandura's claim to fame as a revolutionary in the field of child psychology resulted from his work on the modeling of aggression. Bandura can probably best be described as a crossover psychologist because he was a social behaviorist dabbling in the affairs of developmental child psychology. But it was his interest in children's socialization specifically that made his behaviorist presence palatable to child psychologists.

Even though Bandura may have looked like a behaviorist to those on the outside, he himself was struggling with behaviorist principles, especially the idea that behaviors were learned or eliminated exclusively through reward or punishment. Would we permit an adolescent to learn to drive by trial and error? he questioned. Would we trust a police recruit to manage a firearm without extensive training? he wondered. Of course not. The adolescent and the police recruit have to be taught— through instruction and demonstration.

Bandura concluded that there had to be more to the story than learning through reward and punishment, and modeling was a particularly powerful candidate to fill the gap. In modeling the learner adjusts his own behavior so as to copy or imitate the behavior of the teacher. Modeling had the potential to be far more effective than punishment/reward systems for learning complicated behaviors. As you probably know, most activity classes use modeling as the primary means of instruction. The ballet teacher models the pirouette, the sensei models the roundhouse kick, and the baseball coach models fielding techniques. It's not that rewards and punishment don't also mold our learning, it's just that there are other routes of learning to consider. And some of these routes may be exceptionally powerful.

INTRODUCTION

In their study, Bandura, Ross, and Ross set out to test the hypothesis that aggression was one type of behavior that could be learned through modeling. They focused on children, under the assumption that a large chunk of our adult personality is molded by our childhood experiences. Other research in the 1950s and 1960s had successfully demonstrated the effect of modeling in children, but that research had never tested whether children would carry modeled behaviors into new situations. And the behaviors that were learned didn't come close to resembling aggression.

So Bandura, Ross, and Ross set out to explore whether children who observed aggression in one situation would then behave aggressively in a different situation, even when the aggressive model was no longer present. Why this carryover effect was important will become evident later on. But their expectations were clear: "According to the prediction, subjects exposed to aggressive models would reproduce aggressive acts resembling those of their models and would differ in this respect both from subjects who observed nonaggressive models and from those who had no prior exposure to any models."

Bandura, Ross, and Ross also included a couple of sex variables. Even as early as the 1950s, research was showing that parents were likely to reward "sex-appropriate" behaviors in their children. Bandura, Ross, and Ross reasoned, therefore, that because aggression is a masculine behavior, boys would be more inclined than girls to imitate an aggressive model. Further, they reasoned that children were probably used to being rewarded for imitating same-sex parents and punished for imitating opposite-sex parents. Accordingly, they thought children ought to be more likely to imitate behavior coming from a person of the same sex. So they included both a male and a female model. The predictions were simple: Boys should be more inclined to imitate aggressiveness if it were modeled by a male, and girls should be more inclined to imitate aggressiveness if it were modeled by a female.

METHOD

Participants

Thirty-six boys and 36 girls participated in the experiment. They ranged in age from 37 to 69 months, with an average age of 52 months (about 4.3 years old).

Two adults played the role of the model, one male and one female. These same two people played the role of the model for all 72 children. (Bandura himself played the role of the male.)

Materials

The materials used in the first part of the experiment consisted of potatoes, picture stickers, a Tinkertoy set, a mallet, and a 5-foot inflated Bobo doll. A couple of these items may need a little further explanation. The potatoes were used to create ink stamps. If you cut potatoes in half, you can make cute little designs in their flesh by carving out excess potato material. If you then dip the face of this design in ink, you can stamp out on paper a whole series of copies of the design you just created. So potatoes were used here as an art material. Tinkertoy sets aren't as popular as they used to be. In the old days they consisted of little wooden sticks, blocks, and wheels and such, and were used to build things. (These days Tinkertoy sets are made of plastic.) Finally, we have the Bobo doll. The Bobo doll was so central to Bandura's experiments that these days they're usually called "the Bobo doll studies." A Bobo doll was simply an inflatable plastic doll that had the likeness of Bobo the Clown printed on the surface. It also had a compartment filled with sand built into its base that kept it standing upright; so even if you pushed it over, it would pop right back up again. At 5 feet tall, it loomed larger than most of the children in the study.

Procedure

Forty-eight children were assigned to the "experimental condition" and from there to either an "aggressive" or a "nonaggressive" condition. Children in the aggressive condition saw a person behaving aggressively; this person was called the "aggressive model." Children in the nonaggressive condition saw a "nonaggressive model." Half of the children in each group were boys, and half were girls. Finally, half of these children saw a female model and half saw a male model. Altogether there were eight possible groups:

- Girls who saw an aggressive female model
- Girls who saw an aggressive male model
- Girls who saw a nonaggressive female model
- Girls who saw a nonaggressive male model
- Boys who saw an aggressive female model
- Boys who saw an aggressive male model
- Boys who saw a nonaggressive female model
- Boys who saw a nonaggressive male model

There was an additional group of 24 children who were assigned to the "control condition." These children saw no model at all but were otherwise treated exactly the same as the children who saw the models. These "control children" served as a comparison group, and with them Bandura, Ross, and Ross could determine what children would do if they saw no model at all.

Experimental Conditions

Each of the 48 children in the experimental conditions was taken, one at a time, to the experimental room by the experimenter. When the child and experimenter arrived at the room, a stranger would be standing in the hallway just outside the room. The experimenter invited the stranger into the room to "come and join the game." The child was then taken to a small table in one corner of the room and shown how to play with the potato prints and the stickers. The experimenter then took the stranger to a different small table in the opposite corner of the room. Here was found the Tinkertoy set, the mallet, and the Bobo doll. The experimenter told the stranger that these toys were for him/her to play with, and then left the room.

Nonaggressive Condition.   In the nonaggressive condition, the stranger assembled the Tinkertoys "in a quiet subdued manner totally ignoring the Bobo doll." At this point, we can now call the stranger a "model" because s/he was "modeling" behavior for the benefit of the child.

Aggressive Condition.   In contrast, the model in the aggressive condition played with the Tinkertoys for only about a minute, and then began beating up the Bobo doll. The original description of the beating-up procedure is too funny not to quote in its entirety. "The model laid Bobo on its side, sat on it and punched it repeatedly in the nose. The model then raised the Bobo doll, picked up the mallet and struck the doll on the head. Following the mallet aggression, the model tossed the doll up in the air aggressively and kicked it about the room." This beating-up sequence was repeated three times, and was interspersed with verbally aggressive phrases such as: "Sock him in the nose," "Hit him down," "Throw him in the air," "Kick him," and "Pow." Two nonaggressive comments were also made: "He keeps coming back for more" and "He sure is a tough fella."

After 10 minutes, the experimenter returned to the experimental room, told the model/stranger good-bye, and informed the child that she would be going to another room with games. The other room was located in a separate building. It was in that other room where the children were tested for their levels of aggression.

Aggression Arousal

Bandura, Ross, and Ross wanted to test the children for aggressive behavior under conditions that would allow them to express it. Bandura realized that when children were around unfamiliar, official-looking adults, they might be inclined to put on their best behavior. But this would be a problem because if they did put on their best behavior, their efforts at being polite might override any aggressiveness they might be harboring, and Bandura's study might be foiled. For that reason, Bandura, Ross, and Ross set up an artificial situation that would more or less *pull* aggression out of the children. So they did something they knew would have the effect of ticking the children off. Here's what they did.

As the children were escorted to the second experimental room, they had to pass through a smaller room, called an anteroom. The anteroom contained a number of highly attractive toys, including a jet fighter plane, a cable car, a colorful spinning top, and a doll set complete with wardrobe, doll carriage, and baby crib. Notice the equal representation of sex-typed toys. The experimenter told the children they could stop and play with these toys, which they proceeded to do. But after about 2 minutes, just when the children were really getting involved with the toys, she remarked that these were her "very best toys, that she did not let just anyone play with them, and that she had decided to reserve these toys for the other children." In other words, the children had just been dissed. The experimenter explained that although they weren't allowed to play with the toys in the anteroom, they were free to play with any of the toys in the main room, which they subsequently proceeded to enter.

Test for Delayed Imitation

In the experimental room, the children found a number of toys. Some of the toys were similar to those used by the aggressive model: a 3-foot-tall Bobo doll and a mallet. Others were toys not used by the aggressive model, but that still could be used for aggressive purposes: two dart guns and a tetherball suspended from the ceiling with a face painted on it. Still other toys were ones that weren't likely to be used for aggressive purposes: a tea set, crayons and coloring paper, a ball, two dolls, three bears, cars and trucks, and plastic farm animals. The play materials were arranged exactly the same way for every child that entered the room.

Response Measures

Bandura, Ross, and Ross measured aggressive behavior in several different ways. By my count, they used seven different measures, including (1) the amount of physical aggression that was imitated, (2) the amount of verbal aggression that was imitated, and (3) the amount of verbal nonaggression that was imitated. During the process of scoring the aggression, the authors realized that some of the imitated behaviors were only partially imitated, but they decided to count them anyway. The most common partial imitations were (4) sitting on the Bobo doll without any additional aggression and (5) using the mallet to hit other things in the room besides the Bobo doll. Finally, there were instances in which children behaved aggressively, but without imitating any of the model's behaviors. These behaviors included (6) using verbal and physical assaults invented by the children themselves (saying "Shoot the Bobo," "Cut him," or "Stupid ball" or punching the tetherball), and (7) shooting the dart gun at real or imaginary things.

RESULTS

So what were the results of the study? First of all, kids who saw the aggressive model were off the charts in imitating the aggressiveness of the aggressive models compared to kids who saw no model or who saw the nonaggressive model. The aggressive-model kids were also more likely to go around banging on stuff with the mallet than were the kids who saw the nonaggressive model. But importantly, these kids weren't aggressive across the board. They didn't run around shooting things with the dart guns any more than did the other children, for example. So to the extent that aggressive-model kids were aggressive, they were mostly aggressive in the same ways as the model they observed.

In terms of sex differences, boys were more likely to engage in physical aggression than were girls; but boys and girls did not differ from one another in verbal aggression. Moreover, boys were significantly more likely than girls to imitate the male model; but the reverse was not true for female models.

One interesting finding was that children who watched the male, nonaggressive model turned out to be significantly *less* aggressive than the children in the control group (who saw no model). As the authors described it, "[I]n relation to the control group, subjects exposed to the nonaggressive male model performed significantly less imitative physical aggression, less imitative verbal aggression, less mallet aggression, less non-imitative physical and verbal aggression, and they were less inclined to punch the Bobo doll." So not only did the *aggressive* model cause kids to show *more* aggression than kids in the control group, the *nonaggressive* model caused kids to show *less* aggression than kids in the control group.

DISCUSSION

The most revolutionary product of Bandura's study was the finding that children were capable of using models as a means for picking up new behaviors they otherwise wouldn't have produced. This was largely unheard of in the behaviorist-dominated scientific community at the time. Of course, laypeople were familiar with the power of imitation, as evidenced by the popularity of the phrase "monkey see, monkey do." But in the old-school scientific community, modeling wasn't seen as very important. Old-school scientists believed that kids only came across new behaviors by accident; and only if behaviors were rewarded would they continue. But from this point of view, it was essential that the kid produce the behavior himself, and be directly rewarded for doing so. Now along comes Bandura claiming that children can pick up behaviors almost magically simply by watching other people. Not only that, but they produced behaviors without being rewarded for them!

The social-political implications of these findings were HUGE! Not only was it clear that children could pick up aggressive behaviors simply by watching someone else, but they applied these newly acquired aggressive behaviors to new situations when no other aggressive people were present. Apparently, seeing aggression happen in somebody else was enough to bring it out in a child at a later point in time. In Bandura's study, the "later point in time" was later that same day. But an extremely important question raised by this finding was, How long would these aggressive tendencies last? A day? A week? The implications were obvious. If a child saw Bugs Bunny knock over Elmer Fudd on Saturday-morning cartoons, would he carry over that aggression into recess on Monday afternoon? The finding that children could delay their imitation of aggression had wide-ranging implications indeed.

But for whatever reason, all of this was predicated on the aggressive model's being male. A closer look at the results showed that the female model didn't have much success in getting kids to imitate *her* aggressive behavior. Why would this be? One possible explanation for why the male model of aggression was more successful than the female model of aggression was that the male was modeling behaviors viewed to be sex-appropriate. Females weren't supposed to be aggressive. In fact, when the female modeled aggression, the children seemed shocked. They made comments like, "You should have seen what that girl did in there. She was acting like a man. I never saw a girl act like that before. She was punching and fighting but no swearing." Comments about the male model focused much less on the inappropriateness of aggression than on *how well* the aggression was carried out. One girl said, "That man is a strong fighter, he punched and punched and he could hit Bobo right down to the floor and if Bobo got up he said, 'Punch your nose.' He's a good fighter like Daddy."

Of course, all this focus on the modeling of aggression ignores the other side of the coin. Children who observed the quiet model were calmer and less aggressive than the other kids. Apparently, when quietness is modeled, quietness is the behavior exhibited. Bandura, Ross, and Ross concluded that "exposure to inhibited models not only decreases the probability of occurrence of aggressive behavior but also generally restricts the range of behavior emitted by the subjects."

CONCLUSIONS

Follow-up Study

Before I go on to discuss the impact of Bandura's study on the rest of the world (indeed its core findings are under heated debate to this very day), I'd like to acquaint you with a follow-up experiment Bandura published in 1965. I alluded earlier to the possibility that children might imitate aggression modeled in a television cartoon. But this suggestion may have been a bit premature since Bandura's first study didn't address whether children would imitate *televised* aggressive models. However, he remedied this shortcoming with a 1965 follow-up experiment, in which he had children watch a televised model engage in aggressive behavior. He also tested what would happen if children saw the model receive a consequence for his aggressive actions. So Bandura had children view an aggressive model on TV under one of three conditions: Either the model was punished for beating up the Bobo doll, he was rewarded for beating up the Bobo doll, or he received no consequences for beating up the Bobo doll. The results revealed that children who saw the televised model rewarded for his aggression were themselves likely to behave aggressively. The importance of this study is that television can be a powerful medium for transmitting aggressive actions to passively observing children.

Television, Video Games, and Violent Lyrics

As I already mentioned, Bandura's results were huge. I suppose on the one hand they only showed that people will copy the behavior of other people. Duh. But more than that, they showed that aggressive behavior can be copied, and that young children will do the copying. In the confines of Bandura's lab, these results may be relatively harmless. But beyond the safety of the lab, there's no telling what lengths children might go to, to carry out imitated aggressive behavior; there's no telling the range of media that might prompt children to behave aggressively; and there's no telling the range of aggressive behavior children might respond to. Bandura's research opened a Pandora's box of possibilities.

What's scary is that today's children are being bombarded by media images the likes of which the world has never seen before. Now this wouldn't be so bad if the images were positive ones, say where Bambi risks his life to rescue Thumper from the forest fire. But the images usually aren't positive ones. They're replete with violence, aggression, and bloodshed; and that's just the cartoons! Bandura's research raises the very real possibility that these images may be finding their way into the daily routines of our children. Aggressive models don't even have to be important figures in the children's lives; they can be complete strangers. Imagine the impact made by models whom children respect, like movie stars, sports heroes, WWF characters, or pop music icons. Consider these recent stories quoted from popular media sources:

- *The Boston Globe*, 10 December 2000: A recent study from the Mayo Clinic shows that anorexia has been increasing by 36% every five years since the 1950s. Today, some 8 million people—mostly women, but increasingly men, too—suffer from anorexia nervosa and bulimia nervosa, a related disorder characterized by binge eating and purging. Less obvious to many of us, however, is the way in which popular culture and eating disorders intertwine. For instance, the highly popular television series "Friends" took anorexic chic to new heights last year by putting an ad on a South Dakota billboard that read: "Cute Anorexic Chics" alongside the three, very slim female stars of the show. Surveys show that 80 percent of women are dissatisfied with their bodies. Girls as young as 9 and 10 are dieting, even though they are at a normal weight.

- *Newsweek*, 4 December 2000: In 1995, Elyse Pahler was lying on her parents' bed, watching TV, when the phone rang. The 15-year-old was invited to a nearby eucalyptus grove to hang out with friends. But once there, three acquaintances wrapped a belt around Pahler's neck and stabbed her to death. What drove the teens to murder? The killers, devotees of the heavy-metal band Slayer, believed they needed to commit a "sacrifice to the Devil" to give their garage band, Hatred, the "craziness" to "go professional."

- *Denver Post*, 10 June 2001: When a 13-year-old Connecticut boy laid himself across a barbecue grill last February and suffered severe burns, his misguided attempt to become some sort of human kabob prompted hand-wringing at the highest levels. But it wasn't aimed at the boy himself, who arguably should have known the risks involved with straddling a lighted grill. Instead, the darts were aimed clear across the country, at MTV and its "Jackass" show.

- *Chicago Sun-Times*, 10 March 2001: Ignoring a multitude of pleas for clemency, Broward County Circuit Court Judge Joel Lazarus sentenced 14-year-old Lionel Tate to life in prison without parole Friday for killing a girl playmate while allegedly demonstrating professional wrestling techniques on her. "The acts of Lionel Tate were not acts of immaturity," Lazarus said. "The acts of Lionel Tate were cold, callous and indescribably cruel." Tate's victim, 6-year-old Tiffany Eunick, was found beaten to death July 28, 1999. Her killer, Tate, was twice his victim's age at the time and, at 170 pounds, more than three times her weight. An autopsy showed that Tiffany suffered a fractured skull, a lacerated liver, a broken rib, internal hemorrhaging and numerous cuts and bruises. She was stomped, flung against a wall and beaten while on a table.

• *Denver Post,* 22 April 1999: News of Tuesday's massacre and the killers' involvement in Columbine High School's Trench Coat Mafia has triggered questions about how a youth underworld of nihilism and rage could emerge in conservative, cushy south Jefferson County. Masked gunmen Eric Harris, 18, and Dylan Klebold, 17, are said to have hung out with the so-called mafia, a small, self-styled group drawing on the satanic "goth" scene and neo-Nazi paramilitarism. Classmates say Klebold and Harris—who apparently killed themselves—wore swastikas and worshiped Adolf Hitler. Some say their clique drove hearses, tested friendships by cutting each other with knives, engaged in endless hours of macabre Internet chatter and relished a fantasy game called "Doom" on their computers.

In every one of these instances, media images were implicated as being causally related to the bizarre behavior patterns of the individuals involved. Of course, it's impossible to say whether or not these media images really were responsible; you'd have to have a God's-eye view to know that. But based on the scientific experiments conducted by Bandura, and dozens of other scientists since, we know at least that children are highly inclined to imitate behaviors modeled by other people. Although it's the children who carry out the acts, the media may need to shoulder much of the blame.

Media Bashing

The question of who should take responsibility when children conduct criminal acts based on models in the media is highly controversial and emotionally charged. Most social scientists familiar with the modeling research are inclined to lay much of the blame on the media. In fact, in 1999 the American Academy of Pediatrics issued a recommendation that parents should avoid exposing their children to *any* television prior to the age of 2 years (although I've often wondered how they arrived at 2 as the magical age).

On the other hand, I can already hear the counterarguments. "Hey, whatever happened to free will? Humans *choose* to imitate what they see in TV shows, video games, or on billboards. Millions of teenage boys play the video game Doom and listen to the band Slayer, *without* slaughtering their classmates!" (This is the most frequent view expressed by my students.) You might argue that perpetrators like Tate, Harris, and Klebold are simply bad apples who chose to follow the path of evil, that they must've had something wrong with them in the first place. As you can imagine, this is a very popular view. Media companies are also strongly aligned with this position. They stand to lose a lot of money if one of the most attractive features of their product, its violent content, is removed.

But there are a couple of different issues intertwined here. First, blame-placing doesn't need to be an either-or, black-and-white kind of thing. Human beings are highly individualized creatures who differ from one another greatly (which you already know from your own personal experiences). So why assume that everyone would have to respond to media-portrayed violence the same way? Just because you played Doom before and didn't go out and kill someone doesn't mean the game didn't influence your behavior in some small way. Perhaps you once kicked the dog afterward, or maybe you got a little snippy with your parents. And there are thousands of kids out there trying fancy and dangerous wrestling moves on their little brothers and sisters every day who *don't* kill and maim them. When I first moved into my present home, I noticed that one of the adolescent boys in the neighborhood had a full-size wrestling ring sitting in his back yard! He and his friends were always slamming one another onto the mat and drop-kicking each other into the ropes. Apparently, no one ever got seriously injured because I never saw any EMTs rushing down the street. But I doubt he would've had a wrestling ring in the first place if the WWF hadn't had such a powerful influence on him.

So why would social science be so much at odds with popular beliefs? For one thing, not everyone's aware of the Bobo doll studies. But even if they were, many people would probably still deny their validity. I think this stems in large part from popular misconceptions about how social science works. Social science works by describing the behaviors of large groups of people. There are bound to be exceptions to the rule. Even in the Bandura study, where we know for sure that children's aggression was enhanced by the aggressive model, not all the children performed at the same level of aggression. Some children were more aggressive than others. There was probably even one child who was the most aggressive of all. Would we be justified in concluding that the aggressive model had no influence on most of the kids simply because most of the kids failed to behave as aggressively as the most aggressive kid? Of course not. For this reason, I'm not inclined to buy the "bad apple" argument. Imitative behaviors can be extreme, and most kids don't behave extremely violently, but that doesn't mean these kids are *unaffected* by the violent images in the media. They're just not all affected to the same degree.

Whether we like it or not, the balance of the evidence places a large portion of blame on the media. But let me be clear that I don't think the media *intend* to promote violence in the society with their violent imagery. Most media sources are in it for the money—and unfortunately, violence sells. And to be sure, media sources would stand to gain very little by promoting a violent society, if for no other reason than that, over time, they would have fewer customers. Still, the media are subject to scientific scrutiny, and science doesn't have a whole lot of positive things to say about the media images being distributed. Unfortunately, the media have a long history of turning a deaf ear toward scientific concerns.

Consider the following. Way back in the 1970s, Surgeon General William H. Stewart was directed to form an advisory panel to examine research relevant to the effects of television on children. He wanted the committee to be made up of representatives from the scientific community, the broadcasting industry, and the general public. To make up the group of scientists, he requested nominations from social science organizations such as the American Sociological Association, the American Psychiatric Association, and the American Psychological Association. Some 200 names of prominent scientists were submitted. The surgeon general narrowed the list down to 40 and forwarded the names to the presidents of the National Association of Broadcasters, the American Broadcasting Company (ABC), the National Broadcasting

Company (NBC), and the Columbia Broadcasting System (CBS). The presidents were asked to say which individuals, if any, would *not* be "appropriate for an impartial scientific investigation of this nature." The presidents (with the exception of CBS's) blackballed 7 scientists. Guess who was on the list. Albert Bandura! Bandura, the most prominent expert on the potentially negative influences of television, was eliminated by the television broadcasters themselves from the most esteemed presidential advisory committee addressing the issue. What were they so afraid of?

On a Positive Note

If media have been the cause of the problem, they can also be the source of the solution. What tends to be forgotten in media-blaming sessions is that the existence of media isn't at issue. We couldn't live without them. It's the content of the media that causes concern. That's what children imitate. A lot of good science has shown that children exposed to positive media are inclined to display prosocial behaviors. For this reason, Senator Joe Lieberman and former Vice First Lady Tipper Gore have been at the forefront of a movement to pressure media sources toward increasing the amount of positive media programming. The few prosocial programs we have, children's shows like *Barney, Sesame Street,* and *Mr. Rogers,* have done wonders for exposing children to behaviorally positive daily routines. As just one example, a 2001 monograph put out by the Society for Research in Child Development showed that children who watched *Sesame Street* had higher grades in school, engaged in more leisure-time book use, participated more in art class, and exhibited lower levels of aggression than children who didn't watch *Sesame Street.* One can only hope that in this capitalist society, media distributors can find an attractive profit motive for exposing children to more positive media imagery.

Final Comment

Bandura revolutionized child psychology because he approached the field as somewhat of an outsider. He was interested in the very general matter of how people can pick up behaviors they've never been rewarded for and apply them to new situations. But the fact that he focused on the aggressive behavior of children made it all the more important to the scientific community, and to the public at large. His major finding, that children would imitate behaviors they saw modeled by other people, was elementary. Yet, because it was aggressive behavior that the children were picking up, it was at the same time of grave sociopolitical importance. To this very day, scientists and the media industry are locked in a battle over how to allocate blame for what is feared to be an unprecedented rise in social negativity and apathy. The results can't yet be foreseen, because the battleground expands with every techno-media innovation that presents itself before us. If there is a consensus, it's that the battle is an important one, because it may be for the mental health of today's children. Now—back to my heavyweight boxing career.

Bibliography

Anderson, D. R., Huston, A. C., Schmitt, K. L., Linebarger, D. L., & Wright, J. C. (2001). Early childhood television viewing and adolescent behavior. *Monographs of the Society for Research in Child Development, 66*(Serial No. 264).

Bandura, A. (1965). Influence of models' reinforcement contingencies on the acquisition of imitative responses. *Journal of Personality & Social Psychology, 1,* 589–595.

Grusec, J. E. (1992). Social learning theory and developmental psychology: The legacies of Robert Sears and Albert Bandura. *Developmental Psychology, 28,* 776–786.

Liebert, R. M., & Sprafkin, J. (1988). *The early window.* New York: Pergamon Press.

Questions for Discussion

1. Does the media have any responsibility to the public to portray positive images? How about musical celebrities or movie stars?

2. Is learning aggression through imitation a new phenomenon? Or is it possible that children have been imitating aggressive models throughout history? What would be some examples of the latter?

3. Would you expect there to be age differences in children's and adult's susceptibility to aggressive models? At what age do you think children would be most susceptible to portrayals of aggression? At what age are children most susceptible to peer pressure? Do you think adults would be immune to models of aggression?

15

The Ethic of Care:
It's a Woman Thing

IN A DIFFERENT VOICE: PSYCHOLOGICAL THEORY AND WOMEN'S DEVELOPMENT.
Gilligan, C. (1982). *Cambridge, MA: Harvard University Press.*   (RANK 10)

Are you a moral driver? I mean, when you make decisions about what you do when you drive, what are your real motivations? Lawrence Kohlberg outlined six levels of moral reasoning that may give us some insight into the level of our driving morality. Borrowing from and extending Piaget's theory of cognitive development, Kohlberg believed that our moral behaviors are a reflection of our mental reasoning abilities. When we reason at low moral levels, it's because we're not very sophisticated thinkers. And when we reason at the highest moral levels, it's because we're capable of high-level, principled, abstract thinking. Normally, we pass through each of the six levels one at a time as we grow older and gain intellectually maturity. We first reason at Stage 1, then Stage 2, and so forth, up through Stage 6 (if we ever become smart enough). Of course, not everybody thinks sophisticated thoughts in adulthood, so there's no guarantee that everyone with a driver's license is guided by high-level moral principles.

Kohlberg launched his theory of moral development based on his study of boys' and men's responses to the now-famous "Heinz dilemma." The Heinz dilemma is a fictitious story about a man named Heinz, whose wife is dying from cancer. There is a druggist in Heinz's town who has developed a drug that could cure the wife's cancer, but he is charging $2,000 for just a single dose. Unfortunately, Heinz can only muster up half the money. The questions put to the participants in Kohlberg's study were: (1) Should Heinz steal the drug? and (2) Why?

Kohlberg analyzed the men's and boys' responses to this question and found that it didn't matter so much whether they said Heinz should or shouldn't steal the drug. Rather, the most important issue revolved around the *reasons* they gave for why Heinz should or shouldn't steal the drug. The respondents were assigned to one of the six levels of moral reasoning, based on the rationale they provided.

According to Kohlberg, we find that at the earliest stages of morality, which we usually experience in early elementary school, our behaviors are motivated primarily by punishments and rewards. If we do something so that we won't get into trouble, we're at Kohlberg's Stage 1. If we do something to gain some sort of reward, we're at Stage 2. In these most primitive moral stages, our thinking is tied directly to the bad consequences that can happen for not doing something or the concrete rewards we get for doing something. Kohlberg called moral reasoning at Stages 1 and 2 a **"preconventional" level of morality**.

Higher levels of moral reasoning, such as those found in Stages 3 and 4, are reflected in behaviors we do because we're supposed to. People expect it of us. In these stages, our morality is tied to the thoughts we have about the thoughts other people will have about our chosen plans of action (Stage 3) or to the thoughts we have about doing our duty and adhering to a set of conventional rules (Stage 4). At these stages, we're no longer concerned about what happens to us directly, we're mostly concerned about staying in line, not letting other people down, and not rocking the boat. These two stages represent a **"conventional" level of morality** in Kohlberg's conceptualization.

When our mental abilities develop to the point where we can think abstractly, when we can consider how our behaviors affect all of society or even all of humanity, we're at the most sophisticated levels of morality. At these upper-level stages, our moral choices are no longer based on what will happen to us directly, nor are they based on what will happen to our family and friends, nor even on whether we're breaking any rules or laws. Instead, we base our decisions on whether or not something is "the right thing to do" given the circumstances (Stage 5), or whether something is consistent with some set of "universal ethical principles" we've developed (Stage 6). Stage 6 moral reasoning is reserved for only the rarest, smartest, most sanctimonious among us. People like the Reverend Martin Luther King and Mahatma Gandhi fit the bill here. Unfortunately, so few people ever reach Stage 6 that Kohlberg eventually gave up on it and dropped it from his list. In any case, Stages 5 and 6 represent a **"postconventional" moral approach**.

Now, I expect that most of us would like to regard ourselves as creatures of high moral character. We'd like to believe that we'd do the right thing when our friends and neighbors call upon us. Surely we'd help an elderly person who has fallen down, or try to make a crying child laugh. But why does all our moral wisdom seem to fly out the window when we get behind a steering wheel? Let's consider *your* driving morality. As a case in point, let's consider why you speed.

Oh c'mon. Everybody speeds. Well, maybe not everybody. We know from scientific research that as we get older we tend to slow down—mostly because we're compensating for our slower reflexes. But for the rest of you who do speed, what are your reasons? Do you speed because you want to get somewhere fast? Do you gain pleasure from getting to your destination quickly? If so, then you're at Kohlberg's Stage 2. This is the stage where we do things because they benefit us directly. Remember, Stage 2 is a fairly primitive level of moral reasoning.

But maybe you speed because you're afraid of being late to work or school and fear that you might get scolded by your boss or professor. If this applies to you, then you're reasoning at an even lower moral level than before. This is Kohlberg's Stage 1 of moral reasoning. In Stage 1, your actions are controlled by the avoidance of punishment. If you speed to avoid getting in trouble, then you're functioning at the moral level of a kindergartner.

However, you can speed using higher levels of moral justification. If you're supposed to meet your in-laws at a restaurant but you're running late, you might speed to avoid having your spouse feel embarrassed at your absence (Stage 3). Or you might speed to get to class on time because your course syllabus says that lateness is inexcusable, and after all, "a rule is a rule" (Stage 4). About the only way that you can speed at higher moral levels would be in situations along the lines of getting a pregnant women to the hospital in time to give birth. In this instance, your rationale would be that the traffic laws weren't set up for emergency transportation situations and that sometimes it's okay to break the law. Here you'd be reasoning at Stage 5.

But you may not be morally high and mighty if you always obey the speed limit either. Your level of morality in following the law, just like the morality of breaking the law, also depends on the reasoning you use. If you obey the law because you want to avoid getting a speeding ticket, you're in Stage 1: punishment avoidance. If you drive 55 because it's the law, you're in Stage 4: law-and-order orientation. You'd reach the highest levels of moral reasoning if your legal cruising speed were based on a belief that traffic laws were set up by the community for a good reason. For example, it's always seemed to me a pretty good idea to have residential speed limits set to 25 mph. At this speed you'd have a pretty good chance of being able to stop in time when you see a basketball bounce out into the street, knowing that a child may be in fast pursuit.

Of course, it's not my goal to change your driving morality. That's something you'll have to come to grips with on your own. My goal is simply to illustrate Kohlberg's theory of morality as it applies to an everyday behavior you're familiar with. The two key points to remember about Kohlberg's theory are (1) that Kohlberg links moral development directly to thinking ability, and (2) that because it is linked to thinking ability it "improves" over time.

*****

Now you may be wondering why I've spent that last several paragraphs talking about some guy named Kohlberg and his theory of moral development when the chapter is supposed to be about someone named Carol Gilligan and the psychology of women! The answer is that you can't really understand Gilligan's theory without also knowing something about Kohlberg's. Although Gilligan was a student of Kohlberg, she was so opposed to his theory about the development of morality that she ended up creating her own. So to understand where Gilligan was coming from, you need to understand the intellectual climate that she was rebelling against. For it was this climate, and the child psychology community more generally, that she revolutionized when she published her 1982 book *In a Different Voice* (ranked 10th most revolutionary overall).

What stuck in Gilligan's craw about this whole Kohlbergian morality thing was simply that too much of mainstream psychology was dominated by research involving nothing more than men and boys. It was as if men and boys were the default, the standard, and any deviation was an exception. As a result of ignoring women and girls, Gilligan argued, most theories about human nature couldn't avoid being based on a masculine perspective. This complaint applies to theories as popular as Piaget's and as old as Sigmund Freud's. If you remember, Freud's major claim was that personality development was essentially based on a boy's recognition that (1) he had a penis, and (2) he wanted to use it. In Freud's theory, girls were by definition defective because they lacked a penis. In fact, he argued that girls spent their lives trying to regain their missing penis. He labeled this motivation "penis envy." Obviously, if "normal" personality development is based on the discovery and intentional use of one's penis, then half the human population is bound to have a serious personality disorder! Does this seem biased to you?

In her first couple of chapters, Gilligan outlined a history of psychology that showed how psychology had systematically neglected the views and voices of women. She really makes a convincing case. She singles out Freud and Piaget among others. But the lion's share of her criticism is aimed at Kohlberg's theory. Throughout the remainder of her book, she wields data like a sword to carve out an alternative to the traditional male view of the moral world.

Although you might be tempted to think that the alternative to a masculine view is a feminine one, Gilligan is quick to point out that such an overgeneralization would be premature. The alternative view she describes may indeed be typical of women's ways of knowing about the world, but men are also capable of embracing it. So rather than focusing on separate men's and women's moralities, she encourages thinking about the two approaches in terms of an **ethic of care** versus an **ethic of justice**. The ethic of justice was the kind described by Kohlberg's theory, the kind that mostly applies to men and boys. But Gilligan argued that the ethic of care was just as important and valid as the ethic of justice. Unfortunately, no one had worked out a developmental theory detailing how a morality could be based on an ethic of caring. So Gilligan's goal in her book was to provide just such an outline.

INTRODUCTION

Gilligan begins her book by writing, "Over the past ten years, I have been listening to people talking about morality and about themselves. Halfway through that time, I began to hear a distinction in these voices, two ways of speaking about moral problems, two modes of describing the relationship between other and self. . . . Against the background of the psychological descriptions of identity and moral development which I had read and taught for a number of years, the women's voices sounded distinct. It was then that I began to notice the recurrent problems in interpreting women's development and to connect these problems to the repeated exclusion of women from the critical theory-building studies of psychological research."

The data for Gilligan's own theory building came from three different studies. The "college student study" consisted of 25 male and female sophomores selected randomly from among students enrolled in a course on moral and political choice. These students were interviewed as seniors and then again 5 years after graduation. However, Gilligan also noticed that of an additional 20 students who dropped that course, 16 were women. This disproportionate gender difference was so striking that Gilligan also contacted and interviewed these women.

The "abortion decision study" was based on interviews with 29 women, who ranged in age from 15 to 33 years. All of the women were pregnant and considering having an abortion, and were referred to Gilligan's study through pregnancy counseling services and abortion clinics. Gilligan collected complete interview information on 24 of these women, and 21 were interviewed again 1 year after they made their choice.

Finally, the "rights and responsibilities study" consisted of interviews taken from males and females at nine different ages: 6–9, 11, 15, 19, 22, 25–27, 35, 45, and 60 years of age. There were 8 males and 8 females at each age, making a total of 144 participants. Two males and females at each age also participated in a more intensive interview process. Let me be clear that Gilligan didn't interview the same people at each age. This would've taken over 50 years! Rather, Gilligan interviewed different people at each age. This approach is called a **cross-sectional design**.

The characteristic feature of all three studies was that Gilligan used an interview procedure for collecting the data. In her methodology, Gilligan began each participant's interview with the same standardized set of questions. During the course of the interview, however, questions were developed on the spot so as to follow up on some interesting point a participant might've made in response to an earlier question. The general purpose of the questions was to explore people's understanding of themselves and their own morality. Follow-up questions were developed as needed to probe deeper into each person's line of reasoning and logic as it pertained to themselves and their own morality.

Although Gilligan's book is based on the results of her three studies, very little detail is given about any study in particular. To give you a sense of the procedures she used in her research, I'll focus on describing what seems to be the most popular study of the three—her abortion decision study. However, to provide these details I have to move beyond the 1982 book and refer to an earlier chapter that documented the abortion decision study. This chapter was published in 1980 and was coauthored by Mary Field Belenky.

METHOD

One of the most serious limitations of Kohlberg's theory, besides that it was based on the responses of only men and boys, was the fact that it was based on responses to a *hypothetical situation*. That is, none of the men and boys were actually in a position of needing to steal a drug to save their wife's life. So what they *said* Heinz should do may or may not have reflected what they themselves would *actually* have done in the same situation. To remedy the problem of having to rely on responses to a hypothetical situation, Gilligan chose a sample of women who were actually undergoing a real-life moral dilemma. Gilligan's rationale here was that people undergoing an inner emotional struggle would be more in touch with their own personal moral values, and so would give more realistic indicators of their underlying moral belief system.

Participants

As already mentioned, the 24 participants who started out in the study were all pregnant women who ranged in age from 15 to 33, and who were referred to the study by pregnancy support services and abortion clinics. Some of the participants were also referred through private physicians or through a university health service. To be included in the study, Gilligan and Belenky required that each woman be in the first trimester of her pregnancy and be considering having an abortion for one reason or another.

The women came from a wide variety of social, racial, and cultural backgrounds. Some were married, others single. Some had had previous abortions. Three already had a child at home. Gilligan and Belenky chose women from such a wide range of backgrounds so that they would bring with them a wide range of cognitive and moral functioning that could also be explored. This was important because it increased the generalizability of Gilligan's findings. If you remember from the Baumrind chapter (Chapter 13), Baumrind's study suffered from the fact that it was based on only white, well-to-do, high-IQ people. At least this same criticism can't be applied to Gilligan's study.

Materials and Procedure

The women were interviewed two times. The first interview took place sometime between the 8th and 12th week of pregnancy. The second took place 1 year after their abortion decision was finally made. Twenty-one of the original 24 women were available for the 1-year-after follow-up interview.

The interview questions during the initial interview were designed to probe the women's understanding of (1) the problems posed by their pregnancies, (2) the decisions they were facing, (3) the various alternatives they were thinking about, and (4) what they thought about each of the alternatives. The start-up interview question was, "How did you get pregnant and how have you been thinking about it so far?" Based on the women's responses to this question, the interviewer then asked follow-up questions designed to unravel the thinking processes used by the women in their answers. After this line of questioning was complete, additional questions were asked about the women's senses of self ("How would you describe yourself to yourself?") and their moral judgments ("Is there a difference between what you want to do and what you think you should do?" "Is there a right thing to do in this situation?" "Right just for you or anyone?"). The 1-year follow-up interview was basically the same as the initial one, but the women were also asked about their experiences after they made their abortion decision ("Thinking back now about the decision you made a year ago, what was your thinking about what to do?").

To have a point of comparison with Kohlberg's study, the women were also given the standard Heinz dilemma. Their responses to the Heinz dilemma were scored using two different scoring manuals. One scoring manual was the one originally developed by Kohlberg. The other manual was developed by Mary Field Belenky and represented an adaptation of the Kohlberg manual to better fit the moral responses of women.

Difference Scores.   Because Gilligan and Belenky had information about women's responses to real as well as hypothetical moral dilemmas, they were able to compare women's responses across both these two situations. In addition, because they had interview data from the women before and after their abortion decisions, Gilligan and Belenky were able to invent a scale to measure changes in life circumstances that took place between the two interviews. This scale measured whether there were any changes from Time 1 to Time 2 in the areas of love and work, and in the women's feelings about their lives. If there were any changes, the changes were rated as "better, worse, or same." Gilligan and Belenky gave the example of a student who was out of school during the pregnancy but who had returned to school after making her abortion decision. This woman "reported a change for the better in her life, had better friends, and had a more satisfying relationship with her parents." This kind of change would be scored as "better." Another woman "who had abandoned her occupation at Time 2 and was bedridden, alone, and full of self-doubt" was scored as "worse." The number of different *better*s, *worse*s, and *same*s were weighted and averaged together to produce a Life Outcome Score.

RESULTS

Now, talking about the results of the abortion decisions study is tricky because in the original 1980 write-up of their results, Gilligan and Belenky didn't focus so much on how women's ethic of care differed from men's ethic of justice in influencing their moralities. Instead, they focused on how women's morality changed from the time of the initial interview to the time of the follow-up interview. Gender differences in moral reasoning are underscored in Gilligan's 1982 book. So the following results are extracted from the 1982 book and not the 1980 chapter. It's also important to point out that the results Gilligan described aren't your run-of-the-mill, everyday experimental results. She didn't rely on numbers, averages, or correlations, for example. Instead, she relied on a **narrative research design** in describing what she found, giving special emphasis to the women's own voices as they illustrated their ethic-of-care ideology.

The most significant finding from the abortion decision study is that the women often expressed their moral understanding in terms of their relationships with others. They focused on their relationships with their developing babies, their parents, their sexual partners, and their friends. And what they talked about most frequently when they talked about their relationships was care and responsibility. Diane, a woman in her late 20s, described her conception of morality as:

> Some sense of trying to uncover a right path in which to live, and always on my mind is that the world is full of real and recognizable trouble, and it is heading for some sort of doom, and is it right to bring children into this world when we currently have an over-population problem, and is it right to spend money on a pair of shoes when I have a pair of shoes and other people are shoeless? Is it part of a self-critical view, part of saying, "How am I spending my time and in what sense am I working?" I think I have a real drive, a real maternal drive, to take care of someone—to take care of my mother, to take care of children, to take care of other people's children, to take care of my own children, to take care of the world. When I am dealing with moral issues, I am sort of saying to myself constantly, "Are you taking care of all the things that you think are important, and in what ways are you wasting yourself and wasting those issues?"

In sum, Gilligan found women's moral reasoning to be like a fabric interwoven from spools of relationship, care, and responsibility.

But even though the women seemed to have a different moral voice than men, they still differed from one another in their levels of moral reasoning. Gilligan wrote, "Women's constructions of the abortion dilemma in particular reveal the existence of a distinct moral language whose evolution traces a sequence of development. This is the language of selfishness and responsibility, which defines the moral problem as one of obligation to exercise care and avoid hurt. The inflicting of hurt is considered selfish and immoral in its reflection of unconcern, while the expression of care is seen as the fulfillment of moral responsibility. The reiterative use by the women of the words *selfish* and *responsible* in talking about moral conflict and choice, given the underlying moral orientation that this language reflects, sets the women apart from the men whom Kohlberg studied and points toward a different understanding of moral development." Gilligan then went on to describe a sequence of three levels of moral thinking in women's ethic of care that roughly corresponded to Kohlberg's three levels (preconventional, conventional, and postconventional) of moral thinking in men's ethic of justice.

The First Level: Orientation to Individual Survival

Remember that in Kohlberg's preconventional level, men's and boys' moral reasoning focused on avoiding punishments and gaining rewards. Here, benefiting the self was the central focus of moral action. Similarly, the most primitive level of women's moral thinking is based on caring for the self in order to ensure survival. Gilligan's women had to deal with a pregnancy they didn't want and the possibility that their life's goals could be forever corrupted. Faced with this realization, and feeling disconnected from the world, many women felt angry and ripped off at not being able to do a lot of things they planned to do. And their initial moral actions were based on decisions aimed at protecting the self. Betty, an adopted 19-year-old with a history of repeated abortions, disorderly conduct, and reform school, responded to the Heinz dilemma this way:

> The druggist is ripping him off and his wife is dying, so the druggist deserves to be ripped off. (*Is this the right thing to do?*) Probably. I think survival is one of the first things in life and that people fight for. I think it is the most important thing, more important than stealing. Stealing might be wrong, but if you have to steal to survive yourself or even kill, that is what you should do. (*Why is that?*) Preservation of oneself, I think, is the most important thing; it comes before anything in life. A lot of people say sex is the most important thing to a lot of people, but I think that preservation of oneself is the most important thing to people.

The Second Level: Goodness as Self-Sacrifice

At Kohlberg's conventional level, the focus for men moved to doing one's duty. Gilligan's women also began seeing themselves as needing to do their duty. But unlike Kohlberg's men, Gilligan's women equated "duty" with "caring for others." They began to see their earlier focus on the self as, well, selfish. As they pondered their conditions more fully, some of the women began to realize their essential role in caring for their upcoming baby. This focus, in turn, motivated a more general *responsibility* orientation, where these women tied their values as people to their efforts at caring and providing for others. At this level, to "do good" meant to "do for others." But the problem here was that women tended to go over the edge in caring for others, and they frequently neglected caring for themselves. Caring is what you do for other people, not something you do for yourself. Sandra, a 29-year-old Catholic nurse, really struggled with the issue. As she reflected on her decision to get an abortion, she found it very difficult to hear what her own voice had to say. She said:

> On my own, I was doing it not so much for myself; I was doing it for my parents. I was doing it because my doctor told me to do it, but I had never resolved in my mind that I was doing it for me. Actually, I had to sit down and admit, "No, I really don't want to go the mother route now. I honestly don't feel that I want to be a mother." And that is not really such a bad thing to say after all. But that is not how I felt up until talking to [my counselor]. It was just a horrible way to feel, so I just wasn't going to feel it, and I just blocked it right out.

The Third Level: The Morality of Nonviolence

In Kohlberg's postconventional level, the aim of men was to do what's right even if it comes at great personal cost or dereliction of duty. For the men in Kohlberg's study, this often amounted to acting according to internalized principles of conscience that were based on doing the greatest amount of good for the greatest number of people. Although concern for people was central, "people" was an abstract concept and didn't really refer to any individual person. Even war could be a perfectly legitimate response to a large-scale infraction of personal liberties, despite the potential for hundreds of thousands of people to die.

The highest level in Gilligan's vision was conceptualized a little differently. As the women in Gilligan's study entered *their* third level, they realized they had been neglecting and in some ways even losing themselves in their role as provider and protector of others. Upon further reflection, they realized that they were intimately connected with other people in their lives, and that by neglecting themselves, not only were they harming themselves, they were harming others as well. After reaching the third level, they developed a new understanding of the interconnections between themselves and important people in their lives. The focus shifted away from caring only about the self or only about others to caring about relationships. But in all cases, the relationship between themselves and significant others took top priority. Abstract principles of justice were much less meaningful. The response of a college woman (who wasn't part of the abortion decision study) exemplifies this point. To the question "Why be moral?" she responded,

> My main principle is not hurting other people as long as you aren't going against your own conscience and as long as you remain true to yourself. . . . There are many moral issues, such as abortion, the draft, killing, stealing, monogamy. If something is a controversial issue like these, then I always say it is up to the individual. The individual has to decide and then follow his own conscience. There are no moral absolutes. Laws are pragmatic instruments, but they are not absolutes. A viable society can't make exceptions all the time, but I would personally. . . . I'm afraid I'm heading for some big crisis with my boyfriend someday, and someone will get hurt, and he'll get more hurt than I will. I feel an obligation not to hurt him, but also an obligation not to lie. I don't know if it is possible not to lie and not to hurt.

DISCUSSION

Gilligan summarized differences between women's morality, which is most often based on an ethic of care, from men's morality, which is most often based on an ethic of justice, this way: "The moral imperative that emerges repeatedly in interviews with women is an injunction to care, a responsibility to discern and alleviate the 'real and recognizable trouble' of this world. For men, the moral imperative appears rather as an injunction to respect the rights of others and thus protect from interference the rights to life and self-fulfillment. Women's insistence on care is at first self-critical rather than self-protective, while men initially conceive obligation to others negatively in terms of noninterference. . . . In the development of a postconventional ethical understanding, women come to see the violence inherent in inequality, while men come to see the limitations of a conception of justice blinded to the differences in human life."

Whew! That's a mouthful. Let me try to simplify a few of these ideas. What Gilligan was saying here was that men seem to have as their ultimate moral goal the protection of certain fundamental rights. You can think of these fundamental rights as being along the lines of the rights to life, liberty, and the pursuit of happiness. Anything that gets in the way of these rights is called "injustice." Men with high levels of morality value these principles so much that they might even assign greater priority to them than they do their relationships with their parents, their wives, or even their own children. Women, in contrast, place the value of meaningfully embedded personal relationships above such abstract, individualistic principles. Injustice for women comes in the form of anything that threatens the sanctity of relationships. Unlike men, whose concern with these abstract principles may or may not have any bearing on their own life situation, women's are almost exclusively focused on real-life situations. Women concern themselves with actual attempts at alleviating human trauma and violence in real-life circumstances, whereas men are more inclined to denounce the principle or rule that led to the trauma and violence in the first place.

As I sit here writing these words, America is still reeling from a series of disastrous terrorist attacks that took place on September 11th. Since then, the country has continuously witnessed images of destruction in the media that resulted from four wide-bodied passenger airplanes being hijacked and intentionally crashed into the Pentagon and the two World Trade Center buildings. More than 2,000 occupants of those buildings were killed. At the time, I offered up my class time to talk with my students about whatever was on their minds concerning the attack. The gender differences in the discussion were astounding! The men, almost without exception, wanted to go in and "bomb the crap" out of Afghanistan. The women, again almost without exception, thought that bombing the crap out of anybody wouldn't help anything, and that it would only make matters worse.

The men were arguing from the principle of justice. The terrorist attacks on our fellow U.S. citizens were viewed by them as a complete breach of our rights to life, liberty, and the pursuit of happiness. The men showed little regard for the loss of life that would result from any counterattack the United States could muster. Many of the men even expressed an interest in joining the military to lead the charge.

The women in the class expressed a completely different sentiment. They defined the tragedy not as a violation of abstract principles and rights, but as a violation of the sanctity of human relationships. They were opposed to any American counterattack, which they believed would only kill more people and cause more emotional damage, all to no apparent end. The women were also extremely troubled by the possibility of losing their friends to the military, not just because their friends might die in the war, but for an even more basic reason: that their friends would have to go away.

The moral of the story is that the moral reasoning of women and men comes in different flavors. Whereas men are inclined to believe that abstract moral principles transcend the specifics of any situation, women focus on the relational details of the situations they are reasoning about. Now, keep in mind that Gilligan wasn't saying that women's ways of being moral were any better or worse than men's. They're just different. But it seems the same can't also be said about Kohlberg's scheme. When Kohlberg came up with his original moral classification system, he based it on men's responses to hypothetical dilemmas. It never seemed to occur to him, nor perhaps to any of the many scholars who adopted his system, that what applied to men might not apply equally well to women. In fact, Gilligan notes throughout her chapters that many of the women participants who reasoned at high moral levels using an ethic of care would be classified at a lower level using an ethic of justice, corresponding to Kohlberg's Stage 3. So Kohlberg's scale seems to undervalue women's moral rationale. Had Gilligan singled out the ethic of caring as superior to the ethic of justice, she would've been guilty of the very misattribution made by Kohlberg that got her so fired up in the first place. The punchline is that you can get into trouble when you try to evaluate the morality of one gender through the eyes (or the measurement scale) of the other. You just can't mix and match the two.

CONCLUSIONS

Gilligan revolutionized child psychology because she opened up our eyes to the possibility that women may not follow the same developmental route into morality as men. But much more than that, her work has forced us to consider the problem of gender-biased samples in psychological research far more generally. Developmental theories based only on samples of men paint only half the picture. By proposing her own theory, based on life stories being told by women, Gilligan helped complete the picture. She gave the field of child psychology a new vision and a new understanding of the path of moral development in women.

Importantly, Gilligan's influence extended well beyond the field of moral development. Her work has had a particularly strong impact on the role of gender differences in cognitive development. Riding Gilligan's tidal wave, for example, Mary Field Belenky and her coauthors published a landmark book in 1986 that documented how the thinking of girls and women seems to follow a different developmental path than the thinking of boys and men. The book, *Women's Ways of Knowing: The Development of Self, Voice, and Mind,* follows Gilligan's lead by documenting a series of transitional points in thinking that adolescent girls progress through as they experience the world and develop into adult women. And as with Gilligan's work, *Women's Ways of Knowing* was written as somewhat of a rejoinder to the then prevailing boy-based understanding of late-adolescent cognitive development inspired by William Perry.

Challenges to Gilligan

Although Gilligan played a central role in painting a new view of the American psychological landscape, one that included the voices of girls and women, her work has also caused a firestorm of controversy. The controversy appears at two levels. On a more basic level, her work caused some scientists to become suspicious about the scientific integrity of making grand claims exclusively on the basis of interview data. One of the most obvious problems with any interview procedure is that interviews are notoriously susceptible to biased interpretation. The argument is that if you're expecting to find something, no matter what it is, you can find it using an interview procedure. But even if Gilligan's interviewing techniques turned out to be just fine, her theory was still criticized for being based on such a small sample size. In the abortion decision study, for example, she was criticized for making sweeping generalizations about the morality of all women based on only a sample of 24 women; and even then they were women who were in the very unusual situation of having to consider whether or not to have an abortion.

But in her defense, Gilligan did conduct a number of other studies with women who weren't pregnant and who weren't considering an abortion. And in defense of her small samples, she writes, "To claim that there is a voice different from those which psychologists have represented, *I need only one example* [emphasis added]— one voice whose coherence is not recognized within existing interpretive schemes. To claim that common themes recur in women's conceptions of self and morality, I need a series of illustrations. In counterposing women's conceptions of self and morality to the conceptions embedded in psychological theories, I assume that a psychological literature filled with men's voices exemplifies men's experience. Therefore, in listening to women, I sought to separate their descriptions of their experience from standard forms of psychological interpretation and to rely on a close textual analysis of language and logic to define the terms of women's thinking."

Other criticisms have come from studies that failed to find sex differences in moral reasoning. In one study, for example, Friedman, Robinson, and Friedman strike pretty hard at the foundation of Gilligan's theory. They concluded, "[Our] results indicated that neither gender nor sex-differentiated personality attributes are reliably associated with the type of moral judgments that individuals make. The composites based on the two dimensions that we deduced from Gilligan's theory are very unlikely to have differed by more than a trivial amount as a function of sex. Very few of the 48 individual items [used to measure moral judgment] showed sex differences and most were in a direction inconsistent with the theory. Furthermore, men and women showed highly similar patterns in rating the importance of individual items in each [Heinz-type] dilemma. Taken together with previous studies using Kohlberg's procedure . . . these findings seem to cast doubt on the validity of Gilligan's claims."

But Gilligan has a defense against these criticisms too. The problem with studies like this, she says, is that researchers rely too heavily on the Heinz type of hypothetical moral dilemma. Gilligan herself has conducted studies where she found no gender differences in reasoning about Heinz. The Heinz dilemma is *designed* to bring out justice-based reasoning—from both men and women—because it was designed by a man who believed that morality was justice-based to begin with. But although both genders are *capable* of using justice-based reasoning in the Heinz dilemma,

Gilligan argues, the two genders wouldn't be equally likely to frame up a moral dilemma this way. Use of the Heinz dilemma reduces women's opportunity for framing the moral conflict their preferred way, in terms of an ethic of care. Women would rather not frame moral dilemmas according to universal principles of rights. The question Gilligan wants to answer is how women frame moral conflicts to begin with, which is why she chose to use the interview method. Through relatively unstructured, open-ended interview questions, the researcher can avoid framing a moral problem in advance. The respondent can frame the moral situation however she chooses. Consider how Ruth struggles to reframe the Heinz dilemma in a way that makes more sense to her,

> I don't even think I use the words *right* and *wrong* anymore, and I know I don't use the word *moral*, because I am not sure I know what it means. We are talking about an unjust society, we are talking about a whole lot of things that are not right, that are truly wrong— to use the word that I don't use very often—and I have no control over that. If I could change it, I certainly would, but I can only make my small contribution from day to day, and if I don't intentionally hurt somebody, that is my contribution to a better society. And so a chunk of that contribution is also not to pass judgment on other people, particularly when I don't know the circumstances of why they are doing certain things.

I would like to conclude the chapter by reminding you that after all is said and done, after all this talk about women's ethic of care and men's ethic of justice is laid out on the table, there is nothing that inevitably leads women to reason differently about morality than men. They *do* seem to reason differently, but they don't *have to*. Many women may indeed reason according to a justice ethic, and many men may similarly reason according to an ethic of care. For this reason, Gilligan prefers to think of these two approaches as reflecting different "themes" of moral reasoning. The point is that by ignoring the voice of women throughout its history, psychology has done a disservice to itself by failing to discover that there are alternative ways to be moral. And for any science that wishes to seek out the truth of the human condition, it would be a big mistake not to listen to all the voices involved.

Bibliography

Belenky, M. F., Clinchy, B. M., Goldberger, N. R., & Tarule, J. M. (1986). *Women's ways of knowing: The development of self, voice, and mind.* New York: Basic Books.

Friedman, W. J., Robinson, A. B., & Friedman, B. L. (1987). Sex differences in moral judgments? A test of Gilligan's theory. *Psychology of Women Quarterly, 11,* 37–46.

Gilligan, C., & Belenky, M. F. (1980). A naturalistic study of abortion decisions. In R. Selman & R. Yando (Eds.), *Clinical-Developmental Psychology: New Directions for Child Development, 7,* San Franciso: Jossey-Bass.

Kohlberg, L. (1969). Stage and sequence: The cognitive-developmental approach to socialization. In D. A. Goslin (Ed.), *Handbook of socialization theory and research.* Chicago: Rand McNally.

Larrabee, M. J. (1993). *An ethic of care: Feminist and interdisciplinary perspectives.* New York: Routledge.

Puka, B. (1994). *Caring voices and women's moral frames: Gilligan's view.* New York: Garland Publishing.

Questions for Discussion

1. Based on Gilligan's findings, how might the office of the President of the United States of America be different if it were filled by a female president? How might foreign policy be affected? How might domestic policy be affected?

2. One extension of the attention Gilligan brought to research on gender differences in morality is that maybe there are gender differences in other domains as well. In fact, maybe the whole enterprise of science reflects a male bias because, historically, science itself was invented by men. How might science look if it were designed by women?

3. Can you think of any examples from either your own romantic relationships or those of your friends, in which the man had a different point of view than the woman? Did these views conform to Gilligan's notions of the *ethic of care* and the *ethic of justice*? Do you think your male friends or your female friends are more likely to say something like "But it's the principle of the thing that matters"?

16

"If You Were Born First, I Would've Stopped"

TEMPERAMENT AND BEHAVIOR DISORDERS IN CHILDREN.
Thomas, A., Chess, S., & Birch, H. G. (1968). *New York: New York University Press.*   (RANK 6)

At my niece's second birthday party last year, I overheard a longtime family friend remark that had her third child, Kristi, been born first, she probably would have stopped having children! Kristi was apparently a rather challenging child to parent. I suppose it was a good thing for the sake of the other two kids that Kristi came last. Still, even though her mother viewed her as a difficult child, Kristi seemed to use her difficultness to great advantage. She's now in her mid-30s, leads a successful life, pursues a professional career, and has a really big house. As far as I can tell, she seems to be a pretty normal adult, although I reckon she occasionally seems a bit intense. I know her well because she's married to my brother, and it was their daughter's birthday party I was attending.

The fact that brothers and sisters can be so uniquely individualistic is really quite a wondrous thing. How can siblings be so different when they're raised under the same roof with the same rules and same daily routines, especially when they get their genes from the same two parents? Behavioral psychologists would no doubt say that sibling individuality comes from receiving different patterns of reinforcements and punishments. But this explanation doesn't go very far in helping parents understand why a reinforcement works so well for one child and fails miserably for the next. Developmental behavior geneticists would probably remind us that full-blooded siblings, despite their genetic similarity, are still not genetically identical.

Alexander Thomas, Stella Chess, and Herbert Birch earned their revolutionary status because they placed children's individuality at the center of their microscope. Their book, ranked sixth overall, was a rather radical departure from mainstream child psychology, because the status quo at the time was to follow a nomothetic approach. Pursuing a **nomothetic approach** is just a fancy way of saying that child psychologists spent most of their time documenting universal laws of development that could be applied to all children. Piaget applied a nomothetic approach to his research on cognitive development, Bowlby applied a nomothetic approach to his research on attachment, and Bandura applied a nomothetic approach to his research on modeling. Studying universal laws is just one of those things we're trained to do when we're scientists.

However, like so many other revolutionaries we've been discussing, Thomas, Chess, and Birch were pretty displeased with the standard nomothetic approach. They were even more displeased that the only other theoretical dishes on the menu included behaviorism tartare, which developmental psychologists had been force-fed for years, and the ever-popular Freudian psychoanalysis flambé. Thomas, Chess, and Birch found both courses difficult to swallow, and found both left a strong, bitter aftertaste. So like good little revolutionaries, they catered their own theoretical banquet. They had a lot at stake too. As child psychiatrists, their primary concern was understanding and eliminating the many bizarre, maladaptive behavior patterns they often observed in their child patients. So they not only had to come up with a scientific explanation for children's individuality, they also had to come up with scientifically valid ways for fixing behavior problems at the extreme ends of the range.

INTRODUCTION

The purpose of their 1968 book was to present the results of a monstrous longitudinal study of children's individuality, which they began some 12 years earlier. A **longitudinal study** is a study of a single group of people over a certain period of time. A short-term longitudinal study might follow a group of kids from, say, age 4 to age 5, to observe what happens during the transition to kindergarten. A longer-term longitudinal study might follow a group of kids from, say, age 13 to age 18, to investigate what happens as adolescents transition into adulthood. But Thomas, Chess, and Birch's study began in 1956 and was still going strong until 1988, 20 years after their book was published! The study is so famous these days that it has its own name, "the New York Longitudinal Study."

As I said, a primary goal of their study was to document children's individuality from early infancy through later childhood. They focused not only on how the environment influences individuality, but on internal contributions as well. These internal contributions were collectively called **temperament**. The authors believed that to get a full-blown explanation of children's individuality, you would need to know not only their temperamental starting point, but also how the rest of the world reacted to that temperamental starting point. But you wouldn't stop there; you would also need to know how children's temperament changed as a result of the world's response to their temperamental starting point. But you wouldn't stop there either. You would next need to know how the world responded to the changed temperament, which changed as a result of the world's response to the temperamental starting point. And so on, and so forth. I think you get the picture. It's kind of like the children's song about the old lady who swallowed a fly. The authors argued that a child's individuality at any one point in time would result from a complicated history of the cyclical interplay of temperament and environmental reactivity to that temperament.

Before describing the role of temperament in the development of children's individuality, Thomas, Chess, and Birch first had to come up with a workable definition of temperament. Being pioneers, they had to be sure their definition captured the essence of what they were describing, but they also had to be sure that it would be sufficiently palatable to other scientists in the field. Since most other child psychologists in 1956 had a strong behaviorist orientation, Thomas, Chess, and Birch were painstakingly careful to describe temperament in terms of children's actual physical behaviors. They might not have been accepted into the scholarly community otherwise. Moreover, they weren't particularly interested in *what* children did, or *why* they did it, but rather in *how* it was done. They described it as a *style*.

Imagine three different boys on a baseball team going up to bat. Top of the order, nobody out. The pitcher on the opposing team is known for throwing a lot of balls and very few strikes. One by one, each boy trots up to the plate, takes four wild pitches, and gets a walk. Boy 1 seems extremely pleased with his walk. He tosses his bat aside, and with giddy excitement, sprints to first, grinning ear to ear at the first-base coach. Boy 2 seems to have little interest in his walk. He sets his bat down gently, looks casually around at the fans, and walks tranquilly to first base, combing his hair the whole way. Boy 3, on the other hand, is furious. He throws his bat down, makes some candid gestures to the opposing team, spits at the pitcher, and trots stridently to first. Three boys, three walks, three very different behavioral styles. This is the essence of temperament.

As you might imagine, when the authors began their study temperament wasn't considered to be a very worthy topic for psychological investigation. It was viewed as being beneath a scientist's dignity. The dominating behavioral theories of the time held strongly to the belief that children's behaviors were entirely products of their environment. Bad behavior was simply due to bad parenting. But Thomas, Chess, and Birch held strongly to their own convictions that temperament was important for three reasons. First, there rarely seemed to be a one-to-one correspondence between the environmental consequences of a child's behavior and her future behaviors. Second, children seemed highly variable in how susceptible they were to environmental stressors. And third, as we saw in the beginning, children from the same family could differ drastically in response to similar parenting practices.

So Thomas, Chess, and Birch launched their study. They had three explicit goals in mind. First, they wanted to figure out how best to study temperament. Remember, they were pioneers, so they were on their own in coming up with ways to study temperament. Second, they wanted to use their temperament classifications to identify children who were at risk for developing behavior disorders. Here you see their child psychiatry training showing through. And third, they wanted to carefully document the environmental conditions in which their participants were being raised. To accomplish this last goal, they had to carefully chart how the children were cared for, as well as the kinds of environmental stresses the children encountered in their day-to-day activities.

METHOD

Because Thomas, Chess, and Birch were dealing with the hairy subject of individuality in children, they thought it would be a good idea to reduce the "noisiness" from the outset by using a relatively homogeneous sample in their study. So they chose families who were middle and upper class, all from New York City and a few surrounding suburbs. This strategy would help reduce the number of environmental factors they would have to take into consideration. For example, they wouldn't have to worry about explaining the individuality of small-town kids because all their kids were from a big town (a *very* big town). They began enrolling families in their study in 1956 (as I already mentioned) and continued until they ended up with a total of 85 families. Once a family was enrolled, any new children that were born into the family were observed as soon as they popped out.

Participants

A total of 136 children were included. Five children were lost during the study because they moved away. Forty-five families had 1 child, 31 had 2 children, 7 had 3 children, and 2 families had 4 children. By 1966, 10 years after the study began, they had 40 10-year-olds, 25 9-year-olds, 18 8-year-olds, 16 7-year-olds, 15 6-year-olds, 10 5-year-olds, and 12 4-year olds. About half of the children were boys (69) and half were girls (67). Seventy-eight percent of the children were Jewish, 15% were Protestant, and 7% were Catholic. At the beginning of the study, the mothers ranged in age from 20 to 41 years and the fathers ranged in age from 25 to 54 years.

A subset of the entire sample was designated the "clinical sample." These were 42 children who had symptoms of concern to their parents or their school and who were diagnosed through clinical psychiatric judgment to have a "significant degree of behavioral disturbance." Examples of behavioral disturbance were (1) significant delay in such areas as language, perceptual, or motor development; (2) self-destructive or self-endangering behaviors; (3) significant unresponsiveness to the environment; (4) flagrant flouting of social conventions such as masturbating in public; (5) significant isolation from friends; (6) persistent bullying; or (7) failure in school without having an intellectual deficiency. Although it's never a good thing when children have behavioral disturbances, it was extremely important for the study that some kids did have behavior problems, because one of the goals was to see if temperament was related to behavior disorders. Thomas, Chess, and Birch couldn't have gotten very far if all their participants were normal.

Materials

Because it was a study of such huge proportions, Thomas, Chess, and Birch used a lot of different materials to measure the psychological well-being of the children and their parents. For starters, all the children were given standard tests of cognitive functioning (in other words, IQ tests) at 3 and 6 years of age. In addition, when the children were 3 years old, the parents were tested about their attitudes toward child-rearing and were asked about their actual child care practices.

Children in the clinical sample sometimes needed additional testing, depending on their specific behavioral problems. The additional testing came in the form of psychiatric play interviews, for example, or neurological workups. The results of this additional testing were also included in the study.

Probably the most relevant measurement device for our consideration was the one Thomas, Chess, and Birch used to measure children's temperament. Remember, there were no temperament measurement instruments available at the time of their study, so they had to invent their own. They ended up developing a series of parent and teacher interviews, containing meticulously devised questions, in which parents and teachers were asked about very specific behaviors of the children that occurred under very specific circumstances. The interviews focused on behaviors that took place in typical daily routines such as feeding, sleeping, dressing, playing, and so on. For example, parents might've been asked about how their child responded to an interruption in the daily feeding or bedtime routine. Or teachers might've been asked about how easily a child responded to transitions from naptime to recess. Throughout the interviews, the authors gave special emphases to children's responses to new people, things, and situations. In addition, only examples of real behaviors were counted. If parents or teachers made *interpretations* of children's behaviors, such as "The baby hated his cereal," or "This child always gets angry if he doesn't get his way," an extra effort was made to press the parents to say exactly what the child did that led them to their conclusions.

In addition to the interviews, school observations were made of each child during a 1-hour free-play episode. During these episodes, an observer sat "unobtrusively in a corner of the schoolroom." According to the authors, "The observer noted the general and specific attributes of the setting and every observable verbal, motor, and gestural interaction of the child with materials, other children, and adults. All notations of behavior were made in concrete, descriptive terms. Inferences as to the meaning of the child's behavior were avoided."

Procedure

Unfortunately, Thomas, Chess, and Birch didn't give us a lot of detail about the precise procedures that they followed, at least not in this book. But we do know that they were quite systematic in interviewing the parents and teachers. The parents were first interviewed as soon as possible after they were enrolled in the study. The interviews were then conducted at 3-month intervals until the child was 1½ years old, at 6-month intervals until the child was 5 years old, and at yearly intervals after that.

Eighty-nine percent of the children attended nursery school, what we would call preschool today, so it was possible to begin interviewing the teachers in nursery school for the majority of the children. The first teacher interview occurred during a child's "initial adaptation to the nursery school situation, and the second took place during the latter portion of the school year." Interviews appeared to continue on a yearly basis afterward, through a second year of nursery school (if it happened), through kindergarten, and then through first grade. It's not clear from the authors' descriptions whether teacher interviews continued beyond first grade, but it seems that they did.

RESULTS

Defining Temperament

As noted earlier, one of Thomas, Chess, and Birch's first goals was to come up with a way to measure temperament. Based on their interviews and classroom observations, the authors came up with a nine-dimensional definition of temperament. Whew! In other words, they thought children's temperament should be defined as a series of scores on nine different kinds of behaviors. The nine dimensions of temperament they came up with were: (1) activity level, (2) rhythmicity, (3) approach or withdrawal, (4) adaptability, (5) intensity of reaction, (6) threshold of responsiveness, (7) quality of mood, (8) distractibility, and (9) attention span and persistence. This is quite a bit to swallow in one bite, so let's look at the dimensions one at a time in a little more detail. As we pass over each one, it might be useful for you to consider where you might score (if you were a baby), so for each dimension I'll ask you a college student–level question that might probe where you fall on that dimension.

Activity Level. The dimension of **activity level** measures how fast and how often a child does some behavior, and it always includes a measure of movement. Kids who splash a lot in the bathtub, crawl all over the house, run all over the playground, or are squirmy to hold would score high on activity level. Kids who sit quietly in the bathtub, who remain in one place in the house or at the park, or who are easy to pick up and hold would score low. (*College student–level question: Do you fidget or bounce your leg when sitting still? Would you prefer the slow pace of life in a small town, or would you prefer the hustle and bustle of a big city?*)

Rhythmicity. **Rhythmicity** focuses mostly on the regularity of bodily functions. Kids who go to sleep, wake up, get hungry, and poop at roughly the same time each day would score high on rhythmicity. Kids who go to sleep, wake up, get hungry, and poop at different times each day would score low. (*College student–level question: Do you get sleepy, wake up, get hungry, and poop at about the same time each day?*)

Approach and Withdrawal. In **approach/withdrawal**, the focus is on how children deal with new things. The new things can be people, places, toys, or routines. Children who tend toward the approach end of the scale are likely to smile when they see new people, or they'll want to play with new toys. Children at the withdrawal end do just the opposite. They tend to fret in the presence of strangers, they back away from new toys, or they might cry when they go to the doctor's office for the first time. (*College student–level question: Does the idea of dining at an exotic foreign restaurant appeal to you? Would you rather pull your own teeth than travel to a foreign city like Tokyo?*)

Adaptability. The **adaptability** dimension overlaps a little bit with approach/withdrawal. But whereas approach/withdrawal was focused on the child's initial reaction, adaptability is focused on how easily the initial reaction can be modified or soothed in the direction desired by the parents. Examples of high adaptability given during the parental interview were things like, "He used to spit out cereal when I gave it to him, but now he takes it fairly well," "Now when we go to the doctor's he doesn't start to cry till we undress him, and he even stops then if he can hold a toy." Children low in adaptability never fully adapt to the situation in the parents' desired direction. For example, "Every time he sees the scissors he starts to scream and pull his hand away, so now I cut his nails when he's sleeping," or, "He doesn't like eggs and makes a face and turns his head away no matter how I cook them." (*College student–level question: If you and a group of friends were on your way to see a movie you've really been wanting to see, and the rest of your friends decided they'd rather go hiking, how easy would it be for you to go along with their decision? Are you able to shake off pesky little things pretty easily?*)

Intensity of Reaction.   The **intensity of reaction** dimension focuses on how much energy a child puts into her response when she responds to something. It doesn't matter if the reaction is positive or negative. Children at the high-intensity end of the scale tend to overrespond, or respond beyond what would seem normal. A baby who sees balloons at a restaurant might squeal loudly with excitement. Another baby might cry for half an hour if the sun gets in her eyes for the briefest time. Children at the low end of the scale barely respond to things at all, but they give evidence that they noticed the thing by responding a little bit. They might look at the balloon for a while, or might squint slightly at the bright sun. (*College student–level question: Do you "blow up" when something irritates you? Or do you let it slide off your back?*)

Threshold of Responsiveness.   This measure reflects how intense something has to be before a child will notice it. Children with a high **threshold of responsiveness** may not respond to the loudest of sirens or the brightest of light, even though all their senses are working perfectly. Older children playing at a downtown city park may not even seem to notice the wails of a fire truck speeding by. Babies with a high threshold can tolerate wet diapers for hours. In contrast, children with a low threshold of responsiveness will look around when they hear the softest of sounds or smell the slightest of smells. When these children play at the city park, not only do they take notice of the fire truck, but they also pick out the song of the sparrow and the chatter of the chipmunks above all the traffic noise. Low-threshold babies begin crying the moment they wet their diapers. (*College student–level question: When you're taking an exam, does it bother you if somebody starts tapping his pencil, or if someone with a cold keeps sniffing? On your drive back from the beach or the pool, do you feel uncomfortable if you're still wearing your wet bathing suit?*)

Quality of Mood.   Here the focus is on whether reactions tend to be positive or negative. Babies with a positive **quality of mood** spend a lot of their day being happy. They smile and laugh a lot, they're frequently content, and nothing seems to be particularly bothersome to them. One parent said this about her positive child, "He loves to look out of the window. He jumps up and down and laughs." Babies with a negative mood quality, on the other hand, appear stressed out by a variety of things they encounter throughout the day, and other people may find it rather difficult to tolerate them. As an example, "I've tried to teach him not to knock down little girls and sit on them in the playground, so now he knocks them down and doesn't sit on them." (*College student–level question: Would your friends and family describe you as a Happy Camper? Or would they more likely call you a Grumpy Gus?*)

Distractibility.   Children high in **distractibility** are easily interrupted from whatever they're doing. This is a good quality to have when a child is mildly injured, because parents can easily get him to forget about his injury by redirecting his attention to the pretty yellow flower in the garden or the bluebird gliding through the air. Children low in distractibility, on the other hand, would go right back to crying despite their parents' efforts at redirecting their attention. (*College student–level question: Do your friends ever call you "loopy" or "scatterbrained" behind your back [or in front of your back for that matter]? Can you get so absorbed in a good book that you lose track of time?*)

Attention Span and Persistence.   This dimension is actually two different measures rolled into one. **Attention span** refers to the length of time a child stays engaged in a particular task when there's little interference. **Persistence** is more along the lines of how long a child will keep doing something despite interference. A child high in attention span, for example, might "play Barbies" for hours on end. If the child is also high in persistence, she will continue playing Barbies even when her big brother keeps coming into her room and taking her Barbies away from her. A child low in attention span doesn't stay engaged in any one thing for very long, and so might switch from playing Barbies to playing dress-up to watching a cartoon on TV. A child low in persistence will break off from playing Barbies if something interrupts her flow of activity, such as when her dog comes into her room and licks her face. (*College student–level question: Does it get under your skin if you're watching TV with someone who likes to channel-surf? Do you enjoy taking phone calls when you're studying for an exam or writing an essay for a class?*)

Temperament and Severe Behavioral Disturbances

If you remember, one of Thomas, Chess, and Birch's goals was to see if children's temperament had anything to do with the emergence of severe behavior disorders. So they conducted a second analysis to see if children in the clinical sample were different from the rest of the kids in terms of each of the nine dimensions of temperament. They began by dividing the clinical sample into two general groups: children with active behavior disturbances and children with passive behavior disturbances. These two groups of children were more or less at opposite extremes in terms of behavior disorders. The active behavior disturbance group engaged in what today would be called "acting out" behavior, or an **externalizing disorder**. These were kids who generally had behavior control problems. They might bully other children, for example, or they might defiantly disobey the teacher. You can probably best understand the passive behavior disturbance group as kids who are extraordinarily shy. They didn't participate in group activities when requested, but they didn't show outward signs of anxiety or fear either. They were "wallflowers." These behaviors would be characteristic of what today we'd call **internalizing disorders**.

Thomas, Chess, and Birch found that a number of temperament measures predicted whether or not a child would develop a behavioral disturbance. Now this is not to say that children's temperament *made* them have behavioral problems. Temperament was only *predictive*. You might think of temperament as a risk indicator. Not all the children who were in the clinical sample had deviant temperaments. And not all the children with deviant temperaments developed behavior disturbances. We're simply talking about group *tendencies*. Here is a summary of how each of the two behavior disturbance groups differed from "normal" on the various temperament dimensions. I'll also point out how the various temperament dimensions changed over time for the two clinical groups. We'll begin with the active behavioral disturbance group.

Temperamental Profile of Kids With Active Behavior Disturbances.   Not surprisingly, children in the active behavior disturbance group were higher in *activity level* and more *intense* in their responses to the world. You can almost picture this child from your own elementary-school days as the kid who could never sit still and who constantly made loud, rude comments to the teacher and other students. These children were also less *adaptable* and more *persistent* than normal. This means they were hard to calm down once they got on a roll, and because they were *persistent*, once they got on a roll, they stayed on it. On a few of the temperament dimensions, children with active behavior disturbances were at first indistinguishable from normal children. It was only as they got older that their temperamental profiles began deviating from normal. One temperament dimension that followed this pattern was *threshold of responsiveness*. Active behavior kids started out being no more sensitive to the sights and sounds in the surrounding environment than normal kids, but with age they became more and more sensitive to them. Similarly, at the younger ages, these kids were no more *distractible* than the normal kids, but they got more and more distractible as they got older.

Temperamental Profile of Kids With Passive Behavior Disturbances.   As a rule, the temperamental profiles of kids in the passive behavior disorder group were far more complicated, and they changed greatly from one age to the next. There were a couple of across-the-board differences. Specifically, and as you might expect, passive behaviorally disturbed children were much lower in *activity level* than normal children. But these kids were also far more negative in *mood*. In other words, they were stationary, unhappy little children. But for the rest of the dimensions, the temperaments of these children varied quite a bit depending on how old they were. In terms of *rhythmicity*, the passive kids were initially far more regular and predictable than normal children, but over time they became as unpredictable as normal children. For five other dimensions—approach/withdrawal, threshold of reactivity, intensity, distractibility, and persistence—they started out on one side of the normal children, and then as they got older they moved completely to the other side of the normal children. For example, the passive kids started out being much more likely than normal kids to be interested in new things, but later were much more likely to withdraw and shy away from new things. They started out having a low threshold of reactivity, meaning they didn't seem to notice much going on around them, but after a few years they ended up being hypersensitive. They started out being much less intense in their reactions, but eventually became much more intense. They also started out being much less persistent, but ended up being much more persistent. Finally, they started out as more distractible, and ended up being much less distractible. Of course, these age-related changes are extremely complicated and we can't really spend much time on them here. But the point is that early temperament was a predictor of children's likelihood for developing a behavior disturbance.

Temperament Clusters

If there's a single feature of Thomas, Chess, and Birch's work that made the headlines, it was their identification of *clusters* of temperament characteristics that led them to describe three general *types* of children. Through a number of highly technical statistical analyses, they found that a number of temperament dimensions tended to go together. For example, they found that children who tended to have high withdrawal (shying away) scores also tended to have biological irregularity, tended to have a negative mood, tended not to be adaptable, and tended to have high-intensity reactions. They called children with this temperament cluster **difficult children**. Children with this temperamental profile were royal pains in the keister to deal with and have sometimes jokingly been called "mother killers" at professional meetings. But on the other side of the coin were children who were interested in new things (high in approach), who tended to be biologically regular, who tended to have a positive mood, who tended to be high in adaptability, and who tended to have low-intensity reactions. These were labeled **easy children**. Children with this tempcramental profile are the kind parents imagine having before they actually have them. Thomas, Chess, and Birch also discovered a third cluster of temperament dimensions, which they thought characterized the **slow-to-warm-up child**. The slow-to-warm-up child is initially high in withdrawal and slow to adapt, but has low-intensity negative reactions. In many ways, reactions of the slow-to-warm-up child mirror the reactions of the difficult child, but differ in that he eventually comes around and gets along just fine in new situations.

DISCUSSION

Goodness of Fit

Having identified nine dimensions of temperamental individuality among children, along with three major temperamental clusters, Thomas, Chess, and Birch laid out the blueprints for what they called "a dynamic theory of child psychiatry and development." The essential feature of their new theory was, of course, children's temperament. Now, being the major innovators of this newfangled temperament theory, they admitted to being tempted to place temperament at the central core of their theory. But they realized that if they gave temperament an exclusive role, their theory would have no grander perspective than the "static" theories of their time, behaviorism and Freudian psychoanalysis, which they were rebelling against.

What made these other theories static was the assumption that the direction of influence was always a one-way street, that the children themselves didn't have much say in the development of their own individuality. For example, the static feature of the behavioral theories was that they placed almost exclusive emphasis on environmental punishments and reinforcements in producing children's individuality. The static feature of the Freudian-type theories was that they placed too much emphasis on unconscious motivating forces. Thomas, Chess, and Birch didn't want to fall into the same trap by placing the entire developmental burden in their theory on temperament. No, they thought a realistic account for the development of children's individuality would have to be much more dynamic.

The "complex dynamic" they thought would be better at explaining the development of children's individuality went something like this: Children with certain temperamental profiles would elicit characteristic responses from the environment, and these characteristic environmental responses would then bounce back and further influence the specific temperamental characteristics of the children. The now-changed temperamental characteristics of the children would then have additional impacts on the surrounding environment, which would then bounce back once again and have an additional impact on children's temperament. The cycle of temperament → environment → temperament → environment could go on forever. This isn't necessarily a bad thing, especially if the child is well adjusted and mentally healthy. But if the cycle resulted in the development of behavioral disturbances, the cycle would need to be broken, either through psychotherapy or through improved parenting skills. Children who cried and whined a lot, for example, might be inclined to bring out frustration and impatience on the part of their parents. As these parents got irritated at their children because of the constant crying and whining, the parents would be inclined to get angry at their children and were at risk for resorting to excessive punishment. The punishment given by the parents would then further increase the amount of crying and whining of the children. The only way this cycle could be broken would be if the parents learned to be more patient with their children. The role of psychotherapy, then, might be nothing more than offering parents alternative strategies for dealing with their crying, whining children.

Accordingly, Thomas, Chess, and Birch introduced the concept of **goodness of fit**. The goodness-of-fit idea reflected how well a child's environment would accommodate his unique temperamental profile. Good fits between children's temperaments and their environments would be likely to produce mentally healthy, well-adjusted children. Poor fits between children's temperaments and their environments would be likely to produce children with behavioral disturbances, or at least put them at risk for behavioral disturbances. So, although children with difficult temperaments were difficult to deal with, if they had understanding parents, they wouldn't necessarily develop behavioral disturbances, because their environments could accommodate their temperamental difficulty. On the other hand, although easy children were easy to deal with, they *could* develop behavioral disturbances if their environment didn't fit them well. For example, parents who are always on the go may become intolerant of a child who doesn't share their enthusiasm.

CONCLUSIONS

Thomas, Chess, and Birch revolutionized child psychology because they developed a whole new temperament-based theory that launched wave after wave of research on the developmental impacts of children's individuality. Early temperament research focused on the role of temperament in the development of behavioral disturbances, following essentially the same trail blazed by the authors. But more recently, researchers have taken temperament for a ride in all manner of developmental areas. A number of researchers, for example, have investigated whether temperament might be related to the development of children's intelligence. As you may have noticed, a couple of Thomas, Chess, and Birch's temperament scales are closely related to measures of cognitive functioning. Attention span, for instance, has a long history of being drawn into measures of intelligence. On standard IQ tests like the Wechsler Intelligence Scale for Children, attention span is routinely assessed.

The results of some of this research have revealed some very interesting findings that make for some rather fascinating possibilities. In two studies, for example, children with difficult temperaments were actually found to be cognitively advanced! This should give us cause to pause before making any overly negative generalizations about temperamentally difficult children. But why would difficult children be cognitively advanced? Well, if you think about it beyond a surface level, it does make some sense. One thing that makes some children more intelligent than others is the fact that they know a lot of things and are able to solve problems quickly. If they know a lot of things and solve problems quickly, it stands to reason that under many circumstances they're going to become bored more quickly than less intelligent children. And if they become bored more quickly than less intelligent children, it also stands to reason that they would become cranky and discontented more quickly than less intelligent children. Being cranky and discontented is one characteristic of the temperamentally difficult child. So being temperamentally difficult isn't necessarily a bad thing. It could be an indication of better intellectual functioning!

On the other hand, temperamental difficulty has also been associated with slower language development. This also makes some sense. Language development proceeds most rapidly when children have people to talk to; and if a child is temperamentally difficult, she may not be the most pleasant conversational partner. Temperamentally difficult children simply may not get as many opportunities to engage in long, extended conversations with other people. Temperamentally easy children, in contrast, make for delightful conversational partners.

Researchers have also been exploring the biological underpinnings of temperament. Thomas, Chess, and Birch's goal of maintaining a strict behavioral definition is laudable, especially since they wanted to make sure parents and teachers weren't reading too much into children's behaviors. But still, the behaviors have to come from somewhere, and the most likely candidate would probably be underlying brain activity. These days, modern temperament researchers have been exploring which parts of the brain might be most responsible for temperament-related behaviors. In a wonderfully thorough and recent review article, Mary Rothbart and John Bates have highlighted a number of neurological factors that might be responsible for producing a variety of temperamental characteristics. (If you're interested in knowing, most of these are located in the brain's limbic system.) Once the brain parts responsible for extremely maladaptive temperamental characteristics have been identified, it may eventually be possible to develop medications for their treatment.

Measurement Issues

Thomas, Chess, and Birch have received a lot of criticism for basing their temperament measures on parent and teacher interviews. So a lot of researchers have been developing alternative techniques for measuring temperament. At least a half-dozen different checklists have been invented for measuring temperament, but they usually still depend on parents' perceptions in filling them out. Other techniques have been invented to measure temperament directly, through laboratory observations. But the problem with laboratory observations is that they reflect children's behaviors in only a single situation. Because temperament is believed to wind its way through *all* of children's day-to-day experiences, laboratory observations simply have to be supplemented with observations in a variety of alternative settings. Whether we should employ parent-reported temperament or laboratory-observed temperament is actually the source of quite a bit of controversy these days. But then again, revolutionaries are known to kick up a little dust in their path.

As with any other scientific topic, additional refinement of what temperament is, what it means, and how it's measured will only take place one study at a time. And it may not take all that much longer. At its current pace, temperament researchers are pumping out scientific studies at the rate of over 130 investigations per year! We can only hope that a continued focus on children's individuality will continue sharpening our understanding of the psychological development and well-being of our children. Once the temperament concept loses its effectiveness, we'll have to brace ourselves for another revolution.

Bibliography

Dixon, W. E., Jr., & Smith, P. H. (2000). Links between early temperament and language acquisition. *Merrill-Palmer Quarterly, 46,* 417–440.

Rothbart, M. K., & Bates, J. (1998). Temperament. In W. Damon & N. Eisenberg (Eds.), *Handbook of child psychology, vol. 3, social, emotional, and personality development.* New York: Wiley.

Smith, P. H., Dixon, W. E., Jr., Jankowski, J. J., Sanscrainte, M. M., Davidson, B. K., & Loboschefski, T. (1997). Longitudinal relationships between habituation and temperament in infancy. *Merrill-Palmer Quarterly, 43,* 291–304.

Questions for Discussion

1. Although it's hard to raise temperamentally difficult children, is it possible that temperamental difficulty would give any children an adaptive advantage? Why? Who gets more attention from parents, difficult or easy children? How might this influence children's later development?

2. What kinds of parenting strategies would work best with temperamentally easy versus tempermentally difficult children?

3. Temperament researchers have shown that mothers and fathers show only moderate agreement when it comes to judging the temperament of their children. Why might mothers and fathers rate their children differently when it comes to temperament? What are some specific examples of how mothers and fathers might perceive their children's temperament differently?

17

Armadillos Aren't the Only Mammals That Grow Armor

JOURNEYS FROM CHILDHOOD TO MIDLIFE: RISK, RESILIENCE, AND RECOVERY.

Werner, E. E., & Smith, R. S. (2001). *Ithaca, NY: Cornell University Press.*   (RANK 17)

BUILDING HOPE

When I started to think why did something have to make a difference for me, I came up with a list. The first risk factor on the top of the list was for where I was at that time in my life growing up on the island of Kauai, I was culturally wrong. My mother was Hawaiian, born and raised on the island, and my father is from New Jersey. Where I grew up was what we call Hawaiian Home; it's similar to the idea of a Native American reservation. . . . You must be Hawaiian to live there. . . . This was back in [the] early sixties. Though Hawaii is the melting pot of the world today, and there is a mixture of all kinds of cultures and people and ethnicities, they didn't mix back then.

Number two, we lived in a blended family. My mother had three children from a first marriage. My father had six children from a first marriage. Then they proceeded to have four more. And I was the oldest. . . .

Number three, we were poor. . . . There were times when there was no food on the table. We never, ever, ever had new clothes, never. . . . We never had shoes. It's a good thing in Hawaii you don't need them; it doesn't get cold enough. Bare feet are fine, and that's how we existed. . . .

Number four, my father was an alcoholic. When he wasn't working, he was drunk. And when he was drunk, mom was angry. Lucky for us mom didn't drink. . . . My mother would rage when dad was drunk. I remember walking into the kitchen one day where she had grabbed his bottles, and busted [them], and was going after him. There was blood all over the kitchen, and there was blood all over her. As children, you don't stick around to watch your parents hurt each other. You take off. . . . I remember watching my mother chase my father down with the car. He was drunk. She was angry, and she chased him with the car through the pasture fence, knocked him over. I don't know how the man lived to die a natural death, but he did.

I remember a time when I was in the second grade when my mother was institutionalized because she had a nervous breakdown. What was very difficult for me was that the elementary school was on a little one lane road, and the hospital was right across the street. So I would sit in my classroom and I would look out the window and know that my mother is over there. I didn't understand why she had to be there with all those funny people and why she couldn't go home. . . .

The first thing I think made a difference for me was that we were expected as children to work, and we were expected to work hard. If we didn't we would get lickings. We would get beat. That was all there was to it. . . . We did laundry by hand for nine people. If there's no food, there's no washing machine. If there's no food, there's no lawn mower to clean the yard. So we did it with sickles and hoes and what we call cane knives. . . .

Number two, probably the most important for me were caring and supportive people throughout all of my life. I was fortunate to have such people. . . . For me, the first and foremost was my grandma. . . . She was a wonderful, wonderful, quiet Hawaiian woman. . . . I remember a couple of things you need to know. Number one is we were "those children." You know what "those children" are? The ones where you as parents say, "I don't want you playing with "those children." I don't want you going to "those people's house." We were "those children" that nobody wanted around. . . . Grandma Kahaunaele never treated me like one of "those children.". . . My Grandma Kahaunaele is the only person I remember who would comb my hair. I remember going to school one day and the teacher said to me, "Doesn't anybody ever comb your hair? Doesn't anybody ever wash your face?" I guess I was dirty. Grandma Kahaunaele was the only one who would comb my hair. . . .

Third thing . . . that made a difference for me was education. . . . When I was twelve years old, I left Kauai and went to the main island of Oahu to go to that school—all of the money comes from King Kamehameha. . . . Personally I would not send my child away at age twelve. There is too much that goes on in the life of a twelve-year-old. But for us it was one of the best things my parents did.

At age sixteen, as a junior in high school, I became pregnant. The policy at Kamehameha at that time was when you're pregnant, you're gone. I was taken to the office of the dean of students; her name was Wynona Reuben. . . . She basically said, 'Well, I'm sorry. You've got to leave.' She put me on an airplane back to Kauai to tell my parents.

We had to make some decisions. The decision at that time was that I would get married. So at age sixteen, I got married. At age seventeen, I had my first child. . . . We went back up [to] Wynona Reuben's office. I don't know how or what happened, but I was allowed to go back to school, pregnant and married. It had never happened in this institution before. A few years ago, I wanted to find out what happened, so I called my counselor who was still counseling at that school. I said, "Tom, how come they let me come back?" He said Wynona Reuben called the counseling department—they had been looking at the problem of teenage pregnancy in students—and she said to them: "You know the parent-student program we've been talking about? I want you to push it and I want this student to be the first one in it. She is not a bad student. She just made a mistake."

The other thing that going away to Kamehameha did for me, it broadened my vision a whole lot. It helped me make some choices that I never knew I could. All around me in my neighborhood was alcoholism and abuse. Uncle Sonny across the way, every day, all day long, he sat on his porch with his bottle of Primo Beer. Uncle Henry next door was a policeman but when he got angry, he would beat his children. I remember one day his littlest son came out of the house with an iron burn on his back because his dad was angry with him. All around me, that's what I saw. . . . When I went away, I realized that it wasn't the way it had to be. There were people who had fathers who didn't drink. I realized that I could make choices.

The fourth thing that made a difference for me—when there was no Grandma Kahaunaele, . . . when there was no Wynona Reuben, [or] the many, many others who cared—was that somewhere, someplace down the line, somebody had taught me, "There is somebody greater than us who loves you." And that is my hope and my belief. Whatever that translates for you—a belief in God, a belief in a religion, a goal, a dream, something that we can hang on to. As adults, we need to give our young people hope and something to hang on to.

In this chapter we consider the groundbreaking work of Emmy Werner and her colleague Ruth Smith, who dedicated their lives to tracking the origins of resilience in children. In their major longitudinal study, ranked 16th most revolutionary in the field of child psychology, Werner and Smith traced the development of a whole community of children born and raised on the island of Kauai (the northwesternmost of the Hawaiian islands, pronounced "cow-EYE") from 1955 onward. Their 2001 book is actually the most recent installment of a series of books reporting on the development of these children and, as such, represents the culmination of their landmark longitudinal study. The narrative reproduced above, was excerpted from their book.

The children on the island of Kauai were ideal candidates for an exploration of resilience because the population of the island underwent dramatic change during the time of the investigation. The study began prior to Hawaii's inclusion as the 50th state of the union and continued well into a period of massive economic, cultural, and social upheaval as Hawaii transitioned at head-spinning pace from an agricultural- to an industrial- to a tourism-based economy. And if that wasn't enough, in 1982, and again in 1992, the island was devastated by Hurricanes Iwa and Iniki. The tourism industry was especially damaged after Iniki struck, wiping out 85% of the available lodging space.

Werner and Smith wanted to understand whether children can cope when tremendous stress is placed on them under conditions of large-scale cultural and social upheaval. In their own words, Werner and Smith wrote that their primary goals "were to document, in natural history fashion, the course of all pregnancies and their outcomes in the entire island community from birth to age forty, and to assess the long-term consequences of perinatal trauma, poverty, parental psychopathology, and adverse rearing conditions on the individuals' adaptation to life." Although they didn't start out with a plan to study resilience directly, the amazing success stories of many of the Kauaian children naturally led Werner and Smith into a detailed investigation of the development of resilience.

INTRODUCTION

In their introductory chapters, Werner and Smith outline a number of characteristics of their longitudinal study that made it unique among the long-term longitudinal studies of the time. Perhaps its most remarkable feature was that their participants were rural, village-dwelling, multiracial folks. Many of the other studies focused on white, middle-class, city-dwelling types. And as we've already seen in the Baumrind chapter (Chapter 13), what applies to the majority culture doesn't necessarily apply to minority cultures. Werner and Smith described the population of Kauai as "a kaleidoscope of ethnic groups: Japanese, Filipino, part- and full-Hawaiians, Portuguese, Puerto Ricans, Chinese, Koreans, and a small group of Anglo-Caucasians." The children were mostly descended from immigrants who traveled to Hawaii to work on the sugar and pineapple farms, which made up the lion's share of the island's agricultural industry.

The other longitudinal studies going on at the same time as Werner's were revealing that a lot of children were capable of turning out to be just fine despite a variety of physical and environmental hardships. These children were often described as **resilient**. *Resilience* means that the children seemed to be affected very little by all the traumatic circumstances going on in their lives. They were kinda like human Bobo dolls; you know, the inflatable doll that you can knock down but it always pops back up for more? So even though some children were growing up under the most outrageous conditions in the most terrible homes, they seemed to turn out okay anyway. But the problem with those other studies was that no one really knew why the resilient kids *became* resilient. So Werner and Smith started with the most resilient children in their own sample, and began looking for clues as to what made them resilient. They took into account both the biological and the psychological makeup of the kids, as well as the environments that they were growing up in. Werner and Smith hoped to identify a set of characteristics that served to buffer the resilient children against otherwise overwhelming odds. The no-brainer implications here are that if such **buffering agents** could be identified, they could be used to benefit future generations of children who are also at risk for developmental disabilities and poor qualities of life.

Werner and Smith kept tabs on the whole Kauaian community of children across four decades of their lives. They began in 1954 by developing a list of all the occupants of all the villages on the island, and paid special attention to the women of childbearing age (12 years old and older). These women were asked to report as soon as they became pregnant. Werner and Smith then began collecting data on all the children born the following year. The sample consisted of all babies born in 1955. The babies were evaluated for a number of characteristics that were associated with **prenatal** and **perinatal complications**. (Prenatal and perinatal complications are those that take place during the pregnancy and during the time of birth.) Mothers of these babies were interviewed right after the babies were born and then again when the babies reached their first birthday. Medical exams were conducted during the second year, usually when the babies were about 20 months of age. Finally, there were 10-year, 18-year, 32-year, and 40-year follow-ups, at which time a whole battery of additional evaluations and assessments were completed. Imagine what it must've been like for the authors to dedicate 45 years of their lives to a single scientific study. That's what I call commitment! But their efforts didn't go unnoticed by the Hawaiian state government, which initiated several public service efforts to help reduce the incidence of a variety of developmental difficulties for future generations of Hawaiian children. Their efforts also didn't go unnoticed by the child psychology community, which recommended by vote that I include their study in this book. Now, on to the details.

METHOD

The detailed examinations that Werner and Smith made of the Kauaian children from infancy through middle age is no doubt one of the most outstanding features of the study. In fact, it's probably because their evaluations were so comprehensive that they were able to capture so well the aspects of the Kauaian children's lives that fostered the development of resilience in so many of them.

Participants

The initial cohort of the Kauai study consisted of all 698 children born in 1955 on the island of Kauai. Broken down by ethnicity, there were 217 Japanese, 147 part- and full-Hawaiian, 115 Filipino, 42 Portuguese, and 17 Anglo-Caucasian babies. The remaining babies were described as coming from other ethnic mixtures, including Chinese, Korean, and Puerto Rican heritages. The vast majority of the babies came from lower-class homes, although there was also a good-sized chunk of babies from middle-class homes too. Very few babies came from upper-class homes, although there were some.

Materials and Procedures

As noted above, the children were evaluated before birth, during birth, right after birth, about a year after birth, about 2 years after birth, then at 10 years after birth, 18 years after birth, 32 years after birth, and finally at 40 years after birth. The types of evaluations used, of course, differed depending on how old the children were at the time of the evaluations.

Pre/Perinatal Complications.   For each baby, a pediatrician scored whether or not any of some 60 complications or risk-indicating events took place. If such events did take place, they were scored for their severity. Of course, I can't go over all 60 things that the babies were evaluated for, but here are a few examples. For the prenatal (before birth) evaluations, the pediatrician looked for such complications as vaginal bleeding, placenta previa (when the placenta covers the opening from the uterus to the vagina, thus preventing normal vaginal birth), abnormal fetal heartrate, abnormal positioning of the baby in the uterus, and congenital syphilis (when the fetus itself has syphilis). Perinatal (time of birth) complications included things like breech birth (being born foot- or butt-first), delayed onset of breathing after birth, birth injuries, being very small for gestational age, or having abnormal reflexes.

Home Visits in Year 1.   In the first year, public health workers and social workers interviewed mothers in their homes. They asked mothers to rate the temperaments of their babies, including activity levels, social responsiveness, and ease of handling. They also asked mothers whether their babies had any distressing habits like frequent head-banging, frequent temper tantrums, or irregular sleeping or feeding routines.

Pediatric and Psychological Examinations in Year 2.   Two pediatricians conducted medical exams on the children when they were about 20 months old. They evaluated all the toddlers' organ systems and looked for evidence of congenital (from birth) and acquired (after birth) defects. They evaluated nutritional intake, sleeping and feeding habits, and speech, motor, and social development. Finally, the pediatricians made global evaluations of the overall physical and intellectual status of each toddler by rating him or her as "superior," "normal," "low-normal," or "retarded." Two psychologists made official intellectual assessments using the Cattell Infant Intelligence

Scale and the Vineland Social Maturity Scale. The psychologists also made observations of the toddlers' social behaviors during the actual testing sessions and asked their mothers about any stressful events that had taken place between Year 1 and Year 2.

Family Environment in Year 2.   The quality of the family environment was measured by taking note of the quality or social status of the father's occupation, the mother's educational level, the family's standard of living, the conditions of the family's housing, and how crowded the home was. Also, family stability was measured based on whether the father or mother was absent, how much marital discord happened, and whether alcoholism was present in one or both parents.

Child Competence in Year 10.   When the children were 10 years old, a concerted effort was made to determine how advanced they were in both social and intellectual skills. The major determinant here was whether the children had developed serious physical, intellectual, behavioral, or emotional problems that interfered with their performance in school. The children were also given tests of mental abilities using the Bender-Gestalt Test and the Primary Mental Abilities Test, which measured reasoning skill as well as verbal, numerical, spatial, and perceptual-motor skills.

Family Environment in Year 10.   Nurses and social workers visited the home in Year 10 to once again find out about the quality of the family environment. As in Year 2, the quality of the father's job was taken into consideration, as was the condition of the housing. In addition, the children's home environments were rated for how educationally stimulating they were, and a clinical psychologist scored how emotionally supportive each child's social environment was.

Year 18.   In Year 18 the authors began focusing on how successfully the children were adapting to their young adult lives. Using a variety of publicly available information, Werner and Smith were able to find out how frequently the teens had been in trouble with the law, how many had developed serious mental health problems requiring some form of medical treatment, and how many girls had become pregnant. They were also granted access to the teens' test scores on the School and College Ability Test and the Sequential Tests of Educational Progress. Both of these tests were routinely given by the school systems, and the scores more or less reflected the students' levels of educational achievement. Personality tests were also given to some of the teens, and they were interviewed about their attitudes toward school, their career plans, and their level of satisfaction with their work and social lives. They were asked about their friends, their relationship with their parents, how comfortable they felt around their family, and how much they identified with their parents.

Year 32.   The big question in the adult years really was how well the people's lives were going. So when the kids reached their early 30s, Werner and Smith collected information about how well the participants had transitioned into the work world, how successful their marriages were, and how they were doing as parents of their own children. They were also given the Life Events Checklist, which is a down-and-dirty measure of how many stressful events had occurred in their lives, and the Rotter Locus of Control Scale, which is a measure of how much control they felt they had over their own lives. Finally, public records were again searched to find out how often these individuals had a run-in with the legal system or sought out assistance for mental and physical disabilities. Through these public records, Werner and Smith found out about crime rates, divorce rates, lawsuits, delinquent child support payments, child and spouse abuse, restraining orders, and the frequency of visits to the hospital.

Year 40. The 40-year follow-up measures were again aimed at finding out about the participants' life circumstances. Measures of employment and marital status were taken, as were counts of the number of children in their households and the number of serious health problems they or their family members experienced. Because this cohort had just experienced Hurricane Iniki 3 years earlier, the authors also collected information about any hardships the families suffered as a result of Iniki. The participants were again interviewed about their relationships with their parents, their spouses, their children, and their friends. They were asked about their goals for the future and about how satisfied they were with a variety of aspects of their lives. They were given the Life Events Checklist and were additionally tested on their "psychological well-being" using the Scales of Psychological Well-Being test. Finally, criminal, court, and hospital records were checked to determine how many times the participants had run-ins with the law, the legal system, and the medical system.

RESULTS

Amazingly, 489 of the original 698 babies were still participating in the study by the time of the 40-year follow-ups. This corresponds to a whopping 70% retention rate! Although Werner and Smith provided a broad range of information about their 1955 cohort from birth to age 40, I'm going to focus mostly on the participants who were considered "at risk" for a host of problems throughout their lifetime but who overcame their hardships anyway. Of these folks, more than 80% were still participating in the study by the time of the 40-year follow-up.

Of course, one of the big questions that arose during the course of the study was how well the adults had adapted to their life circumstances. To measure life quality, Werner and Smith developed an Adult Adaptation scale, which took into account six dimensions of life quality. These six areas of life, as well as what it took to be classified as "successful," included:

Work. The successful individual was employed or enrolled in school *and* was satisfied with work or school achievement.

Relationship With Spouse or Mate. The successful individual was married or in a long-term committed relationship *and* was satisfied with his or her partner and had little or no conflict *and* had no record of desertion, divorce, or spouse abuse.

Relationship With Children. The successful individual thought very highly of his or her children *and* was very satisfied with his or her role as a parent *and* had no record of child abuse or delinquent child support payments.

Relationship With Parents and Siblings. The successful individual evaluated father, mother, and siblings positively *and* had little or no conflict with them.

Relationship With Peers. The successful individual had several close friends who provided emotional support when needed *and* the individual was very satisfied with the relationship *and* had no record of assault, battery, rape, or other criminal offenses.

Self-Assessment.   The successful individual was very happy or mostly satisfied with his or her life *and* had no alcohol or drug problems *and* had no psychosomatic illnesses *and* had no record of psychiatric disorders.

An amazing 47% of the participants met Werner and Smith's criteria for good adaptation to adult life at age 40; and another third of the participants were judged to be functioning adequately. Unfortunately, about 16% of the sample were judged to be doing poorly—for any of a number of possible reasons. Men were more than twice as likely as women to be among the poorly functioning group.

Pathways of Resilience

Werner and Smith's study will go down in history as one of the most intensive long-term investigations of human development from birth to midlife. But perhaps the most revolutionary contribution made by their study was their identification of the factors that contributed to the resilience of a number of participants in their group. Roughly 30% of the participants in their study encountered a variety of "potent" biological and psychological risk factors when they were growing up. Werner and Smith noted summarily, "They experienced perinatal stress, grew up in chronic poverty, were reared by parents who had not graduated from high school, and lived in a family environment troubled by chronic discord, parental alcoholism, or mental illness."

Most of the children who experienced at least four of these risk factors by age 2 wound up having serious learning and behavioral problems in school by age 10 or had run-ins with the law, mental health problems, and unplanned pregnancies by age 18. But, and here is the clincher, one third of the children who experienced these adversities turned out to be successful in adulthood anyway! Werner and Smith called these individuals "vulnerable but invincible." Apparently, there was just something about these people that catapulted them into a successful healthy adult lifestyle, despite all the obstacles thrown in their way. In Werner and Smith's words, "they had developed into competent, confident, and caring persons who expressed a great desire to make use of whatever opportunities came along to improve themselves."

The fact that these 72 people turned out to be "invincible," despite the apparently overwhelming odds against them, and the fact that Werner and Smith had been following them from even before they were born, gave Werner and Smith the perfect opportunity to identify the factors that contributed to resilience. All they had to do was look to see what these invincible people did for themselves and had going for them that the other less successful people didn't.

Child Predictors of Resilience.   One of the earliest factors that distinguished resilient babies from their more unfortunate peers was their temperament (see the Thomas, Chess, and Birch chapter [16] for more on temperament). Specifically, resilient babies had temperaments that brought out positive, happy responses from the people around them. Resilient babies were very active, affectionate, cuddly, and easy to deal with. Also, their sleeping and eating habits were less distressing to their parents. In toddlerhood, the resilient kids were more alert, independent, and outgoing than their less resilient peers; they had better communication skills; and they were good at getting things they wanted without asking for help from others. By school age, the resilient kids got along better with other kids in their classes and tended to have better problem-solving skills, but they weren't especially intellectually gifted. And interestingly, the resilient kids were less likely to pursue sex-typed interests and activities than the nonresilient children, which meant they had a more flexible range of ways to interact with their surroundings. Resilient boys, for example, may have been just as happy playing with Barbie dolls as with Tonka trucks. Nonresilient boys would've had a major problem if they had to play with Barbie dolls.

The resilient children tended to have fewer than four siblings, and the spacing between them and their brothers and sisters was about 2 years. They were also less likely to have long periods of separation from their primary caregivers, and they had at least one caregiver with whom they were able to establish a close emotional bond. These caregivers weren't necessarily the mother or father either. They were often a grandmother or grandfather, a sibling, or some other authority figure in their lives. The children were also involved in close relationships with others outside of the family. These external relationships often came in the form of close personal ties with friends and church youth group leaders, but also came in the form of being involved with civic organizations such as the YMCA/YWCA or 4-H. The fact that emotional closeness with another person appeared so important for the development of resilience makes sense given what we know of John Bowlby's research (Chapter 11) on the importance of attachment.

Young Adulthood Predictors of Resilience.   As the children entered their late teenage years, a period we commonly call young adulthood, a number of additional factors became associated with resilience. For one thing, resilient teens had a relatively positive view of themselves and believed they had control over their own destinies. Indeed, resilient children were, as a rule, highly motivated to achieve. And resilient girls were especially assertive and independent.

Middle Adulthood Predictors of Resilience.   Once they reached middle adulthood, defined as the 32- and 40-year age periods, the resilient individuals continued to differ from their trouble-prone peers in a number of ways. For one thing, the resilient ones were more likely to go to college and to have and hold jobs. Very few resilient individuals were unemployed. And even though their fathers tended to have low-paying, unskilled jobs when they were children, they themselves tended to have professional and managerial positions.

In terms of family life, the resilient men and women had fewer children and viewed parenthood more positively than did the nonresilient men and women. The resilient men's attitudes toward parenting was especially noteworthy. Not only did they enjoy the opportunity to care for their children, they saw child-rearing as an important characteristic of their own self-development. Their nonresilient male peers were more likely to view child-rearing as a burden.

A very interesting difference that arose between the resilient adults and the risk-prone group was in how they dealt with their parents. Although both groups had troublesome parents, either because the parents were still alcoholics or were mentally ill, or because their parents' marital relationships were still in a state of disharmony, the resilient adult children were much more likely to simply "disconnect" from their parents' problems. That is, they detached themselves emotionally. The risk-prone adult children, on the other hand, still seemed to get caught up in the turmoil of their parents' lives. This finding is interesting because under most circumstances, you wouldn't think it a good idea for people to emotionally detach themselves from their parents. You might think detachment would be unhealthy. But for the resilient folks, detaching themselves from the mess of their parents' lives seemed to be a good thing for them in order to maintain their own mental health.

Finally, one of the biggest differences between resilient people and their trouble-prone peers was in the goals they set for themselves in terms of personal achievement. As noted by Werner and Smith, "Career or job success was the highest priority on the agenda of the resilient men and women, but the lowest priority on the agenda of their peers with problems in adolescence."

DISCUSSION

Because I've focused on the specific theme of human resilience, I've not been able to do justice to the vast amount of additional and vital information Werner and Smith have pulled together from their Kauai study about what it's like to grow up vulnerable. All I can do here is point out that their book has a number of additional chapters documenting developmental outcomes from a variety of perspectives. For example, they have chapters on the impact of teenage pregnancy, the impact of learning disabilities, and the impact of juvenile delinquency on adult development. Should your curiosity demand greater fulfillment than what I've been able to supply here, I direct you to these chapters.

In summarizing the results, the bottom line is that unique characteristics of the person *as well as* unique characteristics of the environment are both powerful contributors to long-term well-being and life success. In particular, Werner and Smith identified five characteristics of the person and five characteristics of the environment that seem to best promote resiliency in the individual. The personal factors are (1) *autonomy and social maturity*, (2) *scholastic competence*, (3) *self-efficacy*, (4) *temperament*, and (5) *health status*. Taking these in combination, individuals most likely to succeed in troubled times include those high in social maturity and whose who perform well in school. Resilient folks believe in their own abilities, are socially outgoing (extraverted), and are less susceptible to diseases and accidents. The most important environmental factors are (1) *maternal competence*, (2) *sources of emotional support in childhood*, (3) *sources of emotional support in adolescence*, (4) *sources of emotional support in adulthood*, and (5) *the number of stressful life events experienced*. Taking these factors in combination, environments that are most likely to promote life success are those that provide emotional support, those that provide emotional support, and those that provide emotional support! Although it's fairly easy to separate out personal factors from environment factors on paper, in real life it's easy to imagine how an individual's personality characteristics would interact with his environment to bring about a socially supportive network. Obviously, a child who is socially mature and socially outgoing would probably have an advantage in constructing socially supportive environments since more people would enjoy being around him. But regardless of how socially supportive environments are formed, socially supportive relationships help buffer vulnerable children from the turmoil and discontent going on all around them.

Now that we're aware of the human potential for resilience, along with some of the components that help foster it, what can society do about it? Werner and Smith point out that in the United States we are amazingly ineffective in taking action to deal with known contributors to life difficulties. So even though we know that "the quality of the mother-infant interaction, the spacing of her children, the health status of the young child, reading skills and scholastic competence in the early grades [are] *all* important protective factors that equip us to weather adversities, both in our formative years and in adulthood . . . [we live in a country] where the majority of mothers with infants are now in the labor force and where nearly half of the fourth grade students and more than one-fourth of the eighth graders score below basic reading level, we have no universal policies for (paid) parental leave, no universal access to high-quality child care programs and early childhood education, no universal health care or insurance for our children, and no national standards or accountability for the teaching of reading in our schools. . . . we spend considerably more money in trying to 'fix' serious coping problems . . . than in preventing them!"

Werner and Smith conclude by suggesting that the gateway to success in helping out vulnerable children will likely be opened by smaller local and state public efforts and by private endeavors. They point out a number of instances where relatively small programs have made huge impacts on the successful outcomes of vulnerable children. They describe one study conducted by the research firm Public/Private Ventures that examined the role of the Big Brothers/Big Sisters organization in helping to reduce negative outcomes in a group of at-risk children. About 1,000 kids participated in that study, mostly from poor, urban, disadvantaged households. Forty percent of the kids came from homes with a history of substance abuse, and 30% came from homes with a history of domestic violence. The most striking feature of that study was just how much having a Big Brother or Big Sister reduced the likelihood of vulnerable children succumbing to adversity. Among children who had a Big Brother or Big Sister, first-time drug use was down 46%, absenteeism in school was down 52%, and violent behavior was down 33%, compared with kids who were put on a waiting list! And these effects were equivalent across race and gender.

CONCLUSIONS

Werner and Smith's study was revolutionary because it accomplished the Herculean goal of documenting the lifelong development of resilience in a group of highly vulnerable individuals, and perhaps more importantly, identified factors that predicted resilience. They were able to accomplish this feat because theirs was a **prospective** study, which means that it explored factors in very early life that were associated with success in later life. Similar studies either hadn't taken resilience into consideration beyond a limited time frame, explored resilience only **retrospectively**, or didn't explore resilience at all.

Perhaps one of the most important outcomes of Werner and Smith's study is that it causes us to take a moment to reflect on our stereotypes of disadvantaged children. We often assume that children raised under dire conditions and rough life circumstances are doomed to fail. And consequently, if we hold such stereotypes, we're at risk for assuming that anything we might try to do to give such kids a helping hand would likewise be doomed to failure. But assuming that intervention efforts would be futile is obviously not warranted. Some children, the resilient ones, can thrive despite overwhelming misfortune. And now that Werner and Smith have given us a sense of how these kids do it, we can use this information to pave a pathway for other disadvantaged children so that they might also benefit from the safeguards employed by the resilient children. Indeed, Werner and Smith believe so strongly in the potential for vulnerable children to succeed that they're donating royalties from the sale of their book toward helping the current generation of vulnerable children on the island of Kauai! And the Hawaii state legislature has provided funds to establish mental health teams to provide services for troubled children and teens, based, in part, on the monumental findings of Werner and Smith's study.

Now, you might think that any scientific findings that show that vulnerable children can overcome incredible odds would be a source of great satisfaction and pride for most people. You might think that government figures and ordinary citizens alike would be jumping for joy knowing that battered children can rise to the challenge of adversity. And indeed this is largely what has happened in Hawaii. Yet I feel obliged to share with you that knowing vulnerable children can overcome adversity doesn't always inspire jubilation. No, there is also a dark side to this knowledge. Apparently, there is political risk associated with claiming that disadvantaged children and troubled teens can escape the skeletons of their past. What risk could there possibly be? Consider a recent event that may become one of the darkest chapters in the annals of social science research. It's a story about another social science research project that investigated resilience in young adults.

The story begins in July of 1998, when Bruce Rind, Philip Tromovitch, and Robert Bauserman published a study on the long-term impacts of child sexual abuse on later life success. In their study, they reviewed and analyzed some 59 previous studies on the relationship between childhood experiences of sexual abuse and later mental health problems in college. The study was published in *Psychological Bulletin*, one of the premier journals in the field of psychology. After statistically analyzing the results of the 59 studies, which together comprised information on some 37,000 men and women, Rind and his colleagues found that *sexual abuse in childhood had no overall systematic relationship with psychological or emotional problems in adulthood.* Now, wouldn't you think this is good news? Wouldn't you expect people around the country to run out into the streets and shout "Hooray!" in honor of the resilience and fortitude exhibited by child sexual abuse victims?

On the contrary, not only was the study not publicly celebrated, it was actually publicly condemned! In July of 1999, just about 1 year after the article was published, the United States Congress actually voted unanimously to renounce the study! What a display of scientific illiteracy by our elected government officials! Why was Congress so outraged? Why weren't they happy to find out that child sex abuse victims could turn out okay? Because they believed that this finding would encourage pedophiles to perpetrate sex crimes against children, that's why. Of course, this isn't what Rind and his colleagues endorsed at all. The authors were simply reporting that child victims of sex crimes aren't necessarily going to turn out to have a lifetime of mental problems. But rather than rejoicing in the celebration of human resilience,

Congress voted instead to shoot the study down. Rather than authorizing additional government funding to study how the sex abuse victims were able to overcome their traumatic experiences, they voted to deny that it was even possible. As noted by psychologist and freelance writer Carol Tavris, because Congress couldn't stomach the message, they chose to shoot the messenger. We can only hope that in the future, cooler and more scientifically literate minds will prevail.

I hope that reading this chapter leaves you with three take-home messages. The first is that even the most vulnerable children aren't doomed to fail, so long as they have the proper physical and social supports in place. Second, the single most important social prophylactic that guided the resilient kids into a successful adulthood was the availability of social and emotional support from important figures in their lives. Finally, I hope you remember how a team of researchers were so devoted to finding out how resilience works that they dedicated 45 years of their own lives to explore the topic. Now that Werner is in her 70s, one wonders what lies in store for readers interested in the continuing saga of the children on the island of Kauai. Will her students continue her work? Will the story draw to a close? Based on the dynamic and energetic personal conversations I've had the pleasure of sharing with Dr. Werner, I get the impression that she herself will be directing the study as the children of Kauai enter their own retirement years.

Bibliography

Rind, B., Tromovitch, P., & Bauserman, R. (1998). A meta-analytic examination of assumed properties of child sexual abuse using college samples. *Psychological Bulletin, 124*, 22–53.

Tavris, C. (1999, July 19). Headline: Commentary; Perspective on Psychology; Uproar Over Sexual Abuse Study Muddies the Waters; Suppressing Credible but Unpopular Scientific Findings Won't Reduce the Number of Incidents. *Los Angeles Times*. Times Mirror Company.

Questions for Discussion

1. One of the factors correlated with resiliency was the number of siblings a person had. Vulnerable people with fewer than four siblings were more likely to be resilient than vulnerable people with four or more siblings. Given this finding, would it make sense to encourage fewer children among at-risk families? Why?

2. Can you think of any celebrities who've overcome adversity?

3. Werner and Smith found emotional support to be one of the most significant environmental factors that helped buffer vulnerable children and adolescents against traumatic life experiences. Do you know anyone who's having a tough life to whom you could lend emotional support?

4. Do government officials have a responsibility to incorporate the findings of psychological research when making new laws to help people? Do government officials have a right to deny the findings of psychological research when the findings don't agree with their own personal beliefs?

18

Keep the Baby
and the Bathwater

REPRODUCTIVE RISK AND THE CONTINUUM OF CARETAKING CASUALTY.

Sameroff, A. J., & Chandler, M. J. (1975). *In F. D. Horowitz (Ed.), Review of Child Development Research. Vol. 4. Chicago: University of Chicago Press.*   (RANK 12)

I may be biased, but I'd be willing to bet that of all the subdisciplines of psychology, child psychology is the most popular. I think so for a couple of reasons. For one thing, when I was shopping around my idea for this book, every publisher told me that the market share for child psychology was second only to the market share for introductory psychology. But second, when you think about it, just about every other subdiscipline of psychology has a vested interest in knowing how its area applies to children. The very large subdiscipline of social psychology is interested in children's social development. The subdiscipline of cognitive psychology is interested in cognitive development. And clinical psychology, which comprises the greatest number of professional psychologists of all, is interested in the development of children's mental and emotional health. No doubt, this translates into a very exciting and lively field of study. The downside is that it's impossible to keep abreast of all the scientific developments taking place in child psychology. A quick search of the PsycINFO database, using the search terms *infants*, *children*, and *adolescents*, reveals that nearly a quarter million manuscripts have been published since 1966 alone!

To help manage the overwhelming scientific progress in child psychology, researchers from time to time will publish what are called "review articles." Review articles summarize the most important scientific discoveries that have taken place on a particular topic over a particular period of time. These articles are immensely useful to scientists not only because they bring together a wide array of findings into a single place, but also because the authors of review articles usually give some indication of the limitations of past research and some direction of where future research is headed or should be headed. Needless to say, authors of review articles perform an extremely vital service for the rest of the scientific community. The review article written by Arnold Sameroff and Michael Chandler in 1975 proved to be so important to the field of child psychology that it even achieved revolutionary status (ranking 12th most revolutionary overall).

Sameroff and Chandler were concerned with the state of research on children's developmental outcomes. Of course, all child psychologists are interested in children's developmental outcomes, but they differ in how much attention they pay to normal versus deviant outcomes. In many areas of child psychology, the goal is to understand **normative development**; that is, researchers just try to understand which factors need to be in place for children to develop normally. But in other areas of child psychology, especially clinical child psychology, special attention is paid to factors that disrupt normal development. The belief here is that if we can identify disruptive factors, maybe we can do something to get rid of them. In their article, Sameroff and Chandler reviewed 156 different articles dealing with factors thought to contribute to poor developmental outcomes in children.

Not surprisingly, disruptive factors fall into two general categories: biological and environmental. After all, what else is there? Accordingly, the articles reviewed by Sameroff and Chandler focused on these two general classes of problem-makers. The biological factors most frequently investigated came in the form of genetic defects and complications of pregnancy or birth. Sameroff and Chandler suggested that these biology-related problems fell on a "continuum of reproductive casualty." The environmental problem-makers most frequently explored were social class and caretaking behaviors, which Sameroff and Chandler placed on the "continuum of caretaking casualty." Putting the two together, you can see how they derived the title of their article, "Reproductive Risk and the Continuum of Caretaking Casualty."

What follows is a summary of the main themes found in the articles reviewed by Sameroff and Chandler, as well as what they take each set of findings to mean. They divide their paper into several sections, based on the general findings of the research they reviewed in each. I will follow their general tack and adopt the same section headings they used.

INTRODUCTION

Sameroff and Chandler began their review by pointing out that great strides had been made in protecting children from the traditional hazards of growing and developing. To be sure, every generation witnesses medical advances that ensure more children survive to maturity than in any previous generation. Despite these scientific advancements, each year many millions of children still die or succumb to diseases or disorders that might otherwise have been prevented. Of course, the best way to protect children from the three Ds, death, disease, and disorder, is to identify as early as possible the risk factors associated with each of them. However, much of the research aimed at identifying early risk factors has met with only moderate success.

Sameroff and Chandler pointed out that a major limitation of the prevention research has been its overreliance on *retrospective* designs. Retrospective research begins by identifying children who have a disease or disorder, and then looks back at their histories to try to isolate any potential risk factors that might've contributed to it. But, as Bowlby argued in Chapter 11, there is a major problem with this approach. Sameroff and Chandler agreed. They wrote, "Efforts to reconstruct events that may have led to the occurrence of a disease by studying persons who currently suffer from it often create the impression of inevitability of outcome." In other words, just because a child with a particular disease or disorder experienced a particular event earlier in his life, it doesn't mean that other children who experience the same event will inevitably develop the same disease or disorder later. To make the goofiness of retrospective reasoning clearer, suppose we do a study on child-onset depression and we find that all children with child-onset depression experienced birth. Can we then conclude that all children who experienced birth will develop child-onset depression? Of course not. The growing disenchantment with retrospective research led many researchers to try to identify risk factors *prospectively*. The prospective approach begins by studying children as early as possible, sometimes even before birth, and then following those same children through as much of the rest of their life as feasible. Although retrospective studies might've had some success identifying *possible* risk factors, prospective studies are necessary for confirming them as *actual* risk factors. Bowlby (Chapter 11); Baumrind (Chapter 13); Thomas, Chess, and Birch (Chapter 16); and Werner and Smith (Chapter 17) would strongly agree with Sameroff and Chandler on the necessity of conducting prospective research.

Continuum of Reproductive Casualty

Sameroff and Chandler then launch into their massive literature review. Their first stop was the literature dealing with biological risks associated with pregnancy and birth. They began by citing some startling statistics from an earlier 1971 study, which reported that of the 5–10 million pregnancies occurring each year, 2–3 million ended in spontaneous abortion (miscarriages) due to genetic defects or poisons taken in by the mother, and 1 million ended in intentional abortions. Of the babies that made it to 20 weeks postconception, 50,000 died before birth, 50,000 died within a month after birth, 50,000 had severe malformations of one kind or another, and another 300,000 had learning disorders that ranged from mild to severe retardation.

It's these learning disorders that child psychologists were most interested in. Learning disorders were usually assumed to be the result of some sort of brain malfunction, even though no brain problems had ever been identified. In fact, what we commonly call ADHD (attention deficit with hyperactivity disorder) today, we might have called minimal brain damage or organic brain dysfunction 30 years ago. Anyway, the term **continuum of reproductive casualty** as used by Sameroff and Chandler, refers to the "range of minor motor, perceptual, intellectual, learning, and behavioral disabilities" appearing in children that may have resulted from complications associated with pregnancy or birth. Below are some of the biological risk factors reviewed by Sameroff and Chandler, which were frequently assumed to contribute to some of these psychological casualties.

Anoxia.   *Anoxia* means lack of oxygen. Many times during childbirth, something bad happens that cuts off the oxygen supply to a baby's brain. Sometimes the umbilical cord gets trapped between the baby and the birth canal so that the baby can't be delivered without pinching off the umbilical cord and cutting off the blood supply. Sometimes the umbilical cord gets tangled around the baby's neck and acts like a noose as the baby is delivered. And even if the birth goes well, babies sometimes take their own sweet time before they start breathing on their own. The problem is that the longer the brain goes without oxygen, the greater the possibility of permanent brain damage. For child psychologists, of course, the important question was whether mild bouts of anoxia contributed to mild problems in psychological functioning.

One way to look for the effects of anoxia on later psychological functioning is to examine correlations between the experience of anoxia during childbirth and later intelligence test performance. When IQ was considered in the literature reviewed by Sameroff and Chandler, it was clear that it *wasn't* clear whether anoxia led to later intellectual deficiencies. Four of the studies reviewed by Sameroff and Chandler showed that anoxia was correlated with low school-age IQ scores, but an even greater number of studies found no correlation between the experience of anoxia and later IQ.

So researchers reasoned that maybe IQ was too general a measure of psychological functioning. Intelligence test scores depend on the adequate functioning of dozens of psychological abilities. Maybe poor functioning on some of these abilities was compensated for by good functioning on others. Maybe the effects of anoxia would become clearer if instead of looking at general IQ, researchers focused on more basic psychological characteristics, such as perceptual functioning and motor control. Studies that examined this possibility still found that although there were differences between anoxic babies and normal babies right after birth, the differences gradually disappeared as the children got older. In fact, one study compared anoxic versus normal children on 21 different cognitive and perceptual abilities when the children were 7 years old. The 7-year-olds who were anoxic as babies were different from the normal babies on only 2 of the 21 measures!

Okay, so maybe anoxia doesn't affect cognitive and perceptual performance. Maybe it has its greatest impact on children's personalities. But even when this possibility was examined, it was found that although babies showed some personality differences early in life, there were few differences even by age 3. In sum, whatever's going on with anoxia, it has its greatest impact during the first few months after birth. As children grow older, the negative impact that anoxia seems to have on children gradually disappears.

Prematurity.   Another expected indicator of later psychological problems is when babies are born too soon. Normally, babies stay inside the womb for 38–40 weeks. But sometimes they're born too early. When this happens, we call them "premature," or "preemies" for short. Prematurity brings with it all sorts of hazards, not the least of which is an immature respiratory system. The respiratory system is one of the last systems to develop during pregnancy, and so when babies are born prematurely they sometimes need to be put on mechanical respirators to make sure they keep breathing. Preemies are also really small, which means they have relatively little body fat to keep them warm and protect them against the elements. So are premature babies at risk for later psychological deficiencies?

Apparently they're at some risk. Sameroff and Chandler reviewed research which found that preemies do score a few points lower on IQ tests at school age compared with children who weren't born prematurely. But this raises the question of why preemies would be at risk for lower IQ scores when children who experienced oxygen deprivation weren't. Sameroff and Chandler suggested that one possible explanation might be that premature babies are easily identified by their parents as premature, and so parents might treat them differently than they otherwise would have. In contrast, babies experiencing anoxia are not so easily identified, and many times parents aren't even aware that babies have experienced anoxia. So anoxic babies might be treated normally. Can you see where Sameroff and Chandler are going here? They raised the intriguing possibility that parents' *perceptions* of their babies' health status might've been more important than babies' *actual* health status in contributing to later successful psychological development.

Socioeconomic Influences.   So far we've considered two more or less biological factors that were commonly believed to contribute to negative psychological outcomes. And as we've seen, neither anoxia nor prematurity had a particularly devastating impact on later psychological development. However, for both of these biological risk factors we've ignored a potentially important buffering agent: socioeconomic status. Socioeconomic status is a general, all-purpose indicator of the quality of a child's surroundings. Socioeconomic status has two parts: a social part and an economic part. The social part usually reflects the amount of prestige a person's job holds in the community. Garbage collection isn't a particularly highly regarded profession, for example. More prestigious professions would include the ranks of doctors, lawyers, and even (shockingly) college professors. The economic part refers to how much money one makes in his job. Doctors, lawyers, and many factory workers make a lot of money, but, alas, college professors do not. Socioeconomic status reflects both the level of prestige of one's job and how much money one makes. Doctors and lawyers have highly prestigious jobs and make a lot of money, and so would be regarded as being among the highest socioeconomic levels. Many factory workers, although they make a lot of money, don't work in highly prestigious jobs and so would be regarded as being at a midrange socioeconomic level. (I don't even want to think about the socioeconomic status of college professors.) People at the lowest socioeconomic levels have jobs that are both low in prestige and low in pay. The potential impact of socioeconomic status on psychological development lies in the fact that people with higher socioeconomic status can draw on a large number of resources in raising their children. People of low socioeconomic status have fewer resources.

The literature reviewed by Sameroff and Chandler revealed striking differences in the psychological outcomes of children raised in higher versus lower socioeconomic households. In general, children from the lowest socioeconomic households were far more likely to experience serious developmental disabilities than children from higher socioeconomic households. In fact, socioeconomic status was the single best predictor of developmental problems. It was a far better predictor than anoxia, prematurity, or any other single index of complications before, during, or after birth. Sameroff and Chandler summarized the literature this way: "In advantaged families, infants who suffered complications [during birth] generally showed no significant or small residual effects at follow-up. Many infants from lower social class homes with identical histories of complications showed significant retardations in later functioning. Social and economic status appear to have much stronger influences on the course of development than [birth complications]."

Two Hypotheses.   As a result of these findings, Sameroff and Chandler constructed two hypotheses about the development of psychological problems. First, they hypothesized that when children who had birth complications experienced later psychological problems, the problems resulted not from the complications themselves, but from a third variable correlated with both the birth complication and the poor psychological outcome. This third variable, they suspected, was socioeconomic status. People of low socioeconomic status were more likely to have children with birth complications and were more likely to have children with poor developmental outcomes. Again, it's not that the birth complications *caused* the psychological problems. Rather, it was more likely that people with little money ran into birth complications during pregnancy (because they couldn't afford high-quality health care, for example) *and* were more likely to live in environments that contributed to psychological problems (because they couldn't afford intellectually stimulating toys and books, for example).

Sameroff and Chandler also hypothesized that the effects of birth complications on poor psychological outcomes would be strongly influenced by the attitudes of the children's caretakers. In other words, it wasn't so important whether children actually experienced difficulties during their birth. What was important was how their parents dealt with it. Parents who *thought* their children were going to be problem prone were more likely to have children who *became* problem prone. Thus, a central component of both hypotheses was that certain elements would be present in children's lives that created an imaginary correlation between early problems and later problems. In the first case it was thought to be socioeconomic status; in the second case it was thought to be parental attitudes.

Reproduction and Stress

Stress and Genetic Abnormalities.   If parental attitudes play an important role in maintaining psychological problems in children, then a corollary might be that parental emotional health can also affect complications during pregnancy. In this regard, Sameroff and Chandler reviewed several studies that examined the relationship between parent emotional health and the presence of birth complications. Fascinatingly, stress experienced by the mother was found to be especially predictive of birth complications. In one study, for example, it was found that women in Great Britain and Germany who gave birth during World War II were at increased risk for having children with birth defects. Apparently, the stress of the war had a significantly negative impact on these pregnancies over and above what could be explained by any nutritional deficiencies. In another study, conducted by the same scientist, it was found that mothers of children with Down's syndrome experienced prolonged distress during their pregnancies relative to mothers of children without Down's syndrome.

Of course, many birth defects are known to be caused by genetic or chromosomal abnormalities. Down's syndrome, for example, is known to be associated with an abnormality of chromosomal pair number 21. Where there would normally be only two number-21 chromosomes, children with Down's syndrome have three. But if birth defects are genetically caused, how could maternal stress have anything to do with it? One suggested possibility was that the unusually high stress experienced by the war mothers and the Down's mothers somehow interrupted their bodies' natural abortive function. What is the "natural abortive function"? When women are pregnant, their bodies sometimes can detect when something has gone awry with the embryo and can, if necessary, end the pregnancy through spontaneous abortion or miscarriage. But when women are emotionally distressed, their bodies might somehow become less sensitive to embryonic malfunctioning and might become less inclined to cause the pregnancy to terminate.

Maternal Emotion and Birth Complications.   Sameroff and Chandler next reviewed several studies that revealed striking associations between mothers' emotional status and the presence of birth complications. The most dramatic influence imaginable would be when the emotional state of the mother is so severe as to cause the death of the fetus. Sadly, a couple of studies suggested just this possibility. In one study of 427 women described as "habitual aborters," it was found that these women had "clear psychic conflicts and little desire for additional children." Apparently it was possible for these women's emotional conflicts to contribute to their multiple miscarriages. Another study compared habitual aborters to women with no history of spontaneous abortion. Again it was found that the spontaneous aborters "demonstrated poorer emotional controls and stronger dependency needs." A third study revealed that women with emotional difficulties were more likely to experience premature birth. Finally, seven studies reviewed by Sameroff and Chandler found high anxiety in mothers to be linked to birth difficulties. Apparently, maternal high anxiety was another culprit implicated in birth complications.

Is It the Smoking or the Smoker?   It's well known that children of mothers who smoke are born small for gestational age. They're about the size of premature babies, but they're full term. What's interesting is that although small babies are about 20 times more likely to die than normal-sized babies, small babies of smoking mothers are no more likely to die than normal-sized babies. So the question is, What makes babies of smoking mothers small, because otherwise they seem pretty healthy? Is it because of the cigarette-based poisons taken in by the smoking mother? Or is it because of the personality of women who are likely to smoke? Sameroff and Chandler reviewed one study that examined these two possibilities. The author of that study found that women who didn't smoke during their pregnancies, but who took up smoking afterward, were just as likely to have small babies as mothers who smoked all the way through their pregnancies. This finding led the author to conclude that it wasn't the smoking that made the babies small, it was their mothers' personalities.

Psychiatric Conditions.   If stress, high anxiety, and inclination to smoke all have an impact on pregnancy and birth, then it stands to reason that more severe psychiatric conditions would also have adverse impacts on pregnancy and birth. A related question has to do with the possibility that severe psychiatric conditions in children could result from complications experienced in pregnancy in birth. To this end, Sameroff and Chandler reviewed a number of studies that dealt with these issues. Consistent with what you might expect, research revealed that mothers with psychiatric illnesses such as schizophrenia and depression were more likely to have birth complications than were women without these illnesses. Moreover, the more severe the illnesses were, as measured by the number of times the women were hospitalized for their mental illnesses, the more difficulties they had with their pregnancies and deliveries.

It was also found that children who themselves had psychiatric conditions were more likely to have experienced birth complications than were normal children. This finding held true for children with either autism or schizophrenia. For example, in one review article that Sameroff and Chandler reviewed, the authors found "a higher incidence of prenatal complications, in particular bleeding, toxemia, and severe maternal illness, in the birth records of schizophrenic as compared to normal control groups."

Continuum of Caretaking Casualty

Throughout most of the preceding discussion, we've focused on what Sameroff and Chandler called the continuum of reproductive casualty. The idea was that certain biologically related factors associated with pregnancy and childbirth, such as anoxia or prematurity, could have a devastating impact on children's later psychological development. Generally speaking, we saw little evidence that they do. Stronger evidence suggested that the mental and emotional health of the mother might've played a more important role in producing negative psychological outcomes in children than any direct biological insults experienced by the fetus. One of the most interesting possibilities considered was that pregnant women undergoing emotional stress might be more likely to carry babies with genetic abnormalities to term than women without stress. Such a finding raises the possibility that stress may somehow interfere with the body's natural abilities to detect and spontaneously abort fetuses with genetic abnormalities.

In this section, Sameroff and Chandler considered the **continuum of caretaking casualty**. Here the focus was on the caretaking environment that babies experience after they're born. In reviewing this literature, Sameroff and Chandler pointed out that it would have been impossible to take into consideration all the relevant research at that time. They wrote, "Because the list of parental and other environmental hazards to a child's normal development is almost endless, our attempt to review the research literature on these topics must be selective and incomplete. Since anything from nutritional standards to disciplinary techniques might be legitimately included, some arbitrary delimiting of this domain was required." Consequently, they chose to focus on the most "flagrant" forms of deviant caretaking, where the "hazards to the child are immediate and unqualified." Specifically, they looked at the research on child abuse and neglect.

The transition from inside the uterus to the outside world is a rough one for babies. The uterus is an exquisitely constructed masterpiece, designed by millions of years of evolution to protect the developing fetus from all manner of unsavory environmental insults. But once the baby leaves the uterus at birth, she's thrust into an uncertain and sometimes even hostile caretaking environment. There's no guarantee that her parents will know how to take care of her. And even though evolution has also operated on parenting for millions of years, the product of that evolutionary molding has for some reason been to produce parents who have the capacity to choose to harm their newborns if they feel like it.

The Battered Child.   There are no limits to the variety of ways that parents can harm their children. They can beat them, burn them, cut them, poison them, or have sex with them. The immediate consequences of such tragic physical assaults are obvious. But the status of physical abuse as a risk factor depends in part on the long-range psychological outlook of children who are abused. In 1975, few studies looked at the long-term psychological outlooks of abused children. In one of two studies Sameroff and Chandler reviewed, 20 children who were treated for abuse over a 13-year period were found not to have an especially positive outlook. "At the time of the follow-up, 90 percent of the study population evidenced some form of residual damage. More than half of the children studied were judged to be mentally retarded, and more than half were thought to be emotionally disturbed. Growth failures, speech disturbances, and a variety of other signs of developmental delay and arrest were present to such an extent that only two of the study children were judged to be completely normal at the time of follow-up."

How could parents be so cruel to their own children? There seem to be two general contributing factors. First, abusive parents were found to differ from nonabusive parents on a number of psychological factors. In one study, abusive parents were found to be "less intelligent, more aggressive, impulsive, immature, tense, and self-centered than nonabusive parents." But more than that, one of the most striking features of abusive parents was that they were typically abused themselves as children. When abusive parents have a history of being abused themselves, it means they grew up never seeing examples of good parenting practices. As parents, they may have maintained unrealistic expectations for their own children. And why shouldn't they? Their own parents never had realistic expectations for them.

Children's Contributions to Their Own Abuse.   Sameroff and Chandler pointed out that there is more to the parent-child relationship than just the parent. Following the lead of Thomas, Chess, and Birch (Chapter 16) and Richard Bell (Chapter 20), Sameroff and Chandler remind us that children may play some role in contributing to their own abuse. Now wait, we're not talking about blaming the victim here. It's not like children should be viewed as doing anything on purpose that causes their parents to abuse them. Rather, what Sameroff and Chandler meant was that some abnormalities in children may predispose them to being abused by their parents.

One example is prematurity. Babies born prematurely place a heavy burden on their parents emotionally, physically, and financially. A mother who might not normally abuse her child, or who might be on the edge of abusing her child but who is inclined not to, might be pushed over the edge when confronted with the special needs of her premature child.

In support of this possibility, the scientific literature reviewed by Sameroff and Chandler showed that abused children were frequently in need of special caretaking practices. In one major national survey, abused children were found to be deviant from normal children socially, physically, intellectually, and behaviorally. Of course, with correlational data like these, we can't be sure which came first, the abuse or the deviance. But many of the parents reported that their abusive behaviors were precipitated by the unusual behaviors of their children. Sameroff and Chandler concluded by noting, "the preliminary data on abused children would suggest that there are relatively high rates of bio-psycho-social deviance in the victims, as well as in the perpetrators, of child abuse and that any singular emphasis on one of these factors to the exclusion of the others fails to come to terms with the true interactional character of child abuse."

Failure-to-Thrive Syndrome.

Failure-to-thrive syndrome is a label applied to groups of children who for one reason or another fail to show normal physical growth. A baby's main job for the first few months of life is to gain weight. But babies who fail to thrive show a pattern of gaining no weight and might actually lose weight (but don't confuse this with the normal weight loss newborns sometimes experience right after birth as they begin taking in food on their own). Failure-to-thrive syndrome is often caused by physical problems such as disease or hormonal imbalance, but here we're concerned with the failure to thrive that results from parental neglect.

No doubt neglect is a type of child abuse, but it differs from other forms of abuse because rather than parents doing things to the child, neglect results from parents *not* doing things for the child. Still, from a scientific point of view, neglect shares many features in common with other forms of child abuse: Neglected children have poor long-term psychological outcomes, their parents have personality characteristics that differentiate them from non-neglectful parents, and the children themselves have characteristics that differentiate them from non-neglected children. One study found that neglected children were often described by their parents as "having fussy eating habits, poor food intake, and frequent regurgitations," and the children themselves were often found to have histories of chronic diarrhea and intestinal allergies. Consider what effects these dietary habits might've had on parents who were on the edge of neglecting their children, but who hadn't yet done any neglecting. Whenever these parents fed their dietarily deviant children, the children might have thrown up, or a nasty mess might've come out the other end. From the parents' point of view, feeding may have been an extremely "punishing" event. On the other hand, when they didn't feed their babies, the neglecting parents didn't have to spend any time cleaning up bodily waste, and consequently may have felt "rewarded." From the parents' point of view, neglecting their children may have been a positive experience.

Bidirectionality of Child-Caretaker Effects.

As I said before, by pointing out that babies may be partially responsible for contributing to their own abuse, Sameroff and Chandler weren't placing any blame whatsoever on the children. Child abuse and neglect is extremely tragic and should be eliminated at all costs. Their point was more of a scientific and clinical one. If we're going to have any hope of understanding child abuse and neglect so that one day we can eliminate it, we have to realize that there's more involved than just the abusive and neglecting behaviors of the parents. If we know that some children might push their parents over the edge, either because of their physical or intellectual deviance or because of their finicky eating habits, then we can design programs of intervention to teach parents what to expect and how to cope.

Sameroff and Chandler mentioned some of the temperament research to make their point. They made specific reference to Thomas, Chess, and Birch's research on children with "difficult temperaments" (see Chapter 16). If you recall, Thomas, Chess, and Birch found that babies who were classified as having difficult temperaments were at increased risk for developing later behavior problems. But whether or not temperamentally difficult babies would remain temperamentally difficult throughout childhood was influenced by how their parents responded to them. If the parents were able to adjust to the difficult temperament, good outcomes happened. But when parents failed to adjust to the temperamental difficulty, children's behavioral problems were exacerbated.

DISCUSSION

To try to pull the main themes of Sameroff and Chandler's review together, we can draw a number of summary conclusions. First, in terms of the "continuum of reproductive casualty," it seems that most children who have complications during pregnancy and childbirth, although they might have problems shortly after birth, have not been found to have especially pronounced difficulties in later childhood. Second, in terms of the "continuum of caretaking casualty," it seems that children who are abused or neglected have parents with particular personality characteristics, but Sameroff and Chandler also noted that not all parents with these personality characteristics abuse their children. Third, the best way to characterize children's longterm psychological prognosis is to combine their reproductive risk status with the continuum of caretaking casualty. Child psychologists should consider that children and parents both contribute to long-term successes or failures in the development of children's psychological health.

Sameroff and Chandler concluded their review by promoting the widespread adoption of what they call a **transactional model** of child development. A transactional model of child development stresses both the flexible nature of children's environments and their own active role in their own psychological development. Consistent with Werner and Smith's conclusion (Chapter 17), children seem to have natural "self-righting" tendencies that allow them to overcome all but the most severe biological insults incurred during pregnancy and childbirth, but these self-righting tendencies have to be nourished and facilitated by a supportive caretaking environment. Sameroff and Chandler argued that "rather than being considered separately, [reproductive and caretaking] risk appear to be closely interrelated in the production of positive or negative developmental outcomes. Where the child's vulnerability is heightened through massive or recurrent trauma, only an extremely supportive environment can help restore the normal integrative growth process. A seriously brain-damaged child requiring institutional care would be an instance of such an extreme case of reproductive casualty. On the other extreme, a highly disordered caretaking setting might convert the most sturdy and integrated of children into a caretaking casualty."

CONCLUSIONS

Sameroff and Chandler's revolutionary contribution to child psychology was to challenge the age-old assumptions about the origins of poor developmental outcomes. They cautioned child psychologists not to assume that reproductive difficulties and poor parenting practices must always result in negative psychological outcomes. Rather, the extent that either produces a negative psychological outcome depends quite a bit on the quality of the other. In this regard, they suggested that reproductive risk and the caretaking environment not be viewed in absolute, black-and-white, good or bad terms, but that each be viewed as a continuum reflecting a range of possibilities.

As we've seen in many other revolutionary contributions in this book, it's not always easy for child psychologists to practice what they preach. These days, few child psychologists would deny that children's developmental outcomes result from complex transactions between characteristics of the child and characteristics of her caretaking environment. Still, every now and then we seem to lapse into an either-or mode of thinking about psychological development. Perhaps the most recent, highly publicized example of this black-and-white kind of thinking is the hysteria that surrounded the discovery of so-called crack babies in the early 1990s.

Crack babies earned their name because of the crack cocaine smoked by their mothers during their pregnancies. From the very beginning, health professionals and the public assumed the worst—that crack babies were doomed to suffer lives of misery. And at the time, this seemed like a reasonable conclusion. After all, the negative effects of cocaine on adult users had been well documented for years. It only stood to reason that if adult users of cocaine experienced health problems, then fetuses, whose biological systems are only in the process of developing, ought to be profoundly affected. The crack-baby hysteria was coupled by frequent images on TV and in magazines of these very small, prematurely born pathetic little creatures who were placed on ventilators and who looked to be struggling for every breath they took. Their prognosis was indeed bleak. If the truth be told, some of the earlier scientific studies seemed to confirm these gloomy expectations. Crack babies often *were* found to suffer long-term negative psychological consequences.

Then, in March of 2001, Boston University scientist Deborah Frank published an article in the *Journal of the American Medical Association* challenging all the gloom-and-doom hysteria surrounding crack babies. In her article, she reviewed the results of 36 previous crack cocaine studies dating all the way back to 1984. Her earth-shattering conclusion was that prenatal exposure to crack cocaine wasn't consistently linked to later negative psychological outcomes. She noted that a common problem throughout the early research was that researchers failed to consider whether crack-using mothers were also using a host of other substances like tobacco, alcohol, and marijuana, as well. In addition, crack-smoking mothers were almost always from low socioeconomic backgrounds. Frank argued that to blame children's poor psychological outcomes on crack cocaine was to completely miss the point. Children of crack-smoking mothers are born into environments that are poor to begin with, so it's not surprising to find that crack babies run into developmental problems. In Sameroff and Chandler's terms, crack babies are born into environments at the high end of the caretaking casualty continuum. But it's simply not true that crack babies are necessarily doomed. Should they have the good fortune to be born into an otherwise healthy environment, crack babies turn out just fine.

Research on developmental outcomes has continued to flourish in the 30 years since Sameroff and Chandler published their revolutionary review. And just as the sheer amount of research was beyond the scope of what they could've hoped to review back then, the volume of scientific knowledge is even greater today. But the basic recommendations they set forth for understanding psychological development remain firmly grounded in modern child psychology theorizing. We can only hope that as future generations of prevention researchers face the formidable challenge of eliminating reproductive and caretaking casualties, they keep in mind the complex transactions continually taking place between child and environment.

Bibliography

Frank, D. A., Augustyn, M., Grant Knight, W., Pell, T., and Zuckerman, B. (2001). Growth, development, and behavior in early childhood following prenatal cocaine exposure. *Journal of the American Medical Association, 285,* 1613–1625.

Questions for Discussion

1. One of Sameroff and Chandler's main points is that to understand poor psychological outcomes, it's important to understand the child's own role in contributing to those outcomes. Is this a valid point? Could a similar point be made that to understand crime, it's important to understand the victim's own role in contributing to the crime?

2. We know that, in general, there are racial differences on standardized tests such as the SAT or the ACT. How might Sameroff and Chandler's conclusions be applied to this statistic?

3. Can you document from your own personal history how your environment of upbringing buffered you against various biological/environmental insults? What are some examples?

19

Choreographing the Nature-Nurture Dance

HEREDITY, ENVIRONMENT AND THE QUESTION "HOW?."
Anastasi, A. (1958). *Psychological Review, 65, 197–208.*   (RANK 14)

I imagine most psychology instructors have developed some pretty thick skin when it comes to the flack they have to take about psychology not being a "real" science. You might not know it, but many people don't think too highly of psychology. We psychologists get dumped on both by laypeople and by our colleagues in other science departments. If you have friends who're majoring in one of the so-called natural sciences, like physics or chemistry, ask 'em what they think of psychology. You'll see what I mean. Of course, a lot of the criticism leveled at psychology is really just a matter of ignorance. Many people just don't understand what psychology is. Fortunately, ignorance can usually be rectified by a little education.

What really stings is when people *do* know what psychology is and question its integrity anyway. If there's one valid criticism that people on the outside can raise about psychology, it's that psychology lacks a single guiding theme or focus. Can you think of any common thread that runs through all of psychology? You can't say that all psychologists study human behavior, because some psychologists study nonhuman behavior. And it doesn't help much to modify the sentence to say psychologists study animal behavior of any type, because some psychologists study brain activity, which may or may not have anything to do with behavior. In any case, the wide variety of topics that psychologists pursue is also the Achilles' heel of the discipline as a whole, because it makes psychology seem fragmented and disconnected.

So, when you get right down to it, it's rather hard to pinpoint any single unifying theme that permeates all of psychology and ties everything together. But in 1958, Anne Anastasi hit the nail on the head when she identified the nature-nurture issue as central to all of psychology. I'm sure you've heard of the nature-nurture issue. It's one of the main themes we discussed in Chapter 1. It's usually framed as a genes-versus-environment question. "How much of our intelligence is inherited?" "How much of our math phobia comes from how we're raised?"

Now Anastasi wasn't the first person to bring up the matter. The nature-nurture issue has been a central philosophical question for thousands of years. And depending on whom you ask, human individuality could be said to be all, partly, or not at all due to our genes (or environment). You can trace differences of opinion about the nature-nurture issue all the way back to the great Greek philosophers. Plato was a firm believer in the central role of nature, that is, of genes (although genes weren't known to exist at that time). But his student Aristotle begged to differ. He believed that the environment played the crucial role in the human condition. Ever since that time, philosophers and psychologists have gone back and forth, to and fro, ebbing and flowing about whether genes or environment played the most important role in explaining human development. But in her article, rated 14th most revolutionary by the child psychology research community, Anastasi shouted, "Enough is enough, people! Let's get down to business!"

The personal history of Anne Anastasi is an interesting one in its own right. She was a product of the early years of psychology, back when women were rarely admitted into graduate programs, and when they were, they were expected to pursue psychology as an applied discipline. It was rare for female psychologists to do raw, basic, experimental research. And Anastasi pretty much conformed to this trend. But the fact that Anastasi pursued graduate training at all was extraordinary. Like Piaget and Vygotsky before her, she was one of those child geniuses who simply couldn't be held back. She was home schooled in New York City for much of her early years, and when she finally ventured into an elementary school in 1917, at the age of 9, she was promptly bumped up a grade. But she soon dropped out because she had to sit in the back of an overcrowded schoolroom and found the work too confusing. Giving public school another try the following year, she found herself skipping two more grades, and she eventually completed elementary school at the top of her class. She tried high school on for size, but again found the classrooms overcrowded and so dropped out once more. Not to be outdone, she decided simply to skip high school altogether. After passing several College Board Entrance Exams, she entered Barnard College at the age of 15.

Although Anastasi started college with an interest in mathematics, she was also enchanted by a couple of psychology courses she took at Barnard. She soon found herself being pulled in two directions, toward mathematics, which she loved, and toward psychology, which fascinated her. Fortunately, she found her calling in an area that combined her interests in both mathematics and psychology: psychological testing, an area that nourished her throughout the rest of her life. She graduated from Barnard in 1928 at the age of 19 and published her first professional journal article that same year. She earned her Ph.D. from the graduate program at Columbia University in 1930, when she was only 21. I'm sure you're aware that most college students are only juniors at that age!

Anastasi enjoyed a very notable, and maybe even profitable, career in the field of psychological testing. Her textbooks on psychological testing were mainstays of the field for several decades, and thousands of psychologists learned their trade from her tuition. But most important for our purpose was that her expertise in testing catapulted her smack into the middle of the nature-nurture debate. Here's what's at issue. Whenever someone takes a psychological test, his score is liable to differ from that of someone else who takes the same test. And sometimes it happens that groups of people take a particular test, and the scores of one group differ from the scores of another. In both cases the question arises, Why do the scores differ? You can imagine what the range of possible answers might be. If the two groups come from different races or ethnicities, say white Americans versus Asians, then you might conclude that the differences in scores are due to differences in genetic makeup. Indeed, many psychologists have drawn exactly this conclusion. But if both groups come from the same race or ethnicity, say poor white Americans versus wealthy white Americans, then you might attribute testing differences to differences in environmental upbringing. But either conclusion amounts to little more than idle speculation. The problem is that people from different races or ethnicities differ not only in their genetic makeup, but also in their environmental upbringing.

In her 1958 article, Anastasi called for an end to such unproductive speculation. She argued that instead of fighting over *whether* nature or nurture is responsible, or *how much* nature or nurture is responsible, psychology should focus on *how both* are responsible. In other words, it was a no-brainer that nature and nurture both influenced psychological functioning, and any further debate along these lines was worthless. Instead, Anastasi implored, the field should move on to more important things, like mapping out how a person's unique set of genes interacted with his unique environment to produce the unique individual that he was.

Anastasi's article wasn't a "study" in the ordinary sense of the word. Rather, it was more of a position paper, an essay. In it she criticized the old ways of thinking about the nature-nurture issue and outlined what she believed was a new, more productive approach. She also made several suggestions for specific research agendas that researchers in the nature-nurture area should follow. Apparently it made quite an impact on the field, for even today, some 40 years after its publication, the paper is heralded as a watershed in the field of psychology as a whole, and appears among the 20 most revolutionary contributions in child psychology.

INTRODUCTION

Anastasi began her article by pointing out that the question of whether genes or the environment contribute to any behavior, characteristic, or psychological trait is a dead one. Since both matter, there is little else to be said about it. But somehow, it's just not very rewarding to say that both matter because it doesn't really tell us anything. She also pointed out that some researchers have tried to make a case for estimating the *proportion* of any behavior, characteristic, or psychological trait that was due to the genes versus the environment. From this angle, a researcher might try to determine if bicycle-riding ability is 10% genetic and 90% environmental or maybe 25% genetic and 75% environmental. But Anastasi pointed out that this too was a dead-end proposition because it assumed what she called an **additive** property of the relationship between genes and environment. Quite simply, genes and environment don't work together additively. Does it make sense to say, for example, that something as complicated as intelligence is a result of adding 2 parts genes to 3 parts environment? We need to know *how* the 2 parts genes work with the 3 parts environment to produce intelligence in order to know anything useful.

She argued that a much better way to think about the joint contributions of genes and environment was to think of them as *interacting* with each other. The definition of an **interaction** is that the effect of one thing depends on the quality of the other thing. In the framework of our nature-nurture question, it would amount to saying that the effect of the environment depends on the type of genes, or that the effect of the genes depends on the type of environment.

Okay, I get the sense that we're talking in cloudy abstractions here, so let's move on to a more comfortable real-life example. Consider the effect of a warm, loving, caring family environment on the social development of a child adopted at birth. An adopted child raised in this kind of environment may very well turn out to be warm, loving, and caring herself. In this case, couldn't we say with certainty that the environment had a positive impact on this child's social development? Could the child have turned out otherwise? Sure, the child could've had autism. One of the primary symptoms of people with autism is that they seem uninterested in socializing. Children with autism rarely make eye contact, they rarely respond to verbalizations, and they're rarely interested in displays of affection. So a warm, loving, caring family environment might not have had as much of an effect on a child with autism. This is an example of how the effect of the environment depends on the quality of the genes, of how environment and genes can interact. And this is precisely what Anastasi meant when she called for psychologists to pursue the question "How?". Psychologists should focus on *how* genes and environment interact.

TYPES OF INTERACTIONS

Now, recognizing the need to understand interactions between genes and environment is only the first step in the process. There are a bunch of ways that interactions can happen, and each of these ways may require a different set of methods to study them. In her article, Anastasi listed several types of interactions that might take place between genes and environment. She started by considering a variety of inherited genetic conditions that might be expected to limit the environment's influence on people.

Hereditary Factors

There are a number of conditions that can be inherited through the genes, and they range in how much they can be affected by the environment. Down's syndrome, for example, is an inherited condition that *always* leads to mental retardation. In other words, no amount of environmental intervention can remedy this condition; no amount of education, no drug, no therapy will undo the intellectual disadvantages experienced by a person with Down's syndrome.

On the other hand, congenital deafness may or may not lead to intellectual retardation, depending on the kinds of environmental opportunities that are made available. Anastasi notes, "It has been said . . . that the degree of intellectual backwardness of the deaf is an index of the state of development of special instructional facilities. As the [special instructional facilities] improve, the intellectual retardation associated with deafness is correspondingly reduced." Of course, these days it's unheard of to describe a person who is deaf as having intellectual retardation, but that's precisely because of all the advances we've made in helping deaf people adjust to society. In the old days, deaf people might not have been given any special attention or any special education, and as a result they may not have experienced the same intellectual growth as their hearing peers.

A third example is when a child inherits a *susceptibility* to certain diseases. That is, he doesn't actually inherit a disease, but he inherits a chance to get a disease. The disease might develop, it might not; it all depends on his living conditions, his environment. And whether or not he gets the disease in turn influences what happens afterward. If a child doesn't get the disease, for example, he might venture into the world of sports and become a star athlete or social icon. But if he develops the disease, he might be forced to avoid sports and social activities. If this happened, he might focus his interests on more sedentary, indoor activities like book reading or video game playing, and this refocusing of his interests could have an effect on his later personality development. How his personality turned out could, in Anastasi's words, "run the gamut from a deepening of human sympathy to a psychiatric breakdown." Indeed, many famous scholars became scholars in large part because they were rather sickly and spent a lot of time reading and studying. Philosopher René Descartes and psychologist Alfred Adler come to mind. If you're familiar with the movie *Unbreakable*, starring Samuel L. Jackson and Bruce Willis, you can see the range of possibilities in the two characters: brittle-boned Elijah Price and unbreakable David Dunn. Because of his bone-thinning disease, the Elijah Price character spent his life as a shut-in and enacted several feats of domestic terrorism with the hopes of flushing out a real-life superhero. His ideas were inspired in part by all the comic books he read as a child. Had he not had the bone disease, he wouldn't have led as sheltered a life, and he probably wouldn't have read as many comic books, and he probably wouldn't have developed an obsession with finding a real-life superhero.

Finally, hereditary factors may have an effect on social phenomena such as stereotypes. A kid might not be born with a disease at all, but might be born with a set of physical characteristics that are associated with certain stereotypes. Suppose a child inherits blond hair. In adolescence and adulthood, blond hair is often associated with being "ditzy" or "airheaded," and people with blond hair might be treated as if they were ditzy or airheaded. Of course, blond-haired people are no more ditzy or airheaded than red-, brown-, or black-haired people; but if they are treated by others as if they were ditzy or airheaded, then their own behavior could change to fit or reject that stereotype. Blond-haired people who accept the stereotype might start *acting* ditzy or airheaded, which is something they wouldn't have done had they been born with darker hair. Obviously, the social environment is interacting with the genes for hair color in a way to produce ditzy, airheaded behavior.

In all these examples, there is a certain influence of the environment that depends on the kinds of genes that were inherited. Anastasi points out that the influence of hereditary factors in all these cases varies in terms of their *indirectness*. In the case of Down's syndrome, the hereditary influence on the psychological outcome is very direct. The genes are directly responsible for the disorder. But in the other cases, hereditary influences are more and more indirect. In the case of blondness being associated with ditzyness, the genes are not directly responsible for the ditzyness, although they are responsible for producing the blond hair, the blond hair is responsible for triggering social stereotypes, and the social stereotypes may bring out ditzy behaviors in the blond-haired individual. Ultimately, the ditzy behaviors were caused by the genes, but only very indirectly.

Environmental Factors: Biological

It may sound like an oxymoron to talk about *biological* environmental factors, but the idea here is that after a child is born, her body can suffer a number of environmental insults, which may have an effect on psychological functioning. As before, environmental insults can also influence an individual's psychological profile on a continuum of indirectness. One way that the environment can have a fairly direct impact on psychological development is if some sort of biological injury happens during birth. If a child is born with her umbilical cord wrapped around her neck, for example, the umbilical cord may become constricted and may cut off the blood supply to the baby's brain. If the insult is serious enough, permanent brain damage may take place, resulting in lifelong mental retardation. Now here, there is obviously a biological problem, but it wasn't the result of any conditions that were inherited.

A less direct example of a biological environmental factor would be if a child developed a serious infection in one of her limbs. Suppose the infection got so bad that it resulted in an unfortunate but necessary amputation of the limb. In this case, the amputation might result in the same sort of social withdrawal that we described above having to do with an inherited disease. Accordingly, the same types of consequences might again take place. The amputee might sit around and read a lot and develop into a world-renowned scholar. Or she might withdraw further and further into her shell and develop any of a number of personality disorders.

An even less direct influence of a biological factor borrows again from the idea of hair color and social stereotypes. As Anastasi described it, "Let us suppose that a young woman with mousy brown hair becomes transformed into a dazzling golden blonde through environmental techniques currently available in our culture. It is highly probable that this metamorphosis will alter, not only the reactions of her associates toward her, but also her own self concept and subsequent behavior. The effects could range all the way from a rise in social poise to a drop in clerical accuracy!"

Environmental Factors: Behavioral

We just saw that environmental factors can impose themselves through their impact on the biological makeup of an individual. But environmental factors can also affect a person's behaviors directly. Anastasi noted that, by definition, these kinds of environmental influences always have a direct impact on what an individual does. Take social class membership, for example. A person who belongs to a high-level social class will have a far greater range of opportunities than a person belonging to a low-level social class. A person of high social status will have greater numbers of books available to read, he'll have more money to spend on educational opportunities, and he'll have more money to spend on extracurricular activities like horseback riding, skeet-shooting, and polo playing. Anastasi describes social class as having a very broad environmental impact.

A much more restricted environmental influence, described by Anastasi, was the opportunity that some children might have to learn about specific items on an IQ test. In this case, a child might gain a high IQ test score, not because he is especially high in intelligence, but because he may have received coaching from someone familiar with the contents of the IQ test. Or similarly, children from some cultures may have greater opportunity to come into contact with items that are typically used on an IQ test. Puzzles, for example, may be very popular toys for children from one culture and less popular for children from another culture. Since the most popular IQ tests employ puzzles of one kind or another, children from puzzle-playing cultures will have an advantage. Alternatively, the very procedure that IQ tests follow may be strange for some children. In an individually administered IQ test, a child sits across a table from an examiner, and the examiner gives the child one task after another and watches to see if the child can successfully complete each task. But if a child comes from a culture where sitting at tables is unfamiliar, or where adults don't usually engage with children one on one, or where doing jobs rapidly is discouraged, the child is at placed at quite a disadvantage in taking the test.

METHODOLOGICAL APPROACHES

After pointing out several ways that heredity and environment can interact in influencing psychological development, Anastasi went on to make a number of suggestions about how research could be designed to better answer the "question of 'How?'" In other words, she put her money where her mouth was. She described seven methodological innovations that would likely bear fruit in addressing the nature-nurture interaction question in her revolutionary new way of conceptualizing it. Here I describe four of them.

Selective Breeding

One of the easiest and most obvious ways of identifying how genes and environment interact is through selective breeding. Now wait, I'm not talking about selectively breeding humans of the sort advocated by Hitler. I'm only talking about selectively breeding furry little critters like mice and rats. What you get when you selectively breed these little guys across several generations is the opportunity for producing offspring who excel in a particular talent or ability.

In one classic study, for example, maze learning was bred into a series of generations of rats. The way it works is that you start out with a large group of rats, and you have them run through a maze. Some rats run through the maze quickly, while others run through it more gingerly. Then you take the fastest maze runners and breed them together. These offspring are then run through the maze just as their parents were, and you interbreed the fastest maze runners from this second generation. Of course, you can continue interbreeding rats this way indefinitely, but at the end of the breeding cycle you end up with a group of some pretty darn fast maze-running rats! Let's call them "maze-bright." You could also breed the slowest of the slow through several generations of offspring and end up with a strain of "maze-dull" rats. The final step would be to compare the maze-bright rats with the maze-dull rats to see what other psychological factors go along with being able to run through a maze quickly (or slowly). According to Anastasi, maze-bright rats are not only good at running through mazes, but when you compare them with the maze-dull rats, it turns out that maze-brights differ from maze-dulls on a host of other emotional and motivational factors besides maze running. In other words, maze-brights aren't just fast maze-runners.

Prenatal Environmental Factors

A second methodological approach to examining genetic-environment interactions is to explore relationships between different prenatal environments and later development. We already talked about how being born into a higher social class provides children with greater educational opportunities, and because of these educational opportunities it comes as no surprise that children from higher social classes perform better in school and earn higher IQ test scores than children from lower social classes. But does the influence of the high-social-class environment begin only after birth? Probably not. Expectant mothers from higher social classes also have access to better food. Now, everybody knows that expectant mothers should eat well-balanced, nutritional meals; and everybody knows that expectant mothers should increase their food intake when they become pregnant. But sometimes people forget that the prenatal nutrition that fetuses get is one way the environment interacts with genetically determined development. So if two high-social-class babies are developing prenatally, and one of them gets better nutrition than the other one, the baby with better nutrition will also be physically and psychologically advanced.

Likewise, three pregnant mothers from the same social class may differ in the types of environmental hazards their babies get exposed to. One mother might smoke throughout her pregnancy, one mother might drink throughout her pregnancy, and the third mother might choose a hazard-free lifestyle during her pregnancy. You can keep track of all three babies after they're born, and look for any short-term or long-term differences. At the time Anastasi's article was published, it wasn't well known what would happen to babies exposed to these kinds of prenatal hazards. But now we know that babies of mothers who smoke tend to have lower birthweights and tend to have trouble in some school subjects in later childhood, and that babies of mothers who drink are at risk for fetal alcohol syndrome, which, among other symptoms, is related to moderate to severe mental retardation.

Comparative Child-Rearing Practices

Anastasi suggested that a third way to explore nature-nurture interactions was to consider ways that people from different cultures or subcultures raised their children. Of course, this approach is more on the environment side of things, but it's still helpful to know the range of possible outcomes that can result from a range of possible parenting inputs. Anastasi described a few outcome studies that were already available at that time. In one study, for example, children raised in higher- versus lower-class environments were evaluated for reading readiness upon entry into first grade. In that study, higher-class parents were found to be emotionally warmer and more positive toward their children than were lower-class parents. The result was that lower-class children tended to view adults in general and teachers in particular as rather hostile. No doubt, lower-class children, because of their disconnected relationships with their parents, would be at a disadvantage in school given that they mistrusted adults. Anastasi's call for comparisons across child-rearing practices anticipated Diana Baumrind's revolutionary study on parenting styles, which we covered extensively in Chapter 13.

Twin Studies

One way to really get at the root of the nature-nurture interaction question would be to hold the environment completely constant and look for differences between children raised in that environment. If you did this, then any differences you observed between the children would have to come from differences in their genetic makeup. Another way to get at the root of the question would be to hold the genes constant across a number of children and raise them in different environments. In this case, any differences between the children would have to come from differences in their environmental experiences. The problem, of course, is that you can't really use either one of these research tactics. It would be logistically impossible to expose different children to exactly the same environments. And it would be unethical, and probably illegal, to give two children the exact same set of genes. The only way you could do this would be through cloning! Fortunately for us scientists, nature has given us an arrangement that comes pretty darn close to this research design. They're called twins. Twins are kind of like Mother Nature's own attempt at conducting an experiment to answer the nature-nurture question.

Identical twins result from the splitting of a single ovum that was fertilized by a single sperm. Since one fertilized egg produces both twins, identical twins are called *monozygotic* (meaning "from one fertilized egg"). But most importantly, because both twins come from the same fertilized egg, they are genetically identical. Fraternal twins result from two eggs being fertilized by two different sperm cells, and so are called *dizygotic* (meaning "from two fertilized eggs"). Dizygotic twins are no more alike genetically than any other pair of siblings, who, on average, share only about 50% of their genes.

Now the scientific beauty of twins is that both members of a twin pair experience about as similar an environment as is possible. For all practical purposes, monozygotic twins raised in the same family have the same genetic makeup and experience pretty much the same environment. Dizygotic twins, in contrast, are only 50% genetically alike (on average), but also share pretty much the same environment. To get a sense of the role of genetics, all you have to do is compare how similar monozygotic twins are to each other on some psychological trait such as IQ with how similar dizygotic twins are to each other on the same trait. If monozygotic twins are more alike than are dizygotic twins, then the trait in question must have a genetic component. But of course this isn't good enough for Anastasi, because as we've already seen, everybody assumes that all psychological traits have some genetic component. More interesting for Anastasi would be comparing the behavioral similarity of dizygotic twins to the behavioral similarity of regular biological siblings. Since both types of sibling relationships are based on a known genetic relationship (50% similarity), then differences in similarity must result from differences in environments. The next step would be to document what differences in the environment were correlated with the differences between dizygotic twins versus other biological siblings.

CONCLUSIONS

Anastasi's 1958 article was revolutionary because it demanded that scientists come up with better ways to answer the question of *how* in explaining the interaction between nature and nurture in producing the incredibly varied range of human psychological potential. She argued that it wasn't enough just to say that nature and nurture, genetics and environment, heredity and experience work together. Everybody already knows that. Duh! What was needed was an understanding of *how* they work together.

Anastasi's prompting seems to have worked quite well over the decades since her article was published. But at the time, she gave us the sense that people weren't doing much research on the nature-nurture question anymore. In 1958 she wrote, "Two or three decades ago, the so-called heredity-environment question was the center of lively controversy. Today, on the other hand, many psychologists look upon it as a dead issue." Since 1958, however, there has been a healthy, and sometimes scary, resurgence of interest on the topic. Much of this interest has been motivated by health concerns and has been spurred on by some fairly radical technological innovations in biochemistry, biotechnology, surgery, and brain-imaging techniques. In fact, modern science has advanced so far on the nature-nurture question that it seems to have rendered most boundaries between what is nature and what is nurture so fuzzy as to be imperceptible.

Take gene replacement therapy, for example. Technologies have been developed that actually permit scientists to remove or repair individual disease-causing genes, leaving in their place healthy versions of the same genes. At the M. D. Anderson Cancer Center in Texas, for example, scientists have modified a virus that's known to cause the common cold. They inject the modified virus into patients who have a particular form of lung cancer. But instead of infecting normal body tissues and causing a cold, the virus infects the lung cancer cells and repairs the gene responsible for producing the lung cancer! Now here is a case where the difference between nature and nurture is blurry. If the "fixed" genetic makeup of the cancer patient allows him to return to being normal and disease-free, would you say it's the result of genetics or the environment? You could develop arguments for both sides. On the one hand, you could say that being disease-free was obviously genetic because the adult had a disease-free gene. On the other hand, you could say that being disease-free was environmental because a scientist and his pet virus caused the disease-free gene to come into existence in the first place.

And then there is the whole issue of **plasticity** in brain development. Most people probably have no idea how complicated it is to grow a normal brain. I would imagine that the average person thinks our genes just "tell" our brain cells (called neurons) where to go and what to do. With over 100 billion neurons, each making connections with hundreds or thousands of other neurons, our genes would have to bark out several trillion commands to be sure our brain develops properly! But as it turns out, our brains don't develop that way at all. Rather, neurons in our brain figure out where to go and which other neurons to connect with by communicating with other nearby neurons. Sure, genes set the whole thing in motion, but the final structural architecture of the brain is ultimately determined by hundreds of trillions of little conversations going on between all the little neurons.

How do we know this? Through a wonderful little feature of the brain called plasticity. *Plasticity* refers to the idea that parts of the brain can be extremely flexible in what they end up doing. A lot of animal research has shown that if you take neurons from one part of the cortex, say the visual cortex (which is responsible for processing visual information), and transplant them into another part of the brain, say the somatosensory cortex (which is responsible for processing information about touch, among other things), then you find that the relocated visual cortical cells don't try to reestablish connections with their old visual neuron buddies, and they don't shut down and stop working altogether. The visual cortical cells start acting like somatosensory cortical cells. They adopt the philosophy of "When in Rome, do as the Romans do." The point is that brain neurons get their orders from nearby cells, not from genes. Again, would you say the function of the transplanted visual cortical cells is the result of genes, since the genes were responsible for making them into neurons in the first place? Or is it the result of the environment, because it was the surrounding neurons that coaxed the transplanted neurons to work toward a different goal than what they were designed for?

An extremely hot-potato topic these days has to do with the use of "stem cells." Stem cells are a type of cell, usually extracted from aborted fetuses or discarded umbilical cords, with the potential to grow into or become any other cell of the body. A stem cell could become a blood cell, it could become a neuron, or it could become a bone cell. It all depends on where it's placed. If it's placed among other blood cells, it develops into a blood cell. If it's dropped into the brain, it becomes a neuron. The reason stem cells are so important is that they can be used to help cure a variety of diseases. Stem cells could become insulin-producing cells for treating patients with diabetes, for example, or they might be coaxed into becoming dopamine-producing neurons for treating patients with Parkinson's disease. But if a stem cell is transplanted into the brain to treat Parkinson's disease and becomes a dopamine-producing neuron as a result, is it the result of nature, because genes give stem cells the capability for becoming any cell they want to become? Or is it the result of nurture because it was the surrounding neurons that communicated with the stem cell to tell it to become a neuron in the first place?

Anastasi was regarded as the first psychologist to notice that the old ways of answering the nature-nurture question were going nowhere. But to be honest, her call for new approaches hasn't always been heard. It's easy to find research even today where the goal is to find out what percentage of some psychological ability is genetic and what percentage is environmental. This kind of research is obviously ignoring the question *how*. On the other hand, researchers who have been heeding Anastasi's call, and who already know *how*, are presenting us with some challenging moral questions. For example, if we know how to alter the genetic makeup of our children to get rid of disease, shall we go ahead and alter their genes? Maybe. But what about knowing how to change our children's genetic makeup to make them more attractive or more intelligent? Should we do this? As we move forward into the 21st century, we may find that we become less interested in answering the question *how*, and more focused on answering the question *when*.

Bibliography

Elmes, J. L., Bates, E. A., Johnson, M. H., Karmiloff-Smith, A., Parisi, D., & Plunkett, K. (1996). *Rethinking innateness: A connectionist perspective on development.* Cambridge, MA: MIT Press.

Jackson, N. W. (1992). *Anne Anastasi and the heredity vs. environment problem: A history in psychology.* Unpublished doctoral dissertation. University of Rhode Island.

Questions for Discussion

1. Do you ever wish you'd look differently, or have different talents and skills, than you currently do? Assuming you could change your looks, talents, and skills, how do you think people in your environment would respond to these changes? Would they treat you differently? Would you want them to treat you differently? Would you treat them differently?

2. If your parents had inherited, say, a couple million dollars when you were a child, how might your personality be different today? Would you be willing to trade in your current personality for that one?

3. If you were given the chance to pick and choose which genes you and your mate gave your offspring, would you take advantage of the opportunity? Would you be more or less in favor of doing it for the purpose of enhancing your children's beauty? Enhancing your children's talent? Reducing your children's potential for disease?

20

What Comes Around
Goes Around

A REINTERPRETATION OF THE DIRECTION OF EFFECTS IN STUDIES OF SOCIALIZATION.
Bell, R. Q. (1968). *Psychological Review, 75, 81–95.*   (RANK 11)

It goes without saying that the goal of child psychology is to understand children. And because they're trained scientists, child psychologists tend to rely on doing experiments to help them reach this goal. Experiments are nice because they allow us to hold the rest of the world still while we intentionally change a very small part of children's immediate environment. Then we look to see how children behave as a result of our small environmental change. As you may remember from your Introduction to Psychology course, the part of children's environments that we change is called the **independent variable** and what kids do as a result of our little change is called the **dependent variable**. When we use experiments, changes in children's behavior in response to our environmental tinkering allow us to conclude that they happened *because* of our tinkering. Experiments are our best, most direct tools for understanding what makes children tick.

Unfortunately, some of the most interesting and important features of children's lives are not things we can experiment with. For example, as much as we might be interested in knowing how divorce influences children's development, we can't really go out and do divorce experiments. To experiment with divorce, we'd have to do something like randomly assign 50 kids to a divorce group and 50 kids to a nondivorce group. Then we'd have to arrange for the parents of the kids in the divorce group to get divorced, and for the parents of the kids in the nondivorce group not to get divorced. All that's left would be to watch these kids develop. Any differences we observed between the two groups of kids would come from their divorce experiences. But even if we could carry out such a devilish experimental feat, I'm sure you'd agree it would be a really bad idea.

When experiments aren't an option, the child psychologist's second-best tool is what's called a **correlational design**. Child psychologists who use the correlational

245

approach look for patterns of associations between two variables. One of these variables is often *believed* to cause changes in the other variable, but without the benefit of a true experiment we can never be sure. We can easily apply a correlational approach to studying divorce by comparing the behaviors of children in divorced families to the behaviors of children from intact families. Any differences we noticed between the two groups of children would be *correlated* with their divorce status. Correlational studies of divorce usually find, for example, that relative to children in intact families, children in divorced families temporarily have more behavior problems in school and temporarily suffer from lower self-esteem. Can we conclude that divorce *caused* the behavior problems and lower self-esteem? Unfortunately, no. With a correlational approach, the most we can say is that divorce and behavior problems are correlated with each other. With a correlational design, it's equally likely that children's behavior problems could've caused their parents' divorce. There's just no way to tell which direction of influence is the right one. Generically, we call this the **direction of effects** problem, and it's a problem in all correlational research.

The problem of direction of effects was brought powerfully to the attention of child development researchers by Richard Q. Bell in a 1968 article, which was voted 11th most revolutionary overall. Bell pointed out that despite the fact that most child psychology researchers paid lip service to the direction-of-effects problem, they still went about their business assuming that direction of effects always went from parent to child. Rarely did anyone acknowledge the possibility that children could have just as strong an influence on their parents.

In his article, Bell focused his discussion on research dealing with children's socialization. It was commonly assumed throughout the child development literature that parents played the primary role in socializing their children. Parents taught their children about manners and rules, and they taught them about what expectations society has of them. You're not supposed to hurt other people, you're not supposed to take other people's stuff, and you should lend a helping hand whenever you can. These were just a few of society's expectations about how children should be socialized. But Bell pointed out that children might have just as strong an influence on how parents go about the task of socialization. So, in his classic article, Bell took some of the more popular scientific findings of the time, most of which were correlational and which assumed a parent-to-child direction of socialization, and reinterpreted them to show that there could also be child-to-parent directions of influence.

INTRODUCTION

Bell began his landmark article by illustrating why child psychology researchers historically found it so tempting to assume a parent-to-child direction of effect in the socialization of children. Human babies are among the most helpless at birth, compared with other animals, and it's quite some time before they develop even the most rudimentary survival skills. It usually takes a full 7 months before they're even capable of self-locomotion! Many other mammal babies can walk right after birth. Human babies depend wholly on the good will of their parents to provide for them. Because of this commonsense observation, Bell wrote, "[i]t seems eminently plausible to visualize the human parent as the vehicle for the transmission of culture and the infant as simply the object of an acculturation process. The parent is the initial agent of culture, the child the object." But this approach entirely ignored the genetic factors that infants bring with them into the world. Some babies cry more than others, some are extremely active, and babies differed markedly in their sleep and elimination schedules. Babies are unique from birth, and it would be foolish to think that parents wouldn't respond in unique ways to the special characteristics of their kids. These facts should remind you of the temperament work by Thomas, Chess, and Birch (Chapter 16).

Recent Data Discordant With the Parent-Effect Model

In the first subsection of Bell's article, he draws the reader's attention to some popular studies of the time that called into question the presumed parent-to-child direction of socialization. He called these studies "discordant with the parent-effect model," because they not only showed that parents influenced children, but left open the possibility that children influenced how parents influenced children (did you follow that?). In other words, he argued there was a child-to-parent-to-child direction of influence. Or to use more technical terminology, we would call this a **bidirectionality of influence**. Bell started out by illustrating some bidirectional influences commonly found in human families, and then moved on to some more powerful examples drawn from experiments on bidirectionality in animal families.

Bell pointed out that by their very babyness, human newborns draw an inordinate amount of attention to themselves from the moment they're born. I'm sure this is something you can relate to. Who can keep themselves from ogling over a new baby? Can any of us avoid blubbering goofy little babyisms to those cute little bundles of joy? And when babies are in distress, they draw a feverish response from those around them aimed at reducing the distress. Bell quotes Harriet Rheingold in making this point: "So aversive, especially to humans, is the crying of the infant that there is almost no effort we will not expend, no device we will not employ, to change a crying baby into a smiling one—or just a quiet one." From this fact alone it's obvious that from the earliest moments of life children exert an immense effect on their parents—long before parents begin the process of socializing their children. (These may remind you of the response-eliciting cues John Bowlby talked about in Chapter 11.)

As another type of discordant data, Bell mentioned the case study of a foster mother who was assigned to care for four identical quadruplet foster daughters, all with schizophrenia. The foster mother was extremely restrictive with all four children. But her level of affection was different for each one. The fact that her affection varied shows that she must've been responding to differences between the four children. In other words, the children were influencing how she displayed her affection. On what basis would she discriminate between the children if not on the basis that the kids were different? This is what we might call a "child effect," because the type of socialization experienced depended on the child. And, of course, the amount of loving-kindness displayed by the foster mother would be an important element that children would pay attention to when they're being socialized. This same foster mother was also observed to show very different patterns of reaction to several other children who were later assigned to her (babies this time). If socialization travels only along a parent-to-child route, then this foster mother's behavior should have been the same for every child she cared for. But quite the opposite happened. The affectional behaviors of the foster mother were driven by the characteristics of the children under her care.

In another study Bell described, one involving a large group of biological mothers rather than a single foster mother, mothers were observed for how they reacted to their newborns during times of feeding. To no one's surprise, the mothers responded more positively when the babies were awake than when they were asleep. Again, the babies' states of alertness influenced the mothers' behaviors more than the mothers' behaviors influenced the babies' states of alertness. In a related study, the best predictor of how many weeks mothers nursed their babies after birth was how much breast milk the babies consumed at each feeding. Babies who drank a lot of milk at each feeding had mothers who nursed them for a greater period of time. In this case, the baby's own nursing behavior was a better predictor of length of nursing than the mother's own nursing intentions.

In the animal research, Bell highlighted some very compelling findings on child-to-mother directions of influence in rhesus monkeys (the same species studied by the Harlows in Chapter 10). For example, in one study female rhesus monkeys who were serving as foster mothers to baby monkeys actually began lactating (producing milk) in response to the clinging of the babies! And in deer mice, females who were simply given a litter of 1-day-old mouse pups began licking the pups and building nests—typical mothering behaviors. I think it's safe to assume that neither the female rhesus monkeys nor the female deer mice would've begun engaging in mothering behaviors if not for the presence of the foster babies. Apparently, as Bell suggested, animal researchers are way ahead of the game when it comes to realizing the importance of bidirectional influences between parents and their offspring. If animals, with their highly instinct-driven behavior patterns, are capable of showing such strong effects of bidirectionality, human mother-child relationships are probably even more susceptible to bidirectionality.

Modifiers of Parent Response

Bell pointed out that it really shouldn't be so hard to accept the idea that babies and children can have significant impacts on their parents' parenting behaviors. After all, from the parents' point of view, babies are really just another source of environmental stimulation. Just as they sneeze when they sniff pepper and squeal when they sit on a tack, parents also respond to the stimulation provided by their kids. Bell suggested that a first step toward understanding the kinds of child-driven stimulation parents react to is to understand what he calls the **congenital determinants** of parents' behaviors. By "congenital determinants," Bell meant the unique temperamental profile that each child brings into the world at birth. Differences in children's inborn temperamental qualities can't help serving as different sources of stimulation to parents. Bell emphasized two temperamental characteristics in particular: *assertiveness* and *person orientation*. Modern temperament researchers might not use these exact labels, but both assertiveness and person-orientation have their counterparts in modern temperament theory.

Congenital Assertiveness.   From birth, children differ from one another in their **congenital assertiveness**. Assertiveness is defined as the "maintenance of goal-directed behavior of high magnitude in the face of barriers," and is very similar to the modern temperamental notion of "persistence." In other words, some children keep trying to do something no matter what obstacles get in their way, whereas other children can easily be persuaded to change their courses of action. Differences in assertiveness can have a mighty strong impact on the socialization tactics used by parents to manage their children. If a toddler wants to stick a screwdriver into an electrical outlet, it would be a lot harder for a parent to deal with the kid if he was highly assertive. The parent could try moving the kid to a new location, she could try to interest him in coloring, or she could try to read him a book. But if he's highly assertive, he'll keep going back to that electrical outlet with his screwdriver. The sheer tenacity of highly assertive children requires parents to dig deep into their pool of parenting strategies. Meanwhile, the child low in assertiveness would probably lose interest in the electrical outlet at the mother's first try to dissuade his interest.

Bell drew from two studies to show how child assertiveness influenced parent socialization practices. Both studies focused on sex differences in primitive cultures. In one study, primitive cultures that emphasized the hunting of large animals were found to socialize only boys into the role of animal hunter. In the other study it was found that only boys, across some 224 different primitive cultures, were socialized to be fighters. Bell believed that all this emphasis on training boys to be hunters and fighters had to be due to the greater skeletal muscle development found in boys, which he also believed must've been accompanied by higher levels of assertiveness. He wrote, "It appears reasonable that some potential for use of muscles in physically assertive behavior can be assumed. We would not expect the exclusive allocation of the fighting role to males if they possessed only greater skeletal muscle mass with no accompanying potential for use, or if there were equal distribution of this potential between the sexes."

Congenital Person Orientation. Another characteristic of children likely to influence parents' socialization practices is what Bell called **congenital person orientation**. Person orientation boils down to children's interests in other people. Children high in person orientation pay a lot of attention to what other people, especially their parents, do, and they are quite responsive to their parents' efforts at initiating social interaction. Children low in person orientation tend to be much more aloof. They're more interested in running and jumping or playing with toys, and they tend to be much less interested in social interaction with their parents. Person orientation also has its counterpart in modern temperament lingo, resembling something like "sociability." Anyway, it's easy to imagine that parents would respond differently to children who were socially warm and receptive versus socially distant and disconnected. Bell used two more studies to make this point.

In one study, it was found that babies who were low in person orientation, defined as being squirmy when held, were more likely to avoid being carried, stroked, or kissed. Bell traced this kind of social isolation directly to the child's own aversions to social contact more than to any social ineptitude on the part of the mother. In a different study, focusing on sex differences, 3- and 12-week-old infant boys were found to be more irritable and to sleep less than girls. Bell reasoned that if boys were irritable and cranky all the time, then their mothers' interactions with them would probably be focused mostly on physical caretaking, and much less on pleasurable social engagement. In fact, it wouldn't be surprising if mothers of irritable and cranky boys simply wished to avoid them. Even when the boys were quiet, the mothers might fear that any interaction might fire up the irritability and crankiness again. Following this line of reasoning, Bell argued, boys are at a socialization disadvantage. But importantly, this disadvantage in socialization was due to their own irritability and crankiness, to their own congenital deficiency in person orientation. Perhaps this explains the popular stereotype that males "aren't in touch with their feelings" and "avoid talking about their problems" with their girlfriends and wives! Maybe as boys they never let their mothers get emotionally close enough to them to be taught about proper etiquette for social-emotional communication.

Differentiation of Parent Response

Bell suggested that when parents approach the task of socializing their children, they usually don't have a fixed, limited set of socialization practices they invariably rely upon. Rather, they choose from a range of strategies. Which tactic they choose depends in part on cultural pressures (these days it's culturally unpopular to swat your kid with a tree branch) and in part on the unique characteristics of their children. Bell proposed that parents draw from two levels of socialization tactics. Which level they drew from depended in large part on the specific characteristics of their children. For some children, socialization practices drawn from the lower level are good enough. But for other children, parents might have to use the higher-octane socialization strategies.

Bell described these two levels as **lower-limit control practices** and **upper-limit control practices**. He thought parents could use lower-limit control techniques when their children's behavior fell within an acceptable range of socialization standards. If a toddler spills some food on the floor when she's learning to feed herself, for example, her mom might simply say, "Oops, try to be more careful next time." In this case, the mom might view spilling food as normal for toddlers, in which case she would only have to draw from her lower-limit control options to deal with the problems. On the other hand, if the same toddler decided to throw her whole bowl of cereal on the floor, this action might exceed her mother's limits of toleration. In this case, the mother might have to draw from her upper-limit control repertoire and provide a more severe socialization response, such as giving the kid a time-out. But notice that in either case, the socialization practices employed by the mother depended on the behavior of the child.

In general, then, which level of socialization practices the mother draws from on any particular occasion depends on three factors: (1) cultural expectations, both in terms of how the child's supposed to behave and in terms of how the mother's supposed to respond; (2) the mother's unique expectations for her child; and (3) the unique characteristics of the child. Despite the fact that socialization obviously depends on all three of these factors, Bell chided, the child psychology literature has overemphasized the role of the parent's expectations and trivialized the child's own power in bringing about certain socialization practices. Bell noted that when the scientific magnifying glass is placed exclusively on the parent, "a parent showing extreme upper-limit behavior in several areas is likely to be described as 'punitive,' or 'restrictive,' [while a parent] showing extreme lower-limit behavior [is described] as 'intrusive,' or 'demanding'." In either case, the role of the child in pulling out the mother's socialization tactics are ignored. Paying exclusive research attention to the role of the parent while neglecting the role of the child can only lead to misunderstanding the true nature of socialization.

Reinterpretation of Recent Literature

In the next portion of his article, Bell reinterpreted several popular parent-effect themes found in the scientific literature of the time, in light of the bidirectionality idea he endorsed. One popular theme that made its way through scientific circles was that excessive punishment by parents caused excessive aggressiveness in children. Bell cited two studies that drew such conclusions. One found that spanked 8-year-olds were rated as more aggressive by their friends than were nonspanked 8-year-olds. The other found that spanked 15- and 16-year-olds were more likely to get into trouble with the law than nonspanked adolescents. The results of both studies support the theory that when parents use spanking to socialize their kids, they are really teaching their kids to use aggression to deal with frustration. Obviously, the authors of these studies assumed a parent-to-child direction of influence. But Bell's take on these results was that the parents may have used spanking as a means to deal with children who were high in assertiveness in the first place. Spanking may have been an upper-limit control strategy directly caused by behavior that was outside a tolerable range.

In a study on moral development, it was found that children whose parents socialized them by talking about right and wrong developed higher moral consciences than children of parents who applied spanking for wrongdoing. Again, this study assumes that the socialization strategy used by the parents is what *produced* the higher moral conscience in children. But Bell pointed out that these results could just as easily be interpreted the opposite way. Perhaps the children who were high in person orientation to begin with, and therefore higher in moral conscience, created an atmosphere that allowed parents to use a talking strategy.

In a study of sex-role development, 5- and 6-year-old boys who were very high in masculinity were found to have fathers who were both very rewarding and very punishing. That is, when fathers rewarded their boys for doing something right, they rewarded very strongly, and when they punished their boys for doing something wrong, they punished just as strongly. The authors of that study concluded that the boys *became* highly masculine *as a result of* their fathers' extreme patterns of reward and punishment. Similarly, they concluded that fathers who rewarded and punished less extremely produced boys with lower levels of masculinity. But an equally viable conclusion, from Bell's point of view, would be that the fathers were simply responding to their boys' sex-appropriate behaviors from the start. One part of being masculine is being assertive. Boys congenitally high in assertiveness would already have a lot of features described by most people as "masculine." Therefore, when the highly assertive boys behaved assertively, their fathers may have been pleased, and may have rewarded them accordingly. On the other hand, when the boys acted *too* assertively, it may have been too much even for their fathers, and the fathers might've resorted to upper-limit control strategies such as punishment. From this perspective, fathers' socialization practices shouldn't necessarily be viewed as producing masculinity in their boys; rather, masculinity in the boys might just as readily be viewed as influencing fathers' socialization practices.

A common theme in research on social class differences throughout the 1950s and 1960s was that parents of middle-class children used less physical punishment and more love-oriented socialization techniques than parents of lower-class children. It was also a common finding that children from lower-class households were more likely to have attention disorders and to get in trouble at school. The typical assumption was that the harsher discipline used by lower-class parents *caused* the children to have attention disorders and to get into trouble. But you can also flip the coin. Families in lower-class households also have less money and less access to high-quality medical care. As a result, lower-class families are at greater risk for experiencing complications during pregnancy and delivery, which probably increases the risk for disorders of attention and hyperactivity. Consequently, the harsher discipline used by lower-class parents may have been caused by the increased congenital hyperactivity in their children rather than the other way around.

Examples of Studies Difficult to Reinterpret

Although Bell pointed to a lot of scientific findings that could be reinterpreted as demonstrating a child-to-parent direction of influence, he also identified several studies that couldn't be so easily reinterpreted. The best example of a definite, unquestioned parent-to-child direction of effect is when parents administer drugs to their children. You're probably aware that children with ADHD (attention deficit with hyperactivity disorder) respond well to various forms of drug therapy, such as Ritalin or Adderall. But there's little doubt that when parents administer these prescription drugs to their children, their children's behavior changes directly. (Of course, notice that it was the children's behavior in the first place that caused the parents to seek medical assistance.)

CONCLUSIONS

Bell's 1968 article was revolutionary because it caused child psychology researchers to take two steps back and rethink the relationship between parents' socialization practices and children's behaviors. But Bell's influence has extended far beyond the specific research area of children's socialization. These days, child psychologists who study just about any aspect of the parent-child relationship take Bell's lessons under advisement, with the sensible realization that wherever there is a parent interacting with her child, there is also a child interacting with his parent. You can see Bell's influence on the revolutionary work of Sameroff and Chandler in Chapter 18, when they talk about the child's role in contributing to his own abuse!

Correlation Doesn't Imply Causation

Bell set the gold standard for how to deal with correlational research. As I mentioned at the beginning of the chapter, it's often tempting to draw conclusions about the direction of influence between parents and children even when only correlational data are available. Moreover, many times it seems as though there is only one possible way to interpret the data. But, just to make the point again, there's nothing in correlational data which proves that the direction of influence between parent and child must be one way or the other. When child psychology researchers find a correlation between something the mother does and something the child does, all this really means is that changes in the mother's behavior co-occur with changes in the child's behavior. It doesn't mean that changes in the mother's behavior *caused* changes in the child's behavior, and it doesn't mean that changes in the child's behavior *caused* changes in the mother's behavior. Either interpretation is equally likely. (This is why psychology professors often implant the phrase "Correlation doesn't imply causation" into their students' brains when they get to the correlation chapter in their textbooks.)

Temperament

Bell's groundbreaking ideas also set the stage for the next three decades of research on children's temperament. For all Bell's talk about congenital difference between children and how parents might be influenced by these congenital differences, very little was known about the nature of such congenital differences. The lack of understanding of these congenital differences produced a gaping hole in child psychology theory. Fortunately, in the same year Bell published his ideas, Thomas, Chess, and Birch published their own revolutionary work on children's temperament (see Chapter 16), which quickly filled the gap identified by Bell. The range in variation in children's temperament explored by Thomas, Chess, and Birch, as well as the variety of types of temperament they identified, gave child psychology researchers something to chew on as they struggled to understand the bidirectionality of parent-child interactions.

As a result, the last three decades have seen an explosion in temperament research, most of it focused on how children's temperament can affect the parent-child relationship. Unfortunately, since temperament is one of those independent variables that child psychologists can't manipulate, most of this research has also been correlational. And for this reason, it hasn't been possible to untangle questions about direction of effects. But at least now we have a sense of the many ways that children can differ congenitally.

"Baby X" Experiment

Based in large part on Bell's contributions, there's greater recognition than ever that if child psychology researchers are going to be successful in isolating parent-to-child or child-to-parent directions of influence, they're going to have to rely much less on correlational designs and much more on experimental ones. Of course, experimental research isn't always possible, such as when studying the influence of divorce on children's self-esteem or when studying the influence of temperament on parent-child relationship quality. But there's still a great deal we can learn about directions of influence from experiments that *are* possible. Offhand, I can think of a particularly cute little study that drives this point home.

The "Baby X study" was motivated by the very popular finding in child psychology that parents play with their male and female children differently. Boys are usually played with more vigorously, while girls are played with more tenderly.

Researchers are interested in parent-child play behaviors because they may give us some insight as to the sources of lifelong gender-role stereotypes. The question, of course, is, Why do parents play with boys and girls differently? Is it because they want their boys to be tougher and their girls to be gentler? Or is it because boys are congenitally more assertive and girls are congenitally higher in person-orientation in the first place, causing their parents to treat them differently? This is a classic direction-of-effects problem.

To help answer this question, Carol Seavey, Phyllis Katz, and Sue Zalk conducted their famous Baby X experiment. The objective of their study was to see if adults would play differently with a particular baby depending on whether it was a boy or a girl. Although this research question had been asked many times before, the ingenuity of the Baby X experiment was that every adult actually played with the same 3-month-old baby. Some of the adults were told the baby was a boy, some were told the baby was a girl, and some were not given any gender information. Baby X was actually a girl, but any clues about her true gender were masked by dressing her in a gender-neutral yellow jumpsuit. Pretty sneaky! There were also gender-typed and gender-neutral toys available to play with. For example, there was a football (a "boy" toy), a Raggedy Ann doll (a "girl" toy), and a plastic ring (a gender-neutral toy).

This was sort of a **critical experiment** because you could make two opposite predictions depending on which direction of influence you thought was more important. If there was an adult-to-child direction of influence, then any gender-stereotyped play shown by adults would be due to their own gender-stereotyped expectations; and the perceived gender of Baby X should have a strong influence on the adults' play behaviors. But if there was a child-to-adult direction of influence, then any gender-typed play shown by adults would be caused by the actual gender of the child, perhaps by some sort of "girlyness" clues she gives off; and the perceived gender should have little influence on the adults' play behaviors.

The results were clear-cut. When the adults thought Baby X was a girl, they selected the doll to play with. When they thought Baby X was a boy, they avoided the doll (and, surprisingly, the football) and instead selected the plastic ring. When they didn't know her gender, female adults engaged in a great deal of social interaction, whereas male adults engaged in very little social interaction. The men may have been uncomfortable playing with a baby of unknown gender. But despite not knowing the baby's gender, almost all the adults "decided" that the child was either a boy or a girl based on physical characteristics they noticed. They called her a boy if they noticed her "strong grip" and lack of hair, or they called her a girl if they noticed she was "soft and fragile." The point is that the way adults played with Baby X was strongly influenced by what gender they *thought* she was. Obviously, they had patently stereotyped expectations of how to play with boys and girls, and their expectations influenced their play behaviors. Experimental research like the Baby X study carries a lot of weight in helping the field of child psychology understand the influence of parental expectations on parent-child interactions.

It's difficult to say whether the field of child psychology would have paid as much attention to the problem of direction of effects had Bell not published his revolutionary work when he did. The field of child psychology seemed ripe for a new movement anyway, and Bell may simply have been in the right place at the right time. Other revolutionary authors of the late 1960s were also struggling to understand child-to-parent directions of influence, including the temperament work already mentioned and John Bowlby's (Chapter 11) work on child effects in attachment relationships. On the other hand, it's also possible that the impacts made by temperament and attachment research would've been much less pronounced had Bell not signaled the changing of the guard when he did. I suppose the bottom line is that Bell did what he did when he did it, and he revolutionized child psychology in the process. The rest is history.

Bibliography

Golombok, S., & Fivush, R. (1994). *Gender development.* Cambridge, England: Cambridge University Press.

Seavey, C. A., Katz, P. A., & Zalk, S. R. (1975). Baby X: The effects of gender labels on adult responses to infants. *Sex Roles, 1,* 103–109.

Questions for Discussion

1. Do you think you had a greater effect on your parents, or did your parents have a greater effect on you?

2. Assuming you have brothers and sisters, how might your parents have raised you differently if you were born either later or earlier? What kinds of specific influences did your siblings have on your parents' parenting practices?

3. When you meet new people for the first time, do you treat them differently if they're men or women? If so, how exactly do you treat them differently? And why is it that you treat them differently?

21
Developmental Lessons From Kitten Brains

RECEPTIVE FIELDS OF CELLS IN STRIATE CORTEX OF VERY YOUNG, VISUALLY INEXPERIENCED KITTENS.

Hubel, D. H., & Wiesel, T. N. (1963). *Journal of Neurophysiology, 26, 994–1002.*   (RANK 13)

Throughout the chapters of this book, we've been reviewing one revolutionary study after another that has made a significant contribution to our understanding of child psychology. We've talked about children's cognition, their language, their emotions, their aggression, even their morality. But in talking about all these psychological abilities and capacities you may have noticed there's always a certain amount of abstractness involved. In fact, you can't really do psychology without talking about abstract psychological concepts. The problem is that you can't *see* a psychological ability or capacity; the most you can do is make inferences about it. For example, you never really see a kid thinking; all you really see is what a kid does, and you assume he's thinking. You never really see a kid's happiness; all you really see is a smile on his face or hear him laughing, and you infer that he's happy. You never really see a kid's aggression; you just observe him kicking and yelling, and you assume he's aggressive. The whole field of psychology is loaded with these kinds of unobservable things, and the best a psychological scientist can hope for is to study behaviors that she thinks are driven by those unobservable qualities.

If there's one thing that nearly everybody in the field of psychology does know, it's that these abstract psychological abilities and capacities ultimately come from the neural circuitry of the brain. Children's thinking happens in their brains, their emotions result from what their brains do, and aggression comes from the way their brains interpret social information. So if so much of psychology really comes down to brain activity, why aren't all psychologists doing brain science? Well, there are a couple of responses I can think of.

First, I suspect that most psychologists wouldn't feel comfortable with the assumption that all of human psychology can be reduced to patterns of electrical activity in the brain, at least not in our current state of technology. Human behavior is so exceedingly complicated, so unpredictable, and we know so very little about the range of possible human actions under any set of conditions, that most psychologists aren't even sure what they would want to look for in the brain. How can you look for a neurological explanation for a psychological ability, when you don't even understand the psychological ability in the first place?

But even so, some psychologists do think of themselves as brain scientists. These people sometimes go by titles like *neuropsychologist, biopsychologist, neurophysiologist,* or *psychopharmacologist.* In fact, several divisions of the American Psychological Association are dedicated to supporting brain-based research: Division 6, Behavioral Neuroscience and Comparative Psychology; Division 28, Psychopharmacology and Substance Abuse; Division 40, Clinical Neuropsychology; and the most recently created, Division 55, American Society for the Advancement of Pharmacotherapy. And brain-based psychological research is more popular than ever, aided by a landslide of technological innovations allowing psychologists to peek in at human brain functioning live and on-line, without requiring that the researchers get advanced medical training in brain anatomy. These new tools allow us to study how the brain reacts to all sorts of stimulation. Through positron emission tomography, for example, we are actually able to take a three-dimensional snapshot of the parts of the brain that are most active when a person is sleeping, reading, talking, or doing math problems.

But just because one part of the brain "lights up" on the computer screen when a person is doing math problems, it doesn't mean that that area is where math rules are stored. A highly active brain region could also indicate that a person is experiencing considerable stress while doing the math. So even brain scientists have to make some assumptions about the connections between psychological abilities and brain activity. From a scientific standpoint, one wonders if it wouldn't be a whole lot easier just to poke around in the brain to see what happens. You could electrically stimulate one section of a person's brain and then ask him what memories come to mind. Or you could remove a piece of brain and observe what a person is no longer able to do. But for some strange reason, human volunteers for these kinds of projects are in extremely short supply (and even if they did volunteer, there would be a whole bunch of ethical and legal reasons that you shouldn't go around removing pieces of people's brains).

This has led a lot of psychologists to turn to brain research in animals. Animals, especially mammals, have brains very similar to ours. With animal brains, you can poke, prod, stimulate, and remove stuff to your heart's (or conscience's) desire. Of course, the American Psychological Association and a host of government agencies have very strict rules for how animal research subjects must be treated. And even so, we must admit that animal brains aren't as sophisticated as human brains—animals don't talk or reason, and they can't do math problems. But at least with animal brains you can gain some excellent insight as to how brains are put together. And there are a lot of brain systems that humans and other animals have in common. One of the most thoroughly studied of these is the visual system.

The focus of this chapter is on the groundbreaking research of David Hubel and Torsten Wiesel, on the developing visual system of the cat. Their work not only was rated 13th most revolutionary by the child psychology community, but earned them a Nobel Prize in Physiology or Medicine in 1982 as well. Their research was revolutionary for three major findings. First, they discovered that *individual cells* in the visual cortex of cat brains responded to specific patterns of visual input. (The cortex is the outer surface of the brain. It's made up of that funny-looking, squiggly, wrinkly stuff.) These **cortical cells** mostly responded to simple patterns like edges and lines, arranged in particular orientations. But this was an extremely important finding nevertheless, because it gave us some insight into how we're able to see. Prior to their findings, we knew that rods and cones in the eye responded to light, and we knew that incoming visual information was eventually routed to the visual cortex through the thalamus; but it was a big puzzle as to how our brains put all this visual information together to create nice, well-formed mental pictures of whatever it was we were looking at.

Think of the problem this way. Each of our eyes has about 120 million rods and about 6 million cones. Since rods and cones are both types of nerve cell, whenever a rod or a cone detects some light coming into the eyeball, it sends a nerve impulse to the part of the brain responsible for processing visual inputs. From the nervous system's point of view, this means that at any moment in time, as many as 252 million visual nerve impulses are being produced. Of course, while you're sitting there reading these words, you don't perceive 252 million different points of light. You perceive a nice, smooth image. The puzzle that needed to be solved, then, was how we could start out with 252 million different nerve impulses, and end up perceiving only one crisp picture! Hubel and Wiesel's answer was that our cortical brain cells don't receive individual inputs from rods and cones, they only respond to patterns of inputs. This means that somewhere in the visual system, after the visual impulses leave the rods and cones, but before they reach the visual cortex, they are combined or *summarized* somehow.

The second discovery made by Hubel and Wiesel (pronounced "HUE-bul" and "VEE-zul") was that most of the cortical cells that processed visual impulses processed impulses coming in from both eyes. In other words, they discovered that cortical cells were **binocular** (from *bin*, "two," and *ocular*, "eye"). When a brain cell in the visual cortex receives binocular impulses, impulses from the eye on the same side of the body (called the **ipsilateral** side) are combined with impulses from the eye on the opposite side of the body (called the **contralateral** side). Binocular cells respond most strongly when they receive binocular input. What this means is that a single binocular cell actually responds to two images, one from the left eye and one from the right. You might think that binocularity wastes valuable brain circuitry. After all, why send the same visual information to a cortical cell twice? But binocularity is actually quite adaptive. For one thing, binocularity gives the brain the capability for perceiving depth. When we look at an object, depending on where it's located in space, the object casts slightly different images to each eye. When cortical cells in the brain summarize this information, they have some sense of how far away in space the object is. But besides the role of binocularity in depth perception, it's probably not a bad idea to give cortical cells two chances at detecting what's in the world. If visual information is missed by one eye, chances are the other eye can still detect it. Hubel and Wiesel also found that binocular cortical cells tended to be dominated by one eye or the other. That is, one eye usually produced a stronger response in the cortical cell than the other eye.

The third major discovery made by Hubel and Wiesel was that visual cortical cells were grouped together into little columns in the visual cortex. In more technical terms, we could say visual cortical cells live together in a **columnar microstructure**. These little columns of visual cortical cells are laid out perpendicular to the surface of the brain. To get a sense of what this means, imagine sticking a needle straight into the surface of an apple. The part of the needle that protrudes into the flesh of the apple corresponds roughly to how columns of cortical cells extend below the surface of the brain. Hubel and Wiesel also found that the cortical cells within a particular column all responded to the same types of simple patterns. This means that the cortical cells are regionally organized. Cortical cells in a column in one region of the visual cortex respond to one type of visual pattern, whereas cortical cells in columns in other regions of the visual cortex respond to other types of visual patterns.

But wait: I'm giving you the end of the story before I've even started it. Let's take a closer look at just one of their contributions to the field. In this article, published in 1963, they documented very early neural organization in the visual system of 2-week-old kittens.

INTRODUCTION

Hubel and Wiesel didn't give us much by way of introduction to their study. About the only thing they tell us is that their purpose "was to learn the age at which cortical cells have normal, adult-type receptive fields, and to find out whether such fields exist even in animals that have no patterned visual stimulation." By **receptive field**, they are referring to the pattern of visual input that an individual cortical cell responds to. I mentioned earlier that individual cortical cells responded to simple visual patterns like vertical lines or horizontal edges, but to stimulate a given cortical cell, the pattern also has to be in a particular location in the visual field. For example, if you are looking at something, and there is a vertical line at the top of the image, then that vertical line will fall within the receptive fields of cortical cells that are sensitive to the top parts of images. But if you are looking at something and the vertical line is at the bottom of the image, then the vertical line will fall within the receptive fields of cortical cells that are sensitive to the bottom parts of images. Cortical cells that respond to patterns in the top parts of images do not also respond to the same patterns found in the bottom parts of images. This is because the two sets of cortical cells have different receptive fields.

METHOD

Participants

Four kittens were used in the experiment, 3 of which were from the same litter. The first kitten was 8 days old when the experiment began and had not yet opened its eyes.

The second kitten had both its eyes covered at 9 days by "translucent contact occluders," which were basically eye covers that allowed some light to come in, but not enough to allow the kitten to see anything. This kitten was just beginning to open its eyes at the time the occluders were put into place. The third kitten had its right eye covered by a translucent occluder at 9 days, but the left eye was allowed to open normally. The fourth kitten, the one from a different litter, was brought up normally, without anything blocking its vision. Its eyes also opened on the ninth day. To summarize, when the experiment began 2 kittens had no visual experience, 1 kitten had visual experience in only one eye, and 1 kitten had visual experience in both eyes.

Materials and Procedure

Hubel and Wiesel apparently had a nasty habit of describing the details of their experimental procedure by pointing their readers to earlier publications. In the method section of this article, for example, they wrote, "Procedures for stimulating and recording have for the most part been described in previous papers," and they go on to cite some of their earlier papers. I checked one of these earlier papers to get the details, and to my surprise I found that in that paper they also wrote, "Details of stimulating and recording methods are given in previous papers." I almost get the impression that they don't want their readers to know how they conducted their experiments! Fortunately, they provided a little more detail in a 1962 publication, so I refer in part to that study in describing their methodology below.

Before being tested, each kitten underwent a short surgical procedure to create a small hole in the skull and dura mater, roughly a few millimeters wide, so that a recording electrode could be inserted into the visual cortex. For kittens this young, surgical preparation included a very small dose of barbiturate and a local anesthetic. Hubel and Wiesel wrote, "A few minutes after injection of the local anesthetic the animal usually fell asleep and showed no signs of discomfort during the surgery or the experiment." The electrodes were inserted into the cortex at a number of locations and at a variety of depths. Most electrodes went no deeper than 3 or 4 millimeters. Because the goal was to make recordings of the activity levels of individual cortical cells, the eyes of the kittens were continually stimulated by light patterns as the electrode was advanced into the brain. This procedure made localization of individual cortical cells possible. During the electrode insertion procedure, the kittens' skulls were cemented to a special apparatus that could be clamped tightly, thus holding their heads completely still. Once the electrode was in place and the skull was held securely, the kittens were shown patterned images on a diffusely illuminated screen. Upon completion of the experiment, the kittens' brains were subjected to **histological examination**, which means their brain tissue was examined under a microscope.

RESULTS

Hubel and Wiesel made recordings from eight or nine individual cortical cells in each of the 4 kittens. In general, they found these cortical cells to be much less active than those in adult cats, and some cells were too difficult to stimulate at all. Cells that did respond tended to tire out much more quickly than was typical for adult cats. But similar to those of adult cats, the kittens' cells responded most vigorously to patterned stimuli of a particular orientation (by "orientation" here, I mean the angle of the line). Hubel and Wiesel reported that finding the correct orientation of a line for a given cortical cell was often tedious. While a cell was being recorded, for example, a line or an edge had to be moved back and forth across the kittens' fields of vision, and rotated in various orientations, until the targeted cortical cell began responding vigorously.

Perhaps I can give you a sense of their procedure by invoking a little imaginary experiment. Suppose you're looking straight ahead. Imagine there is a yardstick dangling in space directly in front of you. Now, in your imagination, orient the yardstick so that it's straight up and down; and then imagine the yardstick sweeping back and forth, from left to right. Then mentally rotate the yardstick slightly until the top is at 1:00 and the bottom is at 7:00, and then imagine the yardstick sweeping back and forth across your visual field at an angle perpendicular to its orientation, from upper left to lower right. Now rotate the yardstick so that the top is at 2:00 and the bottom is at 8:00, and sweep it again across your field. If you kept on doing this, you'd get a sense of the range of visual patterns the kittens were exposed to.

Hubel and Wiesel determined that the receptive field for a given cortical cell was wherever the line was in the visual image and whatever orientation the line was in when the cell responded most vigorously. They wrote, "Brief responses were consistently obtained [in one cell] when the [edge] was oriented in a 1 o'clock to 7 o'clock direction whereas there was no response when it was oriented at 90° to this [11 o'clock to 5 o'clock]. A similar kind of preference in stimulus orientation was common to all of the units isolated. Several of the cells, especially those in the 8-day-old kitten, gave responses over a range of stimulus orientations that was unusually wide by adult standards, yet even in these cells stimulating at an orientation of 90° to the optimum evoked no response at all. Moreover, the responses to moving an optimally oriented stimulus across the receptive field were not necessarily the same for the two diametrically opposite directions of movement. As in the adult cat, this kind of directional preference varied from cell to cell; some cells responded equally well to the two opposing directions of movement, while some responded well to one direction and not at all to the other." In other words, not only did individual cortical cells respond most vigorously to a line in a particular orientation, but the vigorous responding happened only while the line was sweeping across the visual field; and even then, sometimes the line had to be sweeping in one particular direction to produce a response.

Binocular Interaction

Hubel and Wiesel found that the great majority of the cortical cells they studied could be influenced by each eye separately. Of the 39 total cortical cells they recorded from, 26 responded vigorously to input from both eyes. Of the remaining cells, there were 4 that responded *only* to input from the contralateral (opposite-side) eye and 1 that responded *only* to input from the ipsilateral (same-side) eye. This pattern of binocular responding was pretty much the same as that found in adult cats, which led Hubel and Wiesel to conclude, "There is little to no difference in ocular-dominance distribution with age or visual experience."

Functional Architecture

Relating to the idea of the *columnar microstructure*, Hubel and Wiesel found that cortical cells contained within a single column all pretty much responded to lines of the same orientation. They found this out by first inserting the electrode into the top cell of a column and then making a recording, then pushing through to the next cell in the column and making a recording, and then pushing through to the next cell in the column and making a recording, and so on. On the other hand, when the electrode was inserted at a slight angle to a column, thus departing from cells in one column and entering cells in another, the line orientations that produced the most vigorous responding shifted. Hubel and Wiesel diagrammed how the line orientations producing the most vigorous responsiveness shifted as the electrode advanced further and further into the brain, traversing several columns of cells: (1) cells in the first column responded most vigorously to a line orientation of 11:00 to 5:00, (2) cells from the next column over responded most vigorously to a line orientation of about 12:30 to 6:30, (3) the next cells responded best to an orientation of about 9:30 to 3:30, and finally (4) the last column of cells responded most vigorously to line orientations of about 11:00 to 5:00 again.

Cortical Differences Based on Visual Experience

In this study, Hubel and Wiesel found that there was basically no difference in the receptivity of individual cortical cells to binocular inputs coming from both eyes, even in kittens who had been deprived of visual experience. They wrote, "What can be concluded . . . is that even as late as 19 days of age a cell need not have had previous patterned stimulation from an eye in order to respond normally to it." In other words, even though some eyes were deprived of visual input from the environment, the impulses being sent by these eyes to the cortical cells were still heard "loud and clear" by the cortical cells. The connections between the temporarily blinded eyes and the cortical cells remained completely intact.

DISCUSSION

The main result of their study was to show that the basic architectural organization of the visual cortex in kittens is unaffected even in kittens deprived of visual experience. This architecture is basically in place at birth and even severe deprivation of visual experience doesn't alter it, at least not by $2\frac{1}{2}$ weeks of age. They wrote, "The present results make it clear that highly complex neural connections are possible without the benefit of neural experience."

CONCLUSIONS

Although Hubel and Wiesel found that depriving kittens of visual experience didn't have any significant impact on how the visual systems of those kittens were organized, it would be premature to conclude that experience plays no role in maintaining neural connections beyond the first 20 days. In fact, in a related study, published in the same journal issue, they found that serious disruptions in visual neural circuitry *would* happen if the kittens were deprived of visual experience for a much longer time. Let's take a closer look at this related study.

Related Study

In this related study, also published in 1963, but with the order of the authors reversed, Wiesel and Hubel studied kittens who had one eye closed for as long as 4 months. In this study, 7 kittens and 1 adult cat were used. The blinded eye was either sewn shut, preventing any light from entering, or covered with a translucent occluder, permitting some very diffuse light to enter. The neural activity of 84 cortical cells was recorded at various points during the period of visual deprivation. They found that unlike in the earlier study, the binocular cortical cells in these kittens showed absolutely *no* receptivity to impulses coming from the visually deprived eye. If you remember from the earlier study, the cortical cells of kittens who were visually deprived for less than 20 days responded well to both eyes. Their cortical cells remained binocular. But in this second study, when visual deprivation was much longer, those same cells simply stopped responding to the eye that provided no visual input. These cortical cells lost their binocularity, through neural atrophy. In other words, connections that were functioning quite well early in life ceased functioning in the absence of continued stimulation.

Some of the kittens in this second study were also given the opportunity to walk around with their good eye covered, but with their visually deprived eye open. Wiesel and Hubel described the kittens' behavior this way: "As an animal walked about investigating its surroundings the gait was broad-based and hesitant, and the head moved up and down in a peculiar nodding manner. The kittens bumped into large obstacles such as table legs, and even collided with walls, which they tended to follow using their whiskers as a guide. When put onto a table the animals walked off into the air, several times falling awkwardly onto the floor. When an object was moved before the eye there was no hint that it was perceived, and no attempt was made to follow it. As soon as the cover was taken off the [good] eye the kitten would behave normally, jump gracefully from the table, skillfully avoiding objects in its way. We concluded that there was a profound, perhaps complete, impairment of vision in the deprived eye of these animals."

Taking these two studies together, the results show that kittens' visual systems are wired up properly from birth, but that portions atrophy over time through disuse. Prior to Hubel and Wiesel's research, most vision researchers thought that the visual system didn't come prewired. They thought that visual experience was necessary to cause visual cells to make connections with each other. Apparently, this wasn't the case. Instead, cells seem to start out connected, but any lack of visual experience makes these connections become ineffective.

So what does all this talk of cortical binocular cells, the visual system of cats, and cellular atrophy through disuse have to do with child psychology? Actually, Hubel and Wiesel's work has quite a lot to do with child psychology. You just have to be willing to put your critical-thinking microscope on a lower power to see the bigger picture. The most direct implication of their research is that it's helped us understand how the human visual system probably works. When a cat stalks a mouse, we know that the cat has to see and to recognize the thing as a mouse. To accomplish this, the cat first has to process visual information in its eyes; the eyes then send the information to a part of the brain called the thalamus, and the thalamus sends the information to the visual cortex. The human visual system also uses eyes, a thalamus, and a visual cortex.

Because the two systems resemble each other so closely, what we've learned from the visual systems of kittens may also apply to the visual systems of humans. Hubel and Wiesel's research additionally revealed that by the time visual information reaches the visual cortex, it comes in the form of a simple pattern. We know this because cells in the visual cortex respond most vigorously to lines and edges of a particular orientation. If visual information reaches the cortex in the form of a simple pattern in kittens, then it's much less of a mystery why we humans don't perceive the world as a jumble of 252 million disconnected points of light.

Of course, the next problem to address is that we don't see the world as a jumble of disconnected lines and edges either. But Hubel and Wiesel's discovery of edge-detecting cortical cells at least gives us a new way for thinking about the problem of why we don't. For one thing, the very existence of edge-detecting cortical cells raises the possibility that higher-level cells could be responsible for detecting higher-level visual patterns. A simple version of the logic goes like this. When a person looks at an edge or line, an image of the edge or line is projected onto the retinal lining along the back of the eyeball. In the lining of the eyeball are rods and cones. When the image is projected onto the retina, rods and cones that make direct contact with the image respond vigorously. The remaining rods and cones remain relatively quiet. The active rods and cones then send signals, through the thalamus, to the visual cortex. Now because we know that individual visual cortical cells respond to edges and lines, and because we know that information about edges and lines is carried to the cortical cells from the rods and cones, it's reasonable to say that individual cortical cells summarize the outputs of large groups of rods and cones. If cortical cells do this with inputs from several rods and cones, why can't higher-level cells perform a similar summarizing function with inputs from several cortical cells?

As it turns out, this may very well be what happens. Hubel and Wiesel called the cortical cells they studied "simple" cells. Simple cells respond to edges and lines, which, as we've seen, represent patterns of input from groups of rods and cones. Apparently, groups of simple cortical cells can also send information to higher-level "complex" cortical cells. Complex cells act to summarize information from groups of simple cortical cells. Imagine, for example, that a complex cell receives input from two simple cells. Imagine that one of these simple cells responds best to a vertical line and the other responds best to a horizontal line. In this case, if both a vertical line and a horizontal line are present in the visual field, say in the form of a right angle, the two simple cells will each respond vigorously. Accordingly, the complex cell they feed into will also respond vigorously. What this means is that the complex cell summarizes the input of two simple cells, and each simple cell summarizes the input of groups of rods and cones. When there is a right angle in the visual field causing the two simple cells to respond vigorously, and when the two simple cells are responding and causing the complex cell to respond vigorously, then we can ultimately say that the complex cell is responding to the visual presence of a right angle. We might just as well call this complex cell a "90° angle detector."

But this logic can be carried further. Groups of complex cells might themselves be connected to even higher-level cells, called "hypercomplex" cells, which summarize the response patterns of the complex cells. The vigorous responding of a hypercomplex cell would indicate the presence of an even higher-level pattern in the visual field. Instead of an angle, it might be a geometric shape. As the level of responding gets higher and higher up the chain, then the amount of visual summarizing and integration that goes on gets greater and greater. There might be hyper-hypercomplex cells, and hyper-hyper-hypercomplex cells. In the end, we may have very high-level cells which are responsible for our ability to detect very complicated visual pictures in the world around us. Some people have even speculated that way up the cortical ladder there may even be a "grandmother cell" that responds vigorously to the visual image of your grandmother!

Admittedly, the picture I've described here is a wee bit oversimplified. And the explosion of research ignited by Hubel and Wiesel's early work has since revealed a number of shortcomings of their early findings. But it was their early work that got the train rolling to begin with, and for this they are duly recognized.

A second, far more general impact of their work was their discovery of *neural plasticity*. The term *neural plasticity* reflects the idea that neural circuits can be altered through experience (*plastic* means flexible here). Neural plasticity has been a hot topic among brain researchers as well as among child psychologists because it directly addresses the nature-nurture issue (see the Anastasi chapter [Chapter 19] for a more in-depth discussion of the nature-nurture controversy). If you remember, Hubel and Wiesel found that the functioning of visual cortical cells can be radically altered if visual input from one eye is eliminated. But the amount of alteration depends on when the visual input is cut off. In cats, cutting off visual input from one eye during the first 20 days of life doesn't seem to have much of an effect on how responsive a cortical cell is to that eye. But if visual input is cut off for the first 2 to 4 months of life, then cortical cells stop responding to that eye altogether, even after vision is restored. The neural circuitry is so badly damaged that when cats are forced to use that eye to negotiate the edge of a table, they just fall off. Because the neural circuitry of the visual system can be altered through experience, it's clearly plastic.

This finding raises the possibility that neural circuitry throughout the rest of the brain might also be plastic. The brain might be operating according to some sort of "use-it-or-lose-it" philosophy. Connections and pathways in the brain that aren't used might just atrophy, whereas connections and pathways that are used frequently will flourish. Plasticity also raises the possibility that if some cortical cells aren't used for their intended purpose, they might be co-opted by other systems that could use them to greater benefit. Some very interesting research conducted by Helen Neville has suggested that the auditory cortex (the part of the brain involved in hearing) of adults born deaf may take on some visual functions. How can this be? She suggests that at birth there may be neural connections between the visual portions of the thalamus and the auditory cortex. Normally, these connections aren't maintained because the auditory system itself takes up residence in the auditory cortex. But in people born deaf, the cells in the auditory cortex don't receive auditory input, so, as in Hubel and Wiesel's cats, these connections atrophy. This leaves intact the preexisting connections between the visual system and the auditory cortex, and because visual input keeps coming in, connections with the auditory cortex continually strengthens. Over time, the visual system may develop quite a camaraderie with the auditory cortex.

The Joys of Good Luck

There's little doubt of the monumental significance of Hubel and Wiesel's work. But theirs is also a story of how important it is to have a good bit of luck on your side as you're struggling to make a name for yourself in a well-established scientific field. We've spent the last several pages talking about how Hubel and Wiesel made single-cell recordings of cortical responses to simple visual patterns like lines and edges. They made their career on these little recordings, and the Nobel Prize awards committee recognized them for it. But very few people outside the neuroscience research community realize how close Hubel and Wiesel came to missing out completely on their revolutionary path of discovery.

As David Hubel told the story in his Nobel Prize acceptance speech, when he and Torsten Wiesel first began trying to make recordings of individual cortical cells they met with little success. For one thing, when you insert an electrode into the surface of a brain, you can't see where it is. And when you can't see what you're doing, well, it might require a lot of trial and error before you can get it right. But they were certain there was nothing wrong with their technique, because it had been developed and used quite successfully by a guy named Vernon Mountcastle to explore somatosensory cortexes in cats and monkeys. Still, for some reason, they initially found nothing that would cause visual cortical cells to respond. Since they knew their recording technique was okay, they next figured that the problem must've had something to do with how they were projecting the visual images to the kittens. As it turned out, they had to project the images onto the ceiling of the lab! Hubel wrote, "Having no other [cat] head holder, we continued for a while to use the ophthalmoscope's head holder, which posed a problem since the cat was facing directly up. To solve this we brought in some bed sheets which we slung between the pipes and cobwebs that graced the ceiling of the Wilmer [Institute's] basement, giving the setup an aura of a circus tent. One day Vernon Mountcastle walked in on this scene, and was horror-struck at the spectacle. The method was certainly inconvenient since we had to stare at the ceiling for the entire experiment." Fortunately, they eventually got their projection system worked out. They ended up projecting simple visual patterns directly onto the retinas of cats using a special contraption that allowed them to insert either a small brass plate with a hole in it, or a small glass slide with a black mark on it. The contraption would pass light through the hole in the brass plate to project a single spot of light on the cats' retinas, or it would pass light through the glass slide in order to project a shadow of the black mark onto the cats' retinas.

Although they began showering their cats' retinas with spots of light and shadows, their initial recordings were still failures. Their initial reaction was that cortical cells just didn't respond to visual images as expected. But after several hours, while recording from cell number 3004, they made their momentous discovery. (Well, they hadn't actually recorded from 3003 other cells. They decided to start numbering their cells at 3000 to impress Mountcastle, whose cell recordings numbered into the thousands.) At cell 3004, they got a decidedly vigorous response. What was most fascinating about this discovery was that the cell wasn't responding to a spot of light or a shadow, the anticipated targets; the cell was responding instead to the edge of the glass slide as it was inserted into the projection machine! Hubel and Wiesel spent the next 9 hours fiddling with the slide to reproduce the vigorous response. At the end of the day, they concluded that the cell responded most strongly to an edge with an orientation that matched the angle of the slide as it was inserted into the projection machine. When the orientation was right, "the cell went off like a machine gun."

You can probably imagine how easy it would've been for Hubel and Wiesel to completely miss this discovery. For one thing, they apparently left the projection machine turned on as they inserted one slide after another. If they had been in the habit of turning the machine off between each projection, then the shadow of the edge of the slide would never have been cast onto the retina of the cat, and cell 3004 would never have responded. It was also a stroke of luck that they were recording from a cell whose preferred orientation matched precisely the angle of the edge of the slide. If they were recording from a cell that preferred vertical edges, they would have failed to trigger the response altogether. But in the end, they did leave the machine on, and cell 3004 was orientationally matched; and about 20 years later, the Nobel Prize awards committee called out their names.

Bibliography

Barlow, H. B. (1982). David Hubel and Torsten Wiesel: Their contributions towards understanding the primary visual cortex. *Trends in Neuroscience, 5,* 145–152.

Hubel, D. H. (1982). Evolution of ideas in the primary visual cortex, a biased historical account. *Bioscience Reports, 2,* 435–439.

Neville, H. J. (1990). Intermodal competition and compensation in development: Evidence from studies of the visual system in congenitally deaf adults. *Annals of the New York Academy of Sciences, 608,* 71–87.

Neville, H. J., & Lawson, D. (1987). Attention to central and peripheral visual space in a movement detection task: An event-related potential and behavioral study. II. Congenitally deaf adults. *Brain Research, 45,* 268–283.

Wiesel, T. N., & Hubel, D. H. (1963). Single-cell responses in striate cortex of kittens deprived of vision in one eye. *Journal of Neurophysiology, 26,* 1003–1017.

Questions for Discussion

1. Remind me. Why is it that a study on the visual cortex of kittens is in a book on the 20 studies that revolutionized child psychology?

2. Although scientists can't ethically cut into live human brains just to play around and do research, do you think it would be okay if the brains were grown under artificial conditions in the lab?

3. Is it justifiable to do research on the brains of other animals, when the goal is just to learn about brain functioning? Is it more okay to do research on the brains of some species than others?

4. Should Hubel and Wiesel be given credit for the discovery of visual cortical cell functioning when their discovery came more or less by accident?

22

Governments, Grade Schools, and Grocery Stores:

Multiple Levels of Influence

TOWARD AN EXPERIMENTAL ECOLOGY OF HUMAN DEVELOPMENT.
Bronfenbrenner, U. (1977). *American Psychologist, 32, 513–531.*   (RANK 7)

Ever since the birth of psychology way back in the late 1800s, the field has faced a century-long struggle to be recognized as a "real" science by its more glorified sister disciplines in the "natural" sciences. Disciplines such as physics and chemistry commonly scoff at the existence of psychology and its claim to "real science" status. Even the kid sister of the natural sciences, biology, who herself has only recently been admitted to the natural science club, has taken some potshots at psychology. The criticisms of psychology are always the same: "It's way too vague," "Humans can't objectively study themselves," "Psychologists just make up stuff as they go along," "Psychology's just a collection of commonsense facts that everybody already knows," and last but not least, "Psychology is just too inaccurate to be called a science."

On the face of it, our critics have a couple of good points. Psychology sometimes really is way too vague. And it really is true that humans can't objectively study themselves. But for that matter, neither can humans study anything else objectively, including physics and chemistry, because humans by their very nature are limited by their perceptual and cognitive belief systems. But the next two criticisms are simply wrong. Psychologists, at least good ones, really don't make stuff up as they go along. And psychology really isn't just a collection of commonsense facts that everybody knows. In fact, a lot of psychological research has proven many, if not most, "commonsense" beliefs to be completely false.

But one of the long-term sore spots of psychology has been the criticism that psychology doesn't do a very good job of making accurate predictions about human behavior. This is undeniably true, at least when it comes to predicting the specific behavior of individuals. But psychologists are actually quite good at making predictions about large groups of people. For example, I always accurately predict that 40% of my introductory psychology students will earn a D or an F on their first exam, give or take a few percentage points. But this is because 40% of my introductory psychology students *always* get a D or an F on their first exam. The accuracy of my group prediction is based on my past group data. However, I would be extremely hard pressed to predict *which* of my students will to get a D or an F. And there's the rub. Psychologists are notoriously poor at predicting the behaviors of single individuals. Psychologists are often summoned to testify at parole board hearings to say whether an arsonist is going to light more fires, or whether a pedophile is going to molest more children. The most these psychologists can do is base their judgments on available data and say something like, "Based on the existing scientific literature, it is my judgment that there is a 28.7% chance that this individual will avoid committing arson should he be released from further incarceration." This does give a fairly strong impression of scientific inaccuracy, doesn't it?

Now compare this level of precision with what we usually learn about in natural science classes. In physics, for example, we learn about laws of gravity, laws of motion, laws of thermodynamics, laws of quantum mechanics, and so on. Using these laws, we learn to estimate with perfect precision what the outcome of some contrived event will be. On one physics exam, for example, I remember calculating how fast a ping-pong ball would have to go in order to stop a moving locomotive in its tracks. The lesson I learned was that an object with very small mass has to go really, really fast to counteract the momentum of an object with a much larger mass, but moving much more slowly. It's all about plugging values for velocity and mass into certain equations, while making certain assumptions about the event. As it turns out, for a 2.5-gram ping-pong ball to completely stop a 220,000-pound locomotive moving at 45 miles per hour, it would have to be traveling at the rate of 1.8 billion miles per hour, roughly three times the speed of light!

Now clearly, wouldn't you say physics has the flavor of a precise science? Well, the devil is in the details (and the assumptions). With the ping-pong ball event, for example, we assume that the ping-pong ball hits the locomotive head-on, and not at an angle. We also assume that the collision takes place in the absence of changing atmospheric conditions; that is, we assume no wind, no rain, and a constant temperature. We also assume there are no bumps on the train tracks, and that the train is traveling on a level surface. These assumptions are what permit us to make highly precise predictions about physical behavior. Without these assumptions, the level of precision a physicist can muster is much closer to the level of precision a psychologist has to deal with.

My standing challenge to anyone who thinks physics is more precise than psychology is to predict with complete accuracy the outcome state of a watermelon being pushed off the roof of a five-story building. (I got this idea from watching the old David Letterman show back in the 1980s.) Now, it's not good enough just to say a watermelon will splatter when it smacks into the ground. I'm talking about a much more precise level of description, the kind most people think of when they think of physics. Where will each of the seeds end up? Where will the rind crack, and in how many pieces will it end up? What size will each of the pieces be? Where will the pieces end up? How will the flesh of the melon be distributed? Obviously, these questions can't be answered with a high degree of precision. There are simply too many variables to take into account. So much would depend on the varying wind speeds at each elevation as the watermelon descends. And the influence of the wind would depend on the orientation of the melon in space. And the rotation of the melon in space would depend on its wobble as it left the surface of the roof. Then there's the structural integrity of the watermelon rind. How it breaks apart would depend on the thickness of the portion of the rind that makes first contact with the ground. And the influence of the ground would depend on which part of the ground made first contact with the melon. Are there any cracks in the concrete? Are there any small pebbles or sticks lying around? You're probably getting the picture by now.

My point in bringing up the case of the falling watermelon is to show that in these kinds of situations, the physicist, like the psychologist, is reduced to making only the most general of predictions. She could predict, for example, that the flesh of the melon will spread out in a fanlike pattern, proportional to the angle and speed of the melon at impact. But I'm not inclined to call this a highly precise prediction. Yet these are the kinds of situations child psychologists have to contend with every day when predicting children's behavior. Children are subject to so many constantly changing internal and external influences that psychologists simply can't describe with any great degree of accuracy the outcomes of their development.

This is where the revolutionary work of Urie Bronfenbrenner comes in. In his 1977 article, ranked seventh most revolutionary overall, Bronfenbrenner proposed an "ecological theory of human development." He developed his theory to encourage psychologists to take into account as many factors as possible in explaining human development. Of course, the social-emotional-cultural factors that influence human development are no doubt very different from the physical factors that influence falling watermelons, but the level of complexity involved in the two kinds of predictions are probably comparable. If anything, children's development is harder to predict since they don't have the emotional stability of a watermelon!

Bronfenbrenner created his ecological theory because he thought too many child psychologists were spending too much time exploring developmental issues that were too narrow for most children under most conditions in most cultures. In a typical case, a child psychologist brings a toddler to the laboratory, gives him a variety of puzzles and tests, and exposes him to a variety of unusual situations. Although the child psychologist might *think* she is measuring the toddler's intellectual ability, in reality she's measuring a great deal more. For one thing, she's measuring her own influence on the toddler. Not only is the toddler responding to questions on a test, but also to the tone and manner of the child psychologist! The strangeness of the laboratory also influences the kid. When children are in a strange place, their responses are bound to be different than in a familiar place. Bronfenbrenner's gripe is that these extra influences are usually ignored or assumed to be trivially important in most child psychology research.

   In his ecological theory, Bronfenbrenner described four levels, or *contexts*, of environmental influence that child psychologists should take into account if they really want to advance the science of child psychology. By taking all four of these contexts into account, Bronfenbrenner believed that child psychologists not only would do better, more accurate science, but also would be more likely to conduct research that really mattered.

INTRODUCTION

Bronfenbrenner introduced us to the limitations of modern child psychology by pointing out that a lot of child psychology research consisted of elegantly designed, tightly controlled studies that bore little resemblance to what happened in the real world. Humorously, he summed up traditional child psychology as "the science of the strange behavior of children in strange situations with strange adults for the briefest possible periods of time." On the other hand, child psychologists who do try to make their research relevant to the real world, and who conduct their scientific studies outside of the laboratory, have a hard time making their studies rigorous and tightly controlled. In other words, child psychology researchers either focus on rigor at the expense of relevance, or focus on relevance at the expense of rigor.

   But Bronfenbrenner rejected the idea that these are the only two options. He believed that naturalistic observations of children's development in the real world could be well controlled, and that observations in the lab could have real-world applications. The trick was to realize that the laboratory environment and the natural environment are both part of children's natural surroundings, and that both can be expected to influence children's behavior. Similarly, the researcher who tested the child and the mother who cared for the child are both people in the child's natural surroundings who can be expected to influence children's behavior. Bronfenbrenner's call to arms for an ecological approach to child psychology was a call to embrace *all* the contexts, both physical and social, in which children find themselves.

   So what exactly is an ecological approach to psychology anyway? Well, let's start with the term *ecology*. In its standard use, **ecology** refers to a branch of biology that studies the relationship between organisms and their surroundings. Ecology addresses such issues as how an organism uses its surroundings to its advantage, and how changes in an organism's surroundings can influence the functioning of the organism. From an ecological perspective, organisms can't be truly understood unless you simultaneously take into account their surroundings. Consider the woodland beaver. You could bring the beaver into a laboratory setting, you could feed it some worms and some leaves, you could give it a doggy chew toy, and you could try to teach it to ride a bicycle. But by removing the beaver from its natural habitat, you would completely miss out on some of its most unique and interesting naturally occurring behaviors. For example, you would never see how beavers fell trees using their teeth, you would never see their crafty ingenuity in building their homes out of wood and mud, and you would never see how they build dams across waterways to preserve their water supply. An ecological approach would demand that you study the beaver in its natural surroundings.

By applying an ecological approach to child psychology, Bronfenbrenner was urging us to avoid thinking of the child as an isolated organism, and to begin trying to understand the child in the context of its own natural surroundings. By taking children's surroundings into account, child psychologists won't miss out on some of children's most unique and interesting naturally occurring behaviors.

In formal terms, Bronfenbrenner defined his **ecological psychology** as "the scientific study of the progressive, mutual accommodation, throughout the life span, between a growing human organism and the changing immediate environments in which it lives, as this process is affected by relations obtaining within and between these immediate settings, as well as the larger social contexts, both formal and informal, in which the settings are embedded." As usual for professional psychologists, this is a rather opaque definition. He was basically saying not only that children should be studied in their natural surroundings, but also that their natural surroundings exist at several different levels. I'll describe each of these levels in more detail shortly, but for now we can note that the levels of surroundings differ in how directly they influence children. The most direct impact comes from children's immediate environments, composed of the things and people children make direct contact with, including their homes and families as well as their schoolrooms, classmates, and teachers. Then there are broader surroundings, which children don't make direct contact with, but which have an influence on the immediate surroundings. These broader surroundings include such environments as the neighborhood, the public school system, and the place where their parents work. Children may not make direct contact with these broader surroundings, but these broader surroundings can still have an impact on the children. For example, if the public school system has a policy that teachers can't accept gifts from students, then this policy has a direct impact on the child when she tries to give an apple to her teacher. And if one of the child's parents gets a promotion at work, then that parent comes home in a happy mood, which in turn has a positive impact on how that parent plays with her child at the end of the day.

But there are even broader surroundings than these, although the term "surroundings" doesn't fit as well here. Perhaps the better word is "context." Consider the context of the American attitude toward public education, for example. The United States government enforces a federal requirement that all children in all communities receive a formal, publicly funded education. Within this context, it is a policy that all local communities must provide a formal education for their children. As a result, local public school systems are formed, teachers are hired, and kids sit in classrooms and learn. Although the mandatory education policy of the United States doesn't have an immediate impact on a particular child, the policy still has an influence on the child as the policy works its influence all the way down the chain of governmental control. The federal public education policy drives the state public education policy, the state public education policy drives the local public education policy, the local public education policy drives how children in the community will be educated, and this affects how teachers teach their students.

Because children's surroundings, or contexts, can influence them at so many different levels, Bronfenbrenner helped clarify the role of each by dividing them neatly into four different categories. Listed in order of their directness of impact (from most to least), he called them (1) *the microsystem*, (2) *the mesosystem*, (3) *the exosystem*, and (4) *the macrosystem*. We'll consider each of these in turn.

THE MICROSYSTEM

In Bronfenbrenner's technical talk, the **microsystem** "is the complex of relations between the developing person and environment in an immediate setting containing that person." The setting can be the home, the school, the playground, or the candy store, just to name a few. In each setting, the child plays a specific role, such as the daughter, the student, the playmate, or the customer. In addition, there are certain objects within each setting that the child comes into contact with, and certain people the child interacts with. To understand the impact of the microsystem on the child is to understand how each of these settings directly impinges on the development of the child. As a child carries out his routine activities during the course of the day, he might, for example, find himself eating breakfast with his little sister, walking to school with his best friend, sitting in a classroom learning about math, practicing with the basketball team after school, eating dinner with his family, sitting at his desk in his bedroom doing his homework, taking a bath, eating a bedtime snack while watching *Monday Night Football*, and reading a book before going to sleep. Each of these activities represents a set of experiences common to the settings of the home, the school, and the peer group, and each activity has the potential to influence the child's development. All of these settings together comprise the microsystem. Bronfenbrenner outlined four "propositions" about the microsystem that an ecological psychology should embrace.

Proposition 1

> In contrast to the traditional unidirectional research model typically employed in the laboratory, an ecological experiment must allow for reciprocal processes; that is, not only the effect of A on B, but also the effect of B on A. This is the requirement of *reciprocity*.

In other words, child psychology researchers must realize not only that the environment can have an effect on the child, but that the child can have just as strong an effect on the environment. Consider the case of the child eating breakfast with his little sister. When the child arrives at the breakfast table to find that his little sister has eaten the last bowl of Cap'n Crunch cereal, he may lash out at her and call her a "loser." Obviously, this environment has had an effect on the boy. But the very act of calling his little sister a loser also affects the environment, specifically, the role played by the sister as part of that environment. The next morning the child may arrive at the breakfast table to find a much more hostile setting. When he sits down at the breakfast table, his little sister may begin the conversation by calling him a "snotface." No doubt this puts a rather antagonistic spin on things. The two might end up in a war of words, and the boy might then go off to school in a foul mood. Of course, the boy's foul mood was indirectly caused by his own name-calling behavior the day before. The point is that when child psychologists do their research, they would be foolish to believe that the direction of influence goes only from the environment to the child. By ignoring the possible child-to-environment direction of influence, they're missing out on half the story.

Proposition 2

> An ecological experiment requires recognition of the social system actually operative in the research setting. This system will typically involve all of the participants present, *not excluding* the experimenter. This is the requirement of recognizing the **totality of the functional social system** in the setting.

When children are invited to participate in research being conducted by a child psychologist, they are entering into a social system that includes themselves, the experimenter, and any of the experimenter's assistants. And just as the little boy caused his own foul mood by calling his sister a "loser," a child can influence his own performance in a child psychology experiment by virtue of how well he gets along with the experimenter. In my own research, I've seen many 21-month-old babies frustrate the bejeebies out of my laboratory assistants. In one of my experiments, for example, babies are asked to locate a ball. But instead of simply pointing to the ball, or handing it over to the lab assistant, some babies will toss the ball across the room (and because it's a rubber ball, it bounces with reckless abandon). Of course, the lab assistant has to get up and go after the ball. After she locates and returns the thing, many babies throw it again. Although I train my assistants to be very respectful and tolerant of these kinds of behaviors, I can't help noticing the look of exasperation on their faces that says they're going to end the session early. In this example, babies who are ball throwers produce lab assistants who move briskly through experimental sessions. And, of course, if lab assistants do move more briskly through experimental sessions, then babies have fewer opportunities to reveal their intellectual abilities. In other words, babies in the lab can indirectly influence how they score on an IQ test, because their behaviors have personal, direct impacts on the experimenters giving the tests.

Proposition 3

> In contrast to the conventional dyadic research model, which is limited to assessing the *direct* effect of two agents on each other, the design of an ecological experiment must take into account the existence in the setting of systems that include more than two persons. . . . Such larger systems must be analyzed in terms of all possible subsystems.

What this means is that when more than two people are involved with each other in a setting, things get complicated real fast. Suppose you've recruited a young girl named Jenny to participate in a research study. Coming from an intact family, not only does Jenny have a relationship with Mom and a relationship with Dad, but Mom and Dad have a relationship with each other. Each of these two-person relationships is called a "dyad," and each dyad is a subsystem of a larger three-person system called a "triad." Bronfenbrenner warns us that we can't understand the Jenny-Mom relationship, for example, without also understanding the other two relationships. If Jenny and Mom come into the laboratory, and we find during a free-play session that Mom seems overly strict and controlling of Jenny's behavior, our initial judgment might be that Mom is overly strict and controlling. But by jumping to this conclusion, we're ignoring the possibility that Mom's behavior during the lab session might have been influenced by Mom's relationship with Dad. For example, maybe Dad was the one who was supposed to bring Jenny to the lab, and maybe he decided at the last minute to back out of his obligation. In this case, Mom picked up the slack, which she may not have been too happy about, and she might have expressed her frustration in her free-play behavior with Jenny. Our initial belief that Mom was unusually strict and controlling is undermined by the fact that her behavior during this particular free-play session is probably not an accurate reflection of her usual, happy-go-lucky self.

Proposition 4

Ecological experiments must take into account aspects of the physical environment as possible indirect influences on social processes taking place within the setting.

Lastly, Bronfenbrenner pointed out that people aren't the only things that exist in children's natural surroundings. There are physical objects too. And these physical objects can have powerful influences on any social activities taking place in a setting. Bronfenbrenner described one study, for example, which suggested that nearly 80% of households reduce their level of conversation when a television program is on. No doubt, the emergence of television viewing in the household during the last half-century has radically curtailed children's opportunities for talking with their parents, as well as parents' opportunities for talking with their children. So before child psychology researchers jump to the conclusion that parents lack interest in communicating with their kids, they would do well to consider something as trivial as how frequently the television is left on or even how many TVs a household owns.

MESOSYSTEM

The best way to think about the next level of surroundings, that is, the **mesosystem** kind, is to think of them as a collection of microsystems that all influence each other. Bronfenbrenner said that a "mesosystem comprises the interrelations among major settings containing the developing person at a particular point in his or her life. Thus, for an American 12-year-old, the mesosystem typically encompasses interactions among family, school, and peer group; for some children, it might also include church, camp, or workplace." The idea here is that influences that take place in one setting can spill over to influence what happens in other settings. When the influences of individual settings spill over into other settings, you have a mesosystem. Bronfenbrenner crafted three propositions that child psychology researchers should think about when studying the mesosystem.

Proposition 5

In the traditional research model, behavior and development are investigated one setting at a time without regard to possible interdependencies between settings. An ecological approach invites consideration of the joint impact of two or more settings on their elements. This is the requirement, wherever possible, of analyzing *interactions between settings*.

For example, a child might stop by the candy store on the way to school to buy a box of LemonHeads. Already you can see the immediate influence of the candy store microsystem on the child because it provided him with a supply of sour, lemon-flavored candies. When the child gets to school, he might start eating the Lemon-Heads during a math test, causing his teacher to scold him for breaking school rules. In this case, as you might already have noticed, there is a *bidirectional* influence between the child and teacher within the classroom microsystem. The child's candy eating influences the teacher, and the teacher's scolding influences the child. But notice that there is also an indirect influence of the candy store microsystem on the classroom microsystem. The scolding arises out of the *joint* contributions of two microsystems that are brought into relation with one another by the child's actions. Without the schoolteacher the scolding wouldn't have happened, and without the candy the scolding wouldn't have happened. It's only through the joint combination of schoolteacher + candy, coupled with the child's willingness to eat the candy during the test, that the scolding happened.

Now the child might go home at the end of the day and tell his mom that he got into trouble for eating candy during the math test. At this point, the mother might ground the boy, both for his willingness to waste his money on candy and for his willingness to break school rules. This represents another joint contribution of microsystems. If the child hadn't bought candy at the store, and if he hadn't broken school rules, and if he hadn't gotten scolded by the teacher, and if hadn't told his mom anything, he wouldn't have been grounded. In the end, having a good understanding of why the child was grounded requires a good understanding of how all the microsystems interacted with each other to produce the grounding. This is what Bronfenbrenner meant by understanding at the mesosystem level. Child psychology researchers who consider the behavior of children at only one point in time are destined to miss out on the much richer sources of influence that are affecting the children's behavior.

Proposition 6

> The design of an ecological experiment involving the same person in more than one setting should take into account the possible subsystems that exist, or could exist, across settings.

When a child has different roles in different settings, such as candy buyer, student, and son, not only can the settings have different separate and joint influences on the child, but people from the different settings can also form systems of relationships with one another. For example, when the mother of our candy eater goes in for the semiannual parent-teacher conference, she meets, greets, and establishes a relationship with the teacher. She may send notes to the teacher on occasion, and the teacher may send notes back to the mother. The mother-teacher relationship that forms is an example of a subsystem that exists across settings. If the child ever decides to eat candy in the classroom again, then the teacher's scolding of the child may in part depend on her relationship with the child's mother. If the teacher thinks fondly of the mother, she may soften the scolding. But if she thinks the mother's a nasty old witch, she may not scold the child at all, under the belief that the child has a hard enough time at home. Instead, she may just quietly remove the candy from the child, without causing him unnecessary embarrassment. The point, of course, is that children are not only a product of their own beliefs, desires, and abilities, but also a product of how their own beliefs, desires, and abilities interact with their surroundings. And the surroundings themselves both influence the child and are influenced by each other.

Proposition 7

A fruitful context for developmental research is provided by the **ecological transitions** that periodically occur in a person's life. These transitions include changes in role and setting as a function of the person's maturation or of events in the life cycle of others responsible for his or her care and development. Such shifts are to be conceived and analyzed as changes in ecological systems rather than solely within individuals.

The idea behind this proposition is that child psychologists should realize not only that individual children change and develop, but that their ecological surroundings change and develop as well. We tend to think of the home setting, for example, as just one setting. But the home setting can change quite a bit if the child and his family move to a new home. He might have a basketball court at his new home, providing him with an opportunity to improve his athletic skills. And the new home may have a much larger yard for him to mow, resulting in his allowance being bumped up to match.

EXOSYSTEM

In the two types of surroundings we've just talked about—the microsystem and the mesosystem—the child was a direct participant in the goings-on. It's easy to think of them as surroundings because the child is directly involved. But there are broader, more remote kinds of surroundings that affect children even when they don't actually make physical contact with them. The first of these is what Bronfenbrenner called the **exosystem**. He defined it as "an extension of the mesosystem embracing other specific social structures, both formal and informal, that do not themselves contain the developing person but impinge upon or encompass the immediate settings in which that person is found, and thereby influence, delimit, or even determine what goes on there." Typical exosystems you're probably familiar with include the work world, the media, the local government, commerce and industry, and the social community. Bronfenbrenner's one proposition about the exosystem only implores child psychologists to take the exosystem into account, without giving any specific dictates about how to do so.

Proposition 8

Research on the ecology of human development requires investigations that go beyond the immediate setting containing the person to examine the larger contexts, both formal and informal, that affect events within the immediate setting.

In my northwestern Ohio community, for example, the local public school system has decided to set aside some of its funds to support special programming aimed at meeting the needs of the community's "gifted" children. Gifted children are kids who score exceedingly high on standard tests of intelligence or achievement. To satisfy the needs of these children, our local school system created a one-day-a-week "pull-out" program. On Thursdays, all the gifted elementary-school kids in the community are pulled out of their regular school classrooms and bused to a special classroom located at one of the elementary schools. There, a teacher certified to work with gifted children runs a gifted classroom with curricular goals specifically matched to the advanced intellectual needs of these children. This is a perfect example of the influence of the exosystem on children's development. The "larger context" here is the decision of the school system to offer extra services to gifted children. Although the kids don't actually make direct contact with the policy, they do make direct contact with a gifted classroom and teacher that were created as a result of the policy.

Let's consider how the exosystem might influence the results of a child psychology research study. Suppose a child psychologist is interested in doing research on the graduation rates of gifted students. Suppose she travels to a dozen counties in her area and collects graduation data from school systems in those counties. After analyzing her data, suppose she concludes that in general, across a number of different school systems, gifted children are no more likely to graduate than other children. Could her conclusions be wrong? Yes! The accuracy of this finding is in jeopardy without considering exosystem influences. The chances that a gifted child will graduate from high school might depend in no small way on the policies of the community school systems toward providing services for gifted children. Gifted children who attend school systems that don't provide a gifted curriculum might get bored with their regular curriculum. As a result, they might actually be more inclined to drop out than other children. But gifted children coming from school systems that *do* meet their needs might be less inclined to drop out compared with other children. The child psychologist has no way of recognizing any differences between these two groups without considering exosystem influences that affect whether or not school systems provide services for gifted children.

MACROSYSTEM

The largest, most global, most omnipresent, and most remote influences on children's development come from the **macrosystem**. Bronfenbrenner defined the macrosystem as "the overarching institutional patterns of the culture or subculture, such as the economic, social, educational, legal, and political systems, of which micro-, meso-, and exosystems are the concrete manifestations. Macrosystems are conceived and examined not only in structural terms but as carriers of information and ideology that, both explicitly and implicitly, endow meaning and motivation to particular agencies, social networks, roles, activities, and their interrelations."

Yet another hefty, obscure psychological definition. The point is only that in any society there are some cultural and subcultural values that are so central to the fabric of that society that members of that society may not even realize other values are possible. In the United States, for example, the value of education is taken as a given. These days, even a college education is expected of most people. As children develop in American culture, they're developing within the context of this cultural expectation. This is not to say that most Americans seek out college educations, but those Americans who don't often feel that they should. Education is a core fiber of the "American way."

Of course, not all cultures place such a high value on education. In some Middle Eastern countries, for example, it's forbidden for women to seek out a college education. And in other countries, especially poor ones, it may be unusual for children to get an education at all. Bronfenbrenner warns us that in child psychology research, we have to be aware not only that child development takes place within the context of major cultural values, but also that as scientists we ourselves espouse certain cultural values, and we need to be sensitive to the effects these values have on how we do science. These realizations provide the fodder for Bronfenbrenner's last proposition.

Proposition 9

Research on the ecology of human development should include experiments involving the innovative restructuring of prevailing ecological systems in ways that depart from existing institutional ideologies and structures by redefining goals, roles, and activities and providing interconnections between systems previously isolated from each other.

Precisely because the macrosystem is so all-pervasive, it's very difficult to see how research could do much to learn about the influence of the macrosystem on children's development. You could do cross-cultural research to compare children from one culture to children from another. But since cultures are different, and since macrosystem influences affect the micro-, meso-, and exosystems so totally, you couldn't be sure if children from different cultures are different because of the macrosystem or because of the subsidiary systems. Bronfenbrenner instead recommends conducting **transforming experiments**. Transforming experiments take children from within a single culture and expose them to radical departures from the existing ideologies of their culture. Of course, the next question is, How do you do this?

The best example of a transforming macrosystem experiment, according to Bronfenbrenner, is the famous "Robbers Cave experiment," conducted by Muzafer Sherif in the 1950s. The setting for that study was the Robbers Cave campground. Twenty-four lower-middle-class boys, roughly 12 years old, were brought to the campground and were at first allowed to engage in a number of community and friendship-building exercises. Just as the boys were getting to know each other, they were separated into two smaller groups. Boys in each of the two smaller groups lived, worked, and played together, and many new friendships blossomed. The sense of group cohesion that developed was very strong. A number of competitions were set up between the two groups, and as a result of the competitions, within-group loyalty increased, as did between-group antagonism. The between-group rivalry was so pronounced that boys in each group developed a rather severe dislike for children in the other group (many of whom had recently been their friends).

You can think of this within-group connectedness and the between-group mistrust that went along with it as a rather pervasive aspect of American culture, one of its macrosystems—not one that we're particularly proud of, but one that exists nonetheless. People frequently define themselves in terms of the positive qualities of their own group, and distance themselves from what they perceive as the negative qualities of other groups. Our discomfort with unfamiliar groups can rise to the level of loathing and bigotry. Anyway, after Sherif established this American cultural ideology in the two groups of boys, he then tried to change it. The method he chose proved highly successful. He set up a number of "emergency" problems that required the cooperation of both groups to overcome. For example, the water supply was cut off and boys from both groups were recruited to work together to help find the source of a presumed water leak. The "transforming" result was that in the end, boys from both groups put aside their differences and worked cooperatively toward the common good. Harmony emerged where distrust had been. Nothing works so well to bring two enemies together than the sudden emergence of a third, more threatening, common enemy.

CONCLUSIONS

Since the early days, Bronfenbrenner's ecological approach has undergone continual refinement and improvement. Although some of the names have changed, most of the central ideas and issues have remained intact. Bronfenbrenner now calls his theoretical approach a "Bioecological Paradigm," and child psychology research that incorporates the bioecological perspective is described as adhering to a "process-person-context-time" (PPCT) model. As in the old formulation, the new model focuses on psychological development in children, the impact of the immediate setting, and the pervasive influences of more remote social and cultural ideologies. But the revised model gives more explicit attention to the role of *time* in children's development (called the *chronosystem*). A comprehensive description of the current state of Bronfenbrenner's ecological theory can be found in an article he published in 1994 in the journal *Psychological Bulletin* with coauthor Stephen Ceci.

Urie Bronfenbrenner's goals in bringing forward his ecological psychology were to get child psychologists to think more clearly about the multifaceted influences of children's surroundings on their psychological development, to consider how children simultaneously influence their own surroundings, and to prompt child psychologists to conduct studies designed to reveal how these influences operate. Although child psychologists had for a long time recognized the importance of the environment in children's development, "environment" had usually been a poorly defined, loosely conceptualized collection of everything that existed outside the child's head. Bronfenbrenner's ecological theory was revolutionary because it broke down the "environment" and identified a number of levels of generality of environmental influence, all operating simultaneously and interactively to influence children's lives. Bronfenbrenner also gave us a common vocabulary to use in referring to each of the levels of environmental operation.

Despite its logical appeal and comprehensiveness, Bronfenbrenner's ecological theory isn't particularly easy to use. It's hard enough to run a single experiment in a single laboratory setting, let alone extend the research to a multitude of other microsystem settings, while simultaneously taking into account the relationships of the people in each of those settings with other people in those and other settings. Perhaps for this reason, the vast majority of child psychology researchers still haven't adopted Bronfenbrenner's approach, at least not in its full-blown version. Still, Bronfenbrenner's admonitions resonate strongly with the spirit of most child psychology researchers, who usually recognize the importance of considering multiple contexts in understanding the psychological development of the child. You can typically find these declarations in the sections of their published research articles where they talk about directions for future research. Although most researchers don't explicitly acknowledge Bronfenbrenner's theory, I imagine that Bronfenbrenner is at least pleased to see so much of the contemporary child psychology community recognizing the need for considering the ecology of the child. There's no telling what the state of child psychology would look like today were it not for Bronfenbrenner's revolutionary reconceptualization of the nature of children's environments.

Bibliography

Bronfenbrenner, U., & Ceci, S. J. (1994). Nature-nurture reconceptualized in developmental perspective: A bioecological model. *Psychological Review, 101,* 568–586.

Moen, P., Elder, G. H., Jr., & Lüscher, K. (1995). *Examining lives in context: Perspectives on the ecology of human development.* Washington, DC: American Psychological Association.

Sherif, M., Harvey, O. J., White, B. J., Hood, W. R, & Sherif, C. N. (1961). *Intergroup conflict and cooperation: The Robbers Cave experiment.* Norman, OK: University of Oklahoma Book Exchange.

Questions for Discussion

1. Can you identify factors from each of Bronfenbrenner's four contexts that are influencing your behavior at this moment? Can you identify factors from each of Bronfenbrenner's four contexts that are influencing your best friend's behavior at this moment?

2. One of Bronfenbrenner's claims is that it's impossible for the experimenter to remove herself from the experimental situation, since her very existence impacts on children's responses to her? Is it possible for the physicist to remove herself from the experimental situation? Does the physicist's existence impact on the physical environment she is investigating? Does the physicist's humanness impact on her interpretation of the results she obtains from her physical experiments?

3. To the best of your knowledge, how are macrosystem influences similar and different for the citizens of Israel versus those of Palestinians living in territories occupied by the Israel? What macrosystem influences might explain why these two groups hate each other so much?

GLOSSARY

Accommodation: (from Piaget's theory) the process that explains how existing schemas adjust themselves to allow for new information.

Achievement oriented: striving to be successful or to achieve an important goal.

Activity level: one of Thomas, Chess, and Birch's temperament dimensions, characterizing the speed and frequency of a child's movement.

Adaptability: one of Thomas, Chess, and Birch's temperament dimensions, reflecting that children can be soothed when distressed.

Additive relationship: in Anastasi's view, the naïve expectation that environmental effects and genetic influences can simply be added together to understand child development.

Agent: in a sentence, the person, animal, or other animate entity who does something or causes something to happen.

Aggression: acting with intent to harm another person physically or emotionally.

Approach/withdrawal: one of Thomas, Chess, and Birch's temperament dimensions, focusing on the extent that children are comfortable with new things and people.

Assimilation: (from Piaget's theory) the process of fitting new information into existing schemas.

Attachment system: a system, selected by thousands of years of evolution, that ensures mothers and babies are attracted to one another, thereby increasing the likelihood of babies' surviving to maturity.

Attention span/persistence: one of Thomas, Chess, and Birch's temperament dimensions, focusing on the length of time children are willing to stay engaged with a task.

Authoritarian parenting: one of Baumrind's major parenting styles, characterized by an emphasis on strict obedience and high expectations.

Authoritarianism: a tendency to exert power strictly and inflexibly.

Authoritative parenting: one of Baumrind's major parenting styles, characterized by an emphasis on the personal growth of the child and flexible dealings with the child, but while maintaining high expectations.

Behavioral psychologist (or behaviorist): a psychologist who believes that all behaviors are learned through experience through some form of classical or instrumental conditioning.

Beneficiary: in a sentence, the person, animal, or other animate entity who receives something as a result of the action expressed by the verb.

Bidirectionality of influence: the idea propounded by Bell that not only do parents influence their children, but the children simultaneously influence their parents.

Binocular cells: cortical cells in the visual cortex that receive input from both eyes.

Buffering agent: a person or thing that helps prevent something harmful from happening.

Columnar microstructure: reported by Hubel and Wiesel, a type of organization found in the visual cortex in which groups of cells that respond to highly similar visual stimuli are arranged in columns.

Complement: in a sentence, something that is brought into existence by the verb. It is called the verb *complement*.

Congenital assertiveness: a type of temperament discussed by Bell, similar to Thomas, Chess, and Birch's *attention span/persistence*, in which a child maintains a goal-directed behavior despite obstacles.

Congenital determinants: inborn factors that contribute to or cause certain types of psychological development.

Congenital person-orientation: a type of temperament discussed by Bell, similar to Thomas, Chess, and Birch's *approach/withdrawal*, in which a child shows a high level of interest in being near and around people.

Content words: the major, heavy-duty words like nouns and verbs, that carry most of the meaning in a sentence. Most English-speaking children tend to pick up nouns and then verbs first, and then later on pick up the little *filler words.*

Continuum of caretaking casualty: from Sameroff and Chandler, the range of entities relating to postnatal care that can contribute to poor psychological outcomes.

Continuum of reproductive casualty: from Sameroff and Chandler, the range of entities relating to the biological processes of child-bearing and childbirth that can contribute to prenatal or perinatal complications, and subsequently to poor psychological outcomes (see *prenatal complications* and *perinatal complications*).

Contralateral: coming from the opposite side.

Control group/condition: the group or condition in which nothing unusual or different happens. It serves as a point of comparison for the *experimental group* or *condition,* where something unusual or different does happen.

Conventional morality: the second level of morality proposed by Kohlberg, in which right and wrong actions are defined by what other people would think of you if you engaged in them.

Correlational design: a research design in which the goal is to look for and detect patterns of association between two variables.

Cortical cells: cells that make up the cerebral cortex.

Critical experiment: a special type of experiment, the results of which will help decide between the validity of two or more competing theories. If the results turn out one way, Theory A is supported, whereas if the results turn out a different way, Theory B is supported, and so on.

Cross-sectional design: a developmental research design in which a researcher observes individuals from each of two or more ages, and makes inferences about the developmental processes that underlie changes across the two or more ages (see *longitudinal design*).

Cute response: a proposed biologically built-in system ensuring that babies will be perceived as "cute" by adults, thereby increasing the likelihood that adults will want to care for babies.

Deep structure: the underlying grammatical relationships between subjects, verbs, and objects that presumably exists universally in all normal speakers of all languages. Deep structure must be transformed into a *surface structure* before you can communicate your ideas through language or writing.

Dependent variable: in an experiment, the outcome behavior of interest that is presumed to be influenced or caused by some other factor (see *independent variable*).

Developmental behavior genetics: a field of study focusing on the extent that behavior and its development can be accounted for by genes and gene expression.

Deviant development: abnormal development of some kind.

Difficult child: a temperament profile characterized by high withdrawal, biological irregularity, negative mood, unadaptableness, and highly intense reactions.

Direction of effects problem: a problem common to all correlational designs in which it's impossible to tell which of two correlated variables is causally related to the other. If variables A and B are correlated with one another, it's not possible to tell whether A is causing B or B is causing A.

Distractibility: one of Thomas, Chess, and Birch's temperament dimensions, reflecting the extent that children are easily interrupted from whatever they're doing by extraneous events.

Dizygotic twins: siblings born at the same time, but who came from two separate fertilized eggs.

Easy child: a temperament profile characterized by high approach, biological regularity, positive mood, high adaptability, and low-intensity reactions.

Ecological psychology: the scientific study of the progressive, mutual accommodation, throughout the life span, between a growing human organism and the changing immediate environments in which it lives, as this process is affected by relations obtaining within and between these immediate settings, as well as the larger social contexts in which the settings are embedded.

Ecological transitions: according to Bronfenbrenner, fruitful contexts for developmental research. These transitions include changes in role and setting as the person matures.

Ecology: the branch of biology that studies the relationship between organisms and their surroundings.

Environment of adaptedness: the specific environment that a species was built, through evolution, to best fit into.

Epistemology: a branch of philosophy that deals with the meaning and origins of knowledge.

Ethic of caring: an overarching concern, most typically expressed and experienced by women, with the well-being of others.

Ethic of justice: an overarching concern, most typically expressed and experienced by men, with being fair and ensuring that justice is equally distributed.

Ethology: a branch of biology that studies how the behaviors of species help them survive in their natural environments.

Exosystem: from Bronfenbrenner's ecological theory, the set of social structures that influence the developing person's immediate surroundings, but that do not contain the person.

Experiencer: in a sentence, the person, animal, or other animate entity who experiences an action or a mental or emotional state.

Experimental group/condition: this is the group or condition in which the experimenter introduces some special treatment or experience, and tests to see whether the special treatment or experience does have an effect on subjects' behavior.

Externalizing disorder: any of a number of disorders, usually first emerging in middle to late childhood, characterized by acting out, impulsiveness, aggressiveness, and hyperactivity.

Filler words: little words like prepositions, pronouns, connectives, and articles that aren't always necessary to understand the basic meanings of sentences, but which are grammatically required by the language. Children tend to pick them up relatively late (see *content words*).

Functionally invariant: this notion was used by Piaget to suggest that even though the contents of thought and knowledge might change and develop over time, the processes that lead to the development of thought and knowledge always function the same way. In other words, they become *functionally invariant.*

Goodness as self-sacrifice: the second level of morality proposed by Gilligan, in which right and wrong actions are defined in terms of whether or not they provide for the well-being of others.

Goodness of fit: the degree of fit between a child with a particular temperament profile and her surrounding social and physical environment.

Grammatical morphemes: see *morphemes.*

Habituation: the decrease in responsiveness that usually happens as a result of repeated presentation of a stimulus.

Higher psychological process: in Vygotsky's theory, the abilities to use language and tools.

Histological examination: a type of examination in which slices of brain tissue are examined under a microscope for neuroanatomical organization.

Hypothesis: an expectation or prediction derived from the central elements of a theory.

Imprinting: a biological process through which a baby *attaches* to an adult member of the species.

Independent variable: in an experiment, the factor that is suspected of causing or influencing outcome behaviors of interest, and is manipulated by the experimenter so as to show what happens (see *dependent variable*).

Infant-mother affectional system: the love relationship between babies and their mothers.

Information processing theory: a theory of cognitive development that uses the computer as a metaphor for thinking about babies' thinking abilities. Just like a computer, babies have inputs (the senses) and outputs (behaviors), and presumably there's some important stuff that goes on in between.

Innate: usually means "present at birth," but also sometimes used to mean "present in the genes."

Inner voice: in Vygotsky's theory, the running inner dialog we carry on when we're attempting to solve problems.

Instinct: in Bowlby's theory, any system of behaviors that (1) follows a similar and predictable pattern in most members of the species, (2) is not a simple response to a single stimulus, but a sequence of behaviors that runs a predictable course, (3) has consequences that are valuable for ensuring the survival of the individual or the species, and (4) develops even when there are no opportunities for learning it.

Instrument: in a sentence, a tool used by the agent to do something or cause something to happen.

Intellectual adaptation: the more general process that subsumes *accommodation* and *assimilation.*

Intensity of reaction: one of Thomas, Chess, and Birch's temperament dimensions, reflecting the amount of energy children put into their responses to the world.

Interactive relationship: the dependence of effect of one thing on the level or quality of another thing.

Internalization: as used by Vygotsky, what happens as processes that start out as *interpersonal* ones move inside our minds and become *intrapersonal* ones.

Internalization of schemes: the process whereby more primitive, sensorimotor schemes eventually become mentally represented. In other words, they become *internalized.*

Internalizing disorder: any of a number of disorders, usually first emerging in middle to late childhood, characterized by excessive anxiety.

Interpersonal function of speech: Vygotsky's notion that sometimes speech between two people is needed to solve a problem.

Intrapersonal function of speech: Vygotsky's notion that children eventually become capable of more or less talking to themselves when solving a problem. They have an *inner voice.*

Ipsilateral: coming from the same side.

Language acquisition device (LAD):   a proposed inborn brain device that contains all possible grammatical, morphological, and maybe even phonological rules for all possible languages, and determines which rules are relevant for a given child based on the language she is exposed to in her surrounding environment.

Location: in a sentence, it's the *location* of the state, action, or process expressed by the verb.

Long-habituators: usually refers to babies who take a relatively long time to habituate (see *habituation*).

Longitudinal design: a developmental research design in which a researcher observes the same individuals across two or more ages, and makes inferences about the developmental processes that underlie changes across those ages (see *cross-sectional design*).

Lower-limit control practices: the set of parenting techniques that parents use to deal with normal, day-to-day child behaviors.

Macrosystem: from Bronfenbrenner's ecological theory, the overarching institutional patterns of the culture or subculture, such as the educational, legal, and political systems.

Mean length of utterance (MLU):   an extremely popular way of rapidly characterizing the complexity of children's speech by calculating the average number of morphemes per utterance. Invented by Roger Brown.

Means-ends sequencing: when one schema is used in order to make possible the use of a second schema. The first schema is used as the *means* to enable the use of the second *schema.*

Mental model: as used in attachment theory, a set of expectations held by a baby, based on experience, about the reliability and responsiveness of the mother.

Mental state words: words that are used to describe mental states.

Mesosystem: from Bronfenbrenner's ecological theory, a collection of *microsystems* that influence one another.

Microsystem: from Bronfenbrenner's ecological theory, the complex of relations between the developing person and environment in an immediate setting containing that person.

Model: as used in Bandura's research, an individual who intentionally or unintentionally exhibits behaviors that are observed and imitated by others.

Modulations of meaning: basically the same as *morphology* (see *morphological rule system*).

Monozygotic twins: siblings born at the same time, but who came from a single fertilized egg that divided after fertilization.

Morality of nonviolence: the last and highest level of morality proposed by Gilligan, in which right and wrong actions are defined in terms of whether they support the establishment and maintenance of human relationships.

Morphemes (also called *grammatical morphemes*):   the smallest units of meaning in a language. There are two main types, free morphemes, which can exist on their own and are sometimes called root words, and bound morphemes, which can exist only when attached to other words at their beginning (called prefixes), their end (called suffixes), or in the middle (called infixes). See *morphological rule system.*

Morphological rule system: the rule system, unique to a particular language, that specifies how *morphemes* are to be combined. In English, the rule for marking a noun for plurality is to add the plural marker at the end (/car/ + /plural marker/ = cars) or in the middle (/woman/ + /plural marker/ = women).

Narrative research design: a form of research that focuses on the stories told by research participants, with special recognition that each story is couched within a unique frame of meaning created by the participant telling the story.

Nativism: a general school of thought that ascribes nearly all of babies' development to inborn, innate sources (see *innate*).

Natural selection: Piaget applied this Darwinian concept to explain the survival of good, well-adapted ideas, and the extinction of bad, poorly adapted ones.

Naturalistic observation: a research design in which the researcher observes behavior in a naturally occurring environment.

Nomothetic approach: a scientific approach that aims to discover universal, underlying laws.

Nonconforming parenting: a style of parenting in which a parent generally acts in ways that violate the norms of society, sometimes behaving downright oddly.

Normative development: normal development.

Object noun phrase complement: this is a fancy phrase that refers to the fact that whole sentences can serve as the object of a verb. In "I hope *Jane picks her nose*," the embedded sentence *Jane picks her nose* is the object noun phrase complement.

Object permanence: the belief that an object continues to exist even in the absence of visual, auditory, or any other sensory information.

Ontogeny: the developmental course of an individual member of a species.

Operational definition: when psychologists measure abstract psychological traits, characteristics, or abilities, they describe the specific operations or procedures they will use to measure them. Whatever operation or procedure they settle on to measure a trait, characteristic, or ability makes up their *operational definition* of that trait, characteristic, or ability. An IQ test score is a typical operational definition of intelligence.

Orientation to individual survival: the first and most primitive level of morality proposed by Gilligan, in which right and wrong actions are defined in terms of whether or not they will promote individual survival.

Passively acceptant parenting: a style of parenting in which a parent is always outwardly accepting of a child, even when the child disobeys.

Patient: in a sentence, someone or something either in a given state or undergoing a change in state.

Perinatal complications: factors emerging at the time of birth which may make childbirth difficult, and which may compromise the health of the baby or the mother.

Permissive parenting: one of Baumrind's major parenting styles, characterized by an emphasis on complete acceptance of the child but without high expectations.

Phonological rule system: the rule system, unique to a particular language, that specifies how sounds are allowed to be used and combined within that language. English has about 36–40 different sounds; some languages have more, others have fewer.

Phrase structure rules: rules for converting sentences from the deep structure form to the surface structure form, depending on the grammar of the specific language.

Phylogeny: the developmental course of a species as a whole.

Plasticity: reflects the fact that brain cells and brain organization are highly flexible and adaptive and are not destined to develop in a specified way.

Postconventional morality: the third and highest level of morality proposed by Kohlberg, in which right and wrong actions are defined in terms of your own internalized ideals and principles.

Power assertive discipline: a form of discipline characterized by reliance on the parent's superior physical, emotional, or financial status.

Pragmatic rule system: the rule system, unique to specific cultures and subcultures, that specifies how language should be used.

Preconventional morality: the first and most primitive level of morality proposed by Kohlberg, in which right and wrong actions are defined by whether or not you will be punished or rewarded for engaging in them.

Prenatal complications: factors emerging prior to birth which may compromise the health of the baby or the mother.

Primary circular reactions: Piaget's second substage of sensorimotor development. A baby does something interesting with or on his own body, and attempts to reproduce it. In this sense, *primary* means "own body" and *circular* refers to "repetition of the act."

Principle of parsimony: a practice adopted widely throughout all of the sciences dictating that the simplest possible explanation for a phenomenon be assumed until evidence to the contrary is uncovered. *Parsimony* basically means "simple."

Prospective science: an approach to doing psychological science in which the goal is to observe behaviors at an early point in time and observe how they change and develop over time. It's a forward-looking approach.

Punitive behavior: behavior aimed at punishing.

Purposive: acting in such a way as to achieve a goal.

Quality of mood: one of Thomas, Chess, and Birch's temperament dimensions, reflecting the general positivity or negativity expressed by the child.

Rebirthing therapy: A controversial form of therapy in which children or adults with various forms of attachment disorder symbolically reexperience birth.

Receptive field: the field of vision for a particular set of retinal cells that is most responsive.

Reflexes: in Piaget's theory, the basic knowledge structures that babies start out with, and therefore the very first schemas.

Relative clause: a type of embedded sentence in which a clause is inserted into an otherwise simple sentence. In "The man *who came to dinner* stayed a week," the phrase *who came to dinner* is the relative clause.

Requirement of reciprocity: Bronfenbrenner's dictate that any decent theory of child development must specify not only how the environment influences the individual, but also how the individual influences the environment.

Resilience: the potential to develop normally despite apparently overwhelming odds to the contrary.

Retrospective science: an approach to doing psychological science in which behaviors are observed at a later point in time, and inferences are made about the precipitating causes of those behaviors. It's a backward-looking approach.

Rhythmicity: one of Thomas, Chess, and Birch's temperament dimensions, focusing on the regularity and predictability of bodily functions.

Rich interpretation: using the immediate social and environmental contexts as clues to help interpret the intent and/or meaning of children's utterances.

Schemas: basic structures that underlie all knowledge; a schema is our internal representation or understanding of an object, a concept, an event, a fact, or anything else that we know.

Secondary circular reactions: Piaget's third substage of sensorimotor development. A baby does something interesting with or on an external object, and attempts to reproduce it. In this sense, *secondary* means "external object" and *circular* refers to "repetition of the act."

Secure base: as used in attachment theory, the role played by the mother in a securely attached mother-child relationship. As long as a baby has his mother as a *secure base*, he will become a competent explorer of the surrounding environment.

Self-efficacy: feelings of having control over your life and your own destiny.

Semantic relations: the roles played by words in a sentence, including such roles as *agent, beneficiary, instrument*, and *patient*.

Semantic rule system: the rule system that specifies the meaningfully possible combinations of words. "Bachelor's wife" isn't a meaningfully possible phrase.

Sensitive responsiveness: from Ainsworth, the key to a secure attachment. Mothers who are sensitively responsive are finely attuned to the needs of their babies and respond accordingly.

Short-habituators: usually refers to babies who habituate relatively quickly (see *habituation*).

Signaling behaviors: from attachment theory, a biologically prepared and evolutionarily significant set of signals given off by babies to inform their mothers of some need or state. Includes crying and smiling.

Slow-to-warm-up child: a temperament profile characterized by being initially high in withdrawal and unadaptability but with low-intensity reactions, and eventually coming around to be tolerant and accepting of the situation.

Socially adaptive behaviors: from Baumrind's theory, behaviors that aid an individual in getting along with other people specifically, and society more generally.

Socioeconomic status: characterizes the general quality of the child-rearing environment, based on both the social status of the parent's job, and the amount of money the parent earns.

Stimulus: any object or event that is detected and/or responded to by an organism.

Strange situation: an extremely popular methodology developed by Ainsworth to measure the quality of mother-child attachment.

Surface structure: the grammatical arrangement that you hear in spoken language and see in written language. It derives from the *deep structure* of the speaker or writer through a set of transformational rules.

Surrogate mother: as used by the Harlows, refers to the wire and cloth "mothers" that many infant monkeys were raised with.

Syntactic rule system: the rule system, unique to a particular language, that specifies how words can be grammatically combined based on the grammar of that language.

Syntax: the rules for how to form sentences based on the grammar of the language. In normal, declarative English sentences, the *subject* precedes the *verb*, which precedes the *object*. But other languages have their own syntax.

Telegraphic speech: speech in which the *filler words* are omitted, but in which the basic message still is conveyed.

Temperament: a set of biological and behavioral predispositions to respond in a certain way to sources of stimulation in the environment.

Tertiary circular reactions: Piaget's fifth substage of sensorimotor development. A baby does something interesting, and attempts to reproduce it while varying the details of the event each time to "see what will happen."

Theory of mind: refers to children's increasingly more sophisticated understanding that other people have beliefs, wishes, and desires; that is, they develop their own little *theory of mind*.

Threshold of responsiveness: one of Thomas, Chess, and Birch's temperament dimensions, indicating how strong a stimulus needs to be before a child responds to it.

Totality of the functional social system: Bronfenbrenner's dictate that any decent theory of child development must take into account the fact that experiments involving humans are themselves a social system, and that children's behavior in these experiments will inevitably reflect that social system.

Tractable: easily handled, easily controlled.

Transactional model: a theory of child development that stress both the flexible nature of children's environments and children's own active role in their psychological development.

Transforming experiment: a type of experiment in which children are exposed to radical departures from the existing belief systems of their own culture.

Upper-limit control practices: the set of parenting techniques that parents use to deal with extreme or unusual child behaviors.

Visual acuity: how well you can see. "Normal" visual acuity is 20/20.

Zone of proximal development: this extremely popular notion refers to the fact that children can perform at higher levels when they are guided by a more mature or more experienced person. The zone is technically defined as the difference in ability when performing alone and when performing with the more experienced person.

CREDITS

Text

Page 25: From J. Piaget, *The Origins of Intelligence in Children*, Margaret Cook, translator. Reprinted by permission of International Universities Press, Inc., & Routledge & Kegan Paul Ltd., London. Originally published in French, 1936.

Page 37: Vygotsky, L. S. (1978). Reprinted by permission of the publisher from *Mind in society: the development of higher psychological processes*. J. Cole, V. John-Steiner, S. Scribner, and E. Souberman, Eds. and trans. Cambridge, Mass.: Harvard University Press, Copyright © 1978 by the President and Fellows of Harvard College.

Page 45: Table 4.1: Vygotsky, L. S. (1978). Average number of errors in answering the questions with and without the availability of color cards. Reprinted by permission of the publisher from *Mind in society: the development of higher psychological processes*. J. Cole, V. John-Steiner, S. Scribner, and E. Souberman, Eds. and trans. Cambridge, Mass.: Harvard University Press, Copyright © 1978 by the President and Fellows of Harvard College.

Page 51: Fantz, R. L. (1961). The origin of form perception. *Scientific American*, 3, 64–72.

Page 60: Baillargeon, R. (1987). Object permanence in 3 1/2-and 4 1/2-month-old infants. *Developmental Psychology*, 23, 655–664.

Page 74: Premack, D. & Woodruff, G. (1978) Does the chimpanzee have a theory of mind? *Behavioral and Brain Sciences* 4:515–526.

Page 87: Chomsky, N. (1975). *Syntactic structures*. The Hague, The Netherlands: Mouton.

Page 100: Brown, R. (1973). Reprinted by permission of the publisher from *A first language: The early stages*. Cambridge, Mass.: Harvard University Press, Copyright © 1973 by the President and Fellows of Harvard College.

Page 116: Harlow, H. F. & Harlow, M. K. (1965). The affectional systems. A. Schrier, H. F. Harlow & F. Stollnitz (Eds.), *Behavior of nonhuman primates: Modern research trends*. Reprinted with permission of Academic Press. Academic Press is an imprint of Elsevier Science. All rights reserved.

Page 127: Bowlby, J. (1969) *Attachment and loss*. Vol. 1. Copyright © 1969 John Bowlby. Reprinted by permission of Basic Books, a member of Perseus Books, L.L.C., and Random House Group Ltd.

Page 140: Ainsworth, M.D.S., Blehar, M.C., Waters, E., & Wall, S. (1978). *Patterns of attachment: A psychological study of the strange situation*. Hillsdale, NJ: Erlbaum.

Page 153: Baumrind, D. (1971). Current patterns of parental authority. *Developmental Psychology Monographs*, 4(1, pt. 2). Reprinted by permission of the author.

Page 167: Bandura, A., Ross, D., & Ross, S. (1961). Transmission of aggression through imitation of aggressive models. *Journal of Abnormal and Social Psychology*, 63, 375–382. Copyright © 1961 by the American Psychological Association. Reprinted by permission of the American Psychological Association and the authors.

Page 180: Gilligan, C. (1982). Reprinted by permission of the publisher from *In a different voice: Psychological theory and women's development*. Cambridge, Mass.: Harvard University Press. Copyright © 1982 by the President and Fellows of Harvard College.

Page 194: Thomas, A., Chess, S., & Birch, H.G. (1968). *Temperament and behavior disorders in childhood.* New York: New York University Press.

Page 207: Werner, E.E., Smith, R.S. (2001). *Journeys from childhood to midlife: Risk, resilience, and recovery.* Copyright © 2001 Emmy Werner and Ruth Smith. Reprinted by permission of Cornell University Press.

Page 220: Sameroff, A. J., Chandler, M. J. (1975). Reproductive risk and the continuum of caretaking casualty. In: Horowitz, FD, Hetherington, M., Scarr-Salapetek, S., Siegel G, (Eds.) *Review of Child Development Research.* Vol. 4. Copyright © 1975 Arnold Sameroff. Reprinted by permission of the University of Chicago University Press and the author.

Page 233: Anastasi, A. (1958). Heredity, environment and the question "how?" *Psychology Review,* 65, 197–208. Copyright © 1958 by the American Psychological Association. Reprinted by permission of the American Psychological Association.

Page 245: Bell, R. Q. (1968). A reinterpretation of the direction of effects in studies of socialization. *Psychological Review,* 75, 81-95. Copyright © 1968 by the American Psychological Association. Reprinted by permission of the American Psychological Association.

Page 256: Hubel, D.H., Wiesel, T.N. (1963). Receptive fields of cells in striate cortex of very young, visually inexperienced kittens. *Journal of Neurophysiology,* 26, 994–1002. Reprinted by permission of The American Physiological Society.

Page 268: Bronfenbrenner, U. (1977). Toward an experimental ecology of human development. *American Psychologist,* 32, 513–530. Copyright © 1977 by the American Psychological Association. Reprinted by permission of the American Psychological Association and the author.

Photos

Page abbreviations are as follows: (L) left, (C) center, and (R) right.

Page 25: AP/Wide World Photos; *p. 37:* Dr. Michael Cole, Courtesy of A.R. Luria; *p. 51:* Courtesy of Case Western Reserve University Archives; *p. 60:* Renee Baillargeon/University of Illinois; *p. 87:* Copyright © Bettmann/CORBIS; *p. 116:* (L) Courtesy of Harlow Primate Laboratory/University of Wisconsin, (R) Courtesy of Harlow Primate Laboratory/University of Wisconsin; *p. 121:* (L) USDA/APHIS/Animal and Plant Health Inspection Service, (R) USDA/APHIS/Animal and Plant Health Inspection Service; *p. 140:* Mary Ainsworth, University of Virginia; *p. 153:* Courtesy of Dr. Diana Baumrind, Institute of Human Development, University of California, Berkeley; *p. 167:* Albert Bandura; *p. 180:* Harvard Graduate School of Education; *p. 194:* (L) Courtesy of Dr. Stella Chess & Dr. Alexander Thomas, (C) Courtesy of Dr. Stella Chess & Dr. Alexander Thomas, (R) Courtesy of Herbert G. Birch Services, 275 7th Avenue, New York City, 10001; *p. 207:* (L) Courtesy of Dr. Emmy Werner/University of California, Davis, (R) Courtesy of Dr. Ruth S. Smith; *p. 220:* (L) Bill Wood/Sommese Design, (R) Courtesy of Michael Chandler; *p. 233:* Courtesy of Fordham University/Department of Psychology; *p. 256:* Copyright © AP/Wide World Photos; *p. 268:* AP/Wide World Photos.

INDEX